The Best of the Independent Rhetoric and Composition Journals

The Best of the Independent Rhetoric and Composition Journals
SERIES EDITOR: STEVE PARKS

Each year, a team of editors selects the best work published in the independent journals in the field of Rhetoric and Composition, following a competitive review process involving journal editors and publishers. For additional information about the series, see http://www.parlorpress.com/bestofrhetcomp.

THE BEST OF THE INDEPENDENT RHETORIC AND COMPOSITION JOURNALS

2011

Edited by Steve Parks, Brenda Glascott, Heather Christiansen, Brian Bailie, and Stacey Waite

Parlor Press
Anderson, South Carolina
www.parlorpress.com

Parlor Press LLC, Anderson, South Carolina, USA

© 2013 by Parlor Press. Individual essays in this book have been reprinted with permission of the respective copyright owners.
All rights reserved.
Printed in the United States of America

SAN: 254-8879

ISSN 2327-4778 (print)

ISSN 2327-4786 (online)

1 2 3 4 5

Cover design by David Blakesley.
Printed on acid-free paper.

Parlor Press, LLC is an independent publisher of scholarly and trade titles in print and multimedia formats. This book is available in paper and digital formats from Parlor Press on the World Wide Web at http://www.parlorpress.com or through online and brick-and-mortar bookstores. For submission information or to find out about Parlor Press publications, write to Parlor Press, 3015 Brackenberry Drive, Anderson, South Carolina, 29621, or email editor@parlorpress.com.

Contents

Introduction   *vii*
    Steve Parks, Brenda Glascott, Brian Bailie,
    Heather Christiansen, and Stacey Waite

Across the Disciplines   2

1 The Pittsburgh Study of Writing   *3*
    David Bartholomae and Beth Matway

Community Literacy Journal   68

2 "Phenomenal Women," Collaborative Literacies, and Community Texts in Alternative "Sista" Spaces   *69*
    Beverly J. Moss

Composition Forum   96

3 E-Book Issues in Composition: A Partial Assessment and Perspective for Teachers   *97*
    Michael J. Faris and Stuart Selber

Composition Studies   118

4 Changing Research Methods, Changing History: A Reflection on Language, Location, and Archive   *119*
    Jessica Enoch

Enculturation   150

5 Exposing Assemblages: Unlikely Communities of Digital Scholarship, Video, and Social Networks   *151*
    Alex Reid

Journal of Second Language Writing   173

6 A Biliteracy Agenda for Genre Research   *174*
    Guillaume Gentil

The Journal of Teaching Writing   209

7 Flow and the Principle of Relevance: Bringing Our
Dynamic Speaking Knowledge to Writing   210
Deborah Rossen-Knill

Journal of Writing Research   233

8 Writing in Natural Sciences: Understanding the Effects of
Different Types of Reviewers on the Writing Process   234
Melissa M. Patchan, Christian D. Schunn, and Russell J. Clark

Kairos   263

9 How the Internet Saved My Daughter and How Social
Media Saved My Family   264
Marc C. Santos

Pedagogy   295

10 New Media Scholarship and Teaching: Challenging the
Hierarchy of Signs   296
Ellen Cushman

Reflections   314

11 "Found" Literacy Partnerships: Service and Activism at
Spelman College   315
Zandra L. Jordan

Writing on the Edge   337

12 "In Our Names": Rewriting the U.S. Death Penalty   338
Kimberly K. Gunter

About the Editors   347

Introduction

Steve Parks, Brenda Glascott, Brian Bailie,
Heather Christiansen, and Stacey Waite

As scholars and teachers in Rhetoric and Composition, we often talk about engaging our students with the process of revision; we might even hear ourselves explaining revision as a kind of looking again, a continual process of re-examination—even re-imagination. And perhaps one of the most important aspects of our scholarship is that we reflect that very revision we ask of our students in our own writing about them, about our field, and about the difficult work of composing. The essays gathered here, and representing the best of the independent journals in 2011as selected by teacher-scholars representing the diverse identities and career trajectories of our field, reflect, in the best possible ways, our field's most treasured asset—the desire to revise our own histories, terms, and methodologies, to see again (and perhaps question) what we know or what it means to know in the first place.

Jessica Enoch's, "Changing Research Methods, Changing History: A Reflection on Language, Location, and Archives," for example, articulates (through a reflective consideration of her own scholarship that focuses on three Chicana teachers and their contribution to our understandings of rhetorical education) actual methodologies that might enable scholars of composition to revise dominant histories of the field, to compose histories that "account for marginalized rather than enfranchised students and teachers." And it is difficult to read this collection of essays without noting writers like Beverly Moss and Zandra L. Jordan, who each seem to answer Enoch's call. Moss's essay, "'Phenomenal Women,' Collaborative Literacies, and Community Texts in Alternative 'Sista' Spaces," engages in an ethnographic study of an African-American women's community club called *Phenomenal Women Incorporated*. While Moss's essay is not explicitly interested in rewriting history in the precise way that Enoch's is, her close analysis of this alternative literacy site actually illustrates how Enoch's research methodologies might also be thought of as a means of researching the present, seeing the current moment again, seeing it better.

Additionally, Jordan's "'Found' Literacy Partnerships: Service and Activism at Spelman College" asks us to not only consider the places literacy happens *outside* the institution but to also move our students outside their institutional locations through service learning that creates a dynamic and politically powerful "partnership" through community engagement. Rhetoric and composition's move into the realm of public rhetoric and community partnerships has directed the discipline's gaze away from conventional histories, understandings, and locations, and consequently, focused the work of scholar-teachers within the field on both the scholarly and pedagogical enrichment that results in exploring spaces outside the academy. An example of this is Kimberly K. Gunter's "In Our Names: Rewriting the U.S. Death Penalty," which thinks carefully about how students might respond to moving out of the classroom and into a world that asks them to write for specific purposes with real, material world goals and consequences. This movement, Gunter's piece suggests, is quite different from a teacher asking students to write *about* the world outside the classroom—a world they can see, but not touch from inside the classroom location.

As we revise and reconsider the field and move outside of classrooms, we must also contend with the idea of moving outside of alphabetic texts, of imagining reading and composing that privileges sound, image, video, and motion. New media and digital composition scholars ask of us perhaps the ultimate revision: to, at times, move composing away from texts. Ellen Cushman's essay, "New Media Scholarship and Teaching: Challenging the Hierarchy of Signs," enacts this movement in her discussion of "learning new sign systems" as we learn to de-privilege the alphabetic text as the primary mode for literacy. In "E-Book Issues in Composition: A Partial Assessment and Perspective for Teachers," Michael J. Faris and Stuart Selber offer a provocative case study, exploring the impact of the Sony Reader as the "text" of their course and offering up both the pleasures and difficulties of electronic texts as they become more integral to the teaching of writing and reading. In a focused discussion of video composition, Alex Reid's "Exposing Assemblages" encourages scholars to produce scholarship in a variety of media and articulates how digital media might offer scholars a unique opportunity to compose and think in new ways, ways that will enrich the field itself. Reid mentions the journal *Kairos: A Journal of Rhetoric, Technology and Pedagogy* as a place where this new media scholarship takes place. This is no surprise given that one of this year's selected essays appeared there: "How the Internet Saved My Daughter and How Social Media Saved My Family" by Marc Santos—a multi-media essay that makes its argument both through its content and through the reader's engagement with its various components of photographs, hyperlinks, page composition, narrative, and theory. Its multi-media form allows its multi-dimensional arguments *about* media, about suffering, about writing, and about philosophy and rhetoric to sound off in their different registers creating a unique symphony of argument, sound, image, and motion.

In order for any field to continue to revise itself, its scholars and teachers must be willing to call into question their most taken for granted terms, to ask questions about what it means to *know* in a given field and about how they come to know what they know. In this sense, to be a scholar in composition is almost always to be invested in epistemologies. Guillaume Gentil, in "A Biliteracy Agenda for Genre Research," calls into question traditional notions of genre as they connect to conventional understandings of language competence. We cannot read Gentil's essay without asking important questions about what it means to know a genre, to know a language and how those knowledges are connected to reading and writing. In "The Pittsburgh Study of Writing," David Bartholomae and Beth Matway offer the results of an assessment project at the University of Pittsburgh. The results of this study, containing some interesting quotations from teachers of writing in a range of disciplines calls the concept of assessment into question. By considering what a textured and ethnographic assessment project looks like, the essay asks what assessment means in the first place. Also reflective of Pittsburgh's Study of Writing is the essay "Writing in natural sciences: Understanding the effects of different types of reviewers on the writing process" by Melissa M. Patchan, Christian D. Schunn, and Russell J. Clark, an essay which also offers a complex and productive sampling of instructor comments and student response. Reflected in all the essays gathered here is a profound concern for teaching, of course. And Deborah Rossen-Krill's "Flow and the Principle of Relevance: Bringing our Dynamic Speaking Knowledge to Writing," not only demonstrates deep investment in practices of teaching, but also illustrates the rich possibilities of inquiry by pressing in to the term "flow" and considering the dynamic tension between speaking and writing. It is the impossibility of certainty, the vast expanse of the very terms *rhetoric* and *composition* that make the field a shifting, malleable, and (re)visionary location, a place where complex questions of reading, composing, and teaching can echo—so that we might hear them again and again.

Each one of these essays enacts its own innovative set of revisions to the field and these revisions (also understood as interventions and contributions) were part of the criteria used in ranking and selecting these essays, criteria we described as threefold:

1. Essay must demonstrate a broad sense of the discipline, demonstrating the ability to explain how its specific intervention in a sub-disciplinary area intersects addresses broad concerns of the field.

2. Essay must make an original contribution to the sub-disciplinary field, expanding or rearticulating central premises of that area.

3. Essay must be written in a style which, while disciplinary-based, attempts to engage with a wider audience.

The essays gathered here were submitted by their respective journal editors and selected by reading groups at several institutions across the United States. The reading groups consisted of professors, lecturers, graduate students, and part-time faculty who read the essays and carefully considered the criteria above in order to rank the essays on a scale from 1 to 4 (1 being an essay that exceeds all disciplinary criteria and 4 being an essay that fails to meet those disciplinary criteria). The editors gathered these scores to compile the final essays that appear here, essays that both reflect and shape work in rhetoric and composition both in 2011 and beyond.

Lastly, we would like to say that this project would not be possible without the organization, dedication, and careful consideration of our reading group members. For their thoughtful readings and rankings of the essays that reflect some of the best work in rhetoric and composition in 2011, we want to extend our sincerest thanks to all the associate editors who participated in our reading groups: Angela Asbell, Noelle Ballmer, Lesley Erin Bartlett, Jean Bessette, Amy

Lynch-Biniek, Mary Boland, Jen Bray, Jennifer Brewer, Bridgette Callahan, Steph Ceraso, Moe Folk, Nicole E. Green, Carol Haviland, Kelly Jarvis, Marcus Meade, Danielle Koupf, Lance Langdon, Kevin Mahoney, Libby Martin, Bobbi Olson, Gabrielle Owen, Patricia Pytleski, Chloe de los Reyes, Dahliani Reynolds, Jessica Rivera-Mueller, Abraham Rooney, Karen Rowan, Frances Suderman, Elaina Taylor, Jaclyn Vasquez, Scott Zimmerman, Tami Zwick.

Finally, we are also profoundly grateful to Dave Blakesley, Parlor Press, for supporting this project's aims of having funds generated by sales go to support independent journals.

The Best of the Independent Rhetoric and Composition Journals

ACROSS THE DISCIPLINES

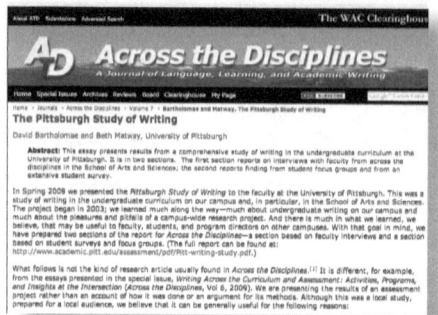

David Bartholomae and Beth Matway's article appears in *Across the Disciplines* on the Web at http://wac.colostate.edu/atd/articles/bartholomae_matway2010/index.cfm

Across the Disciplines is a peer-reviewed journal dedicated to publishing the best scholarly work in interdisciplinary writing, WAC/WID, and communication across the curriculum. The journal (originally called *Language and Learning Across the Disciplines*) began publication in 1994 and merged with the online journal *Academic.Writing* in 2004 under its current title. It is now a part of the WAC Clearinghouse site, hosted by Colorado State University. *Across the Disciplines* receives an average of 4,500 hits a day. In 2011, the journal recorded more than 1,700,000 hits by scholars, students, and other users who visited its site.

"The Pittsburgh Study of Writing" by David Bartholomae and Beth Matway

David Bartholomae and Beth Matway offer the results of an assessment project at the University of Pittsburgh. The results of this study, containing some interesting quotations from teachers of writing in a range of disciplines, calls the concept of assessment into question. By considering what a textured and ethnographic assessment project looks like, the essay asks what assessment means in the first place.

1 The Pittsburgh Study of Writing

David Bartholomae and Beth Matway

In Spring 2009 we presented the *Pittsburgh Study of Writing* to the faculty at the University of Pittsburgh. This was a study of writing in the undergraduate curriculum on our campus and, in particular, in the School of Arts and Sciences. The project began in 2003; we learned much along the way—much about undergraduate writing on our campus and much about the pleasures and pitfalls of a campus-wide research project. And there is much in what we learned, we believe, that may be useful to faculty, students, and program directors on other campuses. With that goal in mind, we have prepared two sections of the report for *Across the Disciplines*—a section based on faculty interviews and a section based on student surveys and focus groups. (The full report can be found at: http://www.academic.pitt.edu/assessment/pdf/Pitt-writing-study.pdf.)

What follows is not the kind of research article usually found in *Across the Disciplines*.[1] It is different, for example, from the essays presented in the special issue, *Writing Across the Curriculum and Assessment: Activities, Programs, and Insights at the Intersection* (*Across the Disciplines*, Vol 6, 2009). We are presenting the results of an assessment project rather than an account of how it was done or an argument for its methods. Although this was a local study, prepared for a local audience, we believe that it can be generally useful for the following reasons:

- It provides a closely textured look at a program with some national recognition.
- It can serve as a model for anyone interested in a similar assessment project—ethnographic rather than outcomes based.
- It can be useful in faculty workshops. The framing in the report provides an everyday, practice-based theoretical language

that can advance discussion.[2] And, because readers hear faculty colleagues speaking in the report, it can create additional space for faculty colleagues to speak in turn.[3]

- It can be useful in undergraduate and graduate seminars, where it is always difficult to find materials to represent individual writing programs.[4]

BACKGROUND

This project began several years ago, in Fall 2003, before our campus had fully committed to outcomes assessment, but when assessment was much in the air. Our Vice Provost called the English department chair (Bartholomae) to say that while the Provost knew we had a strong and highly regarded writing program, he wondered what measures we had to test and to demonstrate its effectiveness. And, he asked, "was I at all interested in an assessment project?" The Vice Provost, Jack Daniel, was an old friend and made it clear that this was a loaded question, that a wise chair would say "yes, of course," that an assessment of student "outcomes" was on its way, and that my department had a chance to get out ahead of this juggernaut as it made its way to our campus.

I said that I was and I wasn't interested in an assessment project. I said that in the Arts and Sciences we had developed a curriculum that promoted student writing across the four years of undergraduate study. The curriculum produced these outcomes—students were writing regularly and with close instruction in a first year writing course and then in two writing intensive courses, one of them in the major. This writing would not necessarily be produced otherwise, and certainly not in the forms that had been developed through our WID program (which made revision the primary point of instruction and sequencing the basic format for a writing course). Outcomes assessment, then, could be descriptive.

I said that we would not learn much from an SAT-like test of general writing ability, an instrument that was being peddled across the nation at the time; I said that what we needed was detailed knowledge of what was happening on the ground. We needed something like an ethnographic study of the "culture of writing" on our campus. I said, "I have been a member of this faculty for 30 years and for 30 years directly engaged with student writing, and yet (with a few exceptions) I could not provide a detailed, documented, or comprehensive account of what goes on in the courses taught outside the English department—in History or Economics or Chemistry." Nor did I know in detail what the faculty, in general, think about these courses or their students or their students' writing. And so, with Beth Matway, who leads our WID program, we proposed a study designed to learn what we could about the culture of writing in the undergraduate curriculum. To make this manageable, we decided to focus for the time being on undergraduate writing in the School of Arts and Sciences. Our Dean, John Cooper, agreed to the plan and we were off and running. (I should quickly add that we were fortunate to have a Dean who understood the importance of writing as a part of intellectual work at any level, and who was truly interested in a detailed account of writing in Arts and Sciences.)

In announcing the project, the Vice-Provost said that the study should document the "core values and practices associated with writing at Pitt." Our goal was to bring forward the experiences and expectations of students and faculty, to hear what they had to say in their own terms and their own voices. And this, we believe, was the great strength and pleasure of the report. It included, verbatim, comments from a wide variety of students—some pleased with their courses, some not so pleased. Their comments were pointed, thoughtful, eloquent, sometimes critical, always useful. The report also included, verbatim, comments from faculty colleagues across the disciplines, who provided detailed accounts of their courses—their writing assignments; their methods for responding to student writing; their expectations; their frank assessments of what their students do with ease and where they struggle. We had said at the outset that one goal of the study was to give voice to students and to faculty and to make their daily practice as writers and teachers visible.

And so we were pleased to see that, once the report was released, what travelled most widely and most quickly were particular statements by students and their teachers. Actually there were two areas of the report that travelled widely and quickly across campus: these statements by students and faculty, but also lists of faculty members and their courses. The project included a survey, and in this survey we asked students to list the courses that had been most useful to them as writers and to list faculty who had made a difference. We organized both lists by department, and these were quickly picked up by department chairs (and by the Dean), slipped under doors and passed from hand to hand as colleagues looked to see how they and their departments fared in comparison with others.

But we are getting ahead of ourselves. Let us briefly describe the project. Then we will present some selected findings.

The Design of the Study

The study had four primary areas of inquiry, each with its own instruments.[5]

1. We did an inventory of existing courses and requirements. From the record of course descriptions across Arts and Sciences, we wanted to learn what we could about writing beyond the two required writing intensive courses (w-courses). We also wanted to look closely at the existing writing intensive courses, to document the various ways departments made sense of the requirement by developing w-courses as part of advanced study in their disciplines. We summarized other assessments of writing at Pitt.[6]

2. We conducted a series of focus group meetings with students drawn from upper-division, writing intensive courses. We asked the participants what they had learned, as writers, in their courses at Pitt; how their writing had changed; how they understood faculty expectations; we asked about their best and worst experiences. We learned a lot. And we used what we learned to design a survey.

3. We designed and administered an on-line survey in the Spring Term, 2005. (For this, we relied on substantial support from our University Center for Social and Urban Research.) 1000 juniors and 1000 seniors were invited to take part. The response rate was 32%, a relatively high rate of response for surveys of this type. We had representative participation across the three primary areas in the Arts and Sciences: Humanities, Social Sciences, Natural Sciences. The survey was designed to give us a detailed account of the genres of academic writing in use on campus, and of the ways our students' understood and valued these genres.[7] We gathered information about writing and teaching both in and out of writing intensive courses. And we asked students, in general, about the importance of writing to their education and future careers. 90% said that writing was important, very important or extremely important to their education at the University of Pittsburgh; over 1/3 said it was extremely important.

 We also had a section of open ended questions. In the report, for example, we provided a list of courses and teachers that students said "made a significant difference" to their education as writers. And we asked, in more general terms, for comment on the courses they had taken or for advice they would offer the faculty—and the report features what we heard. (One student said, "You should have asked us if we thought long papers due at the end of the semester are useful—they aren't!!") These student comments were thoughtful, interesting and useful. We were impressed with the time they took to tell us what was on their minds.

4. And we interviewed 27 members of the faculty, nine from each of the three divisions: Humanities, Social Sciences and Natural Sciences. We developed the pool by writing to Department Chairs and asking for a list of faculty from across the ranks whose courses included writing and/or who thought of themselves as particularly interested in or concerned about student writing.[8] The report summarizes the interviews by highlighting common themes or issues. Our report, then, provided a rich menu of best practices from our colleagues across the disciplines.

Below, we will provide a more detailed account of what we learned from the student focus groups, from the student survey, and from the faculty interviews. These are excerpts from our report to the campus community.

Part One. The Faculty Interviews

In Fall 2004 we wrote to department chairs in A&S asking them to identify up to 5 members of their faculty from across the ranks (including Lecturer) whose courses included writing (in whatever forms). We were looking for people who thought of themselves as writing teachers. From this list we created a pool of candidates representing departments across the disciplines. We planned for 30 and we completed interviews with 27 members of the faculty equally distributed across the three areas: Humanities, Social Sciences, Natural Sciences. 24 of the 27 were tenure track faculty (some very prominent professionally and on campus); the other three were lecturers, one in each of the three divisions.

Although we had a core set of questions, the interviews took their own shape and direction; they lasted from 30 minutes to 90 minutes. The interviewers had course materials on hand. We wrote up each individual interview and returned the transcript to the faculty colleague for comments or corrections. As we began to think about the full range of interviews, the study became a study of key words, and so we then organized our findings according to the primary themes or concerns that emerged across the group, and we created subdivisions as they seemed useful and/or appropriate. We will list those, with commentary, below. The text is drawn from the final report. The language we use, and the key terms, all came to us from the interviews themselves. We used colleagues' names, of course, when we released the report on campus. We were eager to identify best practices across departments. Here we use initials.

Negotiating Academic Writing

1. Writing Beyond the First Year
Most instructors we interviewed agreed that the quality of student writing, and the quality of students' preparation for a course with

writing, have improved over the last decade. Most felt that A&S students came to their advanced courses with appropriate skills, while acknowledging that students come (as people come) with a range of abilities, some writing with apparent ease and others struggling. A. O. (Religious Studies) reflected on this range in remarking that with some "naturally gifted" writers, he can work on "subtle improvements in style," while with others he teaches at a "more basic level." In general, however, faculty members agreed that most students in advanced courses are ready to make progress in their writing. With faculty support, students can move beyond prepared forms (such as, they said, the 5-paragraph theme, the Term Paper, the Report, the 5-page critical essay), and overcome common bad habits (such as "empty prose" or the broad generalization that "supports all claims and requires no evidence").

Some teachers spoke about the necessity of requiring students to attend to the details of proofreading and correction. M. G. (History) proposed an "institutional policy promoting the use of Standard English."

2. Clarity and Coherence

Almost everyone we interviewed mentioned "clarity" and "coherence" as important qualities in student writing, and almost everyone said that these qualities were often lacking. Thinking about what students need to learn, K. S. (History of Art and Architecture) remarked, "I find that they're not writing as precisely as they need to be." Several faculty members noted that students struggle to accurately describe and represent what they see, study or read. They have not, that is, yet learned to use the lenses or optics of a particular discipline; they work, rather, through a more general cognitive/intellectual lens—often "describing" in terms of expectation, habit or cliché.

- P. S. (Chemistry) notes that "teaching writing in the sciences poses special challenges" because science is "thing-centered and number-centered" and most students have more experience writing about beliefs and opinions than about things.
- J. N. (History & Philosophy of Science) gives the following advice on working with primary historical materials: "Many of you mixed modern day judgments of the science in with the historical narrative. While these judgments are certainly

important, they must not be allowed to take over the narrative. Our goal is to understand an historical episode in its own terms...."
- F. G. (Economics) is particularly concerned about training students to use charts and graphs to represent data. "Students have to be able to describe what is really out there in order to theorize or to explain the forces and consequences of economic adjustments in the steel industry."

Many faculty members saw the lack of clarity and coherence in student writing as an intellectual problem: students, they say, need to learn how to "focus." Faculty commented that students do not get to the point; they have too many ideas working at one time; they are overwhelmed by all that they have read or learned; they do not know how to eliminate extraneous information. They need to learn to choose and select and focus on a single issue or question. They need to frame a problem, to summarize and to justify their findings. And they need to do this economically–that is, they need to know what can be left out.

- I. F. (Psychology) says, "Students have difficulty limiting the information they provide to only that which is relevant to their hypotheses."
- K. M. (East Asian Languages and Literatures) feels that she is working against the current trends in her discipline. In her view, much "successful writing" in film analysis tends to be obscure, complicated, and filled with jargon; she also, however, says that she teaches her students to write clearly, simply, and without jargon.

Faculty members used a variety of phrases to describe what constitutes coherence in student writing. They spoke of the need for students in their discipline to "construct an argument" or "develop a narrative," to "organize" or "structure" a whole piece of writing, or to move from beginning to end in a "logical" manner. It appears that although faculty colleagues agree on the value of coherence, it takes different forms in different disciplines. In the context of advanced courses and the intellectual demands they make on students, the virtues of clarity and coherence do not travel well; they are not easily portable or generalizable. For example, a "clear and coherent" narrative in a history class is different from a "clear and coherent" account of an experiment or a "clear and coherent" analysis of a set of readings in political theory. What was most often represented in faculty concern for "clarity" and for "coherence" was the desire to see students master specific materials and represent those materials appropriately within the expectations of the field.

- S. C. (Economics) believes that her students' difficulties with structuring an argument correspond to their difficulties in knowing how to analyze economic information. "The lack of structure is as related to not quite understanding analysis as it is to not knowing how to get it [the analysis] on paper."

As students work with complex materials in advanced courses, the lack of clarity and/or coherence in their writing may represent an uncertainty about disciplinary methods and expectations. It is also evidence of students struggling to get intellectual purchase on complicated material.

3. Complexity

Alongside their concern for clarity and coherence, some faculty asserted the value of complexity in student writing. They want students to develop the ability to handle multiple sources, ideas, or points of view in a single piece of writing. Perhaps the most difficult task for student writers is to negotiate what appear to be competing demands for "clarity" and "control" on the one hand, and "complexity" and "exploration" on the other. As they move beyond the simpler texts they have learned to control, they find themselves struggling to manage complexity.

- S. D. (German) sees complexity as a key goal—the ability to view an issue as not simply a pro/con debate or as right/wrong, but in multiple shadings. She asks students to write on controversial topics, "issues of their heart," where they must learn to negotiate competing arguments and persuade readers by their ability to work through multiple positions.
- J. G. (History) expects students to manage lots of detail and "nitty-gritty data" in their writing; she expects a clarity that is not synonymous with "simple mindedness."

Additional faculty responses are available in Appendix A.

Engaging Students as Writers and Thinkers: Writing Assignments

Making Writing Matter

A common thread across the interviews was a concern to make writing matter, to make it more than a routine and predictable classroom exercise, to present a writing assignment as something other than one more hoop to jump through en route to graduation.

- L. P. (Anthropology) works to convince students that good writing requires more than "meeting the conventions of spelling, grammar, and punctuation." He has students working on a semester-long project. He wants to convince them that this project is not just "another Mickey Mouse exercise in pretend work." He organizes his course so that students carry out an independent, ethnographic research project. He says that those who struggle are those who are unaccustomed to directing themselves. They come to him to ask, "what do you want?" as if they are ready to do whatever necessary to accommodate to the instructor's demands and idiosyncratic taste. He says, "Despite experience and frequent pessimism, I try breaking that frame of enslavement." He thinks that students have been conditioned to regard class assignments as "make-believe." "As students often choose a topic they think will be acceptable because it is timely . . . or academic . . . , I urge them to trust their intelligence and intuition to choose a topic that appeals, however narrow or simple it may seem. I stress that research is not required to prove something. The object of research is to learn what was not previously known."

- L. A. (Hispanic Languages & Literatures) wants her students to understand that "writing gives a space for reflection." Through writing, students come to view themselves as scholars, and have the opportunity to make sense of their "investment of time in college." She wants to convince them that the way they speak and write "has an impact." Writing enables them to "adopt a position, vis-a-vis the set of ideas in question, with proper backing and argumentation."

Additional faculty responses are available in Appendix B.

Taking the Next (Disciplinary) Step

Many we interviewed use writing as a way to compel students to extend their thinking. Short paper assignments may ask students to prepare an argument or develop a thesis not explicitly developed in class; to articulate what "they think" about a particular argument or issue; to apply a theory taught in class to materials that have not been discussed; or, as P.W. (French and Italian) puts it, "to enter into a dialogue with the text they are reading."

Often, in senior seminars or advanced courses, assignments are designed to help students move from one level of thinking to another—to take the next step necessitated by (and valued by) the discipline. These assignments move students from description to analysis, for example, from summary to interpretation or from report to theory.

- M. G. (Political Science) says that students generally enter his classes able to summarize and able to compose a basic 5-paragraph essay. He also notes that most (but not all) have reasonable mechanics. What they tend not to be able to do is "interpolate." They seldom know how to build toward a conclusion via a presentation of sequential steps. They have trouble discussing strategic logic or consequences, or differentiating between proof and surmise. M. G. uses short assignments that prompt students to practice "specific analytical and expository skills" beyond the basic essay.

- D. F. (Music) has designed the writing assignments in his course to lead students from "description" to "criticism." His students work on the intellectual challenges of describing music in prose and then of moving from description to something else–interpretation or criticism. A sequence of short papers moves from the description of a score to a re-writing of that description in service of a larger, more general critical project.
- F. G. (Economics) has created a set of 6 assignments to prepare students for the step from "description" to "explanation." Students must learn to describe and present data visually and mathematically; they also have to learn how to pay attention to the literature–they need to know what to notice, what counts, what matters. In this course students are preparing descriptions on the basis of interviews and reading as well as formal economic analysis. It takes effort to train students to see what is there and to report on it accurately and clearly. Students also need to know how to process the information or data they have described. In the assigned readings, F.G. asks them to pay attention to how a scholar arrived at the findings—to notice the "analytical bridges" that moved from description to explanation so that they can replicate this process in their own writing.

Additional faculty responses are available in Appendix C.

Writing in the Disciplines/ Writing as a Professional

For some of the faculty we interviewed, the long paper assignment models the process of writing an article for a professional journal. In J. N.'s Senior Seminar in History and Philosophy of Science, for example, students are writing articles directed toward the journal, *Philosophy of Science*. This practice was most common, however, in the Natural Sciences.

- W. C. (Biology). In the "Forest Ecology Writing Practicum," his students are prepared to write a "scientific paper"—that is, something appropriate for a journal—appropriate format, appropriate documentation, "graphs, statistics, everything." The first paper is a kind of trial run, in which students write from

data that is provided. W. C. says he wants to "keep the science simple" because writing is the hardest part for them. They also prepare a paper with their research team. The faculty member pushes hard. Sometimes, he says, an A paper or a publishable paper is 10 drafts away. If the student will do the work, he will provide the direction and the motivation and this collaboration may go on well after the course is done. Three of his students, in fact, have published their work with him in the last three years, in some cases with the student listed as primary author.
- L. R. (Neuroscience). In Neuroscience, the "Writing Practicum" draws primarily on the laboratory research, although students are reading in the appropriate neuroscience journals as well. Students work in teams, discussing the readings and the research. The research project, in other words, is carried out as both a lab project and a writing project. With the instructor's oversight, students prepare a paper suitable (ideally) for publication in a journal in the field. L. R. receives a draft of the articles and reads for ideas, for the science, and for organization. She meets individually with students and if there are sentence level problems, she points them out. Students must fix errors in the prose. Students revise with the sense of perfecting their work. In some cases, work prepared by faculty and student teams has been published.

For other faculty, the senior seminar (or writing practicum) is conceived as an introduction to writing in professional business or industrial settings.

- I. F. (Psychology). For her course, "Psychological Aspects of Human Sexuality," the research project, staged out over the semester, is designed, as she says, "to provide the student with firsthand experience in doing professional writing and research on a topic relating to the psychological aspects of human sexuality." The students write a two-part paper on some aspect of sex education. Her instructions tell them:

  > In order to make this project similar to the type of professional writing and research a college graduate might be expected to do, each student should imagine that he or she is working for a company that markets sex education ma-

terials or a government agency that will be implementing a program for sex education. Develop a research question that might be of interest to this company or agency.

- G. N. (Computer Science). In a proposed course, "Project Design and Implementation," students work on a real project with an industry partner, where they are responsible for writing not only proposals and reports (including oral presentation) but also routine correspondence.
- F. G. (Economics). F. G.'s Proseminar is designed to prepare students to do economic analysis, but also to carry out the kind of projects they are likely to encounter in their careers. The final assignment in the course has students preparing an analysis and report as though for a local firm. The "genres" they practice include report, memo and oral presentation; the skills include summary, analysis and the visual presentation of data.

Many instructors include some form of oral presentation in their courses, to give students practice in a kind of writing they will use in their professions: "Being able to give a talk is almost more important" in Physics than being able to write a report. Faculty also regard oral presentations as opportunities for students to learn to prepare abstracts or short-forms of longer written work, or as occasions for students to feel the pressure of audience and the demand for clear organization.

Brief, Informal Writing Assignments

Most of the faculty we interviewed have students writing short (1–3 page) papers, often informally (that is, without grades or commentary). These serve a variety of functions. They are designed to exercise particular skills (often without concern for evaluation)—preparing graphs and charts, writing an introduction or conclusion, writing a summary or précis, generating ideas from data sets. In large lecture courses, short informal assignments are used to engage students but also to assess what they know.

- R. L. (Political Science) has created a useful taxonomy for the short assignments in his courses.

    In class writing assignments, at least one a week, sometimes several a week. These are short and directive; some are unsigned, not all are graded. They are designed to assess prior knowledge; identify prior assumptions; summarize key points in the readings or lectures (one-minute papers); and help students identify key differences in time periods, approaches or concepts ("structured matrix comparisons").

Out of class writing assignments (four per semester, two of them using draft and revision). These are linked so they build toward a medium length paper. Students are encouraged (but not required) to choose a subject they can pursue through the four short papers. The assignments represent different genres, each providing students with a critical perspective on a text or topic: WDWWWHW (Who Does/Did What to Whom, When, Where, How, Why?); assessment of a news source (comparing the treatment of a single topic across media, according to criteria provided to by the instructor); book review; and analytic paper.

- K. S. (History of Art & Architecture) assigns six low-stakes informal writing exercises in his introductory courses, each designed to help students generate and develop ideas. He wants his students to learn that "writing is a tool for them, rather than purely performance—it can help focus their minds and clarify their thoughts."

Sequencing the Task
Many faculty members we interviewed organize their students' writing through a sequence of smaller assignments that lead to a larger project.

- K. S. (History of Art & Architecture) says, "The goal is clear in my mind—it's true at every level: you need to break down the larger product into a sequenced set of smaller assignments. Sequencing is not just a tool for introductory writers but also for accomplished writers." He believes that the extended work in the preliminary assignments allows students to find a "voice" for the larger paper.
- J. N.'s "Junior/Senior Seminar," with a one credit Writing Workshop attached (History & Philosophy of Science) provides a compelling example of sequencing. The goal of the course is

to give students the "direct experience of how someone with a background in the History and Philosophy of Science synthesizes their history of science and their philosophy of science." The course assumes that students can do each of the individual tasks but have not yet learned to synthesize. J. N.'s sequence moves from a "Short History of Science Paper" to a "Long History of Science Paper." The work on the original and the revision focus attention on problems in writing history (and point toward the larger project down the line). These two papers are followed by a "Short Philosophy of Science Paper," one that focuses on the treatment of induction and confirmation (processes that can be applied to the historical materials from the first section of the course). And this leads to a first draft of the term paper, which is meant to be written in the style of the journal, *Philosophy of Science*. The draft is read and edited by students in the course (as well as by the instructor). Students prepare a seminar presentation on their project and a final version of the paper.

- F. G. (Economics) also has a tightly ordered sequence of assignments. The assignments are organized into two parts. "Part I is based on a series of exercises that are completed on an individual basis by each student, culminating in a research report concerning economic adjustment in a steel-producing region." The exercises are written and organized to lead students through a set of lessons that will "have practical value" for them, including practice in the visual representation of quantitative data. "Part II is comprised of three exercises that are completed and graded on a team basis. The team project is comprised of secondary data collection/presentation, primary data collection/presentation, and a brief oral report related to steel industry suppliers in the Pittsburgh region."

Additional faculty responses are available in Appendix D.

Engaging Students as Writers and Thinkers: Working with Student Writing

Responding to Student Writing

The faculty colleagues we interviewed all provide extensive written commentary in response to the student writing they receive. Many also meet with students in individual conferences. Most assert the importance of providing not only evaluation, but also instruction—in forms of feedback that are directed toward the next piece of writing. "In the next assignment (in the next draft), here is what you need to work on. . . ."

- R. L. (Political Science) reads student writing on-line. He makes sentence level editorial changes on the texts, marks sections and inserts comments using MS word reviewing tools. In addition to these marginal comments, he prepares quite extensive written summary statements for each student. These will characteristically direct students to areas where they can improve presentation or improve the research behind the presentation. He speaks as a scholar to young scholars. For example: "You need to spend more time on the main subject of the paper. To do that, you need to broaden your sources. What you have now is mostly a restatement of Swain and Swain and

of Sharman. You need more specialized sources . . , including those I suggested to you in my earlier note." Or, "you switch back and forth from analytic tone to a historical narrative tone, which is fine, but the reader needs to be clearly alerted when you do that."
- P. W. (French and Italian) explains that "the important thing is for students to learn to read themselves, or teach themselves—to see the difference between a good title and a blah title, the difference between an argument that works and one that doesn't."

Additional faculty responses are available in Appendix E.

Revision

All of the faculty we interviewed spoke about organizing their courses so that revision becomes part of the required work and one of the crucial methods students are given for working on their writing. (All officially certified writing intensive courses on our campus are expected to make revision part of the required work of the course.) Some described revision as a way of cleaning up or tightening up a draft. In many courses, however, instructors use the revision process to open a first draft up to question, to provide the context for additional research and new lines of argument, to raise the problem of alternative points of view, to provide the occasion for attention to audience.

- K. C. (Biological Sciences) is concerned about the way students procrastinate on a writing project precisely because rushing through the writing leaves no time for revision. "Students write their way to an argument and main idea through drafts," she says. She requires students to revise so that they have the time to develop more sophisticated arguments.
- S. C. (English) uses revision as a way of teaching students the dangers and limits of the tightly-controlled argument. Students collaborate through a series of drafts and revisions to work their way toward a more expansive, contradictory and demanding form of critical writing.

Writing Guides, Handouts, and Supplementary Materials

Most of the faculty we interviewed provide task or assignment-specific handouts (or on-line guides)—detailed supports that anticipate problems students might encounter in their writing.

- M. G. (History) provides students with a packet of writing materials, including a carefully elaborated set of guidelines on writing "argument-driven essays." She outlines a sequence of procedures students may follow to develop a paper based on "well-honed middle-range conceptualizations that can be supported or refuted with evidence" rather than inflated generalizations.
- J. N. (History & Philosophy of Science) provides a rich set of on-line materials that offer pointed advice about problems particular to writing (and power-point presentation) in his field. Here, for example, is what he says about Voice:

  > Voice. In both textbooks and research articles, scientists are encouraged to write in a passive anonymous voice. The fiction is of disembodied scientific consciousness that is the repository of scientific knowledge. "It was known that. . . ." New discoveries are stripped as much as possible of human form and motivation. "It was observed that. . . ." This locution suppresses the human beings who made the discoveries, where and when they were done, the reasons they thought to observe where they did, their passions and aversions, the rivalries and feuds and the many dead ends. Writing in this style makes it very hard to pay proper attention to context.

- D. F. (Music) sent his senior seminar students additional instructions by email when they were struggling to move from description (of a musical work) to criticism. In his message, he tries to find another language (different from that in the writing assignment he had prepared for them), a language that might connect with the students, and at the same time he strives to represent the project as a writing project—something to be done in sentences and paragraphs. Here are sections of the e-mail:

1. Take the harmonic analysis you have already completed and try to chart it out or summarize it in broad terms: where do the major changes of key or major shifts in the harmonic progression take place? How do these shifts or changes relate to the placement of text in the passage?

2. After getting this broad overview of the harmonic motion of the passage, then think about how the other elements we discussed in class can be related to it. In short, how does the entire "constellation" of musical procedures combine to create an overall musical-expressive effect that relates to or portrays the text?

3. In a few sentences or paragraphs, summarize what you perceive to be this overall musical-expressive quality and the primary means by which it is achieved. Send that statement on to me whenever you have written it. I then can react quickly to your thesis (or hypothesis) before you proceed to write up a draft of your paper.

Use of Models

Many of those we interviewed use models in their teaching—either examples of student papers or examples of professional writing—in order to give students a point of reference for genre, format, and style. With models, students learn that writing comes from within a community rather than out of the blue (or through divine inspiration). In some cases, the models are provided only to those students who are struggling, who don't have a sense of what is expected of them or who need help in imagining "good" writing.

The use of published models also prepares students to read the professional literature—not simply for information but as a demonstration of thought and method.

- K. C. (Biological Sciences) has students read a typical journal article. As part of the writing instruction, she has them read only the first paragraph, the first and last sentences of the succeeding paragraphs, and the last paragraph. This exercise gets student to think about how those particular sentences function in the article, thereby directing their attention to formal structures. "When you provide a structure—not a template—you get more orderly writing."

- L. R. (Neuroscience) believes students need to learn to read the professional literature. She has students read articles from the journals—first "as science" and then as writing, in order to think about presentation.
- J. N. (History & Philosophy of Science) and W. C. (Biological Sciences) have students writing articles as though for particular professional journals, and therefore have them reading regularly from the journals.
- S. C. (Economics) says, "One of the most instructive things I do is to use a journal in Economics that publishes student papers. I have my students read one and write a review." This process helps students get an idea of how an economic argument can be structured.

For some of the faculty we interviewed, using journal articles as a model for student writing was a new idea. Some expressed an interest in having their students read scholars' work as a model of writing within the discipline. Others prefer that students not read the professional literature. One colleague (Anthropology) said that he wants to demystify research and believes that journal articles would make that task difficult, by distracting students from their own decisions about substance and method. Another (History) avoids professional models so that students will attend to primary materials and work from "inside" the problem of narrating a particular history.

A number of faculty members use student writing as models—in addition to, or instead of, professional writing.

- M. G. (History) conducts workshops in class as students are working on a particular project. For example, she might duplicate the first paragraphs of six different papers so that the class can discuss effective introductions.
- S. D. (German) discusses sample papers with her classes using an overhead projector. She asks students to identify "what is good, not so good," and then to merge parts of one paper with parts of another to compose a collective response.

- L. P. (Anthropology) distributes copies of term papers from previous classes to "serve as examples of research topics, how reports have been organized, different acceptable formats, the optional use of tables and figures, and the manner by which papers are critiqued."

Working with Sources

Most of the faculty members we interviewed provide handouts or lessons on the use of sources. Their particular concerns go beyond students' understanding of plagiarism. Students need to learn to evaluate sources, to read them critically and to use the material as the basis for their own thinking and argument (rather than stringing together quotations in lieu of thought or argument). Students have to find a way of using the material and they have to find a position from which to speak, as writers and thinkers, in relation to the experts or the professionals. They need to learn to understand what is new and groundbreaking, what is controversial, and even how to identify a fact or a conclusion.

In several of the courses discussed in the interviews, faculty restrict the range of materials students can work with as they write—often limiting "research" to materials in a course-pack. Instructors gave several reasons for this restriction. Much time is taken, and much backtracking is required, when students head off to the library to try to find appropriate sources. A limited set of sources and a limited topic is also a hedge against plagiarism. Limiting the source materials also allows for comparisons across a class and increased attention to the intellectual or academic task—that is, what students can make from the materials at hand.

Essay Exams

In the survey and in the focus groups, students expressed a variety of concerns about essay exams. The History Department faculty we interviewed, however, were the only ones to focus attention on this genre of academic writing. So much rests on these exams, they noted, and yet students are often unprepared for the task.

- One colleague noted that this difficulty arises not so much because of student deficiencies but because the approach is foreign to them—reading difficult texts and organizing critical answers to complex questions. She provides written comments on the "content" of essay exams but also on the writing. Students can request conferences to discuss the writing in the exam and they can bring in outlines or drafts for comments in advance of a test.

- Another said that if students have never written a "history" essay exam, she invites them to come to see her. She provides a sample exam, which she will read and comment on. Students tend to take her up on this after the midterm! She does not provide models of previous student essay exams because the key, she says, is for students to learn how to engage the material, to work on the problem from the inside. Students must learn that you don't fully know what you want to say until you begin writing.

PART TWO: FROM OUR STUDENTS. FOCUS GROUPS AND SURVEY

Student Focus Groups

We organized eight focus groups with a total of 33 participants, mostly juniors and seniors. Participants were mainly drawn from upper-level writing intensive courses. This was a select group, largely representing majors in the Humanities and Social Sciences, but they were interested in the study and eager to talk about student writing on our campus. Our experience with the first three sessions helped to shape the undergraduate student survey in-

strument and to refine our questions for the later focus groups. The questions were:

- In what ways would you say your own writing has changed in the time you have been studying at Pitt?
- What are the most valuable lessons you have learned for writing in your major? How did you learn these lessons?
- In your major, what do you think your professors value most in students' writing? What seems to frustrate them the most?
- In what courses have you done your best work as a writer? What were you working on? What do you think enabled you to do good work?
- What was your worst writing experience–the least useful or the least satisfying? What made it so unsatisfying? Please do not use the names of instructors in your response.
- What can professors do to enable students to successfully complete their writing assignments?
- What questions haven't we asked you? What more would you like to tell us about your experience of writing at the University of Pittsburgh?

We had tapes and notes from the focus group sessions, and as we reviewed them we organized our report according to the primary themes, topics, and concerns that emerged in the conversations. In our report, we were also careful to use student language as much as possible. For the survey, we needed a vocabulary that would be current and recognizable, and we wanted our colleagues to hear how writing was talked about in the hallways, the bars, and the dorms.

In the report, we organized the discussion by the general categories in our questioning.

What Do Professors Want?

Thought.

Students were divided in their perceptions of their professors' expectations. Some felt that professors mainly want "certain answers, their answers," a view perhaps related to the belief that what professors require is simply written evidence that the student thoroughly understands the course material.

On the other hand, one student summarized a commonly stated view when she said her professors want to see students "putting thought into [their] writing." Others agreed that professors expect students to formulate their own theses, or make interesting and novel claims. In one group, when a participant declared that his professors value "content," others rapidly modified the statement in a string of responses: "accurate content," "supported content," "arguable content," and their discussion of these modifiers indicated the importance of the student's own thinking in the presentation of "content" to the instructor.

Organization.

While students disagreed about the extent to which their teachers value independent thinking, they were quite consistent in their belief that professors expect "organization" in student writing. A logical order, a well-constructed argument, good reasoning, sound structure, and coherence were frequently mentioned, and tended to elicit nods all round the table. Students who directly commented on what most frustrates their professors mentioned lack of organization more than anything else—sometimes describing the problem as "rambling." A few students mourned that adhering to this expectation led them to write standard, formulaic papers, but most seemed to see their mastery of organization as an achievement. They spoke with pride about the way they had learned to compose a coherent and logical paper, in which their claims were "linked" and orderly, and they seemed to see this accomplishment as evidence that they had become better thinkers than they had been when they entered college.

Clarity and conciseness.

The other quality of writing that students consistently said their professors value is "clarity and conciseness." When they were describing the kind of writing valued in their majors, as well as when they were discussing the most important lessons they had learned about writing in the major, students talked about clarity: "economy of expression," "direct and to the point," "no fluff," "precise word choice." Balancing this expectation is their sense that too much conciseness is a liability. They see a double bind here—writing needs to be efficient and to the point, and yet instructors also expect students to "follow through" on an idea, to elaborate or "explore every avenue" in their writing.

Something deeper, something more, something beyond the obvious.[9]

When they spoke about how their writing has changed during their years at Pitt, students frequently described their ability to organize a paper and to make it more concise and clear. Some spoke about how their own "writing process" has changed, especially to note that they now start a project earlier and take more time to complete it.

Perhaps most striking, however, is the students' repeated assertion that a significant change in their thinking has accompanied the development of their writing. While a few students described academic writing as a requirement that "fences you in," most volunteered their belief that learning to write has "expanded" the way they think. "Most of my progress is not in practical aspects," one student explained, "but more in the way of my thinking." Others described "new ways to approach texts," increased confidence in their own informed opinions, the ability to "synthesize" material, or readiness for a "probing application of theory." In many cases, the students initiated conversations about reading when asked about their writing, asserting the importance of "learning to read critically" or to "look for [another] writer's subjectivity and bias" because "so much of writing is based on reading." One group discussed the way writing in their majors had taught them to go beyond their immediate reactions to texts or ideas. To simply "agree or disagree" with another writer, or to pronounce an idea "correct or incorrect," now seems "too easy" or even "rash" to these students. Instead, they now believe that writing a paper requires them to "understand where [other writers] come from, why they would write this, and if it has application to today." In the end, these particular students articulated a balance they strive for as writers, between keeping "an open mind" and developing their own "convictions."

What Enables You to Do Your Best Work?

Heart and soul.

When describing the courses that had enabled their "best work" as writers, students spoke both about assignments and about instructional practices. Over and over, they recalled assignments that had allowed them to write about something they cared about. As one student put it, she did her best work when "I put my heart and soul into it." Another defined the difference between "heartfelt papers" and papers written "just to get the grade." The students' discussions did not make it clear whether this "caring" must precede the course or can be engendered by it, but in any case it appears that the students we interviewed believe rather firmly that they write best when they care about their topics.

This fundamental belief leads to the question of how much choice students want in an assignment. While some students advocated open assignments that give them complete control over their topics (a condition described as "freedom"), most seemed to prefer a range of choices within a field carefully delimited by the instructor. Students on both sides of this divide felt strongly about the issue. Those who favored open-ended assignments sometimes criticized their peers, claiming that professors are forced to provide paper topics only because students "can't think for themselves." On the other hand, some students who sought clear direction from their instructors labeled as "lazy" those professors who leave an assignment "too open-ended."

New ways of thinking.

Beyond the question of choice, students often described assignments that "pushed" them to do new thinking as those that enabled their best work. "I like to write in a way I feel I can grow," one student explained. One group (consisting mostly of History majors) had an animated discussion of an assignment that had asked them to work with primary sources and come to their own conclusions, rather than "making conclusions based on what other people have already concluded." Others spoke favorably of long assignments that allowed them to "dig deep" and to "tie together in my own mind" the themes of a course. They valued longer projects, they said, that asked them to write from "my own research and my own ideas," to draw on learning from other courses, to refute another writer's arguments, or to synthesize the work they had done in earlier, shorter assignments in the course. (Many mentioned their ability to write longer papers when asked how their writing had changed.) A number of students also said that they appreciated assignments that gave them "creative" opportunities or allowed them to depart from common academic format.

Making connections.

When describing their worst writing experiences, focus group participants did complain about writing assignments they were "not excited about," but they objected even more vehemently to assignments that appeared "disconnected" from the rest of the course work. In contrast, when describing to each other the writing assignments that had enabled their best work, the students often talked about how an assignment had helped them forge connections between different aspects of the course, or between that course and other work they had done in the major. When they perceived that a writing assignment was "not related to what we were doing in class," or was "coming out of left field," students said they felt very uncertain about what to do, or why they ought to do it. Their discussions of this issue indicated that they prefer to have an explicit understanding of how a writing assignment relates to the other goals and activities of the course, and of how their other work in the class should prepare them for the writing; they are quite aware of the occasions when these relationships are not made clear.

What Can Professors Do to Help?

When they mentioned instructional practices that had enabled them to do their best work, students recalled receiving feedback on drafts of a long project. In speaking of their worst writing experiences, they repeatedly asserted the difficulty of writing "with no feedback and no guidelines." And when explicitly asked what professors might do "to enable students to successfully complete their writing assignments," the students again asked for clear assignment guidelines and feedback on drafts. The students themselves raised these terms, and their appearance—so consistently across the groups and in answer to so many different questions—deserves some emphasis.

Provide guidelines.

Students agreed that they have trouble tackling an assignment that asks for a particular type of writing but offers no instruction in how to do it. More generally, they find it difficult to succeed in a class with writing assignments but "not much talk about writing." They advise professors to "be specific about what you want" by providing clear statements about what is expected in style, format, depth of research, and so on. Some students suggested that instructors could provide models, or examples of "good papers from last semester." They also made it clear, however, that instructions for a writing assignment can be too rigid, especially if they consist of a long series of specific questions that all must be answered in the paper. As one student put it, "Instead of telling them what to think, help them learn how to think."

Provide opportunities for feedback and revision.

Once they have started writing for a particular professor, students hope for useful feedback (as opposed to a simple grade or a series of "illegible scribbles") in response to their efforts. Many students expressed their wish that professors would give feedback on a draft so that they could revise it before turning it in as a finished product. "I prefer when the teacher requires a draft," was a typical remark. One self-described "fan" of "drafts and revision" explained that this process gives "first work another chance" and enables her to develop "new thoughts." When not given the opportunity to revise, students value extensive comments on an early paper. Their responses indicated that they want comments both about what they call their "writing" (form) and about what they call their "thoughts" or "ideas" (content).

In our conversations about feedback, students often voiced the questions they would have liked to ask after receiving a sparsely-marked paper. "I see what I did wrong, but what should I do?" And, for successful papers: "What did I do well? Why did I get a 95?" The discussion of this issue made it clear that the students were seeking instruction, not just affirmation, in their professor's comments; they wanted to know what to keep doing in their next papers as well as what to do differently. Perhaps even more important, they wanted to hear a response to their thinking. Students receiving good grades described their dismay when an instructor's comments were limited to something like "great job!" They ask, rather passionately, that professors offer "comments on my thoughts" to let the student writer know "if my ideas were good."

Pay attention to timing and to schedules.

One other instructional practice was mentioned often enough to be noted here: the careful scheduling and timely introduction of writing assignments. Students frequently asserted that they want sufficient time to complete an assignment while keeping up with their other classes. They ask professors to "be mindful that their class is not our only class." For these focus group participants, "sufficient time" seems to mean more than a week.

Take care.

Along with descriptions of instructional practices, the focus group questions elicited a surprising number of comments about the teacher-student relationship and its effect on student writing. Students said that they produce better writing when they have instructors who command respect and trust; in this atmosphere, students feel more likely to "find a connection between myself and the material." They also appreciate teachers who are "accessible" or "approachable"—that is, willing to discuss the student's writing in person. One participant asked professors not to be "just a voice behind a desk" but rather to "create compassion between student and teacher." The student accompanied this comment with a gesture: "a teacher-student relationship," he explained (with hands held side by side), "not a teacher-student relationship" (with one hand held high above the other). The compassionate teacher seems to be one who takes students' writing and their thinking seriously, and therefore engages students in serious conversation about their work—"talking to you, not at you," as the student put it. In this relationship, the instructor supports students in developing their own thinking, rather than "telling them what to think." These supportive instructors are apparently the same ones who make it clear that students should be "putting thought into [their] writing" rather than merely reiterating "certain answers" provided in advance by the instructor. The image of the caring teacher seems to mirror students' sense that teachers, too, value "students who care" about their writing and learning.

A "Gap" in the Curriculum

At various times in our focus group conversations, students commented on the "gap" they perceived between their introductory composition course and their w-courses, usually taken late in their college experience. One senior enrolled in a w-course in her major said, for example, "I took [the first year composition course] and made a lot of progress and then didn't work on my writing at all until this year. I wish I had taken [another w-course] earlier." Many participants were enthusiastic, however, about their upper-level instructors; they remarked on the intensity of writing instruction in the w-courses in their majors, indicating that their professors not only demanded a lot but also offered substantial and significant feedback.

Summary

In all the focus groups, talking about their writing led students to talk about their thinking and learning. For students, it seems, learning to write and writing to learn are inextricably linked. The writing assignments they value are those that push them to think further and learn more. They also value writing instruction that helps them develop the skills of organization, clarity, and conciseness.

According to students in the focus groups:

- What professors value in student writing
  - Correct answers
  - Understanding of course material
  - Organization
  - Clarity and conciseness
  - Student thinking—critical, creative, complex
- What students value in writing assignments

- The opportunity to write about something that matters to them
- The opportunity for new thinking and learning
- The opportunity to dig deeply and make connections
- Explicit understanding of the assignment's relation to the course material
- Useful support for student writers
  - Specific and explicit guidelines for an assignment
  - Feedback on a draft, with opportunity to revise
  - Extensive comments on papers, comments that can help students recognize what works as well as what could be improved
  - Response to thoughts and ideas as well as to a paper's form or style
  - Sufficient time to complete an assignment
  - Classroom attention to writing and thinking in the discipline

STUDENT SURVEY

The Sample

In the Spring Term, 2005, 1000 juniors and 1000 seniors were invited to participate. The response rate was 32% (256 juniors and 389 seniors), a relatively high rate of response for surveys of this type.

Who Responded to the Survey?

Students were randomly selected and contacted via e-mail. Students in the Humanities (and with majors in English) were the most likely to respond. There was, however, a reasonable distribution of students with majors across the academic disciplines and the disproportions are not large, as shown in Figure 1.

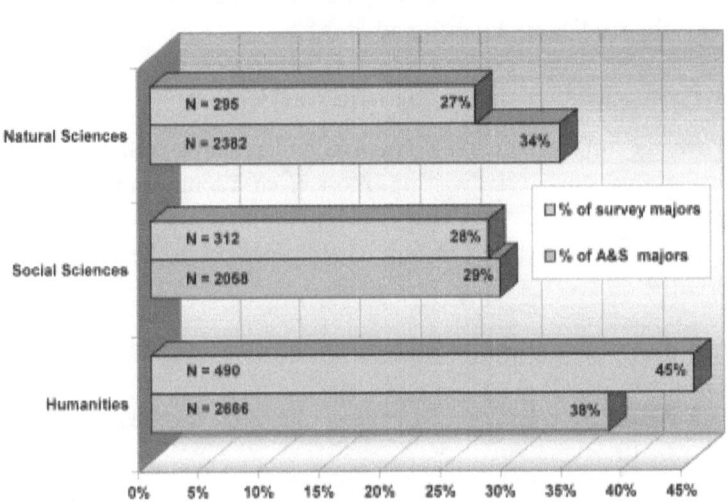

Figure 1: Survey Responses by Area of Study

Students in the Humanities (in particular English Writing majors and Communication majors) were more likely to respond. Students in the Social Sciences responded proportionally (with more Political Science majors responding and fewer majors in Economics or History). Students in the Natural Sciences (in particular, students in Computer Science and Psychology) were least likely to respond.

The Timing of the Required Courses: Seminar in Composition (First Year Writing) and Two W-Courses

We asked students when they took their required courses:

- First Year Writing: 88% took this in the Freshman Year.
- W-designated courses (2 are required): 70% took these in the Junior and/or Senior Year.

We asked students what year was most important to their development as writers: the freshman, sophomore, junior or senior years?

- Both juniors and seniors were in agreement: the junior year was the most important. (This was the same response received in the studies at Harvard and Stanford.[10])

The Presence of Writing in the A&S Curriculum

On average, undergraduates in the Arts and Sciences took 4–6 courses that required substantial writing, most often a long term or research paper.

Students reported that in both the junior and in the senior years, they write on average 7 papers of more than 5 pages:

- Junior Year (mean = 6.9 papers); the range for the majority was 1–10 papers.
- Senior Year (mean = 7.4 papers); the range for the majority was 0–10 papers.

The Genres of Academic Writing

The focus groups helped us to identify and to name the genres of academic writing in courses in A&S. The survey allowed us to draw conclusions about the frequency of the genres and to elicit students' assessments of their usefulness in learning to write and in mastering course content.

The frequency of assignment genres

- The most common:
  - Short response papers
  - In class essay exams
  - Reports (on readings or research)
  - Research (term) papers (using sources or data)
  - Persuasive papers (opinion papers, argument papers, position papers)
- Those in mid range:
  - Personal essays
  - Take home essay exams
  - In-class writing (not an exam)
  - Journals or Reflective Writing
  - Literature reviews, Research reviews

- The least common:
  - Lab reports*
  - "Creative" assignments (such as poetry, short stories, plays)
  - Articles for academic journals (for submission or in imitation)

Note: The low frequency of lab reports is most likely due to the percentage of students in the pool with majors in the Natural Sciences.

Students' assessments of the desirability of the genres

We asked: "How often do you think you received assignments for [this genre]: not often enough, often enough, too often."

There was no clear statement about assignment genres that were too frequent or too common. The most commonly assigned genres (opinion papers, response papers, research reports, for example), had, according to our students, an appropriate circulation in the curriculum. The most interesting responses came to the question about genres students would like to see more often, as shown in Figure 2.

"Not Often Enough" Responses

Genre	%
Journals/Reflective writing	31%
Persuasive/Opinion papers	32%
In-class writing, not an exam	33%
Personal essays	33%
Take home essay exams	43%
"Creative" assignments (poetry, etc.)	52%
Writing as though for an academic journal	55%

Figure 2: Not Enough Writing Assignments, by Genre

Students' assessments of the usefulness of the genres in learning course material and in learning to write

We asked students two questions about genre. How useful was the genre in learning to write, and how useful was the genre in learning the course material?

There was not much difference in the responses and, in retrospect, this makes sense. As students are doing the work of a course, particularly an advanced course, writing papers and working on a subject are pretty much the same thing. Writing is part of the way a student learns to master the subject; attention to writing as something separate from developing an idea or an argument (attention, for example, to questions of style in revision) is often seen as a luxury or a distraction from the task at hand.

Students did, however, find essay exams, lab reports, and informal writing to be more useful in learning subject matter than in learning to write. See Figures 3 and 4.

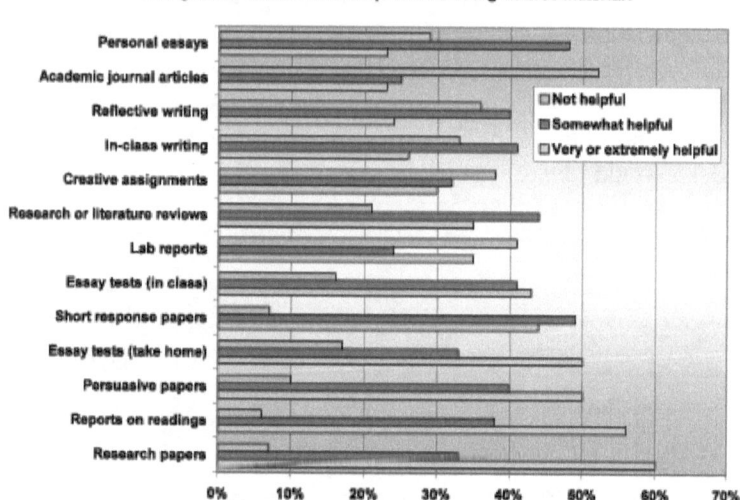

Figure 3: Usefulness of Genres in Learning Course Material

*Note: About 61% of students reported that they had never received this type of assignment, which may account for its low rating here.
**Note: The rating of lab reports may be related to the relatively low percentage of students with majors in the Natural Sciences.

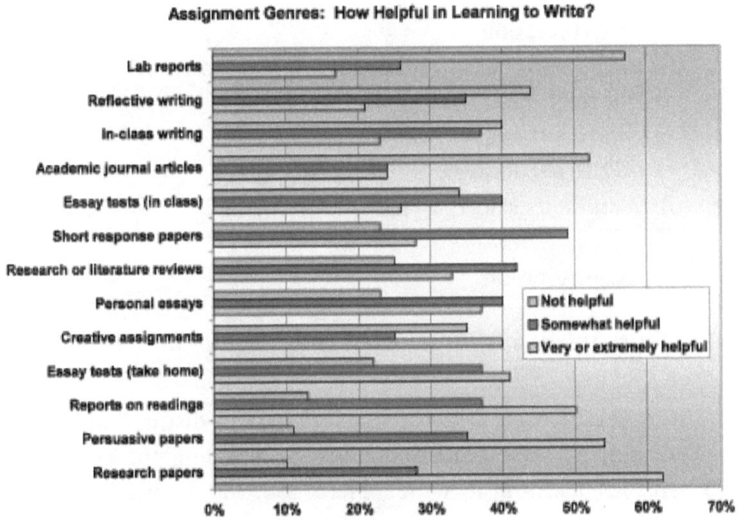

Assignment Genres: How Helpful in Learning to Write?

[Bar chart showing genres: Lab reports, Reflective writing, In-class writing, Academic journal articles, Essay tests (in class), Short response papers, Research or literature reviews, Personal essays, Creative assignments, Essay tests (take home), Reports on readings, Persuasive papers, Research papers — rated as Not helpful / Somewhat helpful / Very or extremely helpful, on a scale from 0% to 70%.]

Figure 4: Usefulness of Genres in Learning to Write

*Note: About 61% of students reported that they had never received this type of assignment, which may account for its low rating here.

**Note: The rating of lab reports may be related to the relatively low percentage of students with majors in the Natural Sciences.

Writing as Intellectual Work

We attempted to measure students' sense of writing instruction as instruction in thinking or in performing specific academic tasks. In order to name these, we used phrases that were common in the focus groups: *regurgitation, summary, analysis, interpretation, developing one's own ideas, working with a thesis, writing persuasively, reflecting*. We asked about the relative frequency of each in the curriculum. From the results, it appears they are all present to about the same degree. There were not significant differences to report here.

Students' assessments of the desirability of the academic tasks

We asked: "How much of this kind of writing have you done: not enough, about right, too much?"

- Students said they had about the right amount of:
  - Summary

- Analysis
- Interpretation
    - Students said they would prefer more opportunities to:
        - Develop their own ideas
        - Prove a thesis
        - Write persuasively
    - And students said they had too many assignments that asked for:
        - Regurgitation

Students' assessments of the usefulness of this writing in learning course material and in learning to write

As in the case above, we asked students to make a distinction between the usefulness of these academic tasks in "learning the course material" and in "learning to write." Here, too, the distinction did not produce strikingly different responses. From students' perspective, the intellectual work and the work of writing appear to be pretty much the same thing.

Students did, however, see "regurgitation" as even less useful to them as they are working on their writing. And they found "persuasion," "developing [their] own ideas" and "proving a thesis" to be particularly useful to them as writing tasks. See Figures 5 and 6.

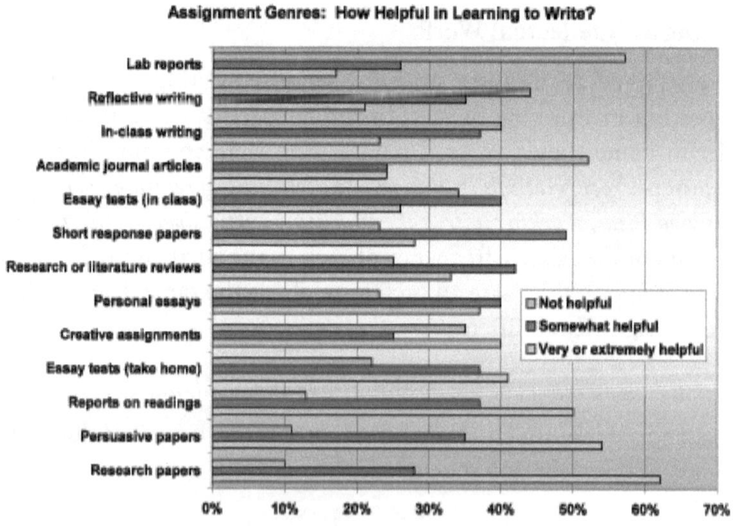

Figure 5: Usefulness in Learning Course Material

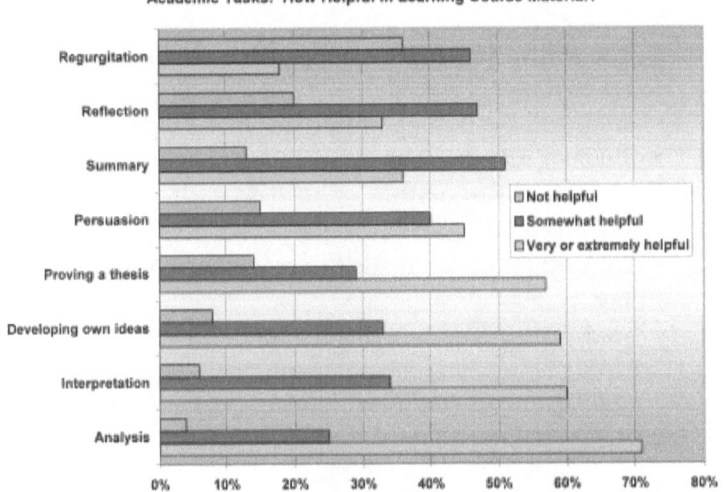

Figure 6: Usefulness in Learning to Write

The Teaching of Writing (in and out of the w-courses)

We asked questions about pedagogical practices in the required writing-intensive courses (the w-courses) and in other courses, courses not designated as w-courses that included substantial amounts of writing. The questions were prompted by our work with the focus groups.

In w-designated courses

- Common practices:
    - Assignments are written out.
    - Students receive handouts with additional guidelines, advice, or strategies.
    - Students must meet firm deadlines.
    - Students work with primary sources (books or research data).
    - Students work with secondary sources (books or journal articles).
    - Students are expected to revise a rough draft after receiving comments from the instructor.

- Students are required to proofread and to correct their work.
- The written work significantly affects the final grade.
- Not so common practices:
  - Students have the opportunity to choose their own topics.
  - Students submit outlines, topic ideas, bibliography, etc., in advance of first draft.
- Seldom practiced:
  - Students are shown models of professional or student writing.
  - Students receive peer evaluation of drafts.

In courses without the w-designation but with significant amounts of writing

- Students were less likely to be required to revise a draft.
- Students were less likely to be provided with written guidelines, advice or strategies.
- The written work was not as important to the final grade.

When students indicated that they had never encountered a given pedagogical practice, we asked them about their preferences. Would they have preferred a particular pedagogical practice in their courses?

- What would students like to see that they don't see?
  - 76% would like to be shown models of student and professional writing.
  - 60% would like to revise a draft after receiving comments from the instructor.
- What practices would students prefer not to see?
  - 63% would not like to use peer evaluation as the basis for revision.
  - 63% would not like to submit outlines, topic ideas, bibliographies, etc., in advance of a first draft.

We asked students questions about the feedback their writing received in w-designated courses and in courses other than w-designated courses with significant amounts of writing.

In w-designated courses

- Common practices:
  - Students receive written commentary.
  - Students receive check marks, x's or editing symbols.
  - The feedback students receive helps in revision.
  - The feedback is constructive and specific.
  - The feedback focuses attention on ideas, arguments and analysis.
  - The feedback focuses attention on style, format and structure.
  - The feedback focuses attention on grammar and mistakes.
- Not so common practices:
  - Student papers are discussed in class.
  - Students have individual conferences with faculty.
- Seldom practiced:
  - Grading follows a table or rubric.
  - Students receive a grade or numerical score only (with no written feedback).

In courses without the w-designation but with significant amounts of writing, students are:

- Less likely to receive written commentary.
- More likely to have checkmarks.
- Less like to have conferences with faculty.
- Less likely to see sample papers.
- Less likely to revise or to receive directions toward revision.
- Less likely to have attention paid to ideas or to style and format.

Again, we asked students who had not received a particular type of feedback about their preferences. Would they have preferred this form of feedback in their courses?

- What would students like to see that they don't see?
  - 58% would like more class discussion of sample papers.
  - 70% would like to have individual conferences with faculty.
- What would students like to have changed in current practice?

- 95% would not like to receive papers with grades but no written commentary.
- 75% would not like to receive feedback that focuses on grammar and/or mistakes.

The Value of Writing

We asked students about the importance of writing to their education and to their future lives and careers.

- 90% said that writing was important, very important or extremely important to their *education at the University of Pittsburgh*.
  - 34% said that writing was *extremely* important to their education at Pitt.
- 81% said that writing was important, very important or extremely important in *helping them to connect with a course and its materials*.
  - 21% said that writing was *extremely* important in helping them to connect with a course and its materials.
- 80% said that writing was important, very important or extremely important *to learning in their major area of study*.
  - 43% said that writing was *extremely* important to learning in their major.
- 81% said that writing will be important, very important or extremely important to their *future professions or careers*.
  - 41% said that writing will be *extremely* important to their future profession or career.

Open-ended Questions

We asked students for the name of the most useful course they had taken, as far as their writing was concerned. We provided a full list in our report. This list, as we noted, garnered considerable attention! The range of courses and departments on this list was interesting and impressive. A substantial number of students mentioned the required introductory course, "Seminar in Composition." And, although the question asked for courses, a substantial number of students referred to the usefulness of the Writing Center.

We asked students for the "one person on campus who has been most important in helping you improve your writing." And we asked, "What can we learn from your experience with this person." A full list of "faculty who made a difference" was included in the report. This, too, garnered considerable interest.

A list of student comments appears in Appendix F.

From students' written comments, teachers were said to have made a difference when

- they had high standards and communicated clear expectations,
- they wrote assignments that were interesting and varied,
- they provided occasions for students to do more than "present information" in a paper,
- they allowed students to follow their own lines of interest and inquiry,
- they showed genuine interest in the student's work and in the student's ideas,
- they knew how to provide close commentary and they knew when to "get out of the way,"
- they were direct and supportive as they led students through the process of revision,
- they were available for conferences on pieces of writing,
- they provided specific guidelines or advice that enabled students to write in a more complex and/or professional manner, and when,
- although demanding, they were also positive and encouraging.

We asked, "What more would you like to tell us about your experience with writing at the University of Pittsburgh?" We included a representative set of responses in the final report. The comments were pointed, thoughtful, eloquent, sometimes critical and often useful. A quick sample is presented below:

> I never expected to write so many papers in college. I've had several papers every semester since my sophomore year and while it was frustrating at times, I'm glad that I had to write them. My writing is far better now than it was my sophomore year, and I don't mind it so much anymore.

I feel writing was an important part of my college education but I had to seek it out myself. There is opportunity at Pitt if you do not like writing or don't feel it is useful to you to avoid it. This may not be a bad thing but it is important to note.

I personally prefer writing papers, at least for my History classes, because I feel that researching your own ideas and then developing them within the paper is much more beneficial in learning the course material than regurgitating information on a test.

I have written more in one-credit Chemistry or Biology labs than I have in most 3 credit courses, including those in which I have received a W. The lab reports are generally 10–25 pages depending on the experiment. I feel that the writing for this course is not worth the 1 credit received.

Long papers for me personally are ineffective. They are usually weighted more when it comes to grades and require so much time they become exhausting. I really appreciate smaller length papers (2–4 pgs) for a number of reasons. It breaks the material down into smaller chunks that are more easily remembered. Research takes less time and more time can be spent on modifying and working on actual writing. It allows more opportunity for improvement because more than one or two papers can be submitted in a semester. There is a cushion allowed for improvement and time for feedback with numerous papers. Writing very short things in class is not helpful to me . . . at all. There is too much pressure, and I think that students should really have time to think and organize their thoughts before handing something in.

Writing has played a central role in my education at the University of Pittsburgh. In both Political Science and Economics, writing played a central role and aided in my understanding of the topics, allowing me a chance to integrate the material I learned. My only critique would be of my Business degree. The CBS program seems to avoid individual writing projects, instead favoring quantitative testing and group projects/presentations. While this helps with learning presentation style, I feel it is a severe detriment that the Introduction-level survey courses do not have a writing component.

I think that students should have more opportunities to write different types of papers. Even though I am a History and Political Science major, I would like to write something other than strictly academic essays.

I think writing is extremely useful in learning most material particularly because it forces you to analyze what you are writing about. The process of writing a paper helps you continue the thought process beyond what you are presented with and make conclusions based on that more than just reading through and sitting through a lecture. The feedback from a paper helps you make your points clearer and more precise and also helps you refine your writing more to help you communicate on more than one level. The writing process should definitely not be underestimated. It has been and will be a vital tool in the learning experience and also in communication in general, something all educated people should be able to do fluently and precisely.

Sometimes papers or writing assignments can become busy work and cause students to lose interest and motivation in the assignment. It is better to have fewer meaningful papers than lots and lots of little ones.

I believe that term papers of ten pages or more in length are key tools for students to learn large amounts of information on a topic, and although time-consuming and more often than not, exhausting to complete, a paper of that size causes a sense of accomplishment and expertise on the subject one completes. The completion of these papers causes students to feel as if they really got their money worth out of the course and learned a lot.

A more complete list of student comments appears in Appendix G.

Part Three. Conclusions

Outcomes

Our project began before "outcomes assessment" hit our campus. Although our study was well-received, it did not, to be sure, serve as a substitute. It did, however, provide a context in which outcomes assessment could be more thoughtful and meaningful, and more of a shared responsibility than it might have been otherwise. It gave departments a very useful context for the evaluation of their capstone, writing-intensive courses. Several department chairs requested copies of the report while it was in draft. Beth Matway led the general assessment of our WID program. Because the study had included so much information on students—their work as intellectual work, their understanding of the value of the work they did, and their sense of its connection to A&S and departmental goals—attention to student outcomes made sense in a way it would not have otherwise. The measurement of outcomes was another way of paying attention to the culture of writing (and learning) on campus; it was not simply a hoop to jump through or a Dean's arbitrary demand.

The study also, however, produced some significant outcomes for the WID program on our campus. After receiving the report, both the Provost and the Dean (and in advance of the later assessment initiatives) offered resources we could use in support of writing in the undergraduate curriculum in the school of Arts and Sciences. There *was* a happy ending, in other words. The report produced action, and that is as much as any report writer can hope for.

In Spring 2007, the Provost provided a full time non tenure track line to add a Lecturer to support and to "build upon the successes" of the initiatives outlined in the study, including a newly designed annual faculty seminar, one that carries a stipend for faculty participants.[11] He offered an additional full time non tenure track line to provide a Lecturer in support of a new program developed in conjunction with our School of Engineering.[12] And, with the Dean of Arts and Sciences, he provided an annual budget of $35,000 to provide additional support to WID. We used these funds initially to develop a program to train talented juniors and seniors in the sciences, who then provide tutorial support for students in large lecture sections and in laboratories.

What Did We Learn?

As we conceived of this project, we thought it to be primarily descriptive and ethnographic. Our charge was to document the "core values and practices associated with writing at Pitt." We did not have the funding (or the ambition) to do a longitudinal study, although our work was very much influenced by the impressive work underway at Harvard and at Stanford. The data base gathered on these two campuses provides a remarkable resource for research on student learning and student attitudes. The collection of student writing provides a corpus that can serve scholars for decades. It is important that institutions with various profiles find a way to contribute to this collection of student writing.

The Pittsburgh study, however, shared some of the primary concerns of the studies at Harvard and Stanford. We were not in a position to speculate on student learning over time (except through student testimony). With Harvard and Stanford, we were interested, however, in gathering information on the genres of student writing. These genres are both local (determined by traditions of local practice) and disciplinary (determined by faculty understanding of writing appropriate for learning in the disciplines). The focus on revision, the sequencing of assignments and the use of professional models are common on our campus and they are, we think, a distinctive part of our academic culture. As in the case of both the Stanford and Harvard studies, it was important to us to be in direct contact with a large number of students and to spend time considering what they had to say. We, too, were careful to feature and to publish the comments of our students. The comment that had the widest circulation after the release of the study was the comment by the student who got an A on her paper, but who was frustrated because the instructor's written comment ("good job") didn't engage with her ideas. Students help to shape the culture of writing on campus; it is our job to learn to listen to and to value what they say (just as it is our job to learn to read and to value their writing).

The faculty interviews provided rich examples of current (and best) practice on our campus, the report made visible (or gave voice to) teachers across the disciplines from whom we had much to learn. (We had seen similar consequences at Harvard.) We did not pay attention to the writing students do outside of class, a major focus of attention in the Stanford study. It seemed beyond our charge and, to be frank, we were already struggling to make the survey instrument more efficient. If we had it to do over again, we would drop the distinction in the survey between "learning to write" and "learning course material." It doubled our questions and turned out to be a meaningless distinction. Our students knew that learning economics by writing was the same thing as learning to write. This would have opened space for other lines of questioning. We would encourage anyone considering a campus-wide study to give as much time and attention to faculty as to students.

We learned much that was helpful to us locally. For example, the student comments led us to realize that while laboratory courses in the natural sciences required substantial amounts of writing, they had not become a focus for writing instruction and were not included among the courses officially designated as "writing intensive." We learned that a surprising number of students were asking for work with models of professional writing (academic and otherwise) and that a surprising number of faculty colleagues were offering them. This knowledge has produced an interesting and useful debate on campus over the appropriateness of asking students to write as though they were writing for professional publication. Our WID program was 20+ years old; the review of w-courses, the ability the report provided to think comparatively across departments and divisions, these led us to see problems, successes, and anomalies that would otherwise have remained invisible.

We learned that our colleagues, on the whole, were thoughtful, inventive and impressive teachers of writing. The template for a writing-intensive course on our campus is pretty basic. What they did with the template, how it was adapted and inflected by individual teachers and through expectations of their disciplines was quite wonderful to see. The most valuable products of the study, then, were the examples it provided of best practice. A course in Biology has become a model for courses in other areas of the natural sciences; a course in the History and Philosophy of Science has become a model for courses across the Humanities. Departments unused to talking about teaching, or featuring the work of colleagues as teachers, had the occasion (at least for a brief moment) to have such conversations and to see a colleague in a new light. Students had a chance to be heard as a collective and, given the chance, rose to the occasion.

In 1945 Raymond Williams returned to the Cambridge University campus after 4 ½ years as a soldier during World War II. When he returned, he had the sensation that things had changed, that the people around him were speaking a different language, even though they were (obviously) speaking in English. He tells this story in the "Introduction" to the first edition of his ground-breaking project, *Keywords. A Vocabulary of Culture and Society*. And he says

> When we come to say "we just don't speak the same language" we mean something . . . general: that we have different immediate values or different kinds of valuation, or that we are aware, often intangibly, of different formations and distributions of energy and interest. (1983, p. 11)

We often use this formulation to think about the linguistic and rhetorical demands of the different disciplines—"we just don't speak the same language." As we started to process all the data we received, including the interview and survey data shown above, one of our goals was to record and highlight the common language on our campus—the shared (rather than different) values and valuations, the shared (rather than different) formations and distributions of energy and interest (to use Williams' terms) and not only across departments but across the community of teachers and students, particularly advanced students, our juniors and seniors. We wanted to pick up keywords and then to use them as organizing devices as we provided an account of undergraduate writing on our campus.

Our point was not to insist that the Pittsburgh campus has its own private language, something unique. However, we did believe it important to give our primary audience a way to think about writing in the disciplines as a shared project of articulation, one where we create (and revise) the key terms used to represent, organize, prompt and value writing on our campus. We do not have our own private language, although we believe there are some distinctive key terms—like revision and sequence and genre. On our campus, it is not unusual to hear student writing referred to as "intellectual work" or as crucial to the work of the disciplines. John Norton, Professor and Director of our Center for Philosophy of Science, stunned us by saying: "If we assume that [students] cannot have a good idea, that they can only rehearse the ideas of others, the field [History and Philosophy of Science] will ossify. A field like HPS depends upon the work of undergraduates in our senior seminars." We also learned that there are some important sites of contestation, as in the different ways of imagining "professional" writing, represented by the disagreement over whether students should or shouldn't read and imitate the writing in academic journals.

We're not in a position (nor do we have the desire) to think comparatively. (It is interesting to note in passing, however, that in the Harvard Study, "thesis" was a key term and "thesis" is a word that seldom appeared in the conversations we had with teachers and students. The Stanford study gives particular emphasis to "performance" and "embodied writing"; on our campus, in the terms and practices of students and faculty colleagues, writing is still represented primarily as textual, represented in books and papers—even if they circulate in digital environments.) The study did much to reanimate conversations about writing and the teaching of writing across the disciplines on our campus. It created new points of reference and rich examples of best practice; it provided a new sense of our students, and what they thought and what they could (and couldn't do) as writers; and it highlighted courses and faculty colleagues that would otherwise have remained invisible.

FACULTY INTERVIEWS APPENDIX 1

L.A. (Hispanic Languages & Literatures) says that in her field, it's not enough for writing to be correct, clean, and clear; instead, it must engage a reader on many levels. She acknowledges that this type of writing, which calls on students to manage multiple texts or disciplines, can be very difficult, and she takes pains to support her students as they attempt it.

R.L. (Political Science) wants students to consider a statement from a variety of points of view, and "to understand trends and to see patterns" in complex bodies of information.

Appendix 2

K. C. (Biological Sciences) notes that students spend four years accumulating content. The role of writing is partly to demonstrate that they've learned something—but, more importantly, having students write compels them to find ways to "communicate information to an audience for a purpose."

M.G. (History) believes students need to write in order to develop their understanding of how a historian thinks. Writing means "learning for understanding," as opposed to learning just to accumulate information. "I don't think I can determine what students truly understand without having them write at some length," she says. "Students can be skillful about memorizing—but it's in the use of that knowledge that I can determine what they truly understand."

G. N. (Computer Science) directs students in his 1000-level course, "Algorithmic Implementation," to write to a lay audience, as in a popular magazine. This is partly to demonstrate their responsibility to a larger public, but also to insure a real or deep understanding of what they have done.

V. P. (Physics) wants his students to understand how important writing is to them as scientists. They can do all the work in the world, he says, "but you have to be able to present your work so that others can understand it or it's like a tree falling in the forest with no one around. It's useless, wasted effort."

J.N. (History & Philosophy of Science) asserts that "undergraduates can be engaged as scholars. . . . If we assume that [students] cannot have a good idea, that they can only rehearse the ideas of others, the field will ossify. A field like HPS depends upon the work of undergraduates in our senior seminars.

J. H. (Slavic) said that her comments on students' papers focus on substance, logic, and mechanics–but also on what she called "excitement." She wants students to explore what excites them, so she stays alert to levels of interest as she reads their papers.

Appendix 3

B. K. (Psychology) notices that "report writing" is the genre students know best when they come into her classes. "They are able to read and summarize what they read," she says. In the Research Methods course, she and her team of TAs have begun to emphasize argumentation in their writing assignments, so that students gain the ability to "integrate, to think beyond what they're summarizing and form an argument."

S. C. (English) says that English literature majors are good at writing the 5 page critical essay. Assigning longer papers (term papers) will not necessarily move them beyond that. That is, the 20 page paper that is a collection of four "5-page critical essays" is not necessarily an advance in learning. His goal is to teach them to complicate the kind of argument represented by the 5-page essay (by considering alternative points of view, or by varying critical style and approach), so that the "long paper" is a different intellectual exercise than the short paper.

R. L. (Political Science) is also concerned to take students out of a "term paper" mode. He works primarily through shorter assignments that put students into positions where they are responding to the news, imagining solutions to real problems, taking positions on quite specific policy issues, even projecting themselves into the role of presidential advisors. R.L. says that he wants to teach students how to pay attention to the news; he wants them to think that they can take a position on current events, he wants them to take a position on what they read (and not just process it as information). He wants them to be aware of how much thinking is based on unwarranted assumptions. His writing assignments are designed to allow students to experience first hand the "pleasures of the extended argument."

Appendix 4

In D. F.'s Senior Seminar (Music) students write a series of four short papers that culminate in a longer "critical" paper. The first short paper assignment asks students to discuss (describe) one movement of the Mozart Requiem with attention to orchestration, to harmonic language and modulation, and to the text to be sung (declamation and expression). The second short paper assignment asks students to place the description in a larger context—and the larger context has to do with the "meaning" of the text and the composer's choices. The assignment announces its objectives: to give students experience "in writing about harmonic progressions in prose rather than labeling each chord"; and to give students experience working with a short passage rather than an entire movement. The third short paper is a return to the project of the first. Students are asked to analyze harmony in one of four prescribed passages from Faure or Verdi. The fourth paper is to be based on the harmonic analysis of the third. It is to be a critical paper and should also take into account "orchestration, vocal setting, and texture." Students are invited to "expand the paper to include a larger segment of the movement, or the entire movement."

L. P. (Anthropology) and I. F. (Psychology) have students conduct a semester-long research project and prepare a research report. A key element for both is the writing of a Proposal or Prospectus. Here students are shown what it means to have a research problem that is specific, manageable and interesting. Both give substantial attention at this early stage; if not, the students' work for the semester can be wasted. From that point on, the assignments are written to organize the student's research and their understanding of the genre and audience for a report.

Appendix 5

M. G. (History) provides extensive feedback in writing and in person. Her marginal comments on a paper are designed to create a dialogue with her students, raising questions about ideas. They are also diagnostic, labeling errors so that students can go to the Diana Hacker website to do the relevant exercises. Finally, a one-page commentary discusses the paper's overall strengths and weaknesses and offers alternatives for revision. While they are revising, students can be in conversation with MG by e-mail or in conferences. She acts as a sounding board for new thesis statements, for topic sentences that will drive the argument—for anything students are struggling with as they write. In addition to her own comments, students in M.G.'s classes receive feedback from each other. "Students tell me that being critics is one of the most difficult tasks of the course," she admits. "They are not accustomed to interrogating another person's prose. But it raises their consciousness about how to persuade, and so on. They learn how to take into account possible disagreement."

F. G. (Economics) points to the importance of directing students back to work they have completed. Instructors can provide advice up front, he says, but it is often lost as students work on an assignment. They need to bring out the knowledge (content knowledge, writing knowledge) that underlies students' work. This gives them "ownership" of their ideas and their projects; it teaches them to work over time (by reflection and revision) to express what they know in words. The feedback in F.G.'s course is staged out. At the opening of the course, he is in very close contact with students; he spends a lot of time working with the writing and with the individuals. This effort serves to establish his standards for their work, but also to show them that they have him as a point of reference and a source of support. They can see that he gives the care and attention to their work that he gives to the work of his profession and his professional colleagues.

From the Students
Appendix 6
Selected student responses: "What can we learn from your experience with this person in class?"

- . . . he helped me add flow to my sentences, tying together my paragraphs, and ultimately creating a 'tight' paper.
- . . . He returns our work with a variety of comments and ideas on how to improve our stories, while still pointing out many positive aspects as well.
- . . . In the past two years of my college experience, she has been an important commentator, reviewer, and critique for my academic writing. She always provides detailed revision suggestions for her students and she has helped them to grow into critical thinking during class discussions, which inevitably makes them better writers.

- Dr. R focused on creating and supporting sound arguments and provided excellent feedback on
- papers. Dr. P focused on stylistic aspects, such as condensing paragraphs and refining sentences for greater impact and clarity.
- Excellent feedback, and he was always willing to discuss writing with me.
- Expectations of all writing assignments were clarified. Intensive feedback if sought would be accommodated.
- He expected so much from his whole class, and had a great way of giving his students feedback.
- He figures out what his students are capable of and then demands that or better on all writing assignments, it is very difficult to impress him with your writing but his demeanor makes one want to try.
- He gave me the best constructive criticism I've ever gotten in my entire educational career. He has a knack for seeing and defining students' styles, and helping them refine them. Respecting him as a teacher made me more eager to provide him with good writing and original ideas.
- He has been particularly helpful in matters of style, documentation, and research skills, and he is one of the few professors I've had that consistently uses peer review in non-seminar courses.
- He helped me to learn how to develop and argue a thesis instead of just presenting information in a paper.
- He helped the class with writing by explaining common grammatical errors as well as ways to appropriately develop a paper. The combination was very helpful and instructive.
- He is always critical yet encouraging in terms of developing my writing style
- He is extremely honest about students' writing even if the feedback is negative. When he gives negative feedback he always gives ways in which the writing can be improved.
- He is great at helping students to develop original ideas by guiding them in research in texts outside of class. He really helps writing on ideas that aren't mainstream.
- He provided positive criticism along with constructive criticism.
- He was extremely helpful in advancing my writing skills, both grammatically and in regards to style. He put a lot of emphasis on thinking through arguments, analyzing texts to support your point, and reflecting upon things from a different point of view than you normally would . . .
- He was one of the only professors who could recognize talent in his students and was willing to let them know. His support and motivating teaching style made you want to learn more. His comments were constructive and fair and he gave you plenty of room for improvement.

- He wrote the usual comments on the papers, but he would also come up to you after class and talk to you or advise one about their writing and understanding of the material. We could come to him with questions or comments, but I found it interesting and cool that he came to us on an individual basis. It felt more personal and encouraging.
- Helped students in the class learn to be more precise in our writing.
- High demands for quality of work.
- His course, History of Mass Media, forced me to write in many different styles, formats, and on a broad range of topics. He was also very quick to return writing assignments with necessary corrections and suggestions for revision, even when a revision was not necessary.
- His term paper assignment was very helpful to me because I became more experienced with using primary sources. Also, he was always available when I needed to discuss my paper with him, and he provided useful feedback.
- I believe that all of my lab instructors have been very influential in my writing development. They have taught me how to analyze data and how to sum up observations without babbling on. Also, my freshman writing teacher C. C. helped me to understand my potential.
- I had always been able to write reasonably well in my philosophy courses, but I believe that his guidance in that class, even though the assignments were rather short, helped me to improve my writing style dealing with often complex ideas and topics in a concise way.
- I have always been a strong writer, but Dr. P. challenged me and didn't give me a good grade off the bat. I worked hard and met with him often and eventually was able to achieve an A in the class. He forced me to think critically and analyze my own work. His writing advice has helped me in every class since.
- I rely on the writing center because the atmosphere is professional and its more helpful and less stressful than dealing with a teacher on a one to one basis.
- In her Junior Seminar course, V exposed us to a lot of theory we were unfamiliar with and showed us how it applied to our writing about literature.
- Introduced me to advanced analytical writing and primary resource writing. Also stressed proof reading.
- It is of the utmost importance to organize your thoughts when you write. G. sets a great example of how one should organize his or her thoughts. I feel that this has helped me tremendously in my paper writing.
- Learned to revise, to clean up my grammatical errors and "spot" good writing. Very honest, direct and monumentally helpful.
- She compelled students to debate with each other anonymous work that they were given in advance; but she herself never made any comments

publicly. Rather, she asked the right questions. This way, students exchanged ideas with each other, but their writing was not trained in any particular style (e.g. hers).
- She designs her assignments so that I am able to write an individual paper using class concepts and also to collaborate with a group for the purposes of writing and presenting material. Class discussion of text makes it easy to think critically and creatively, which is something that was lacking in my GW course. Dr. M-C. does not ask for regurgitation in written work. She actively engages the class in a thorough understanding of the material and facilitates discussion around her findings and the conclusions we draw from various texts and external media.
- She gave me confidence in my abilities by explaining to me the strong points in my writing as well as showing me where the weaknesses in my arguments were. I have taken several literature courses since, including Intro to Critical Reading, and none have helped me develop my writing as much as Intro to Lit with A.M.
- She gave step by step directions for all the students, and anytime I had a question or was concerned, she always helped me through it.
- She has helped me write better as a researcher in doing the papers for Research Methods class.
- She held one on one required conferences and had us do drafts and exchange papers with other students in class. She has contributed to my learning and has helped me to improve my skills as a writer.
- She helped the class to articulate their reasons for liking/not liking certain aspects of theatrical performances that we were required to see which, in effect, helped the class to sharpen their skills in writing persuasive papers.
- She is an extremely engaging and focused instructor. Teaches students to write analytically in a professional academic manner.
- She left the writing assignments very open, and provided extensive comments on formation of our papers thesis and arguments as well as grammar and mechanics.
- She provides helpful ways to improve your writing and sets up conferences to discuss your writing with you on a one on one basis.
- She pushed me in new ways, always helping me bring out the best work I could do. She read my papers carefully, which provided me with constructive feedback that enabled me to successfully revise my work.
- She taught her class how to write clearly and persuasively about literature and gave specific grammar and style tips. Most importantly, she wanted her students to choose words and craft sentences to convey full meaning without fluff. She helped us develop our own topics and argue them well.

- She taught us how to analyze a text closely and to clearly state and support a thesis through interpretation of the text and additional research. She is the first professor I had at Pitt who stressed the importance of a thesis statement.
- She took the time to meet with each student and go over details of research and outline and suggested ways in which we could further develop our work. Furthermore, she pushed us to go beyond our ordinary limit and do better work, thus forcing me to focus on the argument and develop it to a great degree.
- She was an amazing teacher who was willing to work with the students. Allowed for informal discussion that provided an interesting and educational atmosphere. She was one of my very favorite teachers.
- She was clear in her critiques, kept discussions of papers (which she kept anonymous) open and interesting, and made a class that could have been very basic and useless worthwhile.
- She was extremely encouraging, but also a tough grader. She gave you chances to improve work, and assignments were interesting, not just the same type of paper over and over again.
- She was extremely patient and helpful, her class was structured help us be more critical readers and more professional writers.
- She was the first professor I had to really spend a lot of time responding to students' drafts and having conferences with us. I've gotten this kind of attention from teachers in my nonfiction classes, but not in my W classes.
- She was very patient and constructive with our writing, and one of the most important things she did was have one on one conferences with each student to talk about our writing. I think encouraging one on one student-professor talks is critical to a good education and good relationship between the professor in the class. Some (even most) professors seem like they are too busy or could care less if a student drops by his or her office to talk—especially about the work/writing the student is engaged in with that professor's class.
- She would always take time to sit down with me and go over my responses to readings/essays/etc. Not only did she give me comments on paper, but she allowed me to discuss with her my writing, which means so much more.
- The process of becoming a good writer is aided by having contact with other amazing writers and learning their tricks and fusing these tricks into your own writing style.
- The reason I improved during her course was probably a matter of motivation to improve, because she was genuinely interested my improvement and I respected her.

- They have both very much helped me to improve my written Spanish—given opportunities for revisions, specific guidelines and feedback, one-on-one assistance, and small or one-on-one class size which is beneficial to writing classes.
- Through extensive weekly readings and weekly short papers that relate to the readings, students are encouraged to evaluate what they've read, ask questions relating to what they've read, and compare their ideas to those presented.
- W. focuses on making students write in a professional yet interesting and straight forward manner which is essential for a career in science.

[Revised 4/18/2101]

Appendix 7 Pittsburgh Study of Writing Selected student responses: "What else would you like to tell us about your experiences with writing at the University of Pittsburgh?"

- I think that mandatory, brief, one on one interviews between the teacher and the student would tremendously boost academic performance. Speaking is like writing in the air with your vocal chords. For me, it is important that I develop a one on one relationship with the professor. Once the professor demands my respect directly, I find that it is much easier to hunker down and do my homework.
- I think that students should have more opportunities to write different types of papers. Even though I am a History and Political Science major, I would like to write something other than strictly academic essays.
- I think writing is a hard thing to teach, and do well in college. There are so many writing assignments, and each teacher has a particular writing style they want you to adhere to. It is impossible to learn all of the possible styles beforehand, but learning how to adapt to a teacher's specific style is important. I think I have done well here, only because after the first exam or paper, I can realize what the professor wants and is looking for in the papers.
- I was exempt from [the required first year writing course] because of my high score on the AP English test. It was not until I took my W courses that I had any writing-specific instruction. I feel like my writing skills have not improved much since high school. For some time, I blamed my exemption from [first year writing], but everyone I know who has taken it insists it was not helpful to them . . .

- I wish I had more opportunities to work on projects with other media related majors. For example, film studies students and journalism students could be assigned to a project for credit where some written material could be realized in a play or TV show. . . . Another possibility would be computer engineering majors and communication majors perhaps collaborating on a website or something and receiving credit for it.
- I wrote FAR FAR more in my organic chemistry lab than I did in my English, Philosophy, or Spanish classes. Organic Lab should be a W course. I wrote upwards of 15 pages a week in there, while in the other classes I mentioned it might have been around 3 to 5.
- In most of my writing experiences the professors have been liberally biased. I am forced to tone down my opinions in order to receive a decent grade.
- It increased the way I write and think at the same time. I found that it is extremely important to think as you write and revise your thoughts into what you're writing. If you do that you expand your thesis and your general purpose.
- Long research papers are a waste. There is little to no learning involved. All long papers are for most classes is lots and lots of bull shitting and space filler. A shorter paper that can be to the point is always best. If what needs to be said can be said in 6 pages, not 10, why have a 10 page length requirement. Profs need to be realistic when assigning these long papers. They don't want to read them and we don't want to write them.
- My experience in writing at Pitt has been great, and very well-rounded, the only thing I feel that is missing from it is perhaps more social gatherings of writers and more conferences that are free and open to the public, sponsored by the university and not corporations. I would have also appreciated more emphases in my writing classes on using scientific research. I feel that use of research, or at least the perspectives of other people, is something that writers (fiction/poetry/nonfiction, mainly) sometimes steer too far away from.
- One of the main problems with classes that involved writing at the University of Pittsburgh are the essay tests, particularly tests that are given in class. These tests often cause students to feel rushed, thus they simply list information in the form of paragraphs, ignoring style and format, as well as not completely developing their ideas. I think this is detrimental to the students' development as writers because these exams connect writing to anxiety and unpleasantness. Essentially, they associate writing with regurgitation of information.
- Some of the other (non-major, non writing intensive) courses were way too heavily weighted on the writing assignments. If a class is going to have a lot of writing in it, there should be other forms of evaluation in

addition. It's not fair to base the whole course grade on whether or not the instructor likes your writing.
- Some professors are absolute sticklers for mechanics and content in papers and these are the ones that lead to an increase in the writing abilities of their students. These professors are scattered across the disciplines as this drive is a personal one.
- Strangely enough, I learned to think about grammar when I took a foreign language class. I know that as native speakers, we know the rules of how to speak English (for the most part), but it would be most helpful at the beginning of the writing degree to have a type of foundation on many basic rules in addition to the correction received on written papers. To know why a particular rule applies is to reinforce its use in a much deeper sense of the writing process.
- The availability of a writing center is a fantastic resource for those who would like more help or feedback on their writing. So overall, I feel the amount of writing and the skills and resources available through the university are very good.
- The emphasis that this university places upon incorporating writing within its curriculum has
- contributed greatly to my receiving of a well-rounded education, and I believe prepared me to succeed in law school.
- The [required first year writing course] destroys good writers. I had a professor before I took the course and immediately after and he called me into his office hours to ask what happened to the good writer. Limiting the creative license of a writer, limits the potential of that writer. I am still in recovery from that terrible . . . course.
- There hasn't been much room for creative writing for me to pursue at Pitt. Don't let writing be too mechanical.
- There is almost too much writing at the university. Almost every class is like a writing class at another university.
- Unfortunately, many of the professors teaching writing courses (not necessarily W courses) do not do a good job in actually teaching. All they do is assign a grade to your essays, and if the grade isn't an "A," they have a hard time trying to explain what exactly to do to make the paper better. Often times this results in a mediocre grade in the course, unimproved writing skills, and frustration.
- Writing at the University of Pittsburgh does not take a primary place of importance in many of the natural and physical science classes due to the large class size. This impersonal nature does not allow the professors and students to communicate through writing and therefore hinders science students when they are confronted with writing in their other courses.

- Writing is extremely important. Unfortunately, many professors have a different style of writing and a different way papers are to be written. This makes it difficult for a student to remain consistent with how one writes. . . . Perhaps more uniformity across majors and writing for different classes would be helpful. I do understand that writing for a bio class is much different than a poly sci class. However, writing for a poly sci class is not much different than a history or an art class. I also believe that there should be more strict guidelines held for reviewing written work. As an RA for the university for two and a half years, I have corrected many student's writing and have also seen student's with poorly written work receive high grades. This does not seem to be an effective way to improve the student's writing.
- Writing is important, but some of the low level gen. ed classes put too much on structure and grammar, rather than seeking main ideas.
- You should ask if we think long papers due at the end of the semester are useful (they aren't!!!)
- . . . At college I have found that teachers are far less stringent on the style and grammatical correctness of papers. They rather that the general content is acceptable and that you use some form of citation. My major requires me to write lab reports, so the most help and improvement from high school to college has been in that area.
- . . . one of the things that made me come to Pitt was the emphasis on writing.
- All too often, one just receives a grade on a writing assignment. I would like to have the opportunity to improve my writing. A grade alone does not teach me how to improve my writing. I think conferences are a good idea.
- I believe that critical reading and writing are sorely lacking from the physics department. My goal
- is to become a research professor in astrophysics and I am fortunate that I work in a research group which
- encourages reading current papers from scientific journals. I would not have any exposure to writing in my field if it was not for my research group.
- I believe the Professional Writing class should be a requirement for all students. It is a class that 100% of graduating students will apply to their daily work activities. I believe that many students have a distorted/unrealistic view as to what the expectations are in the workforce. I believe they don't know the first thing about writing a memo, or a proposal, or how to prepare a resume. Many don't even know how to put together a business portfolio so they have examples to bring to interview of the type/level of work they are capable of. This class was beneficial in every

way and I can't figure out for the life of me why the University does not make it a mandatory requirement.

- I feel that many times when teachers/grad students grade our papers they're grading them based on their opinion of our paper and not set-in-stone paper critiquing techniques. I'm not sure that best way to get around this, other than maybe having more than one person grade papers and not tell each other what grade they gave and then comparing and taking an average or just going from there.

NOTES

1. We are grateful to Michael Pemberton and to *ATD* for publishing this version of the study. Michael recruited a Dream Team for our referees: Gail Hawisher and Andrea Lunsford. We are very grateful for their suggestions, for their help and support, and for the standards of scholarly care and attention they have established through their careers. We want also to thank colleagues at Pitt who played a major role in the development of the project: Lisa D. Brush, Sociology; Jean Ferguson Carr, English; Nick Coles, English; Jim Seitz, English; Lydia Daniels, Biological Sciences; James Lennox, History and Philosophy of Science; Edward Muller, History; Chandralekha Singh, Physics and Astronomy.

2. The key terms are represented in the section headings below.

3. The Study has provided a useful resource for participants in our semester-long Writing in the Disciplines faculty seminar. For example, Arts and Sciences faculty are especially interested in what students had to say, in the focus groups and in the survey, about the teaching practices and writing assignments that had helped them the most in learning to write. The faculty interviews offer a rich fund of possibilities, inspiring the seminar participants to try new approaches in their own classrooms. Most importantly, however, the report makes tangible for faculty the distinctive writing culture that thrives on their own campus, and includes them in the conversations that will continue to shape that culture.

4. We've used the report in several courses, and we've used these questions to frame discussion: what makes sense to you as a student? What doesn't ring true? What is missing in the report? What is missing in the curriculum?

5. We are grateful to Nancy Sommers who came to campus to consult with us on our project. We began our discussions at Pitt by circulating a copy of her first Harvard Study (1994). Her study combined faculty and student interviews with a student survey and provided the model for our own. Like Sommers, and like Lunsford (see below), we were interested in documenting the genres of student writing on our campus, and we were interested in focusing attention on these genres as forms of intellectual engagement related to or

en route to disciplinary work. (For the 1994 Harvard study, see "A Study of Undergraduate Writing at Harvard," Nancy Sommers, Harvard University, 1994. Unpublished.)

6. The WID program at Pitt provides a variety of support services to the faculty community and to course development. Students are required to take two writing intensive courses, one of them in their major area of study. These are meant to be taken in the junior and/or senior year; most writing intensive courses are senior seminars or one-credit add-ons to senior seminars. The English department supports a first year writing course (required of all students) and a selection of basic and advanced composition courses. For more on the WID program, see http://www.wid.pitt.edu/. For more on the Composition Program, see www.english.pitt.edu/composition/index.html.

7. Our work along these lines was very much shaped by Jim Slevin, who had been to our campus several times and whose book, *Introducing English*, has circulated widely on our campus. See *Introducing English. Essays in the Intellectual Work of Composition.* University of Pittsburgh Press, 2001. The relevant chapters are in sections three and four: "The Context and Genres of Intellectual Work in Composition" and "Composition's Work with the Disciplines."

8. The interviews were conducted by the project directors and members of the Advisory Board: David Bartholomae (11), Beth Matway (9), Lydia Daniels (2), Jim Lennox (2), Lisa Brush (1), Jean Carr (1), and Jim Seitz (1). All were scheduled during the Spring Term, 2005.

9. These were our students' terms—something deeper, something more. They directly echo students in Nancy Sommers' survey at Harvard.

10. When we began to design our project, we were influenced directly by the 1994 Harvard Study, and Nancy Sommers came to the campus as a consultant. For accounts of the more recent longitudinal study at Harvard, see: Nancy Sommers, "The Call of Research: A Longitudinal View of Writing Development." *College Composition and Communication* 60.1 (2008): 152–164; Nancy Sommers and Laura Saltz. "The Novice as Expert: Writing the Freshman Year." *CCC* 56.1 (2004): 124–149; Nancy Sommers. "The Case for Research: One Writing Program Administrator's Story." *CCC* 56.3 (2005): 507–514; and two videos available from the Harvard University Expository Writing Program: *Shaped by Writing: The Undergraduate Experience* (2002) and *Across the Drafts: Students and Teachers Talk About Feedback* (2004). For access to the Stanford Study, see the website http://ssw.stanford.edu/. See also: Andrea Lunsford, Jenn Fishman, Beth McGregor, and Mark Otuteye, "Performing Writing, Performing Literacy." *College Composition and Communication* 57:2 (2005): 224–252, and Erin Krampetz, "Writing Across Cultures and Contexts: International Students in the Stanford Study of Writing" (Masters monograph). Stanford University, 2005.

11. The new line created a permanent position for our WID Director, Beth Matway.

12. We have created a writing intensive freshman course for Engineering, one with goals similar to our first year writing course, but one that meets the expectations of the School of Engineering accreditation agency. See Beth Newborg, "It Takes a Whole University to Educate the Whole Engineer: Narratives of Collaboration," *ASEE Conference Proceedings,* 2008.

References

Krampetz, Erin. (2005). Writing across cultures and contexts: International students in the Stanford study of writing (Masters monograph, Stanford University).

Lunsford, Andrea, Fishman, Jenn, McGregor, Beth, & Otuteye, Mark (2005). Performing writing, performing literacy. *College Composition and Communication, 57*(2), 224–252.

Newborg, Beth. (2008). It takes a whole university to educate the whole engineer: Narratives of collaboration. *ASEE Conference Proceedings.* Retrieved from American Conference for Engineering Education website: http://www.asee.org/conferences/paper-search-form.cfm.

Slevin, James. (2001). *Introducing English. Essays in the intellectual work of composition.* Pittsburgh, PA: University of Pittsburgh Press.

Sommers, Nancy. (1994). A Study of Undergraduate Writing at Harvard. Harvard University. Unpublished. Cambridge, MA: Harvard University Expository Writing Program.

Sommers, Nancy (2002). *Shaped by writing: The undergraduate experience.* [Video] Cambridge, MA: Harvard University Expository Writing Program.

Sommers, Nancy (2004). *Across the drafts: Students and teachers talk about feedback.* [Video] Cambridge, MA: Harvard University Expository Writing Program.

Sommers, Nancy (2005). The case for research: One writing program administrator's story." *College Composition and Communication, 56*(3), 507–514.

Sommers, Nancy. (2008). The call of research: A longitudinal view of writing development. *College Composition and Communication, 60*(1), 152–164.

Sommers, Nancy, & Saltz, Laura (2004). The novice as expert: Writing the freshman year. *College Composition and Communication, 56*(2), 124–149.

Stanford Study of Writing. Website: http://ssw.stanford.edu

Williams, Raymond. (1983). *Keywords. A vocabulary of culture and society.* New York: Oxford University Press.

COMMUNITY LITERACY JOURNAL

Community Litearcy Journal is on the Web at http://www.communityliteracy.org/index.php/clj/index

The *Community Literacy Journal* publishes both scholarly work that contributes to the field's emerging methodologies and research agendas and work by literacy workers, practitioners, and community literacy program staff. We are especially committed to presenting work done in collaboration between academics and community members. We understand "community literacy" as the domain for literacy work that exists outside of mainstream educational and work institutions. It can be found in programs devoted to adult education, early childhood education, reading initiatives, lifelong learning, workplace literacy, or work with marginalized populations, but it can also be found in more informal, *ad hoc* projects. For us, literacy is defined as the realm where attention is paid not just to content or to knowledge but to the symbolic means by which it is represented and used. Thus, literacy makes reference not just to letters and to text but to other multimodal and technological representations as well. CLJ is an independent journal. We receive no funding, and the journal is produced and edited by Michael Moore of DePaul University and John Warnock of the University of Arizona.

"'Phenomenal Women,' Collaborative Literacies, and Community Texts in Alternative 'Sista' Spaces" by Beverly J. Moss

We nominated Beverly Moss's article for inclusion in The BOIRCJ 2011 because it offers keen insights into the collaborative and intertextual nature of literacy practices in communities, while making a strong contribution to the understudied area of contemporary black women's clubs. Moss's ethnographic study explores how the members of Phenomenal Women, Inc. value, use, and shape literacy in a 'sista space,' one of "the shared spaces that African American women create for themselves." Moss moves our field forward with her expansion of Brandt's sponsors of literacy model to include co-sponsors, thus "deemphasizing sponsorship as a top-down approach"; her discussion of community texts created through collaborative reading practices; and her demonstration of how rhetorical strategies, in this case questioning and repetition borrowed from the tradition of call-and-response, can be transported among different alternative genres and spaces as groups "make literacy their own," strengthen community ties, and assume agency through literacy.

2 "Phenomenal Women," Collaborative Literacies, and Community Texts in Alternative "Sista" Spaces

Beverly J. Moss

In June of 2009, I was sitting in a small black church in a rural town in South Carolina at the funeral of my father's last aunt, my ninety-three-year-old great-aunt Alverta, listening to one of her friends talk about how my aunt, as a young woman, had been a member of a black women's club called the "Jollys."[1] It seemed that the Jollys got together so that they could do community service in the black community in this small town and participate in social functions. It was the first time that I had ever heard of any of the women in my family being part of such a community organization as a women's club. I knew that my aunt had been a member of the Eastern Stars—the women's auxiliary organization to the black Masons; however, the Jollys, a club established for Black women by Black women that was not set up in support of a male organization (as the Eastern Stars were), was new to me. I was struck by how I had just spent the past sixteen months researching other Black women in a club when I had a resource, now gone, in my own family. It was at that moment that this research project, which I saw as distant from my own personal life, really encouraged me to think about how Black women in my own family, women with limited means, had created spaces for themselves as Black women, to enrich their lives and the lives of their communities. What stories did they have to tell? What stories had many of them taken to their graves? That moment made the literacy stories of the women of Phenomenal Women Incorporated (P.W. Inc), the Ohio-based African-American women's club featured in this essay, even more important to me.

In calling for more archival and observational research on the literacy of women in the introduction to their edited volume, *Women and Literacy: Local and Global Inquiries for a New Century,* Peter Mortensen and Beth Daniell assert that "Literate activity that is constitutive of gendered identity unfolds all around us all the time—in public institutions, in workplaces, in domestic spaces, in locations marked sacred and profane, in places that provide refuge from violence, and so on—and yet it is barely understood in specific relation to the socioeconomic and cultural particularities of these venues" (31). In considering the literacies of African-American women, I would alter their statement to read that "Literate activity that is constitutive of gendered and *racialized* identity unfolds all around us all the time: in public institutions, workplaces, domestic spaces, and *community spaces.*" Literate activity and behavior in contemporary spaces such as community sites—spaces where people come together based on shared values and goals—provide much needed insight into how individuals, groups, and/or organizations value and use literacy, how they make it their own. To understand the complexities of the literacies which African American women use and how they use them, we must expand the spaces and sites in which we examine these practices. The work highlighted here focuses on African-American women who come together not necessarily to read and write, but who, in their "sista space"—their club—often read and write when they come together. In this space, they promote reading and writing, promote self-help through reading and writing, and use their literacy skills to promote civic action and engagement, and cultural enrichment.

Context of Research

While Anne Ruggles Gere's call for examining writing in the "extracurriculum" speaks to a broad range of contexts ("Kitchen Table"), to date the scholarship that focuses on African-American women's literacy practices, most notably Royster's *Traces of a Stream,* Logan's *We are Coming,* Peterson's *Doers of the Word,* and McHenry's *Forgotten Readers,* has been primarily historical. These important studies establish that African-American women, particularly in the 19th and early 20th centuries, though constrained by racism and sexism, actively engaged in literacy practices that served their personal and public lives. In fact, Anna Julia Cooper, Maria Stewart, Victoria Earle Matthews, Mary Church Terrell, Frances Harper, Harriet Jacobs, Ida B. Wells, among others, stood as exemplars of African-American women whose community service and activism were inextricably bound to their literacy practices. These women rhetors purposely used literacy to advocate for social change, to lift up their race, and to sustain their own intellectual growth. Much of the existing historical scholarship reveals the role of African-American women's clubs, literary clubs in particular, in the activist literacy and discourse practices of African-American women. Because African-American women in the 19th and early 20th centuries were not welcome in most white women's clubs and because they felt a need to come together to promote their own growth and that of their own African-American communities, Black women, particularly educated ones, established their own literary societies. McHenry and Heath remind us that "most often, the clubs created by and for African Americans in the 19th century and early 20th century, were created to meet the intellectual needs of its members because they were denied access to such intellectual and literary societies because of racism and in the case of Black women, sexism" (424). In discussing the Black women's club movement, Royster states that,

> the club movement actually permitted women with different matrices of identity, different perceptions of needs, and different priorities for sociopolitical mandates (cultural, social, political, economic, religious) to form a shared space—a com-

> munity. From the shared space of club work these women articulated a 'common good,' charted courses of action, raised voices in counter distinction to mainstream disregard, and generated at least the capacity—if not the immediate possibility ... to make themselves heard and appropriately responded to. By this process, the club women sustained their roles as critical sources of support for the educational, cultural, social, political, and economic development of the African-American community. (217)

Royster as well as McHenry and Heath point to African-American women recognizing and establishing an alternative space in which they could nurture their collective and individual talents, and from which they could collectively act on behalf of other African Americans. These clubs, as alternative "sista" spaces, the shared spaces that African-American women create for themselves, became important sites for literacy learning and literacy activities. These scholars demonstrate that the literacy practices and literate behavior practiced in these spaces provided these African-American women an opportunity to become visible, effective rhetors on behalf of equal rights for African Americans and women in a time when the received wisdom was that African Americans were incapable of any intellectual, literacy-related activity. While one cannot deny the value of the historical scholarship that has shed light on the literacy practices of African-American women—it is some of the finest work in literacy studies and represents a shift from deficit model scholarship that at one point seemed to dominate research on African Americans' literacy practices—there needs to be more focus on the literacy practices of contemporary African-American women, particularly as they operate in nonacademic spaces. My current research is an attempt to add to this understudied area. I am particularly interested in what we can learn about literacy from adult, primarily middle-class African-American women, a somewhat neglected group, when they come together in their alternative, shared space.

While recent studies introduce us to alternate literacy sites, that is, sites outside formal institutions such as schools, these studies are small in number. McHenry, in addressing twenty-first century Black women's book clubs, discusses alternate sites of literacy as a "challenge to formal institutions and as a place to gain the kind of sustenance that many black intellectuals, especially black feminists, have defined as necessary for their intellectual growth" (314). Recent scholarship that highlights contemporary African-American women's literacy practices—for, example, Lanehart's study of her female relatives in *Sista, Speak,* Richardson's work on critical literacies of young (under 20 years of age) African-American women influenced by hip-hop culture ("she was workin'"), Cushman's work on the critical literacies of a group of inner-city, low-income African-American women—is valuable work which complicates how we characterize African-American women's public and private literacies. But these studies are few in number and limited in scope. Yet, the theorizing that they do about African-American women's literacies acts as a starting point for my study. Specifically, Elaine Richardson, in *African American Literacies,* speaking about African-American female literacies, states that "African American females' language and literacy practices reflect their socialization in a racialized, genderized, sexualized, and classed world in which they employ their language and literacy practices to protect and advance themselves. Working from this rhetorical situation, the Black female develops creative strategies to overcome her situation, to 'make a way outa no way'" (77). This notion of how African-American women use literacy is further enhanced by Royster in *Traces of a Stream,* who states that "the theory begins with the notion that a community's material conditions greatly define the range of what this group does with the written word and, to a degree, even how they do it. The pivotal idea is that what human beings do with writing, as illustrated by what African-American women have done, is an expression of self, of society, and of self in society" (5). What both Royster and Richardson highlight is that African-American women use their literacy skills and practices to create public and private rhetorical spaces for themselves and their communities. They use literacy, among other tools, to negotiate their journeys through paths often littered with racist, sexist, and classist obstructions. While I do not want to argue that literacy is an all-powerful tool that overcomes institutional racism, sexism, and classism—clearly that is not the case—I do want to suggest that contemporary, working- and middle-class African-American women make literacy work for them and their communities through community organizations such as Phenomenal Women Incorporated (more details about this organization follow below). Specifically, they engage literacies in ways that help them meet their needs (see discussion on black history month below). In this study I seek to find out what African-American women in P.W. Inc do with the written word and how the material, social, and cultural conditions in which they operate—the economic, political, social, and religious contexts of their everyday lives—define the range of what they do as well as how they assume agency to define and shape the uses of literacy within the group and their lives. I am particularly interested in how the goals of the organization and the personal and/or professional goals of these African-American women come together to shape how they use and interact with literacy. In this essay, I demonstrate how the women of P.W. Inc use literacy in their "sista space"—the space where they come together as Black women to act as a group and on behalf of their community—for their own cultural enrichment, as a way to strengthen their shared community ties, as a way to teach each other, and to teach other women.

The Study

I have just completed data collection for a 16-month ethnographic study of an African-American women's community service club who call themselves Phenomenal Women Incorporated (see figure 1). I didn't pick this club to study because I was interested in Black women's clubs. I wasn't. What I was and am interested in are the alternative spaces, that is, the non-institutional community spaces, in which African Americans use literacy. P.W. Inc is one such site. Data collection consisted of fieldnotes at monthly meetings, club-sponsored events, and events that the group members attend as official representatives of the club. I audiotaped meetings and audio or videotaped club-related events—like their 2008 Power Brunch in which they invited three panelists who spoke to Black women from the community on HIV/AIDS, diabetes, and financial literacy. I have also interviewed individual members and focal groups within the organization. Finally, I made copies of documents written and/or read by the group at meetings and by individual members in the focal groups. I participated when possible and appropriate (and when invited) in club events; however, I remained primarily an observer-participant.

Figure 1. Phenomenal Women Incorporated

One of my specific goals in the larger study is to document and understand how the women in this organization use literacy as a group and individually to do the work of the group—work that they characterize as "helping the community" and "having a good time." Simultaneously, I am examining how individual women in this organization use literacy in their personal and professional lives to determine which literacy practices, if any, routinely cross the personal-professional-public borders. My primary research questions include the following:

- What are the literacy practices that contemporary African-American women (in this organization) engage in that cross from personal to professional to public borders and vice versa?
- What are the literacy and language practices that define the civic and social practices of this African-American women's community organization, and what is the relationship between those practices?
- What is the role of literacy sponsors (Brandt) in the work of P.W. Inc?

For the purposes of this paper, I will focus primarily on an aspect of the second question: the literacy practices that define the civic and social action of P.W. Inc.

Participants

Phenomenal Women, Inc, located in Columbus, Ohio, has been in existence since 1997. Its membership consists of 15 adult African-American women who range in age from mid-thirties to mid-sixties, with most of the women in their fifties and sixties. Many of them are retired from government county jobs. Only two members have college degrees; one of them—Robyn, the president at the time of the study—has a master's degree in English and the other one—Millie, the vice-president from 2007–2009 and the president who succeeded Robyn—recently completed an MBA. However, several members started college, but for various reasons—marriage, pregnancy, family illness, lack of funds, or lack of interest—never finished.

The Club's Origins

The club came into being because one member, Mawarine (Robyn's mother) wanted to be in a club with other Black women with whom she could socialize and serve her community. Mawarine also saw the forming of the club as a way to continue a legacy of civic engagement and activism passed down by the women in her family. She recalls how, as a child, she and her sister were influenced by her grandmother, great-aunt and mother, who had been active in church groups and Black women's clubs. It was from these women and her childhood experiences that Mawarine's "vision" evolved:

> *Actually, my vision for my club began when I was a little girl. . . . It came from my grandmother. . . . So I think my vision actually started when I was very young, especially, the social part, I think that watching my grandmother and my great-aunt get involved in their church, they led the church choir, they sang in the church choir . . . and I remember all of our church functions, and my grandmother taking us to be involved in the voter elections, she was always a member of the board for the elections, back in the days. And I think that's where I got my first vision 'cause I watched them gather up papers, go out and serve the community and they actually took me and my sister with them. They were involved in Blue Star Mothers, they were involved in . . . there's another program for men that have sons, for women that have sons in the service. So we were always involved with them. We*

> used to go down to the veterans' building. So I actually got my vision for a club when I was 'bout nine, eight, seven, eight, nine years old and then my mother, who's my hero, my mother was involved in a club. And she was very, very social and I remember . . . My mom, I think it was on Fridays, they had their club meetings, every other Friday, or at least once a month, they had a club meeting and they would go over to each other's houses. But I remember sitting there in the rooms listening. (Conference on College Composition and Communication presentation)

As this quote from Mawarine indicates, she is following in the tradition established by the women in her family, a tradition that involved her in community institutions like the church and in civic activities and community activities like the Board of Elections and support groups for veterans and their families. Historically, the African-American church has provided a space for members of African-American communities to engage in leadership training, socializing, activism, and education; therefore, it is not surprising that Mawarine points to church functions and the church itself as an important space in which her vision was nurtured. And a nine-year-old Mawarine noticing "them [her grandmother and great-aunt] gather up papers and go out to serve the community" also connects literacy artifacts—written documents—to the work of community service. Mawarine and her sister Charlene, another founding member, were raised with an awareness of how Black women used club spaces (and other community spaces) to engage in social, political, and community activism. This tradition has been passed down to Robyn, Mawarine's daughter, who is passing it down to her children (whom she brings to the meetings). According to Robyn, Mawarine's daughter, when Mawarine retired she wanted to be active in the community but she also wanted to be active socially with other Black women. Robyn says of her mother that "she always wanted to belong to a club, but not one of those stuffy ones where you had to have a lot of money in the bank." And while most of the members would be considered lower middle- to middle-class, the $50 annual dues and $120-$140 to cover tickets for their annual "Phenomenal Woman of the Year Signature Dinner" in which they honor an African-American woman in the community for her outstanding service, present challenges to some members. Thus middle class, for this study, really is fluid, indicating a more complex, dynamic notion of socioeconomic class for these women.

At the beginning of 2008, I formally began the ethnography. I gained access to the club through Robyn, the president during the time that I did the fieldwork, and her mother Mawarine. I had known Robyn since she was an undergraduate at Ohio State University. Though she was not my student, she had worked for me in a summer program when she was a master's student in my department. After that summer, I invited Robyn (and another graduate student) to my church to hear a famous visiting preacher. Eventually, she, her mother, and aunt, all founding members of P.W. Inc, joined the church to which I belonged. To date, there are five members of P.W. Inc who are members of my church. However, I didn't know the club existed until about a year before I began the study.

There are a couple of things about the signed consent forms that I want to point out. First, the organization decided that they wanted me to use the organization's real name, Phenomenal Women Incorporated, rather than a pseudonym. Each member (without any prompting from me) also decided to waive confidentiality because they thought that it would help me in my research. As Robyn told me after they voted to participate in the study, "they want to be as helpful as possible." In her discussion of major socializing values surrounding African-American females' literacies, Richardson identifies "to serve and protect" as a major value, one that has worked for and against African-American women (*African American Literacies*). When these women agreed to be a part of the study, they felt an obligation to help me with my work—what Richardson would most likely categorize as part of that "serve and protect" value. That value is also evident in their mission statement, which reads as follows:

> The mission of Phenomenal Women, Inc. is to provide women of diverse backgrounds the opportunity to enjoy social gatherings and community service activities that will enrich their lives, as well as the lives of others in the central Ohio area. We are women who hold shared values, interests, and goals. An organization founded by and for women, Phenomenal Women, Inc strives to pursue the following goals:
>
> • Serve the needs of the local community. Our interests include, but are not limited to, promoting the needs of senior

citizens, battered women, and economically disadvantaged women and children
- Organize and participate in social activities which explore various cultures, traditions, and environments
- Provide professional and social networking
- Promote family and friendship
- Respect, honor, and privilege the physical, psychological, and emotional well-being of women (Phenomenal Women Incorporated, 1997)

There are many interesting things about the mission statement. First, it reflects founder Mawarine's goal of having a club that is active in serving the community as well active socially, but social is cast primarily in the role of cultural and social enrichment for the members. Second, the mission statement does not name African-American women as their focus; however, in practice, it is a club for Black women. Third, though never mentioned in the mission statement, the members see the club as a faith-based organization. Each meeting opens and closes with a prayer, as does each club-sponsored event open with a prayer. Church events become club events. For example, Robyn and Charlene invited the club to attend their church to hear Reverend Dr. Jeremiah Wright on his recent visit. Even though the mission statement makes no mention of race and religion, for the women, they are front and center. They never shy away from racial concerns. And even though they do not screen potential members based on any religious affiliation—they never ask about it nor talk about it in the meetings—they feel no need to hide their faith. When asked why the mission statement mentions neither race nor religion, members didn't seem overly concerned. They didn't feel the need to state what they see as obvious. Fourth, the mission statement acts as evidence that the women in the club are acutely aware of the material and social conditions in which they and those they wish to serve operate. And fifth, the mission statement is a collaboratively written document which stands as one of the first literacy artifacts generated by the club.

To fulfill their mission to serve the needs of the community, the members organize Mother's and Father's Day events and buy gifts for the Isabelle Ridgway Care Center nursing home patients (98% African-American), work for the Susan G. Komen Race for the Cure, give two $500 college scholarships to high school graduates, and partner with a battered women's shelter and a community organization that serves the homeless to provide essential items for both populations. They sponsor the annual P.W. Inc Power Brunch for African-American women (mentioned above) which brings speakers who focus on social, financial, and health issues important to African-American women. The Power Brunch is mentioned in a discussion about literacy because it is at this annual event that P.W. Inc arranges for an exchange of information between two parties by bringing together community experts for an audience of African-American women from the community who have a desire for the information provided. The women are given information through oral presentations, question and answer periods, and through the numerous brochures and other print documents passed out or placed on the information table. The service events that I've listed, particularly the power brunch, are examples of activities that illustrate the civic and social activism of the club.

What has become clear during my time in the field is that most often, the social outings, cultural enrichment activities, and the service missions are intertwined; the boundaries are blurred. The monthly meetings are business and social. They conduct their business; they eat and talk. The service activities, the nursing home visits, and Power Brunch, for example, are social activities as well. In fact, serving the community is generally social, and the social serves the community. Located within the service, social, and cultural activities and events are important collective literacy practices which help the women meet the goals as stated in the mission statement. Specifically, these literacy practices, tied to literacy events, as Heath defines them—any activity surrounding print—contribute to P.W. Inc members' focus on enriching their lives and those of their community. As Royster and McHenry—and others who've done work on African-American club women—have established, self-help and self-determination are core missions in these clubs. Deborah Brandt asserts that "by necessity, African-American self-help institutions absorbed into their purview as many politically, socially, and culturally affirming functions as they could" (110). P.W. Inc is no different. The literacy events that I focus on below demonstrate specific socially and culturally affirming functions. I focus, primarily, on one major function—P.W. Inc members' commitment to their own intellectual and cultural growth through one club activity: the club's annual celebration of Black History Month. I argue that both examples of this activity can be classified as literate activities and behaviors because they involve actual reading and writing practices and/or behavior associated with literacy. The examples discussed below are lengthy excerpts by necessity. Readers gain a stronger sense of the nature of the black history month literacy events through the longer examples.

BLACK HISTORY MONTH

Member Gloria felt that it was important that they, as a club, learn more about black history and culture. One of the ways that they have done so is through their Black History Month celebrations. During my very first observation, the February 2008 meeting, the women "prayed out" of their business meeting—that is closed with a prayer, and announced that it was time for their black history month assignments. Each woman had been assigned to read about an important black inventor, public figure, or topic related to African Americans. They were to bring that information to share with the club and assume the responsibility for teaching the club members something about their history and culture. For the women who forgot to do the assignment (three did), club members shared the books or printed texts from which they read or, rather than discussing people that they didn't know, told the club about family members who, for them, fulfilled the requirement of an important black person. Members were encouraged, applauded, and appreciated for however they contributed. For the club, any contribution promotes intellectual growth and cultural enrichment, thus fulfilling an aspect of their mission statement. While on the surface, participation in this literacy event seems to be nothing more than a brief report, for these women, these acts honor where they come from and who they are—their legacy. I share two examples below. First Daryl shares with the club what she learned about Granville Woods, a black inventor who lived in Columbus; second, Sharon reports on Clarence Otis, a corporate executive. In the first example, note how Daryl both reports information and offers an astute critique of the failures of public education:

Daryl: *I'm gonna read about Granville T. Woods. I picked this one because I opened up the front of this book to find something to read. And this is stuff that my grandmother gave my kids when they were little* *because they went to Southwestern City School District and you don't get a lot of Black history there. You only get what's in that little section of the history book. So she wanted them to always, you know, have something. And this is stuff they used to give her when she was in the Black Caucus and stuff before she passed away. And I picked one, Granville T. Woods. He was a Columbus, Ohio native. He developed mechanical and electrical engineering skills quickly as a young man and made important contributions to Alexander Graham Bell and Thomas Edison. Over the span of his career, he earned about 50 patents, including one for an incubator which was the forerunner of present machines capable of hatching 50,000 eggs at a time. Woods' inventions improved and changed America's communications and railroads with such things as steam boilers, brakes systems, and electrical power lines for railroads. One of his most famous inventions assigned to the New Bell Telephone Company enabled operators to speak or use Morse code on telegraph networks. He also developed a system of transmitting messages between moving trains and the new electrical railroad systems which required no exposed wires, secondary batteries, or slided guideways. Woods' inventions were sold to many large companies including the Bell System, as well as Westinghouse, General Electric, and the New Haven Railroad. Um, there's like several different things about different people here and if somebody wants to read one. And there was one thing—I mean this is a list, you know, of different things that happened but I never knew that they actually had documented that the first African-American child born in America was born on January 3, 1624.*

Daryl offers, in her presentation on Granville Woods, a critique of public education for its failure to teach black children about black history and culture. She also references how her grandmother provided material for her children. Thus this literacy event, which acts as a corrective for the failure of public education to do its job, also provides evidence of a tradition, at least within Daryl's family, of actions taken to counter the failure of at least one public school system. Daryl also documents a legacy of community activism in her family when she references, though briefly, her grandmother's involvement in the local Black Caucus. In addition, there is a veiled critique of the publishing industry and history textbooks, in general, when Daryl refers to "that little section of the history book." The implication is that history textbooks, being part of public education, are complicit in ignoring African-American history. Daryl's point that "you don't get a lot of black history there," while uttered about a particular school system, is clearly a sentiment that motivates the women's engagement in this literacy activity. Sharon's presentation continues this act of providing to African-American women what they don't get in school.

Sharon: *Um, mine's on the CEO of Red Lobster and Olive Garden.*
Mawarine (spoken enthusiastically): *Hey, all right!*
Sharon: *His name is Clarence Otis, Jr., and he's the CEO of Darden Restaurants, the largest casual dining operation in the nation. Um, he was born in Vicksburg, Mississippi, and he moved to Los Angeles, when he was six. His father was a high school drop-out who worked as a janitor. They lived in Watts, during the Watts riots in 1965. And, he remembers being stopped and questioned by the police several times a year because of the color of his skin. His high school counselor recommended him to a scholarship to Williams College, and he graduated Phi Beta Kappa from Williams and went on to get a law degree. And he landed on Wall Street as a mergers and acquisition attorney for J.P. Morgan securities. And he joined Darden Restaurants in 1995, and became the CEO in 2004.*
Mawarine: *Wait a minute, wait a minute! You're saying that the CEO of the Red Lobster and Olive Garden is Black?*
[Someone]: *Yeah!*
Charlene: *I did not know that.*
Mawarine: *You all knew that?*
Charlene: *I did not know that.*
Millie: *I saw that a couple months ago.*
Mawarine: *You're kidding! I did not even know that!*
Gloria: *That's why it's important that we need to know us some stuff about Black history.*
[Someone]: *Say the name again.*
Sharon: *Um, Clarence Otis, Jr.*
Mawarine: *Clarence Otis, Jr. is Black?*
Charlene: *I had no idea.*
Mawarine: *I didn't either!*

Mawarine: *Well, I'm just flabbergasted.*
Charlene: *I did not know that.*
Mawarine: *I did not know. So he was the one who started the, he was the—how did he get started with the Red Lobster?*
Sharon: *He just joined the company, uh, and they promoted him to CEO in 2004.*

The conversation that takes place after Sharon's presentation on Clarence Otis, Jr. highlights not only the women's incredulity that they didn't know about him, but it also highlights their pride at finding out that a black man was the CEO of this major restaurant chain. We can also see how this literacy event is situated within the social, cultural, political, and material situation in which they, as African-American women, operate. The club, understanding the exigencies which led to the creation of Black History Month—namely the institutional racism which refused to acknowledge the presence of and the contributions of African Americans in the building of this country—felt an obligation and a need to be agents in promoting the goals of Black History Month—to learn about and celebrate African-American achievements and contributions to the U.S. They are, through this literacy event, as Royster suggests, "raising their voices in counter distinction to mainstream disregard" (217). This particular literacy event emerges out of a non-institutional educational setting, of their own making, in which the women have challenged themselves to become lifelong learners about their history and culture. As Gloria implies in her statement (highlighted above) it is important that they know about their history and culture. They were participating in this literacy event in an alternative literacy site—a club meeting—which Black women have traditionally used since the 19th century to celebrate their cultural heritage.

A closer look at Sharon's excerpt reveals rhetorical patterns that call attention to how these women engage with specific literate texts. Obviously, the talk surrounding the written texts stands out as an important way for P.W. Inc members to participate in the text. Specifically, I want to point out two patterns that the women used often—questioning and repetition. First, questioning appears to be used in two ways: to gain information to clarify a point and/or to confirm a point. For example, Mawarine asks Sharon "how did he get started with the Red Lobster?" Although Sharon had provided that information in her "report" on Clarence Otis, Jr., Mawarine's question is clearly a request for information. However, Mawarine's first question, "you're saying that the CEO of the Red Lobster and Olive Garden is Black?" is not a request for information; it is to request confirmation of a surprising point—that a Black man is the CEO of a popular national restaurant chain. The use of repetition is one of the other major rhetorical strategies which the women employ. Much like the use of questioning to confirm, the women in this example use repetition of clauses/statements for confirmation. Charlene and Mawarine are the primary employers of this strategy in this example:

Charlene: *I did not know that.*
Mawarine*: You all knew that?*
Charlene: *I did not know that.*

While they know the information to be accurate, their repetition of "I did not know that" signals how amazing this information is. The repetition emphasizes the weight of the information that has just been shared as well as the need to have that information confirmed by group members. I find it interesting that for these women the information in the written document is not enough, by itself, to be taken as truth; however, with the confirmation by group members that this information is indeed accurate, the written text is reinforced. The use of questioning and repetition (a strategy drawn from oral traditions) are also prominent patterns in the second Black istory hhHistory Month celebration discussed below.

In February 2009, the club decided to change its black history celebration. Actually, Robyn suggested that rather than have every member bring in a short text to read about an important African American, the club should read Barack Obama's *Dreams from My Father*.[1] Given the recent election of Obama as president, this was not an unusual change. Club members had followed the election closely, held an inauguration party, and one member—Veronica—had complied a book with photographs and newspaper articles documenting the entire election. Therefore, club members were eager to read the book. However, it was the first time that the club had read a book as a group. As individuals, many are voracious readers of mysteries, romance novels, black literature and history. However, they are not a book club. But they embarked down this new path. Each member was assigned two chapters of the book for which they were accountable. I, too, was assigned two chapters.[1] And every person's chapters overlapped with another's. For example, I was assigned chapters 7 and 8, and another member was assigned chapters 6 and 7. Robyn proceeded this way because she didn't want any one member to be responsible for having to read a 400+ page book. The following excerpt is quite lengthy so that readers can see how the club members engage the patterns highlighted and analyzed below. Note what happens in this discussion. Dana, who was responsible for chapters two and three, provides a summary of the chapters for the sake of the people who had not read the chapters she was assigned; in between the summary is analysis and commentary, and most importantly, there is engagement in the discussion.

Dana: *I had chapters two and three. And he talked about, um, Indonesia. They went, they was living in Indonesia, and uh, his mother's second husband, Lolo.*

[Someone]: *Lolo.* **[Others]**: *Lolo.*

Dana*: Talked about him, and um, the conditions and how they lived in Indonesia, and the foods. Ew, my goodness! They ate some things in Indonesia! Some bugs!* **[laughs]** *And iguanas! And all kinds of stuff. Um.* **[pause]** *That's about, he talked, yeah, it was mostly, both these chapters, two and three, and then um, he came, they came back. He came, they, his mother sent him back, and he stayed with his grandparents, and um, they were going, they went through some things, his grandparents, about um, they loved him and they stuck by him. You know, they really did, you know. Um.*

Veronica: *What kind of things did they go through?*

Dana*: Um. [whispers] She's quizzing me!*

Mawarine*: They used to call him names. When he was in Hawaii, and they called him names.*

Charlene*: Were they living there in Hawaii then?*

Dana*: Yeah, they lived in, he lived, his grandparents lived in Hawaii.*

Charlene: *Oh, okay.*

Dana: *They lived in several places, and they ended up in Hawaii.*

Robyn: *Yeah, they started off in Kansas. The mother was born in Kansas.*

Dana: *They started in Kansas. Then they went to, they went to Washington state, I believe.*

Robyn: *Uh huh.*
Dana: *And then, his grandfather worked for a furniture company.*
Mawarine: *Right.*
Dana: *And the furniture company opened up another store in Hawaii.*
Robyn: *That's how they ended up in Hawaii.*
Dana: *So that's how they got to Hawaii. And um—*
Robyn: *His grandmother worked for a bank.*
Mawarine: *But that was later on.*
Dana: *Yeah, but they talked about that later on. They talked about that later on. Um, his grandfather, you know, I think they tried to shield him as much as they could from the racism, but you know, it was there. And um [pause] he talked about the schools he went to. They sent him to a private school, and he called, his grandmother was "Toot."*
Robyn: *Toot. [laughs]*
Dana: *Toot. And his grandfather, and um. [pause] It's been awhile. I started this weeks ago! [laughs] [pause] I think his father, his father, they told him a lot about his father, too. Cause he was six when he—. He was two or three when his father left. Then he came back when he was six, and he stayed for the month. He stayed a month with him.*
Robyn: *Didn't you think that was—? Who had that chapter when the father came back?*
Dana: *And they just took him in!*
Robyn: *Yeah! And I got the feeling that there were some flames still there.*
Dana: *Yeah.*
Robyn: *Did you get that feeling when he came back?*
Dana: *Yeah. She—*
Robyn: *Because Obama walked in, cause they let him have an apartment.*
. . . .
Dana: *They was mesmerized by him.*
Robyn: *Right.*
Mawarine: *Because he was educated. That's why everybody [loved him].*
Dana: *He was very educated.*
[sounds of children playing, running]
Robyn: *But yeah, you definitely got the sense that they, they really loved that man.*
Dana: *He, and the mother met the second husband, and he was a good guy, and his, when he went back to Indonesia, it kind of broke his*

spirit. It broke his—because he went back, he came to America to go to school to go back there to—

Robyn: *Help them.*

Dana: *To help them do things. But when he got back there, them Indonesios wasn't having it. They kind, yeah and um. They really didn't get into— He really I don't think knew what really happened, but something with the government.*

Robyn: *Right.*

Dana: *The government, um, kind of—*

Robyn: *They made it really difficult.*

Dana: *Yeah, they made it difficult.*

Veronica: *For who?*

Dana: *For the guy, the husband, the other husband.*

Robyn: *The second husband. Yeah, yeah. I think he was trying to improve things. And you know how corruption works.*

Dana: *And, and the Indonesians [in the government] are very corrupt. It was very, very corrupt.*

Robyn: *Umm hmm. Umm hmm. And then it seemed like, yeah.*

Figure 2. February 2009 Black History Month discussion of Obama's Dreams from My Father

The entire discussion of the book, which took a little over an hour, followed a pattern: summary, commentary, analysis, and most often, connecting to current issues. The impetus for the entire discussion is the current connection to Barack Obama's election. Throughout this part of the discussion, different members, namely Veronica and Charlene, ask questions for clarification ("what kind of things did they go through?"; "Were they living in Hawaii then?"). Robyn asks questions to solicit opinions from the group ("Did you get that feeling when he came back?"). Other patterns emerge. Specifically, Robyn and Mawarine, at times, act as co-leaders with Dana of this part of the book discussion. They constantly add details to assist Dana as she talks about her two chapters.

Dana: *Yeah. She—*
Robyn*: Because Obama walked in, cause they let him have an apartment.*
Dana*: Yeah, they got—*
Robyn*: There was a separate apartment*
Dana*: They cleaned out an apartment.*
Robyn*: Right, so he stayed cause he was here, he was there for about a month.*
Dana*: Month. Yeah.*
Robyn: *And Obama came in, and the mother was ironing the father's shirt.*
Dana*: Shirt.*
Robyn: *And I got the sense, mm hmmm. [laughs]*
Dana*: And he was like everything, he said for, I think he, didn't he stay, for a minute there, for that time, it was like everything went back to the way it was before his father left.*
Robyn*: Right, right.*
Mawarine*: Because she loved him.*
Robyn*: She did love him.*
Dana*: Everybody. Not only her, but the grandfather.*
Robyn*: Everybody. They all loved him!*
Dana: *They all loved him.*
Mawarine: *Because he was educated.*

Even though Dana is the primary leader of the excerpted part of the discussion, she is clearly not the only one. Robyn and Mawarine collaborate in the direction that this discussion takes. During the discussion of most of the chapters, the collaboration that is evident above is more the norm than the exception. Mawarine collaborates with Dana to reiterate (a form of repetition) the level of education of the senior Obama—clearly a detail that holds significance for Dana and Mawarine and, as they point out, to Barack Obama's family as well. A closer examination of this small excerpt and the longer one from which it is taken also demonstrates how the women of P.W. Inc employ another dimension of the repetition pattern. Again, they repeat words, phrases, and clauses generally to confirm information; however, this pattern is employed in a call-and-response style similar to that practiced in African-American churches. The first example appears at the beginning of the lengthy excerpt when Dana mentions Obama's stepfather's name, "Lolo." Someone immediately repeats his name, "Lolo"; then, several others repeat the name "Lolo." The call and response-repetition pattern is even more evident in the exchange between Dana, Robyn, and Mawarine:

Mawarine: *Because she loved him.*
Robyn: *She did love him.*
Dana: *Everybody. Not only her, but the grandfather.*
Robyn: *Everybody. They all loved him!*
Dana: *They all loved him.*

This kind of repetition can be witnessed in African-American churches all over the United States. Ministers and congregations participate in a dialogue where the congregations answer back (respond) to the ministers' calls. Those responses often come in the form of repeating what the minister has said (see Moss "Community Text" for a more detailed discussion of call and response). Another form of call and response is for the congregation to indicate their approval of the minister's message and preaching style with affirmative words such as "yes" or "you right" among other words. Robyn engages in a similar strategy with Dana with her response of "right" numerous times throughout the long excerpt. Robyn's use of "right" affirms Dana and confirms Dana's summary and analysis. In a sense, the women engage in a kind of intertextuality by importing textual strategies from one genre and venue into texts in a different genre and venue.

Not unlike what happens in book club discussions (though P.W. Inc is not a book club), talk about the written text dominates. The participants rely on their collective conversation about the book as the primary means of engaging in this literacy event. The oral reinforces their literacy practices here. The written text—the book—is the center of the lively discussion.

In addition to the patterns noted above, several times in this excerpt members draw conclusions from the available data in the chapters. For example, the women look at the actions of the family toward Obama's estranged father when he returns to see his son and stays for a month. The club members conclude that everyone in the family loved Obama's father. They conclude that the Indonesian government was corrupt based on how it treated Obama's stepfather. The women are not just engaging in plot summary as they read and discuss this text. They look for evidence in the text to support their assumptions and claims; they pay attention to details (e.g., who is ironing a shirt). Also, through reading the book, the women are learning about cultures foreign to them, and about the newly elected president. However, I would argue that something else is going on. The club, through these literacy activities during the Black History Month celebration, acts as literacy sponsor for its own members. Deborah Brandt, who has turned to *Sponsors of Literacy* [my emphasis] as a conceptual approach, defines sponsors as,

> any agents, local or distant, concrete or abstract, who enable, support, teach, and model, as well as recruit, regulate, suppress, or withhold, literacy—and gain advantage by it in some way.... It is useful to think about who or what underwrites occasions of literacy learning and use. Although the interests of the sponsor and the sponsored do not have to converge (and in fact, may conflict), sponsors nevertheless set the terms for access to literacy and wield powerful incentives for compliance and loyalty (19).

Clearly, P.W. Inc members are the primary agents who enable, support, teach and model, as well as regulate literacy in this specific setting. While one can argue that the occasion of Black History Month is the underwriter and, hence, sponsor of these literacy events, that would erase the agency of these women. It is more reasonable to recognize that these women, through their own agency, see themselves as fulfilling an important aspect of their club mission. They are, in fact, the sponsors *and* the sponsored, thus placing a different spin on Brandt's notion of sponsorship by deemphasizing sponsorship as a top-down approach. The advantage that the women gain, as self-sponsors, is cultural knowledge. At the same time, they fulfill the obligation of self-help. I would also argue that through their collective literacy acts as highlighted in these two different types of examples, the women are not engaged in reading an individual text; they are engaged in the making of community texts. In previous work ("Community Text"), I suggest that a community text is that in which the author and the audience collaborate to complete a text, as in an African-American sermon, where the sermon is seen as a dialogue between minister and congregation. However, in this example from P.W. Inc, the notion of a *community text* has been extended; that is, these women have presented another perspective from which to examine how they co-create a community text. It is not only the public act of reading *as* a group, but also the act of reading *for* their group; each member is reading for their other members. Members' individual readings are situated within the collective reading to make meaning of the book. The whole book is read only when all the individual assigned parts become a whole. The text becomes the group's text—a community text through which they meet goals as set out in the mission statement. In this sense, they engage in collaborative literacies to create these community texts within their sista spaces. As stated earlier, this sista space acts as an alternative literacy site in which these phenomenal women demonstrate how they use the written word to, as Royster suggests, express themselves in society.

Conclusion

The ways that questioning and call and response-repetition patterns are used by P.W. Inc reinforce the collaborative nature of the literacy practices that characterize the 2008 and 2009 Black History Month celebrations. Clearly, collaborative literacy practices are not unique to P.W. Inc. However, the ways in which the women of P.W. Inc use these literacy practices is worth noting because they provide a means for the club to fulfill their mission to "enjoy social gatherings and community service activities that will enrich their lives. . . ." The practices highlighted in this essay, though emerging from only two literacy events, turn our gaze to how literacy, through the creating of community texts and collaborative literacy practices, reinforces sista bonds—those cultural ties that bind this group of African-American women—within this sista space. In addition, the literacy practices on which I focus in this essay point toward the way that literacy practices from multiple community sites, like churches, can act as foundational for literacy practices which emerge in other alternative spaces.

Even though race and gender discrimination still exist and Black women still operate in a society in which they face major obstacles, they are not in the same place as African-American clubwomen in the 19th and early 20th centuries. Yet, many of their goals are similar. The motto coined by the National Association of Colored Women in 1895, "lifting as we climb," is just as relevant for P.W. Inc as it was for African-American clubwomen over a century ago. The activities highlighted here point to P.W. Inc's commitment to increasing their cultural knowledge by uplifting themselves, and thus, their community. They have created, in P.W. Inc, a sista space—a private, community site of their own in which to value, engage, and use literacy as a communal, social act which strengthens their bonds as Black women, enriches their lives, and provides them with the opportunity to, as Royster asserts, "sustain their roles as critical sources of support for the educational, cultural, social, political, and economic development of the African American community" (217).

NOTES

1. Portions of this essay have been presented at Florida State University and Texas Christian University.

2. Robyn was often in the role of what Brandt might describe as a literacy sponsor because she encouraged and sometimes provided opportunities for engaging in literacy practices. Robyn and I suggest that "literacy sponsor" does not adequately cover Robyn's role in the club (see Moss and Robinson," Making Literacy Work: A "Phenomenal Woman" Negotiating Her Literacy Identity in an African American Women's Club," forthcoming in *Literacy, Economy, and Power*. Eds. Christoph et al.)

3. I was also asked to discuss an important black person in the February 2008 meeting as were the children present at the meeting. Members' children are almost always at meetings. During every black history month, the children are asked to participate in sharing what they've learned about black history and culture.

Works Cited

Brandt, Deborah. *Literacy in American Lives.* New York: Cambridge University Press, 2001.

Cushman, Ellen. *The Struggle and the Tools: Oral and Literate Strategies in an Inner City Community.* Albany: State University of New York Press, 1998.

Daniell, Beth and Peter Mortensen. "Introduction—Researching Women and Literacy: Usable Pasts, Possible Futures." *Women and Literacy: Local and Global Inquiries for a New Century.* Ed. Beth Daniell and Peter Mortensen. New York: Routledge, 2007. 1–44.

Gere, Anne Ruggles. "Kitchen Table and Rented Rooms: The Extracurriculum of Composition." *College Composition and Communication* 45.1 (1994): 75–92.

_____. *Intimate Practices: Literacy and Cultural Work in U. S. Women's Clubs, 1880–1920.* Urbana: University of Illinois Press, 1997.

Heath, Shirley Brice. "Protean Shapes in Literacy Events: Ever-shifting Oral and Literate Traditions." *Spoken and Written Language.* Ed. Deborah Tannen. NJ: Ablex, 1982. 91–117.

Lanehart, Sonja. *SistaSpeak: Black Women Kinfolk Talk about Language and Literacy.* Austin: University of Texas Press, 2002.

Logan, Shirley Wilson. *"We Are Coming": The Persuasive Discourse of Nineteenth-Century Black Women.* Carbondale: Southern Illinois Univ. Press, 1999.

Lyons, Mawarine. "Phenomenal Black Women Act: Making Waves, Changing a Community." Conference on College Composition and Communication, San Francisco. 13 March 2009.

McHenry, Elizabeth and Shirley Brice Heath. "The Literate and the Literary: African Americans as Writers and Readers—1830–1940." *Literacy: A Critical Sourcebook.* Ed. Ellen Cushman et al., New York: Bedford/St. Martin's, 2001. 261–274.

McHenry, Elizabeth. *Forgotten Readers: Recovering the Lost History of African American Societies.* Durham: Duke University Press, 2002.

Moss, Beverly J. *A Community Text Arises: A Literate Text and a Literacy Tradition in African-American Churches.* Cresskill, NJ: Hampton Press, 2003.

Richardson, Elaine. "'she was workin' like foreal': Critical literacy and discourse practices of African-American females in the age of hip hop." *Discourse & Society*, 18.6 (2007): 789–807.

_____. *African American Literacies.* New York: Routledge, 2003.

Royster, Jacqueline Jones. *Traces of a Stream: Literacy and Social Changes among African American Women.* Univ. of Pittsburgh Press, 2000.

Beverly J. Moss is an associate professor of English at the Ohio State University where she teaches courses in literacy studies and composition theory and pedagogy. Her primary research interest is in examining African American community literacy practices. Her first book, *A Community Text Arises: A Literate Text and a Literacy Tradition in African-American Churches,* focuses on the African American sermon as a literacy event. She is currently working on a book which examines the literacy practices of a contemporary African American women's club in Columbus, Ohio. This essay is taken from that 16-month ethnography of literacy on the Phenomenal Women Incorporated.

COMPOSITION FORUM

Composition Forum and this article are on the Web at http://compositionforum.com/issue/24/ebook-issues.php

Composition Forum is a peer-reviewed journal for scholars and teachers interested in the investigation of composition theory and its relation to the teaching of writing at the post-secondary level. The journal features articles that explore the intersections of composition theory and pedagogy, including essays that examine specific pedagogical theories or that examine how theory could or should inform classroom practices, methodology, and research into multiple literacies. *Composition Forum* also publishes articles that describe specific and innovative writing program practices and writing courses, reviews of relevant books in composition studies, and interviews with notable scholars and teachers who can address issues germane to our theoretical approach.

"E-Book Issues in Composition: A Partial Assessment and Perspective for Teachers" by Michael J. Faris and Stuart Selber

Michael J Faris and Stuart Selber's "E-Book Issues in Composition: A Partial Assessment and Perspective for Teachers" demonstrates *Composition Forum*'s unique focus on the intersections of composition theory and practice, as well as the journal's commitment to interdisciplinary research and scholarship.

The article provides a sophisticated study of E-book devices (and devices that support e-books) highlighting the ways in which they are becoming increasingly integrated into the working lives of students and teachers. The authors discuss their pedagogical and institutional experiences with the Sony Reader in composition courses at both the graduate and undergraduate level, reporting on dynamics and challenges associated with three key literacy tasks: accessing texts, operating texts, and marking texts. They conclude with a heuristic that can help teachers and administrators adopt and design an e-book initiative. The editorial team at *Composition Forum* has selected this essay because it theorizes practice in an insightful and provocative way, and we are pleased to have it represent the scope and focus of the journal.

3 E-Book Issues in Composition: A Partial Assessment and Perspective for Teachers

Michael J. Faris and Stuart Selber

Book reviews, including the reviews that typically appear in *Composition Forum*, generally focus on the textual content of a book—the ideas and arguments of authors—and they tend to ignore the materiality of the book, unless the book design calls attention to itself. Meanwhile, reviews of e-book devices on sites like CNET, ZDNET, and DigitalTrends consider technological features and functions, but they tend to separate those discussions from considerations of textual content and context. In this essay, we remix the genres of book and software/hardware reviews in order to explore the interconnectedness of texts and technologies in the context of the composition classroom.

Electronic books, or e-books, are no longer an oddity or fringe novelty within American higher education. Although printed books and textbooks still dominate college classrooms, students and teachers can download e-books from a wide variety of places (e.g., university libraries, commercial bookstores, open-source projects) and display them on cell phones, computers of all sorts and sizes, and of course e-book devices like the Amazon Kindle, Barnes & Noble Nook, Sony Reader, and the rest. In addition, e-books tend to cost less than their printed counterparts, and they can sometimes be rented from publishers, a fact not unnoticed by administrators, parents, and others concerned about the escalating expenses associated with going to college or graduate school. For these reasons and a few others, e-books have become a thinkable option for composition courses at both the graduate and undergraduate level.

But there is a lot to think about. With printed books and textbooks, teachers have internalized a whole series of expectations about literacy and learning and how those complex processes unfold and operate in formalized school settings. We ask students to read in a patient and critical manner, for example, assuming they can underline and otherwise mark difficult passages and key ideas and phrases in ways that are useful to them. We ask students to reference their readings in class, assuming they can use page numbers as a reliable and constant navigation aid. We ask students to discuss their readings in class, assuming they can access passages at a pace that does not impede face-to-face conversations and interactions. And yet teachers cannot and should not make such commonsense assumptions, for conventions and expectations from print and speech do not always support and align with student tasks and experiences with e-books.

The same could be said for experiences and tasks on the teacher side of the equation, including work involving computers and other online literacy technologies. E-books may not integrate very well or easily with campus bookstore and library protocols, for example, or with controls placed on university computer networks for installing files and managing electronic devices. E-books may not integrate very well or easily with systems used for bibliography management, course management, or distance education. And perhaps most notable of all, many books and textbooks in composition studies are simply not available in an e-book format. In certain contexts and cases, then, the curricular integration of e-books will require teachers to revisit and reconfigure pedagogical apparatuses and frameworks.

This is a valuable if indirect function of e-books (and of other developments in the evolution of literacy technologies): they can help to defamiliarize the familiar, as sociologists Zygmunt Bauman and Tim May might put it, unsettling assumptions and encouraging teachers to reimagine taken-for-granted patterns and practices. We are not the first researchers to point out this cultural phenomenon, nor will we be the last. It involves a powerful pedagogical perspective that is crucial to critical literacy. In addition, e-books are not the first modern technology to encourage a reconsideration of reading activities. In the early 1990s, for example, hypertext researchers admonished the field to intensify its focus on the counterpart of writing; to that point in time, computers and writing specialists had been somewhat preoccupied with studies of composing. In one prominent strand of work, these researchers contrasted the non-sequential nature of computer-based hypertexts with the sequential nature of printed texts to comment on the ways in which the material dimensions of literacy technologies shape readers and the reception of texts (see Bolter; Johnson-Eilola). We anticipate that the material dimensions of e-books will overlap with, and depart from, those of computer-based hypertexts. These dimensions include physical aspects of media, but also social and pedagogical conditions that enable the production, distribution, and use of e-books.

Our discussion of e-book issues for composition teachers is informed by a collection of classroom experiences with the Sony Reader (model PRS-505).[1] In the 2009 spring semester, 24 students in an undergraduate section of honors composition (taught by Michael) and 10 students in a graduate rhetoric seminar (taught by Stuart) read course texts on this device and used it to support classroom discussions of texts and the preparation of written papers. The themes for both courses focused on literacies and technologies. We interviewed students (on four different occasions) about their experiences, asked them to write reflective commentaries, and analyzed the Readers themselves to understand the ways in which students used and configured them. In addition to e-books and PDF files, students read printed books and several printed essays, and they worked on typical composition assignments as well as reflective commentaries. We reinvented a few components of the courses but on the whole remained committed to the pedagogical approaches of an established composition program. We were curious to see how the Sony Reader might perform in a conventional institutional environment.

We asked our students to read course texts in a very particular way that derives from the values and objectives of our field. What are these values? There are multiple valid answers to variants on this fundamental question, for a complex literacy task like reading can be (and has been) characterized from various useful perspectives, theoretical and empirical. The quick characterization we offer emerges from our sense of an overall course objective that is common to composition: *Teachers ask students to work with discourse and metadiscourse in conventional and rhetorical ways to both consume and produce knowledge for a variety of audiences, goals, and occasions.* The component parts of this general purpose statement help to illuminate reading expectations that have developed in the discipline. Students in composition classes are task-oriented and focused on the applications of texts, on doing things with texts in order to participate in the work of culture. Students read to create as well as learn, using disciplinary and strategic frameworks, and they rely on texts and texts about texts (e.g., reading responses, notes, criticism, reviews) to acquire traction for their own versions of ideas and arguments, whose forms and arrangements attempt to match the ends of a piece of composition. Although there are numerous other ways to represent the many aims of the composition classroom, our (partial) view emphasizes reading as an active, social process for sense-making and meaning-making in educational endeavors.

Thus, what we explored in our classroom study was how these common expectations fared when book technology changed. What pedagogical revisions were invited by the new technology? In what ways did the e-books facilitate status quo practices, and in what ways did they confound and trouble them? Our work with the Sony Reader highlighted three aspects of reading that were, on some level, denaturalized by e-books and their contexts: accessing texts, operating texts, and marking texts. In what follows, we discuss each of these aspects and we comment on the (always) evolving nature of reading and reading matter. We conclude with questions for composition teachers who may be considering using e-books in their courses.

Accessing Texts

Accessing texts is obviously a first-order task for readers, one that has become fragmented and disjointed in the contexts for e-books. On college and university campuses, the distribution channels for print materials are relatively stable and universal. There are well-established routines and procedures for working with libraries, bookstores, and copy centers, which are communicated to new instructors in orientation and beyond and to new students in composition classes and beyond. There are also mature institutional practices for accessing certain types of online texts, including e-books, e-journals, and e-dissertations. As a rule, these practices require users to authenticate themselves with a university ID and password; materials placed on library e-reserves are password protected for students in a course. Under this approach, students can access texts on demand, and in formats that are supported by institutional technologies. Furthermore, the requirements of copyright clearances for texts on e-reserve tend to be handled by librarians or library staff. The benefits of centralized access structures for online texts are not to be minimized.

We were intrigued and surprised by the relationships between the Sony Reader and centralized access structures, ours and those of e-book providers. For students and teachers, these relationships both contracted and expanded access to texts and influenced the ways in which texts were represented and organized for online use. By and large, we noticed access issues from the outside in, from issues associated with options in the Reader bookstore to issues associated with the organizational features of the Reader. Affecting this spectrum of institutional and technical apparatus were our composition pedagogies, which helped to constitute notions of access for our particular explorations of e-books. Despite popular opinion and calls to action, access is not a static or monolithic concept; it comes to mean different things to different people in different contexts.

Options in the Reader bookstore were limited by related market forces. At the inception of our study, Sony had not yet adopted the e-Pub format, which has become something of a standard file format for e-books and their devices. So we could only consider titles that were available in the Reader bookstore. However, as we also discovered through extensive database searches, Sony had not yet established contract relationships with publishers that offer books from the field of rhetoric and composition. The upshot was that Stuart was unable to find compatible titles that were suitable for a graduate seminar, while in the undergraduate course, Michael was restricted to a handful of popular texts on Internet culture. We therefore turned to PDF versions of essays from our library and other information sources to develop reading lists. In profound and unprecedented ways, the content of our courses was provoked by the design specifications of texts and by the strategic role and management of distribution channels.

In the realm of print, access is synonymous with acquisition, but this is not always the case in digital environments. In digital environments, there is the real and continuous challenge of database management, of making files findable in personal collections by both people and machines. Responses to this challenge can be developed by publishers, teachers, and students, all of whom have the potential to assume a role in how files become named and organized in online spaces. If e-book devices were limited to purchased items, then perhaps database management would be less of an issue: Volume matters. But the ease with which people can share and download files expands the scope of accessibility by an order of magnitude. The Reader bookstore, for example, incorporates the content of Google Books, including thousands of free titles in the public domain. Although users can create folders for collections of texts on the PRS-505, this task was less than obvious to students in our courses. Students could not make collections with the Reader software itself; instead, they had to connect the device to a computer via a USB cable and then use the computer's operating system to create and manage folders. In fact, not a single student organized or reorganized files into personal collections.

In addition, filenames contributed to problems of accessibility. We anticipated this issue with required course texts by using author names for filenames, which could be cross-referenced with the syllabus for bibliographic and contextual information, such as which course units or themes the files were associated with. Students, however, tended to retain the idiosyncratic filenames associated with services like JSTOR (e.g., "354886.pdf") and Science Direct (e.g., "sdarticle.pdf"), and they often employed names for their own files that became less than meaningful when uploaded to Readers by others in the class (e.g., "ClassHandout.pdf"). For its part, the Reader used two protocols that created initial problems for students: it appended "Microsoft Word" to the front of filenames for .doc files, thus changing the position of these files in alphabetical listings (e.g., "Microsoft Word – Killingsworth.doc"); and in cases where a Microsoft Word file derived from a personal computer, it used the name of the account owner as the author name. After a period of confusion, we discovered that you can override author defaults with the Properties dialog box in both Microsoft Word and Adobe Acrobat. The design of filenames and folders is not trivial to the networked classroom, but it seems absolutely crucial to the accessibility of e-books.

Let us conclude this section with a perspective on accessibility that begins to involve the aspect of reading we discuss next: operating texts. For people with disabilities, access to physical and intellectual resources for educational purposes has been an expanding and ongoing struggle. In many instances, new media technologies have proven to be inhospitable to the blind, to those with low vision, and to those with other special needs—for example, students with learning disabilities (see Goggin and Newell). To use a clichéd expression for the emergent world of e-books, the more things change, the more they seem to remain the same. In fact, e-books complicate access issues by introducing a layer of mediation not required of print books, or at least one that is more complex and abstract than those of technological antecedents. With print books, providing alternatives means (to a great extent) translating texts into Braille or audio formats. Starting to work with these translations is a rather straightforward operation: you open the cover and read in Braille, or press play and listen to the narrator. We are oversimplifying the matter, but our point is that user interfaces for print have become relatively concrete and transparent for students.

In contrast, e-book devices require users to navigate various interface elements in order to start or continue a reading session. The PRS-505, however, did not have audible menus or text-to-speech functions, so neither the device menus nor course texts would have been accessible to blind or low-vision students. This situation has not been rectified in more recent models of the Reader, and the current approaches from other major manufacturers, including Amazon, have not resulted in e-book devices that are fully compliant with the Americans with Disabilities Act of 1990. For this reason, a number of projects (at places like Princeton, Arizona State, Case Western, and Pace) have been challenged by the National Federation of the Blind (NFB) as violations of the right to equal educational opportunities. The United States Department of Justice shares these very real concerns, and thus encouraged American university presidents, in a June 2010 written memorandum, to avoid e-book requirements until e-book devices are compliant with the law. Challenges from the NFB are beginning to appear for course-management systems, which also tend to lack audible menu systems. In sum, the types of access issues we confronted, which encompass technical, pedagogical, institutional, and legal dimensions, are significant, troublesome, and unsettled, and of utmost importance for both social and functional reasons to the composition classroom.

Operating Texts

In a popular video circulating on the Internet, a monk from the Middle Ages struggles to understand and operate the then-new media of print, to transition from the affordances of papyrus rolls to those of a fundamentally different technology for expression and literacy work. The monk needs the technician from a "Medieval help desk" to show him how to turn book pages, backward as well as forward, and reopen a book using the back cover. In addition, the monk worries over the permanence of print; he wants to be sure that the text has been "saved" for subsequent use, a concern drawn from the future of digital texts to remediate a representation of the development of literacy. In part, this video is popular—it has been played over 2.5 million times on YouTube—because it spoofs computer support in ways that resonate with typical end-user experiences. For instance, the front-line support system (a printed manual for the new book in the video) presents the same navigation problems as the artifact it documents, effectively rendering the support system useless. What makes the video ingenious, however, is the utter cluelessness of the monk. He is confounded by tasks so mundane to our current period that the tasks appear to be conventional (and unlearned at this point) rather than natural. How in the world could someone struggle with opening a book? With turning a page? And what could be so hard about mirroring such simple tasks in reverse? Of course, for print-trained readers, including our students, these questions are belied by years of skilled practice with books, papers, and other physical reading materials. The far-reaching routines of print literacy—in schools, homes, and other locations both official and vernacular—have routinized textual operations in thorough ways and habituated readers to their technological dimensions. But conventional patterns can be disrupted, as the success of the video demonstrates. The video has attracted a considerable audience, in no small part, because on some level people can understand and identify with the challenges of learning a new system for literacy activities. Indeed, the operational struggles our students experienced with e-books were really no different in kind than those of the monk, involving relatively basic functions and procedures.

The previous section mentioned a navigation issue associated with accessing texts (audible menus), one that represents a significant barrier for certain populations of students. Navigation was also a usability matter in the contexts for operating texts. For example, for some unimaginable reason, the PRS-505 did not include a search mechanism, making it impossible for students to move within and across texts using their keywords or those from the course materials and e-books. (Likewise, the Web browser Safari for the iPad did not include a search mechanism until version 4.2 of the operating system.) To navigate, students relied on the three sort features of the Reader—title, author, date—and on bookmarks. Although the sort features seemed to work well enough, modeling queries familiar to search engines, they returned lists of titles and authors that overlapped indexical boundaries created from the alphabet: A-C, D-F, G-I, and so on. As a result, students had to train themselves to focus toward the middle of lists to locate the first item in a sort. There was also an issue with the date sort, which was precipitated by our pedagogical practices. Because we uploaded the course texts more or less all at once, at the start of the term, the date sort became rather useless to a comprehensive search of the Reader. In our academic universe, this feature became useful in very particular ways, for queries of near-past activities, to find texts that had been uploaded in the last few weeks or so (over and above that timeframe, who can remember the dates on which files were uploaded to a digital device?). In this manner, the date sort applied more to ancillaries than to core course materials, to files that included handouts for student presentations, discussion questions for texts, and other periodic updates to our databases of class materials. Finally, students had mixed responses to the bookmarks feature. They employed it with success for navigation purposes, but then they often could not recall the reasons why they had created a bookmark in the first place. As a consequence, students wanted to be able to edit and annotate bookmarks and comment on the text fragments associated with bookmarks. That is, they wanted bookmarks and their contexts to contain semantic elements. From our students, a key recommendation for device designers was to enable users to edit and elaborate the navigational features of e-books.

The navigation practices and issues we noticed contributed to challenges in another operational area: spatial orientation. It is no news to point out that it can be troublesome for readers to establish and maintain their conceptual bearings in online texts. Indeed, back in 1986, for example, Christina Haas and Dick Hayes reported on empirical studies of graduate students and faculty in the humanities who preferred to print computer-based texts for certain complex tasks, including critical reading. Haas and Hayes noticed a causal link between the spatial representations people inevitably develop of texts and the material devices that facilitate and support literacy activities, especially computer monitors and visual aspects of the page and screen. Their findings, in short (and in part), suggested that small and/or low-resolution monitors may be inferior to advanced displays and printed pages for text comprehension and retrieval in tasks involving a considerable amount of reading. Researchers from various fields arrived at a similar conclusion, including those who studied Palm Pilots and other predecessors to e-book devices in educational settings (see Marshall and Ruotolo; Waycott and Kukulska-Hume). Although display systems have improved tremendously over the past twenty-five years, readers continue to describe problems with spatial orientation. Our students were no exception.

We cannot attribute these problems to a low-resolution screen. The Sony Reader (and Kindle, Nook, and many other e-book devices and some smartphones) contains a vivid display system that imitates the high-contrast, high-resolution experience of reading printed texts. The real beauty of the system, which is built on electronic ink technology, or E Ink, is that it delivers a quality viewing experience while drawing very little electrical power from the device itself. Users can turn 7,500 pages or so before the Reader needs to be recharged. And because the display system is not backlit like the iPad, Nook Color, and other devices that have LCD or LED screens, it is readable in direct sunlight. All in all, our students praised the high quality of the monochromatic screen. (Color E Ink is now available and may soon afford a comparable reading experience).

The size of the screen, however, coupled with certain operational features and conditions of the PRS-505, seemed to be a contributing factor to problems with spatial orientation. Recall that we did not assign texts that had been modularized for hypertext or designed for the small screen. Instead, we asked students to read essayistic pieces typical of composition and rhetoric classes—and of classes across the disciplines. Students read these extended (15-30 page) pieces to support a variety of writing projects, and the pieces required them to engage richly developed ideas and connect concepts across numerous text files. We loaded around 60 electronic articles, including argumentative essays and empirical studies, on the Readers for graduate students, and the content for the undergraduates was also widely distributed. Like Haas and Hayes, we were interested in academic reading activities that require patient, careful deliberations and the ways in which those deliberations are mediated and supported. According to students, there were noticeable mismatches between task expectations for our courses and the technologies of the PRS-505.

More than a few students noted that it was often difficult to discern hierarchies in texts, follow the threads of extended arguments, preview and reread texts, estimate progress through texts, and/or associate ideas with authors. These basic tasks were not always well supported by the material realities of the device, which yielded three to five sentences per screen (in middle-zoom mode) in a virtual space with minimal, and predominately linear, operational controls, and required a processing time delay of two to four seconds for navigational commands. This lag could feel like a lifetime in the context of certain active-reading tasks, so students would sometimes abandon tasks like following footnotes, which were not hyperlinked in either the e-books or PDF files, or reviewing passages from earlier pages or other texts. In conceptual terms, these realities produced a more flattened discursive space, and an extensive one at that, in which arguments and authors became entangled and jumbled together. The end results were not thought-provoking textual mash-ups, intertextual interpretations born of serendipitous human-machine collaborations, or new and different options for textual engagement, but troubled and confounded practices for reading with and against the grain of complex texts. As the next section on marking texts discusses, students attempted to solve orientation and retention problems with a variety of personal strategies.

The final issue relates to the level of operational ambitiousness demonstrated with the Readers. The devices themselves were the property of our academic institution; students borrowed them—and the uploaded e-books—for use over a one-semester period. Although students were encouraged to be industrious and to make the Readers their own for the term, we observed rather conservative operational actions and activities, which in some circumstances functioned as impediments to educational development. Generally speaking, students did not deviate from the technical routines required by our assignments, so they did not configure or employ certain features of the Reader that would have been instructive to explore, such as the feature for importing RSS feeds. In the same vein, students were timid about trying third-party software like Calibre, which provided e-book management functions that were useful but not officially supported by the Sony help center, including functions for manipulating file formats. This guarded behavior, in some instances, extended to the texts themselves. In addition to semantic problems, students limited the number and scope of bookmarks because they were concerned about their ability to access them in the future. The relationship between ownership and use raises a real question for e-book rental programs and university initiatives that lend e-book devices: What strategies can teachers use to encourage students to possess, personalize, and test institutional technologies in ambitious ways? Our experiences suggest that answers to this question will need to consider several areas of concern. First, students expected the texts and metatexts to be exportable to other writing and reading spaces and reusable in other projects. They displayed little patience for the types of interoperational problems signified by the Mac versus PC wars and continued by battles over digital rights management. Second, students worried that they might be exposed to personal financial liabilities if the assigned devices were broken, lost, or stolen. Although students should take responsibility for borrowed equipment, the equipment was required for participation in our courses—and the undergraduate course was a general education requirement. What should a user agreement look like for students who are required to borrow institutional technologies? Third, we were surprised by the extent to which our pedagogies domesticated operational uses of the Reader. In our next effort, we will include activities that encourage students to explore e-book environments in a more open-ended fashion.

Marking Texts

If pressed about the affordances of print technologies, digital evangelists will often reference the ability to mark-up texts. It is not easy to discount or dismiss the flexibility and versatility of pencils and pens as ordinary writing instruments. Although these instruments are no more natural to learn and use than a keyboard or mouse (see Baron), they lend themselves well to certain discursive practices that are essential to careful reading and reflection. For example, with a pen or pencil, users are not constrained by the coordinates or characteristics of a page or by a predetermined set of symbol choices. One can mark in any direction or orientation, and in an infinite number of ways. As a result, people can develop highly personal methods of textual annotation. Consider our own idiosyncratic approaches: One of us likes to place the capital letter Q next to paragraphs containing key questions or theses, draw boxes around first-level headings, and write notes lengthwise in the gutter area; the other prefers to summarize key points at the top and bottom of pages, reinforce the cuing devices of authors, and note authorial connections in the margins. For us, and numerous other readers in educational settings, such practices constitute a key component of interpretive engagement, knowledge acquisition, and invention.

The advent of computer-based hypertext encouraged readers to extend their roles by making navigational choices and rewriting original content, but these expansive capabilities did not remove the fundamental need to annotate texts. As is often the case with literacy technologies, new developments exhibit the features of both evolutionary and revolutionary change, simultaneously accommodating and resisting status-quo approaches to textual consumption and production. Although hypertext enabled new and hybrid forms of annotation, there has also been an understandable impulse to investigate online support structures for certain modes and practices from offline contexts. Two areas in composition bear out this claim: electronic grading and peer review. From the outset, teachers interested in these areas have been sensitive to issues of textual markup, routinely considering whether, or to what extent, computers can incorporate traditional grading and editing symbols and permit in-line and marginal comments. In his annotated bibliography of composition software developed in the 1980s, Strickland listed five "representative" programs that "allow comment after critical reading" (29). Teachers of a certain generation may recall their titles: Comment, Daedalus, MarkUp, Prep Editor, Respond, Seen. Programmed by academic faculty as well as commercial software firms, such environments did not work to jettison old approaches for new ones. Instead, they reinscribed particular theories and practices that were considered to be effective and professionally responsible. The user interfaces displayed features with new possibilities, but the programmers did not (and could not, really) operate in a pedagogical vacuum.

Aside from bookmarks, Sony did not build features into the PRS-505 for marking electronic texts. At first blush, this absence seemed to us to be a significant oversight. After all, both stand-alone and embedded annotation tools have been available for decades. On reflection, however, this circumstance is a rather predictable one in the context of patterns of adoption and diffusion for mainstream literacy technologies. As with the Kindle, Nook, iPad, and most other e-book devices and tablet computers with e-book capabilities, the PRS-505 was not created exclusively for higher education. It was targeted at a mass consumer market and then promoted to secondary markets using a variety of technical and social strategies. Although broad and specific contexts are often mutually constituting and inseparable, the practices and motivations of their audiences can be at odds with one another. This rhetorical clash was obvious from the onset of the project, and for a brief period of time we debated the efficacy of studying a device designed for general and leisure reading in an academic setting. A few realities, however, encouraged us to proceed with the investigation. A crucial one was our recognition of the pervasiveness of the situation: Students are constantly contending with literacy technologies that were developed for other contexts or for multiple contexts (an obvious example is Microsoft Word). How might students appropriate the capabilities and features of an e-book device for composition work? This is a new and open question for teachers. Also, we thought it would be profitable to examine an early version of the Reader and provide Sony with concrete feedback: participating in usability evaluations is an organized way for teachers and students to help effect change in future generations of hardware and software.

Our students were interested in mark-up features as aids to memory and recall, especially for face-to-face discussions, and as invention mechanisms for preparing course papers and integrating course readings into subsequent writing endeavors, such as comprehensive exams at the graduate level. They divided their mark-up activities, which for the most part were not supported in a direct manner by the PRS-505, into distinct categories: bookmarking pages, highlighting texts, annotating texts, and note-taking. These activities were denaturalized in pointed ways by our experiences with the device. In response to disruptions in their mark-up techniques, students mobilized a variety of disparate approaches. Some abandoned the use of bookmarks, highlights, annotations, and notes, opting instead to read the texts without making any marks or comments whatsoever. Others employed the bookmarks feature alone, and in a rather cursory fashion (recall the problems with bookmarks enumerated earlier). Still others discarded the device for the capabilities of print-outs or a computer; after a trial period that was disconcerting and even a little maddening, a handful of students gave up on the PRS-505 as a device for active reading. In short, these approaches reverted to familiar practices or attempted to do without them. They did not, in other words, aim to reinvent reading routines.

In contrast, many students devised new methods for marking texts, essentially hacking sociotechnical contexts to produce more hospitable environments for their discourse practices. These methods were simple and complex, and involved notecards, sticky notes, a notebook, and/or a computer. The simple methods were effective at reproducing a version of an established literacy routine: Students wrote down quotes in a notebook instead of underlining them, for example, or took notes in a word-processing program rather than in the margins of a book. Such seemingly superficial recreations, however, did more than just enable an old activity in a new medium. They also transformed the activity itself in evident ways, and in ways considered to be both helpful and potentially harmful. For example, students noted that writing down quotes served as an aid to retention, but also that they copied fewer longer quotes because it was more arduous than highlighting or underlining passages. The complex methods created relatively novel discursive systems for addressing the absence of mark-up features. In one fashion or another, these methods attempted to coordinate multiple interfaces—print and digital—that actively worked to incorporate the PRS-505. Students used word-processing files to elaborate on bookmarks, notepads and notecards to associate page numbers with comments, sticky notes (attached to the inside of the device cover) to record quick reference information like a website URL, and more. In devising such approaches, students drew on the advantages of the PRS-505 while structuring parallel time-space frames for related activities: The mark-up challenges we heard about the most had to do with designing workflows to reintegrate texts and metatexts, which in print tend to have a parasitic relationship (notes are on/in texts). Both the simple and complex methods of appropriation were the result of students being troubled by a system in which certain learned elements of active reading became externalized and unsupported.

Of course, these sorts of hacking behaviors are anywhere and everywhere in educational settings, for mismatches between the embodied assumptions of literacy technologies and those of readers and writers will always exist. To some extent, students and teachers can mediate these mismatches with pedagogical approaches, institutional mechanisms (such as policies and procedures), and hybrid forms of support for reading that leverage the features of a variety of media. Teachers, however, will also want to pay attention to the emergent landscape of e-book devices and the available options for marking texts. In this landscape, we would make a distinction between single-purpose devices like the Sony Reader and multi-purpose devices like the Apple iPad, which includes an e-book program plus many other programs (or apps). The affordances of single-purpose devices have indeed been expanding: current versions of the Sony Reader—there are three different models—include features for highlighting and searching texts, taking notes with a stylus or keyboard, exporting notes, and navigating with a touch screen. The Nook by Barnes & Noble also has a Web browser. In addition, the Amazon Kindle added features for sharing notes publicly and reading public notes and highlights. Multi-purpose devices can function in this very manner: There are well-known apps that emulate the Kindle and Nook on the iPad. But with the iPad there are numerous other apps that can be useful to active readers. Although one can certainly mark-up texts using the current features of single-purpose devices, productivity apps like iAnnotate PDF, GoodReader, Stanza, and Evernote provide an additional range of possibilities, including making audio comments, creating searchable tagging systems, developing document databases of texts and metatexts, and other tasks that integrate writing and reading in more thoroughgoing ways. As a result of these vastly different options, features for marking texts have become criteria for decision making for composition teachers interested in adopting an e-book platform. The world of print has not and does not present a comparable set of decisions.

Conclusions and Questions for E-Book Adoption

Would you purchase a Sony Reader? This was our final interview question for both sets of students, and their responses, which were mainly negative, were not surprising to us in the slightest. In general, students did not welcome the ways in which the PRS-505 defamiliarized classroom activities and the reading practices they had developed—over a period of years—for school settings. The device and its contexts were not considered to be avenues for exploring new directions in literacy or future instructional challenges. Instead, they were viewed as barriers to the perpetuation of productive habits of minds and bodies that students relied on to negotiate and manage educational endeavors. A paramount issue was the lack of alternative mark-up features to support active readers and their tasks. Although word-processing programs confounded the routines of those used to typewriters and pens and pencils, they provided (for better and worse) an environment in which students and teachers could reimagine structures for literacy work, including routines involving printed texts. The PRS-505 had a number of impressive hardware capabilities that are crucial to positive e-book experiences, but its software features were not attuned enough to reading practices in college composition classes. In the final analysis, student appropriation strategies could not bridge this gap.

We should note, too, that the conclusions of students took into account the roles and functions of other electronic devices. In this day and age, students are likely to own multiple devices for consuming, producing, and managing digital content: computers of various forms, cell phones, MP3 players, still and video cameras, and more. How many devices are students willing to purchase and learn? What is the tipping point for dedicated e-book devices? Proponents are quick to point out that the discounted prices of e-books can return the cost of a device in three to four semesters, which is true. This calculus, however, does not factor in what students are spending for other digital devices, high-speed Internet access, data plans for cell phones and other devices that connect to cellular networks, subscriptions to services like Netflix and Rhapsody, and campus computing fees (the campus computing fee at Penn State is $236 per semester). The larger financial picture encouraged our students to question the necessity of dedicated e-book devices with strict systems for digital rights management. Although students could access course PDF files on computers and cell phones, the items from the Reader bookstore could only be operated with the PRS-505. In contrast, students can read Kindle book editions not only on Kindle devices but also on cell phones and computers, including the iPad and other tablet computers that are compatible with the Kindle software (and that make it easier to keep associated work in the same attention space). The debate between closed and open platforms will no doubt continue in earnest. If our experiences are any indication, students will be alert to arguments that take into consideration their full range of digital activities, academic and non-academic. In financial and functional terms, there are limits to what students can and will invest in literacy technologies.

There were other external factors that contributed to our impressions and those of students, most of which have already been mentioned: the activities we asked students to perform, their own literacy practices and habits, our own literacy practices and habits, institutional policies and protocols, publisher offerings, representations of e-books in educational settings and in publications for teachers, and more. Impressions of the PRS-505 from our courses, then, must be located in a particular time and place. This rhetorical perspective is all too often absent from software and hardware reviews. The typical review reports on an experience or two with a technology and then deems it fit or unfit for all of higher education. Our experiences with the PRS-505 were less than stellar, but we can imagine other courses in which it might have faired better with students and teachers. Situated contexts will be central to the ways in which e-books and their devices are interpreted, used, and evaluated for academic purposes.

To help composition teachers reason through situated contexts, we conclude with a series of questions for e-book adoption. Although far from exhaustive, these questions encourage teachers to consider a wide range of technological, pedagogical, and institutional issues that help determine e-book use in composition courses.

Technological Questions

- What assumptions about reading does the device instantiate?
- How does the device support active readers?
- What are the navigation features for e-texts? Are they understandable to print-trained readers? Can they support class discussions?
- What are the marking features for e-texts? What do they enable and encourage? Disable and discourage?
- Can students export their metatexts (e.g., notes, highlights) for use with other literacy technologies? In what ways?

- Which software and hardware systems do you use to support course activities? Is the device compatible with these systems? Does it need to be?
- How does the device handle digital rights management? Is the system proprietary or more open?
- Is the device accessible to students with disabilities? Does the device comply with the Americans with Disabilities Act of 1990?
- Are there add-on components that can expand the capabilities of the device for active readers?

Pedagogical Questions

- What are your assumptions about reading? About writing?
- In your courses, how are reading and writing connected? Reading and learning?
- What do you expect students to do with and to course texts?
- What are the reading practices of students in your courses? How do they engage texts?
- Are your course texts available in an e-book format? If not, are there viable alternatives?
- Have you invented a naming scheme for course files? Can it be extended to e-books?
- What are the workflows for your course activities? Can they accommodate an e-book device? Will they need to be reorganized?
- What is your stance on the relationship between pedagogy and technology? One-directional? Dialectical? Other?
- Does your pedagogy include room for open-ended explorations of technology?

Institutional Questions

- Does your institution lend e-book devices or devices with e-book capabilities? What does the student user agreement stipu-

late? Will students need to create personal accounts (on iTunes or Amazon, for example) to manage the devices?
- How might you encourage students to possess, personalize, and test institutional technologies in ambitious ways?
- Does your institution operate an e-book rental program? What are the offerings in composition?
- Does your institution provide access to e-texts? Are there library protocols for downloading and using them?
- To what extent can you populate an e-book device with library holdings? Does your library subscribe to e-versions of texts that are central to composition?
- How does your institution handle copyright clearances for e-texts? Is there an e-reserve system? Can it be accessed with an e-book device?
- Are there institutional policies that address e-book issues, such as accessibility for the disabled and digital rights management?
- Is there a unit on campus that can provide training services for e-book devices? Does the training cover critical as well as functional concerns?
- Is there a unit on campus that can provide technical support for e-book devices?
- Are there others at your institution who might be interested in e-book initiatives? Are there ways to share costs and resources?

Works Cited

Baron, Dennis. *A Better Pencil: Readers, Writers, and the Digital Revolution.* New York: Oxford UP, 2009. Print.

Bauman, Zygmunt, and Tim May. *Thinking Sociologically.* 2nd ed. Malden, MA: Blackwell P, 2001. Print.

Bolter, Jay David. *Writing Space: The Computer, Hypertext, and the History of Writing.* Hillsdale, NJ: LEA, 1991. Print.

Goggin, Gerard, and Christopher Newell. *Digital Disability: The Social Construction of Disability in New Media.* New York: Rowman, 2003. Print.

Haas, Christina, and John R. Hayes. "What Did I Just Say? Reading Problems in Writing with the Machine." *Research in the Teaching of English* 20.1 (1986): 22-35. Print.

Johnson-Eilola, Johndan. *Nostalgic Angels: Rearticulating Hypertext Writing.* Norwood, NJ: Ablex, 1997. Print.

Marshall, Catherine C., and Christine Ruotolo. "Reading-in-the-Small: A Study of Reading on Small Form Factor Devices." *Proceedings of the 2nd ACM/IEEE-CS Joint Conference on Digital Libraries*, Portland 13-17 July 2002. Ed. Gary Marchionini. New York: ACM, 2002. 56-64. Print.

Strickland, James. "An Annotated Bibliography of Representative Software for Writers." *Computers and Composition* 10.1 (1992): 25-35. Print.

Waycott, Jenny, and Agnes Kukulska-Hume. "Students' Experiences with PDAs for Reading Course Materials." *Personal and Ubiquitous Computing* 7.1 (2003): 30-43. Print.

NOTES

1. We are grateful to Sony Electronics for providing us with e-book devices to study and use at Penn State. We also want to thank colleagues that have supported our e-book initiatives: From English: Robin Schulze, Diana Gruendler, Rebecca Wilson Lundin, and Patricia Gael. From the University Libraries: Mike Furlough, Anne Behler, and Binky Lush. From Information Technology Services: Cole Camplese, Allan Gyorke, Erin Cramer Long, Brian Young, and Jason Heffner. The research presented in this essay was approved by the Penn State Institutional Review Board.

COMPOSITION STUDIES

Composition Studies is on the Web at http://www.compositionstudies.uwinnipeg.ca/index.html

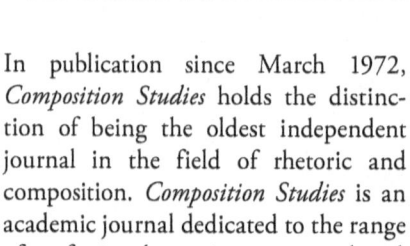

Fall 2012
Volume 40, Number 2

In publication since March 1972, *Composition Studies* holds the distinction of being the oldest independent journal in the field of rhetoric and composition. *Composition Studies* is an academic journal dedicated to the range of professional practices associated with the field: teaching college writing; theorizing rhetoric and composing; administering writing related programs; preparing the field's future teacher-scholars. Currently *Composition Studies* is the only periodical in writing studies to cross international borders, moving from Texas to Winnipeg, Canada in 2010. The current editor is Jennifer Clary-Lemon.

"Changing Research Methods, Changing History: A Reflection on Language, Location, and Archive" by Jessica Enoch

Because *Composition Studies* strives to offer a range of diverse voices and practices relevant to those teaching and researching about writing, we chose Jessica Enoch's piece to help represent that range. Enoch's article not only characterizes the "archival turn" in writing studies but also suggests scholars need to turn a critical eye to their own methods and methodologies. Enoch argues that scholars can investigate the pedagogies composed by and for marginalized populations, exposing unarticulated assumptions of historiographic research practices in doing so.

4 Changing Research Methods, Changing History: A Reflection on Language, Location, and Archive

Jessica Enoch

This essay reflects on the research methods the author employed to write three Chicana teachers into the history of rhetorical education. Her reflections ultimately push beyond her experience to explore how scholars can continue to research and investigate the pedagogies composed by and for marginalized populations at non-elite institutions. In taking up this work, however, she also exposes a number of unarticulated assumptions at the heart of historiographic practice that subtly shape research activities and prevent the diversification and expansion of research, writing, and thinking.

> [W]hen we resist primacy, traditional paradigms for seeing and valuing participation, even in composition studies, are inadequate. They obviously miss the experiences and achievements of many, and they privilege by this process the viewpoints and the interpretations of the officialized few, whether they are acknowledged as prime or not. The challenge then is to broaden the research base, the inquiry base, the knowledge base from which interpretive frameworks can be drawn, not simply to say that we know we don't know but to do the work of finding out. We need methodologies for seeing the gaps in our knowledge and for generating the research that can help us fill those gaps.
>
> —Jacqueline Jones Royster and Jean C. Williams, "History in the Spaces Left," 1999 (582-83)

> *We do not at all mean that our children should not be taught the [English] language of the land that they live in, since it is the means that will enable them to communicate directly with their neighbors, and that will equip them to appreciate their rights. What we simply meant to say was that we ought not disregard the [Spanish] language, because it is the official stamp of the race and of the people.*
>
> —Jovita Idar, "The Mexican Children in Texas," 1911 (1)

Over ten years ago, Jacqueline Jones Royster and Jean C. Williams called scholars in the field to take up two interrelated tasks. The first was to counter officialized disciplinary narratives by composing histories of Rhetoric and Composition that account for marginalized rather than enfranchised students and teachers, as well as nontraditional rather than elite writing programs and pedagogies. The second was to articulate the research methods and methodologies that enable this kind of critical work to come into being. Given the number of histories published over the last decade, the first call has been (and continues to be) answered, with scholars such as Anne Ruggles Gere, David Gold (Rhetoric), Susan Jarratt, Susan Kates, Shirley Wilson Logan (Liberating), Kelly Ritter, Lucille Schultz, and Stephen Schneider composing studies that enrich, expand, and complicate understandings of writing instruction in the United States.[1] In terms of Royster and Williams's second call, however, there has not been as vociferous a response. While scholars have surely discussed larger issues of historiographic method and methodology, we have not spent as much time articulating and analyzing the particular research strategies that allow us to tell a "reconfigured, more fully textured story" of our field's past (Royster and Williams 581).[2]

This essay takes up this latter challenge by identifying and reflecting on the research methods I used to write three teachers, Jovita Idar, Marta Peña, and Leonor Villegas de Magnón, into the history of rhetorical education. In the fourth chapter of Refiguring Rhetorical Education: Women Teaching African American, Native American, and Chicano/a Students, 1865-1911, I analyze the pedagogical arguments these women made through the pages of La Crónica, a turn-of-the-century, Spanish-language newspaper serving Laredo, Texas, that was owned and operated by Idar and her family. As the epigraph above indicates, Idar and her colleagues used the press to call for educational practices that embraced the Spanish language, asserted cultural knowledge, and reformulated civic duties. Their educational articles taught readers to envision themselves as active agents who could promote Mexican cultural traditions while negotiating the realities of their increasingly Anglo and discriminatory Texas society. In assessing their work, I argue that Idar, Peña, and Villegas offered their readers a resistant rhetorical education by providing them with the discursive skills as well as the civic and cultural knowledge necessary not just to participate in, but also to re-shape their Laredo, Texas community. Thus, I use the chapter in my book to claim that because these women composed such revolutionary pedagogical practices inside the pages of La Crónica, their work should revise our understandings of how rhetorical education has occurred in this country.

In this article, I shift my scholarly emphasis to meditate on the research methods that enabled me to write about these teachers and trouble dominant narratives of rhetorical education. It is important to note that my focus in this essay is on methods rather than methodology. Gesa Kirsch and Patricia Sullivan identify the distinction between these terms, writing that while methodology concerns itself with the "underlying theory and analysis of how research does or should proceed," methods are the "techniques or ways of proceeding in gathering evidence" (2). Of course, it is almost impossible to separate completely these two concepts—our theory surely informs the ways we choose to gather evidence and vice versa. But in focusing attention on method, we gain insight on the specific practices that enable us to produce a research project: the work of "locat[ing] and using primary materials [. . . and] achieving access to information" (L'Epplattenier, "Opinion" 69). As Barbara L'Epplattenier explains, "methods make the invisible work of historical research visible" (69). By making research methods visible, we attain a clearer sense of what historians are and are not doing when they compose their narratives. And, through this atomistic view, we have the opportunity to assess the practices that open up and close down historiographic possibilities, learning more about the methodological thruways and roadblocks that allow for and prevent alternative histories to be composed.

This meditation on my research methods ultimately aims to "broaden the research base, the inquiry base, the knowledge base from which interpretive frameworks can be drawn," so that scholars in the field can continue to compose histories that center on marginalized populations and non-elite institutions (Royster and Williams 581). To do this work, I use the major sections of the essay to reflect on the three research methods that I believe distinguished my work: choosing a Spanish-language newspaper as a primary text; locating a history of rhetorical education at the border city of Laredo, Texas; and conducting research at the Webb County Historical Foundation, a small community archive in Laredo. As I make these reflections, I consider how each method brings to light a number of unarticulated assumptions that lie at the heart of traditional historiographic methods. These assumptions not only stand at the center of much historiographic work, but also have the potential to stand in the way of historiographic exploration and revision. My work here, then, is to interrogate these assumptions, suggesting new ways to gather and assess historiographic evidence.

Primary Texts en Español

The road that led me to choose La Crónica as a primary text was a bumpy and circuitous one. As a doctoral student at Penn State University, I embarked on a dissertation project that examined the work of female teachers at the turn of the twentieth century. By 1912, the teaching profession had become an "Adamless Eden," and I was interested in learning more about the pedagogical practices of all of these "Eves" (Bardeen 18). More specifically, I wanted to interrogate the historiographic "fact" that the female teacher was an innocuous nurturer disinterested in the politics of education. So I began my research by looking to moments of conflict when teachers had to address questions of gender, race, culture, and power. The Mexican Revolution was one such moment. This period, I believed, could enable me to explore how teachers living on the Texas-Mexico border responded not just to the influx of Mexican immigrants to Texas, but also to the questions of nation, citizenship, culture, politics, and language that arrived with them.[3]

Thus, I began my research by reading secondary materials about Mexican education in Texas, searching for references and footnotes that would lead to the field-specific artifacts valued by scholars in Rhetoric and Composition Studies such as textbooks, pedagogical materials, and collections of student papers. Time and again I came up with nothing. Disheartened, I felt as if my work was only reifying the "myth of Mexican indifference" that Guadalupe San Miguel Jr. writes about: the idea that "Mexican Americans have not really cared for education or else they have failed to appreciate its importance and benefit to their community in particular and to the society at large" (xvi). Wanting to challenge this myth, I turned to other secondary materials, this time looking for texts that addressed more general themes of Mexican political activity. Finally, I got my lead when I came across Jose Limón's 1974 essay "El Primer Congreso Mexicanista de 1911: A Precursor to Chicanismo." In this article, Limón refers to the Spanish-language newspaper La Crónica as a "remarkable newspaper" that not only was dedicated to the "industrial, moral, and intellectual development" of Mexican people living in Texas, but also was concerned with the particular problem of educational discrimination in the state's public schools (87, 88). Limón referenced the fact that the Idar family owned the press, with daughter Jovita Idar serving as an editor and contributor.

Eager to learn more about the educational agenda of the newspaper and Idar's involvement in it, I requested the microfilm of the newspaper through interlibrary loan. Once I received the microfilm, a quick skim of its contents assured me that this was no dead end. On page after page, La Crónica printed articles in which writers spoke out against school discrimination and offered arguments for change. It railed against Americanization programs that enforced the English language and Anglo culture. It publicized Laredo's escuelitas, the small, community-run schools often headed by female teachers that offered bilingual and bicultural education. And it functioned as an educational space itself, using its pages to teach readers about language, cultural, and civic issues. It did not take long for me to realize that I should pursue this text further, so I embarked on the rewarding and labor-intensive task of translating over 60 articles from the newspaper and focusing attention on the three teachers, Idar, Peña, and Villegas, whose pedagogical arguments spoke significantly to pressing questions about language, literacy, culture, and civic participation that circulate in the field today.[4]

The rewards in choosing La Crónica as a primary text prompt us to consider an obvious yet unarticulated research method central to our field's historiographic work. Scholars who compose histories that investigate writing and rhetorical instruction in the U.S. certainly consult a wide range of primary materials. While more traditional or "curricular" histories rely on lecture notes, course descriptions, department meeting minutes, and so on, "extracurricular" histories—histories of those spaces outside the university where writing and rhetorical instruction occurs—place under examination a different, more varied collection of materials, such as conduct books, club papers, newspapers, and parlor rhetorics (see Gere, "Kitchen"). In consulting an ever-widening range of materials, historians continually redefine what "counts" as a resource that could provide insight to past practice. It is important to note, however, that with few exceptions these texts have one thing in common: they are all written in English.[5] Because of this singular focus on primary texts written in English, our investigations into the history of rhetoric and writing instruction have so far only told one part of a much larger story.

Bruce Horner and John Trimbur write that the field of Composition has consistently enforced a "unidirectional monolingual language policy" through the teaching of writing in English only (607). My work with La Crónica reveals that this univocal monolingual language policy also directs our research practices. Stories like those of the teachers in my study are often not told because we focus our research efforts on texts written in English. Further investigations of Spanish-language newspapers alone would most likely confirm my contention that the implicit and expected monolingualism of our field's research methods necessarily limit our understandings of the history of language and rhetorical instruction. For, even though the pedagogical work of Idar, Peña, and Villegas was exemplary, it was not extraordinary. There are certainly more texts like La Crónica to be studied.

As Herminio Rios and Guadelupe Castillo have found, prior to 1940 there were 372 Spanish-language newspapers published in the southwest region that includes Arizona, Texas, Colorado, New Mexico, and California (Cortés 248).[6] This number does not take into account those presses created in Spanish-speaking enclaves in cities such as Chicago, New York, Tampa, and Miami, or those newspapers published after 1940 and especially during the 1960s that Spanish-speaking students composed at both the high school and college levels (253). Scholars such as Carlos Cortés, Félix Gutiérrez, Doris Meyer, and América Rodriguez have pinpointed the various functions of these publications. While some were more accomodationist and simply translated Anglo news for Spanish-speaking readers, others, like

La Crónica, espoused a more bicultural and activist stance, speaking out as defenders of the community and as agitators against Anglo discrimination. This latter group often worked as "preservers of Chicano history and culture, maintainers and enforcers of language, and strengtheners of Chicano pride" (Cortés 255). As Meyer explains, by taking on the "unofficial role of public forum and community bulletin board," revolutionary newspapers often became sites "where aggrieved citizens could speak out" (406). In terms of the use and regard for the Spanish (and English) language, Cortés outlines the differing positions these presses adopted—positions that reflect their political and cultural investments:

> Some use only traditional Spanish; others champion the use of variations of Chicano Spanish or even bilingual writing that integrates Spanish and English words, sometimes within the same sentence and particularly in poetry. English-language Chicano publications have sometimes functioned as instruments of social activism, cultural reflection, and historical preservation, yet they obviously have contributed little to Spanish language usage in the United States. (255)

As a field, then, we might turn our attention to newspapers such as El Mexicano, La República, La Voz de América, El Mercurio de Nueva York, La Prensa, La Opinión, Las Novedades, Vida Obrera, La Luz, El Obrero, La Mujer Moderna, La Voz de la Mujer, and El Progreso.[7] And these selections are just the beginning since I've only catalogued here Spanish-language presses. Presses published in other languages and by other cultural communities would likely yield similar results. Even so, by investigating just these Spanish-language publications and choosing them as primary texts for historiographic investigation, we would not only enrich our understanding of how Spanish-speaking communities addressed educational debates, but we would also be able to place college writing and rhetoric instruction in a broader context.

In recent years, scholars such as Horner, Trimbur, Paul Matsuda, and Amy Zenger have worked to establish how and why English-language instruction gained prominence in the U.S. university system. For example, Horner and Trimbur investigate the "protracted struggle" (597) that eventually positioned English as the lingua franca of the university through a drastic reduction in attention to classical languages and the "territorializ[ation]" of modern languages like French,

German, and Spanish to "separate departments where students encountered [these languages] as texts to be read, not living languages to be written or spoken" (602). Matsuda extends this conversation, arguing that since its inception, the first-year composition course has functioned as a site of "linguistic containment, quarantining from the rest of higher education students who have not yet been socialized into the dominant linguistic practices" (641). And Zenger's study of student themes at Harvard explains how "required writing, reading, and critiquing" in English was a "means of negotiating a racially inflected identity: speaker of English as the mother tongue" (333).

These studies are revealing in that they chronicle how the composition classroom and the university became sites primarily invested in English-language instruction. However, placed in a broader context and in conversation with educational debates waged in non-English-language publications like La Crónica, this university initiative gains a different nuance: we can understand it as one voice in a multi-vocal and multilingual conversation about language instruction in the United States. Right at the moment when English became the dominant language of the university, La Crónica contributors were speaking out against Americanization campaigns that pinpointed English instruction as a vital part of their programs. Indeed, this broader view allows us to see that instruction in English at the college level did not "merely emerg[e] by default to fill the vacuum left by the classical languages" (Zenger 338). Instead, this shift in university priorities worked in concert with a nationwide Americanization movement that greatly affected educational initiatives at all levels both inside and outside the university.

Thus, choosing non-English language documents as primary texts for historiographic exploration has the potential to reap significant rewards. In terms of research methods, though, the choice requires that we do the difficult work of adding a new "too[l] to the historians' trade" (Ferreira-Buckley 582). As a field, we need to gain greater proficiency in languages other than English. It would only make sense that if we want to learn more about those who spoke to their communities about alternative, non-English language pedagogies or those who advocated for bicultural and bilingual education, we would need to consult texts written in the languages of those writers and their communities.

Of course, for many, studying non-English language texts is not easy; therefore, institutional support would help scholars to add this tool to their trade. For instance, individual departments or national institutions such as NCTE or CCCC might consider offering grants that would assist researchers in translating materials. Graduate courses might focus attention on the "ethnic press" as part of Rhetoric and Composition's extracurricular history. Graduate programs might encourage study in translation courses, comparative literature departments, and other modern language departments. And they might also take language requirements more seriously. As Doug Steward writes, the language requirement has become little more than a hoop to jump through because few English departments stress research in foreign languages (209-10). Rhetoric and Composition programs in particular might re-see this requirement as an opportunity for graduate students to translate educational texts and extracurricular materials that could give insight to alternative pedagogical practices or educational debates. By creating these opportunities for researchers, and especially for graduate students, our field would put scholars in the position to broaden the selection of primary texts we are able to consult and, accordingly, deepen and diversify the histories we produce.

HISTORIOGRAPHIC LOCATIONS

As scholars such as Gesa Kirsch and Christine Sutherland have made clear, going "on location" and actually visiting the places and spaces where historical subjects lived and wrote is an "invaluable" scholarly experience and research method (Kirsch, "Being" 20). For although we can never go back to the moment of inquiry and see what our subjects saw, the process of inhabiting their same spaces and places allows us to get "into closer touch" with their worlds, enabling us to piece the historiographic puzzle together more effectively and efficiently (Sutherland 29).

Kirsch and Sutherland's assessments of this research practice certainly resonates with my own. While reading La Crónica articles in Penn State's microfilm room—almost 1,800 miles from Laredo—I continually encountered references to Nuevo Laredo, Laredo's sister city on the Mexican side of the border; contributors frequently mentioned the Rio Grande, and they consistently wrote of their travels from Texas to Mexico and back again. Looking at Laredo's location on the map, I could see that since the city was a border town, it would make sense that Mexico and cities on the other side of the border would figure into La Crónica writers' contributions. These references, however, gained new meaning once I traveled to Laredo and saw the city and its location with my own eyes.

The moment I arrived in Laredo, I realized that Mexico, Nuevo Laredo, and the Rio Grande were not just sites that were close by or in the same general vicinity. Mexico is a physical presence that is visible from Laredo's city center: the border, the river, and Nuevo Laredo are all within eyesight of Laredo's streets. Being there and assessing Laredo's proximity to Mexico enabled me to understand not only what contributors were referring to but also why these references were so persistent: one could not live in Laredo without acknowledging the presence of Mexico and its border. Simple as it might seem, this observation crystallized understandings about geographic locations that have the potential to expand and challenge our historiographic work.

When researching writing programs and pedagogies from the past, historians often take into account a number of variables that might have affected the way instruction was conducted. We consider the classed, raced, cultured, and gendered status of teachers and students; we assess their use of and access to textbooks and other pedagogical materials; and we reflect on the educational, social, and political climate of the moment. We often do not, however, consider how geographic location inflects pedagogical practice.

Walking the streets of Laredo helped me realize how important a role location can play in pedagogical production; living on the border of Texas and Mexico shaped every aspect of Idar's, Peña's, and Villegas's work. Just as they and their readers crossed and re-crossed the Rio Grande, their pedagogies borrowed and built from both Mexican and American worlds. Ultimately, though, these women's teaching practices were not an even mixture of national and cultural imperatives; instead they were distinctive of and individual to the particular border space in which they lived. For instance, while they argued for their rights as U.S. citizens, they taught readers about Mexican citizenship and culture. And as they rejected English-Only instruction, they did not advocate for Spanish-only instruction but called instead for bilingual and bicultural education in Texas schools. It was because Idar, Peña, and Villegas wrote and taught in what Gloria Anzaldúa defines as the "b"orderlands—the "actual physical borderland" or geographic space where cultures meet—that they created complex pedagogical practices distinguished by powerful and unique cultural and civic negotiations (19). [8]

Nedra Reynolds and Vorris Nunley have convincingly argued that "rhetorical scholarship has undertheorized how spatiality, the politics and poetics of space, mediate rhetorical performances" (Nunley 222). Given my work in Laredo and with Idar, Peña, and Villegas, I extend this claim, adding that historical scholarship in the field has undertheorized how spatiality and geography have affected pedagogical practice. Heidemarie Weidner's research counts as one exception. In her investigation of nineteenth-century composition instruction at Butler University in Indianapolis, Indiana, she writes that because Butler was "situated at what was then the western frontier [. . .] it differed greatly from the eastern schools" (60):

> Less inflexible, more convinced of the necessity to adapt to rapid changes brought on by a growing western expansion [, . . . educators] found it easier to choose curricular change, a decision which resulted in a dynamic, community-centered and practical education. (60)

Here, we see that by attending to questions of location, Weidner can offer a fuller explanation of why Butler's program developed as it did. Thus, the research practice of going "on location" does more than allow us to do the important work of making sense of oblique references or experiencing, in some small way, the worlds of our historical subjects. It also gives us the opportunity to ask larger questions about how the geographic location of the educational site affected the pedagogy produced there.

This awareness of the ways place interanimates pedagogy prompts consideration of another research method: that of choosing a historiographic location. Certainly, Royster and Williams along with Gere have articulated the value of relocating historical studies outside the campuses of prestigious universities, and scholars have in great numbers proven this point true by examining pedagogies produced in Historically Black Colleges, labor colleges, women's colleges, and normal schools as well as parlors, kitchen tables, and rented rooms. Locating my research on the borderlands of Texas and Mexico, however, made me realize that our frame of reference regarding location needs to get incrementally larger because our histories of rhetoric and writing instruction are often situated within a specific and unarticulated terrain.

We not only often situate histories at university sites, but we often locate them in the Northeast corner of the United States.

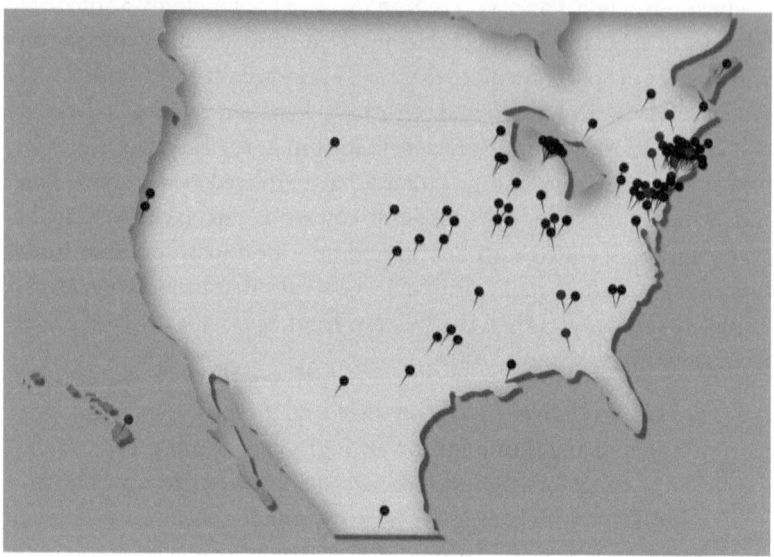

Figure 1:.This map plots the historiographic locations examined in 70 studies of rhetoric and writing instruction.

Figure 1 confirms this point, demonstrating that our disciplinary field is not an abstract one. Out of 70 histories surveyed, scholars have conducted research at 126 curricular and extracurricular sites. Of this total number, 71 historiographic locations are situated along the Northeastern seaboard of the U.S., with an additional 11 studies based at the University of Michigan. Forty-five studies are located outside the "hotbed" of Rhetoric and Composition, with only three engaging work in the Southwest region of North America (see Appendix for the studies I consulted to compose the map).

In creating this map I am not arguing that important and groundbreaking research on marginalized students and teachers cannot happen when scholars situate study in the Northeast, but I am asserting that our field's historiographic understandings have the potential to be enriched if we looked beyond this region. For, if place does indeed inform pedagogy, our histories of writing instruction are eclipsed when we, by and large, only locate our work in one geographic area. Moreover, since as a field we have committed ourselves to exploring contact zones, metaphorical "B"orderlands, transnational as well as multicultural agendas, we might consider how situating our study at actual borderlands like those of Laredo might invigorate our contemporary pedagogical questions, enabling us to learn more about how historical figures living in these spaces taught and learned about rhetoric and writing as well as cultural and civic engagement. By situating our research at new locations, then, we would adopt research methods that challenge disciplinary boundaries and reinforce our theoretical agendas.

As we take up this work, however, we should be critical of our methodological stance and especially of the metaphors we use to conceptualize our research. Reynolds explains that "spatial metaphors" carry with them "certain consequences" (27) in that they often "reflect and construct accepted ways of knowing" (5). Therefore, we should not see this attention to geographic location as an invitation to adopt a colonialist mentality and define our practice as one of exploring new frontiers or examining untouched places. Instead, our prerogative would be to question the boundaries and borders of our disciplinary field, approaching historiographic study with these questions in mind: Where do we implicitly argue that rhetoric and composition happens? What spaces does our field deem worth studying? How might other places and spaces complicate our understanding of writing and rhetorical instruction? By asking and answering these questions, we would come closer to realizing James Murphy's contention that "the place where one stands will have a great influence on what the historian's lever can move" (5). Location matters. Not only does our choice of location condition who and what we're able to see and study, but location itself also inflects the aims and interests of teachers and students, having the potential to act as a major factor in the overarching pedagogical project.

The Community Archive

Most historiographic research is not complete without a visit to an archive. Thus, I complemented my translations of La Crónica and my trip to Laredo with a visit to the Webb County Heritage Foundation (WCHF) to conduct the archival research that would deepen my understanding of Idar, Peña, and Villegas's work. I was especially hopeful that research at this archive would be successful because, in terms of my secondary and primary research, I had found little information about the women in my study besides a small number of scholarly articles on the Idar family and Villegas as well as the republication of Villegas's autobiography, The Rebel. Additionally, these women's names were all but absent from records at major research institutions such as the Library of Congress or the archives at the University of Texas. My hope, then, was that the WCHF, a local, community archive, would contain rich turn-of-the-twentieth-century materials about these women, their teachings, La Crónica, and life in Laredo that would allow me to recover these teachers' forgotten voices and bring their words to "full volume" (Logan, "Introduction" xi). What I found shifted my thinking about the conventional ways scholars of rhetoric and composition discuss their approaches to and work in the archive.

In my research at the WCHF, I certainly found compelling materials that made it possible for me to advance an argument about the revolutionary teaching practices of Idar, Peña, and Villegas. Just as interesting as these findings, however, was my realization that although these women were missing from our scholarly conversations, they were not forgotten inside the city of Laredo. When I entered the WCHF and inquired about Idar, Peña, and Villegas, the archivist did not immediately bring out turn-of-the-twentieth century documents. Rather, she presented me with recent newspaper clippings, public service announcements, and exhibit promotions that the Foundation itself had produced about Idar and Villegas.[9]

For instance, in 1992, the WCHF published a series of biographical sketches entitled "Celebration of our Heritage: Important Women in Webb County's History" for the city's local newspaper, the Laredo Morning Times, and both Idar and Villegas were featured in the series. In Idar's segment, community members learned that she was both a local teacher who "did not have enough text books, or benches or chairs, and on cold days no heat" ("Jovita" 8D) and a community activist who participated in the first Mexican Congress, El Primer Congreso Mexicanista; began a feminist organization, La Liga Feminista Mexicanista;[10] and formed, with Villegas, Cruz Blanca ("The White Cross"), which offered nursing aid to soldiers fighting in the Mexican Revolution. Similarly, in Villegas's installment, the Foundation defined her as a teacher and a political revolutionary—a woman who wrote "fiery speeches" in support of Mexican leader Francisco Madero ("Leonor" 5D).

The WCHF did not just use this series to educate the community about the historical significance of Idar and Villegas. As it informed readers about important women in Laredo's past, it also linked these figures to influential women in Laredo's present-day community.

> The women of Webb County have many times been forgotten in their contribution to the betterment of life in Webb County. Many [w]omen today contribute to the educational wealth and richness of Webb County. This article is dedicated to the 3 women who helped provide the material for this article who are contributing daily to the betterment of hundreds of Laredoans. They are Rose Trevino, Texas Archeological Steward; Dr. Norma Cantu, Laredo State University; and Prof. Lucy Cardenas, Laredo Junior College. ("Jovita" 8D)

In addition to this 1992 series on important Webb County women both past and present, the WCHF also celebrated the work of Villegas six years later by creating a photo exhibit of her kindergarten students and inviting Clara Lomas, Chicana scholar and editor of Villegas's autobiography, to speak at the event. The Foundation once again used this opportunity to connect community members to the history it presented. As one article in the Laredo Weekly Times explains, "Many Laredoans are sure to find themselves, a dear friend, or relative among these memorable photographs" ("Heritage Foundation Slates" 6D).

This effort to encourage community members to connect to and take part in their local history is even more pronounced in other Foundation events and programs. For instance, the WCHF works with local schools and universities to support an oral history project in which students interview community members and then contribute the interviews to the archive. It sponsored a "Save Our Story" campaign which "encourage[d] Laredo, Webb County, and border residents to bring forward their old photographs, documents, letters, maps, and artifacts to be assessed by staff with the possible option of loan or gift to the Webb County Heritage Foundation" ("Heritage," Register 8). And, it also awards the "President of the Rio Grande Scholarship," a $500 scholarship to students who produce essays on their family history.

The innovative work of the WCHF, and other archives like it, calls us to think about how we conceive of both ourselves as researchers and our research methods when conducting work at local, community archives as opposed to large, research institutions. In initial histories of Composition, James Berlin, Robert Connors (Composition), Sharon Crowley, John Brereton, and Albert Kitzhaber consistently consulted resources in university libraries such as those at Harvard, Yale, Iowa, and Michigan. "Our" archives were special collections at these sites, which preserved "those rarest and most valuable of data, actual student writings, teacher records, unprinted notes and pedagogical materials, and ephemera that writing courses have generated but rarely kept" (Connors, "Dreams" 225). As Connors explains in "Dreams and Play: Historical Method and Methodology," the conventional archival practice at these sites is one in which the researcher enters the archive with a specific question in mind and pursues this question, in many ways, like a hunter or a detective.

Connors first equates the researcher with the hunter, writing that she goes to the archive because of a "human instinct to make sense of things [. . . . She] enter[s] that jungle because there is something to track" (226). As the detective, the researcher searches for "inert archival materials" (225) and "dusty mass[es] of past records" (227) to find clues that might offer evidence concerning the mysteries of the past. Once this hunter/detective tracks down her prey or discovers her clues, she activates these materials in ways that help scholars of rhetoric and composition understand who we are and why we teach the way we do. The purpose of working in the archive and writing our history, Connors explains, is for us to tell "stories about the tribe to make the tribe real. [. . .] [W]e are telling the stories of our fathers and mothers, and we are legitimating ourselves through legitimating them" (234).

Such archival practices might make sense for a researcher working in a university archive that holds materials directly related to rhetoric and composition instruction. However, as scholars investigate alternative sites for instruction that often occurred outside university classrooms, they have expanded the range of archives they visit, turning their attention to smaller, local archives like the WCHF as a means to locate materials that would enhance their research. Researching at these archives requires different kinds of approaches than those scholars have used in more traditional archival settings.

My experiences at the WCHF suggest that we might first, as with the historiographic locations, recast the metaphors we use to define our practice in the archive. Seeing the WCHF as an unexplored jungle in need of taming or a crime scene where the researcher-detective discovers clues to a mystery might condition us to ignore the important civic and communal work of archives like the WCHF. The WCHF certainly functions as a place for historic preservation, but it also serves a site for communal involvement and civic engagement. The WCHF is an archive alive with contributions that community members compose, and it is a place where public memory in Laredo is constantly created and re-created. Moreover, the WCHF is not simply a library where scholars can research and compose histories of rhetoric and writing instruction. The WCHF is itself an extracurricular educational space: one of its objectives is to teach the community about its history while also connecting its past to Laredo's present and future. Therefore, as researchers continue to visit local and community archives like the WCHF, it is important that we avoid seeing ourselves as detectives or hunters. We might instead recognize that we are often outsiders to these communities whose members have leveraged very different arguments from these archives and about the figures we study.

This understanding of the work that happens in archives like the WCHF should especially inform the ways we see and "reclaim" figures like Idar, Peña, and Villegas. Through our historiography, we might indeed pinpoint women like these as foremothers whose voices we want to bring to full volume as a means to enrich our knowledge of past iterations of rhetorical education. But we also need to be cognizant of the fact that as teachers of rhetoric and composition, we are not their direct descendents; these women are not figures like Gertrude Buck, Mina Shaughnessy, or Anne Berthoff. Rather, we must appreciate the fact that through the interpretive work of the WCHF, Idar and Villegas are mothers of different lineages; they have been identified as part of a long line of female leaders in the community that continues from 1911 into the present moment. We might be "telling stories of the rhetoric and composition tribe" when we write the work of Idar, Peña, and Villegas into our disciplinary histories, but we should also not forget what other stories women like these are part of and what other kinds of significance they hold.

Reflecting critically on both the metaphors we use to define archival work and the ways we conceive our historical subjects ultimately helps us acknowledge that archives like the WCHF are not "our" archives. These are not spaces like Harvard's holdings of student papers, the Richard Beal collection at the Universities of New Hampshire and Rhode Island, or the Rhetoric and Composition Sound Archives at Texas Christian University. Because they are not "our" archives, scholars need to consider how their role as researchers means they do more than write about their subjects in ethical, respectful, and accurate ways. Researching in spaces other than those we might deem as our own means that we have special responsibilities in terms of the work we do there.

One responsibility of working in the community archive is that we learn not just about the figures relevant to our study but also about the archive itself and the function it serves inside its community: How and why have community members created and shaped the archive? What are its priorities and objectives? What kinds of arguments do archivists and community members create from the historical materials held in the archive? How do figures important to rhetoric and composition "figure into" their community's history and public memory? In answering these questions it does not mean that we paralyze ourselves from conducting our research, but it does mean that we don't just take materials and run.

The challenge of working in the community archive is that we look up from our own research and see the other kinds of work being done in and through the archive. As my experiences at the WCHF make clear, this kind of archive often takes up important communal, civic, and activist work. It is our objective as researchers to learn about this work and to see how our scholarship could reinforce or contribute to these initiatives. Such archival practices underscore and extend the point Royster makes in Traces of a Stream when she writes that "whatever knowledge accrued" through our research should be "presented and represented within th[e] community," making it possible for communal "participation and response" (274). It is the responsibility of the researcher that she "speak and interpret with the community, not just for the community, or about the community" (275). By speaking with archivists about the communal and civic goals of their archive, we elaborate on what counts as a research method. In addition to accessing and retrieving information, we must also see as viable and important the acts of sharing our research and writing with archivists, listening to them, and learning more about what the information we retrieve says not just about our history but about their community's past, present, and future.

New Methods, New Histories

Recent discussions about research methods offer sage advice and important information to scholars interested in conducting historiographic study. From Katherine Tirabassi, Wendy Sharer, Sammie Morris, and Shirley Rose, we learn about the archivist's work and the "organizing principles that gover[n] the construction, maintenance, and investigation of an archival collection" (Tirabassi 171). From Chris Warnick, we learn how to negotiate the various finding aids that might lead to promising primary resources. From Lynée Gaillet, we learn about funding opportunities that enable scholars to go "on location." And from David Gold we learn how to "embrace" and make the best use of serendipitous moments in the archive (see "Accidental").

My work in this essay contributes to and extends this conversation by considering how our investment in articulating research methods might be combined with the field's dedicated interest in composing alternative histories of rhetoric and writing instruction. In combining these interests, I see that we have an opportunity to, in the words of Royster and Williams, "se[e] the gaps in our knowledge" and "generat[e] the research that can help us fill those gaps" (581). But rethinking the language of primary texts, the location where we situate our research, and the practices we use to conduct archival research at local archives is just a start. The goal here is to invite others to the conversation so that we can continue to create new opportunities for listening to new voices and learning about new pedagogies because by changing our methods we change our histories.

Acknowledgments

I greatly appreciate the challenging revision suggestions of the three anonymous reviewers who helped me to rethink my work in this essay.

Notes

1. See also Patricia Donahue and Gretchen Fletcher Moon's collection, Local Histories: Reading the Archives of Composition.

2. For broad-based discussions of historiography in Rhetoric and Composition, see Octalog I and II, Anne Ruggles Gere ("Kitchen"), and Victor Vitanza. For specific discussions of archival methods and methodologies, see

Barbara L'Eplattenier ("Opinion" and "Questioning"); Cheryl Glenn and Jessica Enoch; Gesa Kirsch and Liz Rohan; Alexis Ramsey et al.; Wendy Sharer; Barbara Biesecker; Charles E. Morris II; and the 1999 special issue of College English, Archivists with an Attitude.

3. This is not to say that there were no Mexican people living in the borderlands before this time. The region has been populated by Mexican people for hundreds of years. It was only because of the Texas Revolution of 1836 and the annexation of Texas to the United States that Mexican citizens became Americans when the border "literally migrated" over them (Zavella 77). The Revolution years are exigent for study because of the pressing questions and concerns having to do with political turmoil, war, poverty, immigration, and citizenship that teachers had to contend with.

4. My thanks goes to Penn State University and the University of New Hampshire for funding the work of three fantastic translators, Lisa Lawson, Malena Florin, and Raquel Moran Tellez, who aided me in reading and transcribing these materials.

5. My focus here is on histories of Rhetoric and Composition in the U.S. Surely, histories of rhetoric rely on texts composed in languages other than English. I would contend, however, that these histories focus primarily on texts written in Latin, Greek, and other European languages and rarely consult those written in languages emerging from North and South America. Susan Romano's article "Tlaltelolco: The Grammatical-Rhetorical Indios of Colonial Mexico" serves as one exception.

6. For a recent study of Mexican women journalists in Mexico, see also Cristina D. Ramírez, "Forging a Mestiza Rhetoric."

7. Félix Gutiérrez provides a number of bibliographic resources that point researchers to archives that hold Spanish-language publications. See "Spanish-Language Newspaper Holdings" in the Barker Texas History Collection, University of Texas at Austin; Michael Randall, "Chicano Studies Serials Holdings at UCLA," Univeristy of California at Los Angeles Library; and Ricardo Chabrán, "Listing of 143 Chicano Publications on Microfilm," Chicano Studies Library, University of California at Berkeley (67). In addition, Ramón Gutiérrez's "The UCLA Bibliographic Survey of Mexican-American Literary Culture, 1821-1945: An Overview" would also be helpful in conducting this kind of research.

8. In *Feminist Rhetorical Theories*, Karen A. Foss, Sonja K. Foss, and Cindy L. Griffin explain the difference between Anzaldua's borderlands and Borderlands: "Written lowercase, the word refers to a geographic site—the 'actual southwest borderlands or any borderlands between two cultures.' When she capitalizes it, however, she is using it as a 'metaphor, not actuality' to refer to a state that exists whenever cultural differences exist, whether those cultures involve physical differences such as race, class, or gender, or differences that are less tangible—psychological, social, or cultural" (106).

9. Unfortunately, I was unable to find any secondary materials on Marta Peña. The only information I have about her life and work was culled through the contributions she made to La Crónica and references to her work as a teacher in the same newspaper.

10. To learn more about Idar's feminist investments as well as those of other Laredo women, see Jessica Enoch, "Para la Mujer: Defining a Chicana Feminist Rhetoric at the Turn of the Century."

Works Cited

Anzaldúa, Gloria. *Borderlands/La Frontera: The New Mestiza*. 2nd ed. San Francisco: Aute Lute, 1999. Print.

Archivists with an Attitude. Spec. issue of *College English* 61.5 (1999): 574-98. Print.

Bardeen, C.W. "The Monopolizing Woman Teacher." *Education Review* (Jan. 1912): 17-40. Print.

Berlin, James. *Rhetoric and Reality: Writing Instruction in American Colleges, 1900-1985*. Carbondale: Southern Illinois UP, 1987. Print.

———. *Writing Instruction in Nineteenth-Century American Colleges*. Carbondale: Southern Illinois UP, 1984. Print.

Biesecker, Barbara. "Of Historicity, Rhetoric: The Archive as Scene of Invention." *Rhetoric and Public Affairs* 9.1 (2006): 124-31. Print.

Brereton, John, ed. *The Origins of Composition Studies in the American College, 1875-1925*. Pittsburgh: U of Pittsburgh P, 1995. Print.

Connors, Robert. *Composition-Rhetoric: Backgrounds, Theory, and Pedagogy*. Pittsburgh: U of Pittsburgh P, 1997. Print.

—. "Dreams and Play: Historical Method and Methodology." *Selected Essays of Robert J. Connors*. Ed. Lisa Ede and Andrea Lunsford. Boston: Bedford/St. Martin's, 2003. 221-35. Print.

Cortés, Carlos. "The Mexican American Press." *The Ethnic Press in the United States*. Ed. Sally M. Miller. New York: Greenwood, 1987. 247-60. Print.

Crowley, Sharon. *Composition in the University: Historical and Polemical Essays*. Pittsburgh: U of Pittsburgh P, 1998. Print.

Donahue, Patricia, and Gretchen Fletcher Moon, eds. *Local Histories: Reading the Archives of Composition*. Pittsburgh: U of Pittsburgh P, 2007. Print.

Enoch, Jessica. "Para la Mujer: Defining a Chicana Feminist Rhetoric at the Turn of the Century." *College English* 67.1 (2003): 20-37. Print.

—. *Refiguring Rhetorical Education: Women Teaching African American, Native American, and Chicano/a Students, 1865-1911*. Carbondale: Southern Illinois UP, 2008. Print.

Ferreira-Buckley, Linda. "Rescuing the Archives from Foucault." *College English* 61.5 (1999): 577-83. Print.

Foss, Karen A., Sonja K. Foss, and Cindy F. Griffin. *Feminist Rhetorical Theories*. London: Sage, 1999. Print.
Gaillet, Lynée Lewis. "Archival Survival: Navigating Historical Research." Ramsey et al. 28-39.
Gere, Anne Ruggles. "Kitchen Tables and Rented Rooms: The Extracurriculum of Composition." *CCC* 45.1 (1994): 75-107. Print.
—. *Intimate Practices: Literacy and Cultural Work in U.S. Women's Clubs, 1880-1920*. Urbana: U of Illinois P, 1997. Print.
Glenn, Cheryl, and Jessica Enoch. "Drama in the Archives: Re-Reading Materials, Re-Writing History." *CCC* 61.2 (2009): 321-42. Print.
Gold, David. "The Accidental Archivist: Embracing Chance and Confusion in Historical Scholarship." *Beyond the Archives: Research as a Lived Process*. Ed. Gesa Kirsch and Liz Rohan. Carbondale: Southern Illinois UP, 2008. 13-19. Print.
—. *Rhetoric at the Margins: Revising the History of Writing Instruction in American Colleges, 1873-1947*. Carbondale: Southern Illinois UP, 2008. Print.
Gutiérrez, Félix. "Spanish-Language Media in America: Background, Resources, History." *Journalism History* 4.2 (Summer 1977): 34-41, 65-67. Print.
Gutiérrez, Ramón A. "The UCLA Bibliographic Survey of Mexican American Literary Culture, 1821-1945: An Overview." *Recovering the U.S. Hispanic Literary Heritage*. Ed. Ramón Gutiérrez and Genaro Padilla. Houston: Arte Público, 1993. 309-14. Print.
"Heritage Foundation Slates Photo Exhibit Opening of 'Reading, 'Riting and Revolution—The Kindergarten Students of Leonor Villegas Magnon.'" *Laredo Morning Times* (1 March 1998): 6D. Print.
"Heritage Foundation Declares 'S.O.S.' (Save Our Story) Campaign." *Heritage Register* (Summer 2000): 8. Print.
Horner, Bruce, and John Trimbur. "English Only and College Composition." *CCC* 53.4 (2002): 594-630. Print.
Idar, Jovita. "The Mexican Children in Texas." Trans. Jessica Enoch, Lisa Lawson, and Raquel Moran Tellez. *La Crónica* 3.32 (10 Aug. 1911): 1. Print.
Jarratt, Susan. "Classics and Counterpublics in Nineteenth-Century Historically Black Colleges." *College English* 72.2 (2009): 134-59. Print.
"Jovita Idea [sic] (1885-1946)." *Laredo Morning Times* (6 Sept. 1992): 8D. Print.
Kates, Susan. *Activist Rhetorics and American Higher Education, 1885-1937*. Carbondale: Southern Illinois UP, 2001. Print.
Kirsch, Gesa, and Liz Rohan, eds. *Beyond the Archives: Research as a Lived Process*. Carbondale: Southern Illinois UP, 2008. Print.

Kirsch, Gesa, and Patricia Sullivan. "Introduction." *Methods and Methodology in Composition Research*. Ed. Gesa Kirsch and Patricia Sullivan. Carbondale: Southern Illinois UP, 1992. 1-11. Print.

Kirsch, Gesa. "Being on Location: Serendipity, Place, and Archival Research." *Beyond the Archives: Research as a Lived Process*. Ed. Gesa Kirsch and Liz Rohan. Carbondale: Southern Illinois UP, 2008. 20-27. Print.

Kitzhaber, Albert. *Rhetoric in the American Colleges, 1850-1900*. Dallas: Southern Methodist UP, 1990. Print.

L'Eplattenier, Barbara. "Opinion: Archival Research Methods." *College English* 72.1 (2009): 67-79. Print.

—. "Questioning our Methodological Metaphors." *Calling Cards: Theory and Practice in the Study of Race, Gender, and Culture*. Ed. Jacqueline Jones Royster and Ann Marie Simpkins. Albany: SUNY P, 2005. 133-146. Print.

"Leonor Villegas de Magnon, Hero of the Mexican Revolution." *Laredo Morning Times* (30 Aug. 1992): 5D. Print.

Limón, José. "El Primer Congreso Mexicanista de 1911: A Precursor to Contemporary Chicanismo." *Aztlán* 5:1-2 (1974): 85-117. Print.

Logan, Shirley Wilson. "Introduction: Mounting the Platform." *With Pen and Voice: A Critical Anthology of Nineteenth-Century African American Women*. Ed. Shirley Wilson Logan. Carbondale: Southern Illinois UP, 1995. Print.

—. *Liberating Language: Sites of Rhetorical Education in Nineteenth-Century Black America*. Carbondale: Southern Illinois UP, 2008. Print.

Matsuda, Paul. "The Myth of Linguistic Homogeneity in U.S. College Composition." *College English* 68.6 (2006): 637-51. Print.

Meyer, Doris. "Reading Early Neomexicano Newspapers: Yesterday and Today." *Recovering the U.S. Hispanic Literary Heritage*. Ed. Maria Herrera-Sobek and Virginia Sánchez-Korrol. Vol. 3. Houston: Arte Público, 2000. 402-11. Print.

Morris, Charles E. "The Archival Turn in Rhetorical Studies; Or, The Archive's Rhetorical (Re)turn." *Rhetoric and Public Affairs* 9.1 (2006): 113-52. Print.

Morris, Sammie, and Shirley Rose. "Invisible Hands: Recognizing Archivists' Work to Make Records Accessible." Ramsey et al. 51-78.

Murphy, James. "Prologue: The Politics of Historiography." *Rhetoric Review* 7.1 (1988): 5-6. Print.

Nunley, Vorris. "From the Hush Harbor to Da Academic Hood: Hush Harbors and an African American Rhetorical Tradition." *African American Rhetoric(s): Interdisciplinary Perspectives*. Ed. Elaine Richardson and Ronald Jackson II. Carbondale: Southern Illinois UP, 2004. 221-41. Print.

"Octalog: The Politics of Historiography." *Rhetoric Review* 6.2 (1988): 5-49. Print.

"Octalog II: The (Continuing) Politics of Historiography." *Rhetoric Review* 16.1 (1997): 22-44. Print.

Ramírez, Cristina D. "Forging a Mestiza Rhetoric: Mexican Women Journalists' Role in the Construction of a National Identity." *College English* 71.6 (2009): 606-29. Print.

Ramsey, Alexis, et al., eds. *Working in the Archives: Practical Research Methods for Rhetoric and Composition*. Carbondale: Southern Illinois UP, 2010. Print.

Ritter, Kelly. *Before Shaughnessy: Basic Writing at Yale and Harvard, 1920-1960*. Carbondale: Southern Illinois UP, 2009. Print.

Reynolds, Nedra. *Geographies of Writing: Inhabiting Places and Encountering Difference*. Carbondale: Southern Illinois UP, 2004. Print.

Rodriguez, América. *Making Latino News: Race, Language, Class*. London: Sage, 1999. Print.

Romano, Susan. "Tlaltelolco: The Grammatical-Rhetorical Indios of Colonial Mexico." *College English* 66.3 (2004): 257-77. Print.

Royster, Jacqueline Jones, and Jean C. Williams. "History and the Spaces Left: African American Presence and Narratives of Composition Studies." *CCC* 50.4 (1999): 563-84. Print.

Royster, Jacqueline Jones. *Traces of a Stream: Literacy and Social Change Among African American Women*. Pittsburgh: U of Pittsburgh P, 2000. Print.

San Miguel Jr., Guadalupe. *"Let Them All Take Heed": Mexican Americans and the Campaign for Educational Equality in Texas, 1910-1981*. Austin: U of Texas P, 1987. Print.

Schneider, Stephen. "Freedom Schooling: Stokely Carmichael and Critical Rhetorical Education." *CCC* 58.1 (2006): 46-69. Print.

Schultz, Lucille. *Young Composers: Composition's Beginnings in the Nineteenth Century*. Carbondale: Southern Illinois UP, 1999. Print.

Sharer, Wendy. "Disintegrating Bodies of Knowledge: Historical Material and Revisionary Histories of Rhetoric." *Rhetorical Bodies*. Ed. Jack Selzer and Sharon Crowley. Madison: U of Wisconsin P, 1999. 120-39. Print.

Steward, Doug. "The Foreign Language Requirement in English Doctoral Programs." *Profession* (2006): 203-18. Print.

Sutherland, Christine Mason. "Getting to Know Them: Concerning Research into Four Early Women Writers." Kirsch and Rohan 28-36.

Tirabassi, Katherine. "Journeying into the Archives: Exploring the Pragmatics of Archival Research." Ramsey et al. 169-180.

Vitanza, Victor, ed. *Writing Histories of Rhetoric*. Carbondale: Southern Illinois UP, 1994. Print.

Warnick, Chris. "Locating the Archives: Finding Aids and Archival Scholarship in Composition and Rhetoric." Ramsey et al. 91-101.

Weidner, Heidemarie Z. "A Chair 'Perpetually Filled by a Female Professor': Rhetoric and Composition Instruction at Nineteenth-Century Butler University." Donahue and Moon 58-76.
Zavella, Patricia. "Reflections on Diversity among Chicanas." *Frontiers* 12.2 (1999): 73-85.
Zenger, Amy. "Race, Composition, and 'Our English': Performing the Mother Tongue in a Daily Theme Assignment at Harvard." *Rhetoric Review* 23.4 (2004): 332-49. Print.

Appendix: Historiographic Locations

Bacon, Jacqueline, and Glen McClish. "Reinventing the Master's Tools: Nineteenth-Century African-American Literary Societies of Philadelphia and Rhetorical Education." *Rhetoric Society Quarterly* 30.4 (2000): 19-47. Print.
  *Philadelphia, PA 19104
Berlin, James. *Rhetoric and Reality: Writing Instruction in American Colleges, 1900-1985*. Carbondale: Southern Illinois UP, 1987. Print.
  *Harvard U: Cambridge, MA 02139
  *Columbia U: New York, NY 10019
  *U of Texas: Austin, TX 78701
  *U of Illinois: Urbana, IL 61801
  *U of Wisconsin: Madison, WI 53701
  *Yale U: New Haven, CT 06510
  *Princeton U: Princeton, NJ 08544
  *Williams College: Williamstown, MA 01267
  *U of Michigan: Ann Arbor, MI 48109
—. *Writing Instruction in Nineteenth-Century American Colleges*. Carbondale: Southern Illinois UP, 1984. Print.
  *Harvard U: Cambridge, MA 02139
  *Yale U: New Haven, CT 06510
  *Amherst College: Amherst, MA 01003
  * U of Michigan: Ann Arbor, MI 48109
Brereton, John, ed. *The Origins of Composition Studies in the American College, 1875-1925*. Pittsburgh: U of Pittsburgh P, 1995. Print.
  *Harvard U: Cambridge, MA 02139
  *Yale U: New Haven, CT 06510
  *Stanford U: Stanford, CA 94305
  *U of Iowa: Iowa City, IA 52242-7700
  *Indiana U: Bloomington, IN 47405-7000
  *Amherst College: Amherst, MA 01003
  *U of Michigan: Ann Arbor, MI 48109
  *U of Nebraska: Lincoln, NE 68588
  *U of Pennsylvania: Philadelphia, PA 19104
  *Wellesley College: Wellesley, MA 02481
  *U of Minnesota: Minneapolis, MN 55455
Campbell, JoAnn. "Controlling Voices: The Legacy of English A at Radcliffe College,

1883-1917." *CCC* 43.4 (1992): 472-85. Print.
   *Radcliffe College: Cambridge, MA 02139
—. "Freshman (*sic*) English: A Nineteenth-Century Wellesley 'Girl' Negotiates Authority." *Rhetoric Review* 15.1 (1996): 110-27. Print.
   * Wellesley College: Wellesley, MA 02481
—. "'A Real Vexation': Student Writing in Mount Holyoke's Culture of Service, 1837-1865." *College English* 59.7 (1997): 767-88. Print.
   *Mount Holyoke: South Hadley, MA 01075
—, ed. *Toward a Feminist Rhetoric: The Writing of Gertrude Buck*. Pittsburgh: U of Pittsburgh P, 1996. Print.
   *U of Michigan: Ann Arbor, MI 48109
Clark, Gregory. "The Oratorical Poetic of Timothy Dwight." *Oratorical Culture in Nineteenth-Century America: Transformations in the Theory and Practice of Rhetoric*. Carbondale: Southern Illinois UP, 1993. 57-77. Print.
   *Yale U: New Haven, CT 06510
Corbett, Edward P.J. "The Cornell School of Rhetoric." *Rhetoric Review* 4.1 (1985): 4-14. Print.
   *Cornell U: Ithaca, NY 14853
Crowley, Sharon. *Composition in the University: Historical and Polemical Essays*. Pittsburgh: U of Pittsburgh P, 1998. Print.
   *U of Iowa: Iowa City, IA 52242-7700
   *Harvard U: Cambridge, MA 02139
   *Yale U: New Haven, CT 06510
   *Princeton U: Princeton, NJ 08544
   *U of Michigan: Ann Arbor, MI 48109
—. "Invention in Nineteenth-Century Rhetoric." *CCC* 36.1 (1985): 51-60. Print.
   *Harvard U: Cambridge, MA 02139
   *Amherst College: Amherst, MA 01003
DeGenaro, William. "William Rainey Harper and the Ideology of Service at Junior Colleges." Donahue and Moon 181-198.
   *Joliet Junior College: Joliet, IL 60432
DePalma, Michael-John. "Austin Phelps and the Spirit (of) Composing: An Exploration of Nineteenth Century Sacred Rhetoric at Andover Theological Seminary." *Rhetoric Review* 27.4 (2008): 379-76. Print.
   *Andover Theological Seminary: Andover, MA 01810
Desser, Daphne. "Fraught Literacy: American Missionary Women in Nineteenth-Century Hawai'i." *College English* 69.5 (2007): 443-469. Print.
   *Captain Cook, HI 96704
Donahue, Patricia, and Bianca Falbo. "(The Teaching of) Reading and Writing at Lafayette College." Donahue and Moon 38-57.
   *Lafayette College: Easton, PA 18042
Douglas, Wallace. "Rhetoric for the Meritocracy: The Creation of Composition at Harvard." *English in America*. Ed. Richard Ohmann. Hanover: Wesleyan UP, 1976. 97-132. Print.
   *Harvard U: Cambridge, MA 02139
Enoch, Jessica. *Refiguring Rhetorical Education: Women Teaching African American, Native American, and Chicano/a Students*. Southern Illinois UP, 2008. Print.

*Carlisle, PA 17013
*Laredo, TX 78040

Fitzgerald, Kathryn. "The Platteville Papers Revisited: Gender and Genre in a Normal School Writing Assignment." Donahue and Moon 115-133.
*Platteville, WI 53818-3099

Garbus, Julie. "Vida Scudder in the Classroom and in the Archives." Donahue and Moon 77-93.
*Wellesley College: Wellesley, MA 02481

Gleason, Barbara. "Remediation Phase-Out at CUNY: The 'Equity versus Excellence' Controversy." *CCC* 51.3 (2000): 488-452. Print.
*City U of New York: New York, NY 10019

Gold, David. *Rhetoric at the Margins: Revising the History of Writing Instruction in American Colleges, 1873-1947*. Carbondale: Southern Illinois UP, 2008. Print.
*Texas Woman's U: Denton, TX 76204
*Wiley College: Marshall, TX 75670
*East Texas Normal College: Commerce, TX 75428

Gray, Patrice. "Life in the Margins: Student Writing and Curricular Change at Fitchburg Normal, 1895-1910." Donahue and Moon 159-180.
*Fitchburg Normal College: Fitchburg, MA 01420

Greer, Jane. "'No Smiling Madonna': Marion Wharton and the Struggle to Construct a Critical Pedagogy for the Working Class, 1914-1917." *CCC* 51.2 (1999): 248-71. Print.
*People's College: Fort Scott, KS 66701

Harmon, Sandra D. "'The Voice, Pen and Influence of Our Women Are Abroad in the Land': Women and the Illinois State Normal University." *Nineteenth-Century Women Learn to Write*. Ed. Catherine Hobbs. Charlottesville: U of Virginia P, 1995. 84-102. Print.
*Illinois State Normal U: Normal, IL 61790

Hirst, Russell. "The Sermon as Public Discourse: Austin Phelps and the Conservative Homiletic Tradition in Nineteenth-Century America." *Oratorical Culture in Nineteenth-Century America: Transformations in the Theory and Practice of Rhetoric*. Carbondale: Southern Illinois UP, 1993. 78-109. Print.
*Andover Theological Seminary: Andover, MA 01810

Hollis, Karyn L. *Liberating Voices: Writing at the Bryn Mawr Summer School for Women Workers*. Carbondale: Southern Illinois UP, 2004. Print.
* Bryn Mawr College: Bryn Mawr, PA 19010

Hoogeveen, Jeffrey L. "The Progressive Faculty/Student Discourse of 1969-1970 and the Emergence of Lincoln University's Writing Program." Donahue and Moon 199-219.
* Lincoln U: Lincoln, PA 19352

Jarratt, Susan. "Classics and Counterpublics in Nineteenth-Century Historically Black Colleges." *College English* 72.2 (2009): 134-59. Print.
*Fisk U: Nashville, TN 37208
*Atlanta U: Atlanta, GA 30301
*Howard U: Washington DC 20059

Johnson, Nan. "Rhetoric and Belles Lettres in the Canadian Academy: An Historical Analysis." *College English* 50.8 (1988): 861-73. Print.

*U of Toronto: Toronto, ON, Canada M4B 1B3
   *Dalhousie U: Halifax, NS, Canada B3H 4R2
   *McGill U: Montreal, QC, Canada H3A 2T5
Jolliffe, David A. "The Moral Subject in College Composition: A Conceptual Framework and the Case of Harvard, 1865-1900." *College English* 51.2 (1989): 163-73. Print.
   *Harvard U: Cambridge, MA 02139
Kates, Susan. *Activist Rhetorics and American Higher Education, 1885-1937*. Carbondale: Southern Illinois UP, 2001. Print.
   *Smith College: Northampton, MA 01060
   *Wilberforce College: Wilberforce, OH 45384-1001
   *Brookwood Labor College: Katonah, NY 10536
—. "Literacy, Voting Rights, and the Citizenship Schools in the South, 1957-1970." *CCC* 57.3 (2006): 479-502. Print.
   *Monteagle, TN 37356
Kitzhaber, Albert. *Rhetoric in American Colleges, 1850-1900*. Dallas: Southern Methodist UP, 1990. Print.
   *Harvard U: Cambridge, MA 02139
   *Yale U: New Haven, CT 06510
   *U of Michigan: Ann Arbor, MI 48109
   *Amherst College: Amherst, MA 01003
Larsen, Elizabeth. "The Progress of Literacy: Edward Tyrrel Channing and the Separation of the Student Writer from the World." *Rhetoric Review* 11.1 (1992): 159-71. Print.
   *Harvard U: Cambridge, MA 02139
Lerner, Neal. "Rejecting the Remedial Brand: The Rise and Fall of the Dartmouth Writing Clinic." *CCC* 59.1 (2007): 13-35. Print.
   *Dartmouth U: Hanover, NH 03755
Lindblom, Kenneth, William Banks, and Risë Quay. "Mid-Nineteenth Century Writing Instruction at Illinois State University." Donahue and Moon 94-114.
   * Illinois State U: Normal, IL 61790
Lindbloom, Kenneth, and Patricia A. Dunn. "Cooperative Writing 'Program' Administration at Illinois State University: The Committee on English of 1904-05 and the Influence of Professor J. Rose Colby." *Historical Studies of Writing Program Administration: Individuals, Communities, and the Formation of a Discipline*. Ed. Barbara L'Eplattenier and Lisa Mastrangelo. West Lafayette: Parlor, 2004. 37-70. Print.
   *Illinois State U: Normal, IL 61790
Martin, Harold. "Freshman Composition: Harvard Beginnings." *CCC* 13.3 (1962): 35-36. Print.
   *Harvard U: Cambridge, MA 02139
Mastrangelo, Lisa S. "The Grand Narrative of Fred Newton Scott." *College English* 72.3 (2010): 248-68. Print.
   *U of Michigan: Ann Arbor, MI 48109
—. "Learning From the Past: Rhetoric, Composition, and Debate at Mount Holyoke College." *Rhetoric Review* 18.1 (1999): 46-64. Print.
   *Mount Holyoke College: South Hadley, MA 01075

Mihesuah, Devon A. "'Let Us Strive Earnestly to Value Education Aright': Cherokee Female Seminarians as Leaders of a Changing Culture." *Nineteenth-Century Women Learn to Write*. Ed. Catherine Hobbs. Charlottesville: U of Virginia P, 1995. 103-119. Print.
    *Tahlequah, OK 74464
Newkirk, Thomas. "The Politics of Intimacy: The Defeat of Barrett Wendell at Harvard." *Taking Stock: The Writing Process Movement in the '90s*. Portsmouth: Boynton/Cook, 1994. 115-32. Print.
    *Harvard U: Cambridge, MA 02139
Paine, Charles. *The Resistant Writer: Rhetoric as Immunity, 1850 to the Present*. Albany: SUNY P, 1999. Print.
    *Harvard U: Cambridge, MA 02139 (Channing)
    *Harvard U: Cambridge, MA 02139 (Hill)
Reid, Ronald F. "Edward Everett and Neoclassical Oratory in Genteel America." *Oratorical Culture in Nineteenth-Century America: Transformations in the Theory and Practice of Rhetoric*. Carbondale: Southern Illinois UP, 1993. 29-56. Print.
    *Harvard U: Cambridge, MA 02139
Ricks, Vickie. "'In an Atmosphere of Peril': College Women and Their Writing." *Nineteenth-Century Women Learn to Write*. Ed. Catherine Hobbs. Charlottesville: U of Virginia P, 1995. 59-83. Print.
    *Vassar College: Poughkeepsie, NY 12604
Ritter, Kelly. "Before Mina Shaughnessy: Basic Writing at Yale, 1920-1960." *CCC* 60.1 (2008): 12-45. Print.
    *Yale U: New Haven, CT 06510
Romano, Susan. "Tlaltelolco: The Grammatical-Rhetorical *Indios* of Colonial Mexico." *College English* 66.3 (2004): 257-77. Print.
    *Tlaltelolco, México, D.F. 06995
Rothermel, Beth Ann. "'Our Life's Work': Rhetorical Preparation and Teacher Training at a Massachusetts State Normal School, 1839-1929." Donahue and Moon 134-158.
    *Westfield State Normal School: Westfield, MA 01086-1630
Russell, David. *Writing in the Academic Disciplines, 1870-1990: A Curricular History*. Carbondale: Southern Illinois UP, 1991. Print.
    *Colgate U: Hamilton, NY 13346
    *U of California at Berkeley: Berkeley, CA 94720
    *Iowa State U: Ames, IA 50011
    *Harvard U: Cambridge, MA 02139
    *Columbia U: New York, NY 10019
    *U of Chicago: Chicago, IL 60637
    *U of Kansas: Lawrence, KS 66045
    *U of Missouri: Columbia, MO 65211
    *U of Michigan: Ann Arbor, MI 48109
    *U of Minnesota: Minneapolis, MN 55455
    *Ohio State U: Columbus, OH 43210
    *MIT: Cambridge, MA 02139
    *Central College: Pella, IA 50219
    *Radcliffe College: Cambridge, MA 02139

Simmons, Sue Carter. "Constructing Writers: Barrett Wendell's Pedagogy at Harvard." *CCC* 46.3 (1995): 327-352. Print.
  *Harvard U: Cambridge, MA 02139
—. "Radcliffe Responds to Harvard Rhetoric: 'An Absurdly Stiff Way of Thinking'." *Nineteenth-Century Women Learn to Write*. Ed. Catherine Hobbs. Charlottesville: U of Virginia P, 1995. 264-292. Print.
  *Radcliffe College: Cambridge, MA 02139
Schneider, Stephen. "Freedom Schooling: Stokely Carmichael and Critical Rhetorical Education." *CCC* 58.1 (2006): 46-69. Print.
  *Waveland, MS 39576
Scott, Blake. "John Witherspoon's Normalizing Pedagogy of Ethos." *Rhetoric Review* 16.1 (1997): 58-75. Print.
  *Princeton U: Princeton, NJ 08544
Scott, Patrick. "Jonathan Maxcy and the Aims of Early Nineteenth-Century Rhetorical Teaching." *College English* 45.1 (1983): 21-30. Print.
  *U of South Carolina: Columbia, SC 29208
Soliday, Mary. *The Politics of Remediation: Institutional and Student Needs in Higher Education*. Pittsburgh: U of Pittsburgh P, 2002. Print.
  *City U of New York: New York, NY 10019
Spring, Suzanne B. "'Seemingly Uncouth Forms': Letters at Mount Holyoke Female Seminary." *CCC* 59.4 (2008): 633-75. Print.
  *Mount Holyoke U: South Hadley, MA 01075
Stewart, Donald. "Harvard's Influence on English Studies: Perceptions from Three Universities in the Early Twentieth Century." *CCC* 43 (1992): 455-71. Print.
  *Harvard U: Cambridge, MA 02139
  *Michigan U: Ann Arbor, MI 48109
  *Cornell U: Ithaca, NY 14853
  *Columbia U: New York, NY 10019
———. "Two Model Teachers and the Harvardization of English Departments." *The Rhetorical Tradition and Modern Writing*. Ed. James Murphy. New York: MLA, 1982. Print.
  *Harvard U: Cambridge, MA 02139 (Child)
  *U of Michigan: Ann Arbor, MI 48109
Stewart, Donald C., and Patricia L. Stewart. *The Life and Legacy of Fred Newton Scott*. Pittsburgh: U of Pittsburgh P, 1997. Print.
  *U of Michigan: Ann Arbor, MI 48109
Varnum, Robin. *Fencing with Words: A History of Writing Instruction at Amherst College During the Era of Theodore Baird, 1938-1966*. Urbana: NCTE, 1996. Print.
  *Amherst College: Amherst, MA 01003
Weidner, Heidemarie Z. "A Chair 'Perpetually Filled by a Female Professor': Rhetoric and Composition Instruction at Nineteenth-Century Butler University." Donahue and Moon 58-76.
  *Butler U: Indianapolis, IN 46208
Welch, Kathleen. "Thinking Like *That*: The Ideal Nineteenth-Century Student Writer." Donahue and Moon 14-37.
  *Oberlin College: Oberlin, OH 44074
Wells, Susan. *Out of the Dead House: Nineteenth-Century Women Physicians and the*

Writing of Medicine. Madison: U of Wisconsin, 2001. Print.
  *Philadelphia, PA 19104
Wible, Scott. "Pedagogies of the 'Students' Right' Era: The Language Curriculum Research Group's Project for Linguistic Diversity." *CCC* 57.3 (February 2006): 442-78. Print.
  *Brooklyn College: New York, NY 10019
—. "Professor Burke's Bennington Project." *Rhetoric Society Quarterly* 38.3 (2008): 259-82. Print.
  *Bennington College: Bennington, VT 05201
Westbrook, B. Evelyn. "Debating Both Sides: What Nineteenth-Century College Debating Societies Can Teach Us about Critical Pedagogy." *Rhetoric Review* 21.4 (2002): 339-56. Print.
  *U of South Carolina: Columbia, SC 29208
Whitburn, Merrill D. "Rhetorical Theory in Yale's Graduate School in the Late Nineteenth Century: The Example of William C. Robinson's Forensic Oratory." *Rhetoric Society Quarterly* 34.4 (2004): 55-70. Print.
  *Yale U: New Haven, CT 06510
Zaluda, Scott. "Lost Voices of the Harlem Renaissance: Writing Assigned at Howard University, 1919-31." *CCC* 50.2 (1998): 232-48. Print.
  *Howard U: Washington, DC 20059
Zenger, Amy. "Race, Composition, and 'Our English': Performing the Mother Tongue in a Daily Theme Assignment at Harvard." *Rhetoric Review* 23.4 (2004): 332-49. Print.
  *Harvard U: Cambridge, MA 02139

ENCULTURATION

> *Enculturation* is on the Web at http://enculturation.gmu.edu/

Enculturation started in 1996 by two graduate students. In its fifteen years it has never had institutional support beyond web space provided by a university and has never been affiliated with a press or organization. Currently it is hosted on an individual's server and supported with one RA through the University of South Carolina. All of the managerial, editorial, and production work has been done by young faculty and graduate students in the field of rhetoric and composition. The mission of the journal has generally been to publish broader ranging interdisciplinary work related to rhetoric and composition that is more theoretical or media-oriented.

"Exposing Assemblages," by Alex Reid (*Enculturation* 8, 2010: http://www.enculturation.net/exposing-assemblages)

We've selected "Exposing Assemblages," by Alex Reid. Reid's piece was a part of our special issue on YouTube and Participatory Culture. Guest editor Sarah Arroyo calls this piece stellar and notes that many of her graduate students have gravitated to it this past year and really seem to "get it" in a way that allows them to be productive. Her conclusion is that in the long run it will get a number of citations. Another editorial board member spoke up for Reid's piece because it explores and questions the very conditions for (and the importance of) independent presses and resonates with the spirit of an independent collection. Both pieces also represent the kind of work that *Enculturation* has been publishing since the mid-late 1990s.

5 Exposing Assemblages: Unlikely Communities of Digital Scholarship, Video, and Social Networks

Alex Reid

Over the last decade the crisis in scholarly publication has become as familiar a topic in English Studies as the national decline in undergraduate majors and the disappearance of tenure-track positions. Increasing demands for publication for tenure and promotion have combined with shrinking markets, particularly for monographs. The emergence of online journals has relieved some of those pressures, even though the scholarly reputation of those journals has been slow to improve. More recently, university presses have begun to move to electronic publishing. In March 2009, the University of Michigan Press announced it would adopt digital publication. In an open letter, the Press' Director, Philip Pachoda, writes that "we will publish all new academic monographs primarily in a range of digital formats, while also making high quality print versions available on request for bookstores, institutions, individuals and authors" (Pachoda). Pachoda explains, "Digitized books will be candidates for a wide range of audio and visual digital enhancements--including options like hot links, graphics, interactive tables, sound files, 3D animation and video--allowing authors to better communicate the subtleties of their work." A similar move has occurred at Utah State University Press, where there was a clear acknowledgement of the combination of economic pressures and the recognition of some imperative or at least opportunity to grow in the area of open access, digital publication. Within rhetoric and composition, the Computers and Composition Digital Press (CCDP), which is an imprint of Utah State University Press, was formed in 2007. The CCDP website states that the press "is committed to publishing innovative, multimodal digital projects. The Press will also publish ebooks (print texts in electronic form available for reading online or for downloading); however, we are particularly interested in digital projects that cannot be printed on paper, but that have the same intellectual heft as a book" ("Missions and Goals"). From these initial, but significant, moves from university presses to broader technological shifts, including the growing popularity of e-book readers, it would seem clear that this new decade will mark a decided shift away from the print publication of scholarship.

That said, aside from unique imprints like CCDP and a few journals, like *Kairos*, which have a tradition of encouraging scholars to produce scholarship in a variety of media, the majority of digitally published humanities scholarship continues to replicate nearly all of the features of the print journal article (aside from actually being printed on paper). Pachoda notes Michigan's intention to continue to make publications available in print upon request. This would seem to echo the practice of making PDFs of print articles available through subscription databases, which would be, by far, the most common form of digital scholarship (if one were inclined to count it as such). Beyond digitized copies of print articles, most online articles are as linear and text-based as their print brethren. There are advantages to access and searchability inherent to digital media, and such articles can include active links to online references, but, for the most part, particularly in terms of the composition of such digital scholarship, there is little difference between these digital articles and print ones. That is, as a scholar, one is likely to compose an article for an online journal in the same way as one would compose a print journal article; the reviewing and editing procedures are also fundamentally the same in online and print venues. In fact, this similitude is a compelling argument for valuing online journals as equivalent to print ones. That said, in the last five years, a range of technological innovations have made the basic production and dissemination of video accessible to all scholars (and millions of other Internet users). *YouTube* is evidence of this. While video content may be slowly making its way to scholarly journals, videos of scholars giving course lectures or presentations are now easy to find online. One can also find a growing number of born-digital projects: instructional screencasts, slidecasts of conference papers, video blogs, and so on. In short, video scholarship already exists in a variety of forms, but the relation of these videos to more conventional scholarship, as well as to the rest of the academic community, is uncertain.

This essay neither purports to offer a solution to this situation nor imagines some idealized video scholarship community. To the contrary, as I explore, this confluence of the marketplace woes for academic publishing, the general exhaustion of humanities scholarship, and the emergence of digital media networks creates an opportunity for engaging more fundamentally with the scholarly projects of humanism. That is, digital video scholarship is not a palliative that will allow humanist scholarship to continue trundling along for another decade (or until some other technology replaces it). Instead, as I will explore, the current situation offers scholars the opportunity to investigate the material and social assemblages that have coded and territorialized the humanities over the last century. As I will discuss here through the work of Jean-Luc Nancy, Giorgio Agamben, Manuel DeLanda and others, the investigation of these assemblages can productively operate through an understanding of exposure. Specifically, by understanding how scholarly practices, identities, and communities emerge through exposure to shifting material, technological, and social assemblages, new potentials for humanism might emerge.

Typically, these challenges are framed in technical, rhetorical, and disciplinary terms. Even though the production of digital media, video in particular, has become cheaper and easier, technical hurdles still remain. There is clearly a significant gap between having the basic technical skill and equipment to make a video and having the skill and equipment to make a *professional* video. The issue of technical production standards becomes a rhetorical concern, an issue of authority, but that is not the only rhetorical concern, as video scholars must decide what existing filmic techniques are appropriate for scholarship. Since it would be impractical to imagine digital scholarship as simply replacing print scholarship (i.e. to imagine video as accomplishing the same rhetorical tasks in the same way as print), these concerns are not only rhetorical but also disciplinary. That is, the movement to video cannot be viewed as a means to continue disciplinary work in a new medium. Instead, the move toward digital scholarship (and pedagogy) begins with recognizing that existing disciplinary practices have emerged from exposure to particular historical assemblages of material, technological, and social objects. In other words, though there is no intrinsic relationship between the humanities and the monograph or the journal article, the humanities' exposure to the assemblages of digital media networks will mean a shift in disciplinary practices and identities. The humanities might continue without print scholarship, but it will unavoidably be a different humanities, just at the humanities of the twentieth century differed from that of the nineteenth century. So while the technical, rhetorical, and disciplinary concerns remain salient, they must be understood within the broader context of the assemblages to which the humanities are exposed.

As this essay explores, the conditions of exposure occur in all communities, including traditional, print-mediated scholarly communities, though disciplines have created many mechanisms to close off the possibilities of exposure. Similarly, as the video below investigates, both mainstream and academic discourses have argued for the development of a critical, digital literacy to protect against exposure by and to social, digital media networks. In both cases, digital media are viewed as external forces threatening an existing internal identity rather than as part of a new assemblage through which contemporary identities will be produced. As Agamben notes of such critical gestures, this is "the vanity of the well-meaning discourse on technology, which asserts that the problem with apparatuses can be reduced to the question of correct use. Those who make such claims seem to ignore a simple fact: If a certain process of subjectification (or, in this case, desubjectification) corresponds to every apparatus, then it is impossible for the subject of an apparatus to use it 'in the right way'" (*What is an Apparatus?* 21). That is, it is only through exposure to apparatuses that subjectivities and communities emerge: the question of ethics can only be understood *through* an exposure to these apparatuses not as a shield against such exposures. This observation applies equally to both traditional academic scholarship and social, digital media networks. Both would be apparatuses in Agamben's sense of the term as "literally anything that has in some way the capacity to capture, orient, determine, intercept, model, control, or secure the gestures, behaviors, opinions, or discourses of living beings" (14). That is, for Agamben, the apparatuses of academic scholarship would produce academic subjects (i.e. scholars) and secure their use of the apparatuses (i.e. their production of scholarship) just as thoroughly as social, digital media networks produce user-subjects and manage their use of networks. However, as I will argue it, it would be an error to imagine these as apparatuses as totalizing in their power or as neutral translators of some abstract ideological power. As such, it may be useful to move into a broader conception of assemblage in order to explore these possibilities for emergence through what Manuel DeLanda terms "a realist approach to social ontology" (1). Indeed assemblage theory might allow for moving beyond "living beings" and "social ontology" into a more general mapping of object relations, though the focus here on video and scholarship certainly includes both living beings and social ontologies.

Though I am linking together Agamben's apparatus and DeLanda's assemblage, I do not intend to suggest they are fully equivalent or interchangeable. Agamben clearly differentiates between living beings and apparatuses; assemblages include both. That said, the apparatus cannot simply be subsumed within the assemblage. As Agamben deploys the term, "The anthropological machine of humanism is an ironic apparatus that verifies the absence of a nature proper to Homo, holding him suspended between a celestial and a terrestrial nature, between animal and human—and, thus, his being always less and more than himself" (*The Open: Man and Animal* 29). As he continues elsewhere, "through these apparatuses man attempts to nullify the animalistic behaviors that are now separated from him and to enjoy the Open as such, to enjoy being insofar as it is being" (*What is an Apparatus?* 17). In short, our connection to apparatuses is an integral part of our humanity while also serving as the primary mechanism of an increasingly expansive disciplinary society. For Agamben, this situation calls for "the profanation of apparatuses--that is to say, the restitution to common use of what has been captured and separated in them" (24). This profanation is, at least in part, a process of exposure. As I will discuss, where objects are made sacred by removing them from common use, they are conversely made profane by their exposure to non-sacred spaces. In this context, assemblage theory offers a means to map material, technological, and other social forces and uncover points of exposure and profanation. Here I also turn to Nancy to consider these issues in terms of the interruption of the myth of the writer/author as an immanent force. This interruption, initiated by the experience of exposure, returns the composing from an internal space to external relations. This "being-with," as Nancy terms it, offers a different way of understanding the composing communities of scholarship that might be opened by the experience of exposure presented to us by video and other digital media. Though there are certainly points of difference among these theories, my interest here in is linking them (rather than resolving or adjudicating their differences) to see where they might go. What Gregory Ulmer notes about electracy applies equally well here: "I assume that the ethical dilemma of self/other will not be solved in an electronic apparatus, but simply that it will become irrelevant, just as 'appeasing' the gods, which was the problem addressed by ritual, becomes irrelevant in literacy" (114). Put differently in the terms that will emerge in this essay, the exposure of scholarly practices to new assemblages, including digital media technologies and networks, profanes "sacred" (despite being secular) humanistic practices. Indeed it is particularly the radical redefinition of self/other in the relations of exteriority that characterize assemblage theory that might offer, not a solution, but something other to do.

FROM THE JOURNAL ARTICLE TO THE JOURNAL VIDEO?

In considering what new scholarly practices might emerge, it is useful to give some consideration to the processes that resulted in the development of existing scholarship. Though the first academic journals began with scientific societies in the mid-seventeenth century, the oldest journals in English Studies (e.g. *PMLA*) date to the 1880s. While certainly there are rhetorical and methodological differences between the scholarly discourses of then and now, the deployment of the technological affordances and general purposes of the print journal are largely the same. The creation of *PMLA* was a central topic of the 1884 MLA Convention in New York, where it was agreed that: "Whatever should be done to bring us nearer together and give us a sense of centralized power, this Journal idea was thought to be of the greatest importance, as through it every man could have a chance to make his views known, and to have them criticized by the body at large" ("The Modern Language Association of America" v). As this passage suggests, faculty in English Studies have historically worked independently. In part this might reflect disciplinary-ideological commitments to certain views on the relationship between writers, texts, and readers. It also reflects the material nature of our work. That is, while a scientific laboratory may require several people to operate, a book only needs a single reader, and an essay only requires a single author. The solitary nature of English scholarship has also reflected our increasing specialization. As much as one might happily share research with departmental colleagues, how many would really count as part of the disciplinary audience toward which one's research is directed? (Or more poignantly put, how many of one's colleagues could possibly be included on a list of reviewers for any journal in which one would seek publication?) As the participants of the 1884 MLA convention realized, at the end of the nineteenth century, the print article was the most effective means for speaking with one's colleagues (and potentially with a larger academic or public audience).

Much follows upon the distribution of scholarship in the form of journal articles. Why, for example, are scholarly articles 5-7,000 words in length? Why not 10,000 or 3,000? There is a calculation here that begins implicitly with the managerial and material costs in reviewing and editing submissions and printing and distributing journal issues. Pre-publication review is necessary because of the cost limitations of printing and the pressures of the marketplace. Only so many pages can be printed for a journal, and those pages need to have quality material if the journal is to maintain reputation (and subscriptions). To a large extent, our legacy scholarly practices from monograph publication down to our daily work in our offices have been founded on the principles that communicating with colleagues in our field is difficult, that access to scholarly information is scarce, and that publication is expensive. Very little about our disciplinary practices makes sense in the context of networked media, and the only explanation for our continuing to maintain the shape and practices of our academic community is that disciplinary inertia has not yet been overcome by external exigencies. For 125 years, English scholars have been publishing print articles in *PMLA*. As long as that may seem, it also reflects a distinct historical moment, beginning with the second American Industrial Revolution and reaching to the clearly post-industrial present. It is not difficult to situate the crises of scholarly publication, the job market, and declining majors as symptoms of this larger technocultural shift. Just as the modern profession of English studies took shape through the MLA in the wake of America's electrification, the current crises in our profession mirrors the rise of a new network. While I do not mean to suggest a simple causal or deterministic relationship between these events, I would not be the first to suggest that the emergence of a new technoculture means new opportunities for scholarly community and the chance to build a critical and productive relationship with the emerging post-industrial economy and culture, just as the second industrial revolution offered similar opportunities to English professors in the late nineteenth century. All this provides a backdrop for the particular concern of the role digital video might play in the evolution of scholarship in our field. No longer can we say, as our nineteenth-century colleagues did, that the journal article represents the most cost effective or efficient means for us to communicate and collaborate with other scholars in our field.

Video scholarship arrives amidst this context. The current state of digital video scholarship in the humanities largely takes the form of talking heads. These can be seen on university channels on *iTunesU*, on *YouTube* (or any number of sites similar to *YouTube*, such as *Blip.tv*, *Ustream*, or *Vimeo*) and on more specialized sites like *TED.com*, *BigThink* or *Fora.tv*. In some cases, these videos are little more than home-movie-production-quality documentation of a classroom, conference presentation, or public lecture. Others might have better production quality but are still recordings of events that are given first and foremost for the audience in the room. Less common are talking head presentations that are born-digital in the sense that they were produced for a networked audience. Scholarly videos that go beyond the talking head model to engage with video in different ways remain the rarest variety of digital scholarship. The most well-known example of this genre is Michael Wesch's "The Machine is Us/ing Us," with now over 10 million views on *YouTube*. Wesch's video shows at once the creative power and the limitations for how we have imagined video scholarship. His video is engaging and thought-provoking. It has been the subject of discussions among scholars and often referred to in scholarship on the digital humanities. Certainly, the video skyrocketed Wesch personally to become a new media academic star. But is the video itself "scholarly"? It is only four and half minutes in length. Certainly no one would want to watch a 20-minute video that adopted the rhetorical-compositional strategies of Wesch's video, but a short video cannot hope to develop the kinds of scholarly arguments and analyses we expect of the journal article. One might view Wesch's video as scholarly while simultaneously recognizing that the humanities could not carry forward its research using such videos alone. And this is the primary recognition that ought to arise from an examination of any of these sites or videos: the videos do not "stand alone." Instead they are part of a media network linking the videos to other videos, as well as to text-based discussions. One can see this on *YouTube* where users can post "video responses" and "text comments" or watch "related videos."

Shifting from a focus on the individual video to its networked context reveals a more fundamental, unnecessary assumption at work here. The single-author journal article begins with the assumption that the author is practically separated from her colleagues. Any investigation into the possibilities of digital scholarship must begin with recognizing that our relations with the scholarly community have been altered. Online, every day, one might interact with, potentially, the largest academic conference ever convened. More practically, digital networks offer us the ability to develop and share disciplinary knowledge with a smaller, more manageable group of colleagues in real time. For example, today is November 6th, 2009. I am working on a networked laptop, typing this sentence. Assuming the best outcome, this article will not be published for another six months. Once it is published, it will be static. Alternatively, right now, I could be sharing this document in a variety of networked spaces (Google Docs, for instance) with six, ten, or one hundred colleagues. It wouldn't be "my" document. Instead, we would be working together on the issue of digital scholarship. We wouldn't necessarily be trying to compose a single, 7,000-word essay. How might we understand how that could work? One possible approach requires understanding digital scholarship as part of a social assemblage.

Social Assemblage Theory

Underlying social assemblage theory is a shift from mapping relations between *interiorized* organic totalities to mapping *exteriorized* parts characterized by both properties and capacities. Within the conception of relations of interiority one distinguishes between relations that define identity or totality and those that are extraneous to that definition. As such, for example, being part of a crowd at a stadium would be an extraneous relation that did not impinge on the organic totality of an individual within the crowd. Of course, such relations could shift and alter the individual, as in the case of "crowd mentality," but even give this, the individual would still be an interiorized totality, separable from the crowd. As such, in this model, exposure to the outside always represents a potential threat to the interiorized totality of the organic whole. Conversely, when taking up relations of exteriority, "the properties of the component parts can never explain the relations which constitute a whole" (DeLanda 11). Instead, the properties of the whole "are the result not of an aggregation of the components' own properties but of the actual exercise of their capacities. These capacities do depend on a component's properties but cannot be reduced to them since they involve reference to the properties of other interacting entities" (11). In this model, an individual cannot simply be defined by the properties of the parts that define him or her, as parts also are characterized by capacities that exist in a potential or virtual state and only arise through relations of exteriority. Individuals as subjects are not produced through the interiorized relations of the properties of the subject's component parts; instead the subject only emerges through the exteriorized relations (or assemblages) between parts that actualize particular capacities. In other words, rather than being threatened by exposure, subjectivity can only arise through exposure to the capacities actualized through relations of exteriority.

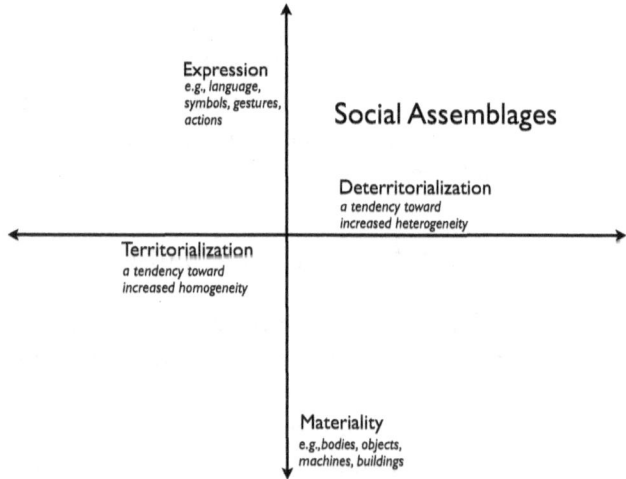

Figure 1: DeLanda's map of exteriorized relations

Taking up the work of Deleuze and Guattari, DeLanda maps the exteriorized relations of social assemblages along two axes (see fig. 1). The first axes travels from materiality to expression; the second axes shifts from territorialization to deterritorialization. Many assemblage components have material roles in a social assemblage, including "a set of human bodies properly oriented (physically or psychologically) towards each other" (DeLanda 12). In addition to bodies, one would also include any objects that are part of a material location: for example, food, furniture, various tools, etc. Those components, along with others, also exercise their capacities for expression. The obvious examples are verbal expressions, but one might include bodily expressions or gestures or the expressive characteristics of objects (e.g., the taste of the food, the comfort of the furniture). Along the other axes, territorialization is the tendency of a space toward organization and increasing homogeneity: for example, a meeting room that is part of a department's offices on a university campus. Deterritorialization then is a tendency to disrupt spatial boundaries or increase heterogeneity. DeLanda notes, "a good example is communication technology, ranging from writing and a reliable postal service, to telegraphs, telephones and computers, all of which blur the spatial boundaries of social entities" (13). As such the homogeneity of the department meeting room might be deterritorialized by video conferencing or even a memo from an external agency. Of course, these examples can only go so far. Certainly, one can see within disciplinary assemblages that the potential deterritorializing effects of scholarly communication are recaptured by the territorializing tendencies of the various spaces through which those messages pass.

In addition to these two axes, Deleuze and Guattari identify two thresholds where expression shifts in function: the emergence of genetic and linguistic codes respectively. It is the second, linguistic threshold that is particularly relevant here.

The temporal linearity of language expression relates not only to a succession but to a formal synthesis of succession in which time constitutes a process of linear overcoding and engenders a phenomenon unknown on the other strata: *translation*... The scientific world {*Welt*, as opposed to the *Umwelt* of the animal) is the translation of all of the flows, particles, codes, and territorialities of the other strata into a sufficiently deterritorialized system of signs, in other words, into an overcoding specific to language. This property of *overcoding* or *superlinearity* explains why, in language, not only is expression independent of content, but form of expression is independent of substance. (62)

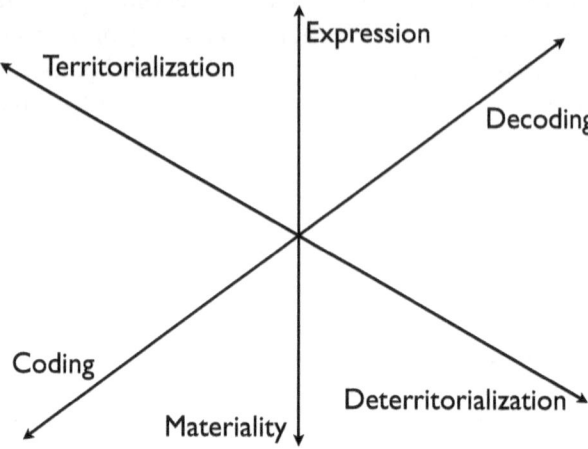

Figure 2: DeLanda's third axis

DeLanda modifies Deleuze and Guattari's approach somewhat to conceive of these processes as a third axis of the assemblage, "in which specialized expressive media intervene, processes which consolidate and rigidify the identity of the assemblage, or, on the contrary, allow the assemblage a certain latitude for more flexible operation" (see fig. 2) (19). The addition of the third axis allows for the investigation of linguistic expressions as secondary processes of territorialization, as *codings*, or alternatively as *decodings* intensifying deterritorialization. This axis is of particular interest for the concerns of this essay, as through it DeLanda provides a means for investigating how media destabilize assemblages.

Taking up DeLanda's examples, one might hypothesize that social assemblages whose materiality and expression are largely mediated by communication networks might have a greater tendency toward deterritorialization and heterogeneity than those where such technologies do not play as integral a role. This is certainly clear in the contemporary classroom, where the students' access to mobile networks deterritorializes the traditional academic territory. In scholarly terms, the traditional location of research (i.e. somewhere in the bowels of an academic library) increased the homogeneity of those with access. Even subscription-based, full-text databases serve this function, though certainly some increase in heterogeneity is visible there. As one moves along the continuum of media networks from open access journals and blogs to videos uploaded to *YouTube*, the deterritorializing effects become more visible. This effect is, in part, the operation of communication networks as destabilizing traditional territorial boundaries but is also the result of potential decoding within the particular media communicated along the media. That said, one should not mistake this observation for a statement about increased political freedom or agency, let alone some inherently liberatory quality of the technology. It is certainly possible, in the future, that academic disciplines might capture media networks as territorializing forces and produce media messages that serve to overcode those territories. That is certainly what has transpired with the print networks and journal media of traditional scholarship. Indeed there is already a fair amount of homogeneity in video scholarship inasmuch as that scholarship is constituted by video recordings of heavily territorialized spaces (e.g. the lecture hall or conference presentation). That said, the scholarly video invested in media networks connects with deterritorializing relations of exteriority, where the coded expressions of scholarly discourse take up new relations and new capacities, and the human bodies, who were once comfortably coded and territorialized as authors and scholarly readers, find themselves exposed to new relations and becomings.

EXPOSURE AND THE MYTH OF IMMANENCE

Unfortunately, this conception of exposure to the exteriority of relations is largely absent from both mainstream and academic conversations regarding social media, and it certainly does not appear to play a role in our discussions of digital scholarship. Despite the discipline's fluency with various theoretical critiques of authorship, as scholarly authors we continue to view our own writerly identities in very traditional ways. Student writers are seen in the same terms. As Diane Davis notes, "Even radical writing pedagogies, that is, which presume that identity is constituted and plural, have a tendency to reproduce the myth of immanence by encouraging students to consider themselves *presentable*" (121). That is, conventional writing pedagogies view students as self-present, internalized subjects, but even those who critique such notions as the production of cultural-ideological forces aim "to help the student writer become conscious of and then to speak from her own radical positioning--that is, to embrace an identity founded on that positioning and to disclose it in writing as the basis for her own arguments and ideas" (121). Typically, we understand our own scholarly authority in the same ways. In the end, after the theorizing of how subjects get produced, we say there remains an immanent being, me, Alex Reid, and I can present myself in this text. Against this widespread conceit, Davis argues that it is necessary "in our field today to begin elaborating a kind of 'communitarian' literacy, a literacy which presumes first of all that writers and readers are in the world and exposed to others, a literacy that can read and write writing as a function of this irreparable exposure, of this irrepressible community" (122). Davis' concerns stand separate from the specifics of digital scholarship. The challenges of externalizing the subject, of inclining toward the community (as Jean-Luc Nancy puts it), as opposed to insisting upon an immanent, self-contained, self-presentable author, exist as much in the world of print as they do within digital contexts. That said, as I have been arguing, the shift in the technological, material assemblages of composition into digital networks reformulates our view of and experience with compositional practices. In short, the externalization of the subject in the emergence of community, which is difficult and abstract in the print world, becomes more palpable and material in digital media networks. Furthermore, this palpability is even intensified by the shift from text into video.

Following along this logic, video might offer more opportunities to pursue a communitarian literacy through the interruption of the myth of the writer. As Nancy explains, where this myth is interrupted, the writer "is not the author, nor is he the hero, and perhaps he is no longer what has been called the poet or what has been called the thinker; rather, his is a singular voice (a writing: which might also be a way of speaking). He is this singular voice, this resolutely and irreducibly singular (mortal) voice, *in common*: just as one can never be 'a voice' ('a writing') but in common" (70). This being-in-common is a *being-with* rather than a being-inside. That is, the conventional notion of community suggests a sharing of interiorized characteristics: a particular religious faith, a passion for a hobby, an ideological viewpoint, etc. Nancy suggests "'with' implies proximity and distance, precisely the distance of the impossibility to come together in a common being. That is for me the core of the question of community; community doesn't have a common being, a common substance, but consists in being–in–common, from the starting point it's a sharing, but sharing what? Sharing nothing, sharing the space between" (Nancy et al.). In this formulation we are each singular beings who arise through our exposure to one another, through a being-in-common, not through a sharing of *characteristics* so much as through the interaction of the *capacities* of the assemblage we produce.

In a more accessible discourse, as captured in the video, Rheingold notes that "the nation state and the online community have something in common, which is that they are imaginary." The first response to imaginary is to interpret this as meaning states and online communities do not exist, that they are not real in the sense that more immediate communities might be. Typically, however, we move to a second definition that accounts for the "imaginary" as an operation of ideology and/or power in which subjects are products of the characteristics they receive from their attachment to these institutions. It is ultimately in such formulations that exposure appears as a threat to the self. Without denying ideological power, in taking up the exteriority of relations, one discovers, as Agamben describes, that "belonging, being-such, is here only the relation to an empty and indeterminate totality" (*The Coming Community* 66). That is, one might be related to a nation-state or online community, but that relation does not pass along determining characteristics to an interiorized being threatened by this exposure. Instead, Agamben echoes Nancy's emphasis on the "space between:" "Whatever adds to singularity only an emptiness, only a threshold: Whatever is a singularity plus an empty space, a singularity that is *finite* and, nonetheless, indeterminable according to a concept. But a singularity plus an empty space can only be a pure exteriority, a pure exposure. *Whatever, in this sense, is the event of an outside*" (66, emphasis original). The imaginary then describes these relations of exteriority, our relations not only with this or that community, but with what Kevin Kelly terms in his TED talk, the "one machine:" our exposure to the collective operation of the web. As Agamben continues, "The *outside* is not another space that resides beyond a determinate space, but rather, it is the passage, the exteriority that gives it access" (67). In other words, as one conceives of this imaginary relation, this being-with or -in-common, this relation of exteriority, as a relation of an "outside," one should not conceive this outside as a beyond but rather as a surface (e.g. as in the phrase "the skin is the *outside* of the body") or more precisely as a threshold or point of access. Nancy takes care to note that in such relations "there is no penetration *into*, there is everywhere only a *touching*" ("Love and Community"). Even in those sexual acts that are typically understood as "penetration," Nancy sees a touching characterized by both proximity and distance. Ultimately what one uncovers here is a different topology from one that ascribes a defined inside and outside. Instead one encounters a fractal or interdimensional space where boundaries do not close-off to define objects as two- or three-dimensional. Hence the imaginary relation, one's exposure to the online community, is a relation of touching, of proximity and distance, along an outside or threshold, where capacities emerge to shape assemblages. The voice, the "authorial voice," can never be the product of an interiorized being, immanent to itself. Instead the voice is always a product of exteriority, of touching: "The body is first a hole, a tube if you want, and around the tube is a skin. The first character of this topology is that it is a resounding thing. The air can go through the tube and you have the skin over it and you produce music. The body is first a certain sound, and that sound is the voice" (Nancy et al.). Obviously there can be no voice without air passing through and over the body's thresholds. In a similar and no more abstract fashion, there can be no writing without a touching of the outside. The text itself is one such threshold, a point of exposure, that writer and reader both touch. Such exposures then must also move beyond these bodily examples as well. While there can be no voice without air passing over the body's thresholds, there can be no language without exposure to an assemblage of material, technological, and social objects. Taking this further, to find one's "voice" in digital video involves exposure to an extensive array of processes as I explore below.

Virtual Community, Virtual Immanence, Virtual Exposure. Available for download via Vimeo http://vimeo.com/14644699

Virtual Immanence, Virtual Community, Virtual Exposure

While social assemblage theory can operate to map the broader picture of digital video entering scholarship, it is arguably even more effective when it begins from a particular site of scholarly production: for example, the production of the video embedded in this essay. To begin, the materials involved in video production are different than those used for composing an essay: new hardware, software, and peripheral technologies come into play. As such, the capacities for expression certainly shift in a radical way in the move from text to video. Though I am using the same computer to write this essay and produce this video, a MacBook Pro, I am clearly using them in different ways, and the differences are not solely in terms of the software I am using. For example, I have used the built-in webcam and microphone to record audio and video. I've also made use of a Flip video camera. If one adds in the access to media networks, heterogeneity increases dramatically. Not surprisingly, in writing this essay I have made extensive use of this network connection to conduct research. Scholars do this today regularly without giving much thought to how a different information architecture or archiving procedure or copyright law would dramatically reframe their research practices. However, the video would quite simply have been impossible without network access to the video footage and background music I downloaded.

Much of the material for the video comes from the BBC "Digital Revolution" collection: video that has been produced for part of a planned series on digital media and released on the web for public use. Other parts come from interviews made for the Internet as Playground and Factory conference. The footage of Kevin Kelly, the founding executive editor of *Wired*, comes from the TED conference. As noted in the works cited, there are a few snippets of video from YouTube, and music taken from a *Creative Commons* music sharing site, *CCMixter*. The video includes web business gurus Charles Leadbetter and Chris Anderson, technology writers Howard Rheingold and Douglas Rushkoff, and a number of academics and researchers: danah boyd, Sherry Turkle, Jean-Luc Nancy, Giorgio Agamben, Mackenzie Wark, Clay Shirky, Nick Monfort, Alex Halavais, and David Weinberger. Even with a relatively simple video editing program like iMovie, it is then possible to cut selections from the downloaded video; adjust color, audio and other qualities of the video; apply simple effects and transitions; add text, voiceovers, and music; and export a video in a format distributable on the web. It is perhaps difficult to think of splicing a video clip in an iMovie window as a social assemblage with "material" dimensions, but, as abstract as the relations may seem, the video ultimately resides in a physical location in memory and storage and the operations undertaken in iMovie make permanent changes to the video's characteristics and capacities. Each of the editorial/compositional actions taken in iMovie has an *expressive* element that, as media, has a secondary *coding* and/or *decoding*. So, for example, in the past, Howard Rheingold sat in his backyard and was interviewed and video-recorded for the BBC. There is an entire social assemblage that one might investigate stemming from that event, but I will forego that here. The result though is that a video of Rheingold is uploaded to the BBC site, where it and he are exposed to web users. I downloaded the video and integrated it as material in a new assemblage that resulted, in part, in the video above. Here, again, Rheingold is exposed to a series of expressions, codings, decodings, territorializations, and deterritorializations, some of which are technical features of the hardware and software I am employing and others of which relate to the rhetorical and disciplinary demands to which I am responding.

Of course, it is more complicated than that. The rhetorical expectations of video are intertwined with technical capacities including everything from sound levels to linking together clips in a manner that results in the experience of some seamless conversation and/or progression of ideas. Disciplinary expectations operate to overcode the potential content of the video, but the video material already comes with its own expressions and codes. As much as Rheingold is exposed to the composition processes I employ, my video is exposed to his facial expressions, intonations, and bodily expressions, as well as the particular content of his interview. Given the general selection of material from these two collections, the BBC and the conference, there was already some built-in continuity. That is, for example, the BBC interviews were produced with the intention that they would be combined into a series of programs; as such they share related content and production strategies. As these pieces are cut and combined, their relations of exteriority activate new potentials, as one clip for one video is juxtaposed with another clip from a different interview. Does it make a difference that danah boyd is interviewed in a mall from a distance while Sherry Turkle is recorded up-close in some indeterminate indoor location? Does it matter that in some videos an interviewer is visible? Each of these characteristics of the video add expressive force to the assemblage. Does the juxtaposition of boyd and Turkle open new capacities for expression that would not have existed if they were not juxtaposed in this manner? As each part is exposed to others, new capacities emerge and the assemblage as a whole shifts. In turn, these assemblages intersect with the production of my video recording myself, in terms of the content of what I say, my nonverbal expression and mood, and the aesthetic-rhetorical approach of the production. Background music adds another expressive mood to particular segments and lends a sense of cohesiveness to the spliced-together clips. While, hypothetically, thousands of *Creative Commons*-licensed audio clips are available for download, there are limitations to how much time one could actually spend searching for appropriate music. Regardless of the selection process, one is ultimately also exposed to the particular material and expressive characteristics of the music and the capacities that emerge between the music and the video. It is only through these relations of exteriority that the video assemblage emerges. This is perhaps most clear in the crescendo-like montage near the end of the video. Here there is an experience of synthesis, of reterritorialization and overcoding. In this case though, the montage is a different rhetorical trick, as I interrupt the process to call attention to the way a video assemblage might obscure the exposures in the video with a turn toward a myth of immanence, where self-immanent beings come together in a totality to which the self remains, in contradiction, unexposed.

Conclusion

Through the mapping of the social-material assemblages of scholarly video production, one can develop tactics for investigating and activating these thresholds, these relations of exteriority. From this perspective, one would see exposure as an integral element of all composition and communication, with the added caveat that, within some assemblages, processes of territorialization and coding tend to limit the potential for mutation. At the current moment, the overcoding and territorializing forces common to print scholarship are not as strong or prevalent for video scholarship, and media networks further deterritorialize these practices by disseminating video beyond the reach of disciplinary organizing forces. Instead, in the crowded space of a social media network where scholars post videos and texts, sometimes in direct response to others, other times as tangential compositions, and yet others as intentionally collaborative efforts, there are regular opportunities for exposure. In a way, it is what scholars fear most: to be exposed (as frauds, etc.). Perhaps it is that fear that keeps many scholars from blogging or Facebook or even posting on email listservs, or perhaps it is the recognition that scholarly identity and authority are secured by remaining within disciplinary territories. In this same moment, however, these overcoding and territorializing forces appear to be approaching a crisis in operation as the traditional mechanisms of scholarly publication, hiring, and student enrollment in our majors falter. It is here that one might think in terms of Agamben's apparatus. The pseduo-sacred qualities of the humanities, if not the university in general, face exposure and profanation in social media. This is both threat and opportunity. Exposure to the decoding, deterritorializing potential of a communitarian video network might present scholars with opportunities to produce new assemblages, new relations of exteriority, that might lead scholarship and discipline into new, more productive and dynamic activities. Davis has already suggested how communitarian writers might take up relations of exteriority: "They do not aim to establish a stable and authoritative ethos nor to put forth an unambiguous message; they aim to amplify the irreparable instability and extreme vulnerability to which any writing necessarily testifies" (139). As such, the point is neither to turn scholarship toward video because it is intrinsically better than print, nor because video represents something exciting or attractive. In fact, scholarly engagement with video may only be transitory on a path elsewhere. Indeed, that engagement will undoubtedly be transitory, if only in the sense that one may now realize that our engagement with print has been transitory. Instead, the "point" is to consider what particular opportunities for transit video networks might offer. This consideration will include an examination of, and experimentation with, the technical, rhetorical, and disciplinary parts of scholarly video network assemblages, where one will engage the particular capacities that emerge among these relations of exteriority. Through video network scholars' exposure to these thresholds new potentials for humanistic scholarship and community might emerge.

Works Cited

Agamben, Giorgio. *The Coming Community*. Trans. Michael Hardt. Minneapolis: U of MN P, 1993. Print.

———. *The Open: Man and Animal*. Trans. Kevin Attell. Standford: Stanford UP, 2004. Print.

—. *What Is an Apparatus? and Other Essays.* Trans. David Kishik and Stefan Pedatella. Stanford: Stanford UP, 2009. Print.

Davis, D. Diane. "Finitude's Clamor; Or, Notes toward a Communitarian Literacy Author(s)." *CCC* 53.1 (2001): 119-145. Print.

DeLanda, Manuel. *A New Philosophy of Society: Assemblage Theory and Social Complexity.* London: Continuum, 2006. Print.

Deleuze, Gilles, and Félix Guattari. *A Thousand Plateaus: Capitalism and Schizophrenia.* Trans. Brian Massumi. Minneapolois: U of MN P, 1987. Print.

"Mission and Goals | Computers and Composition Digital Press." Computers and Composition Digital Press | Peer-reviewed ebooks and scholarly projects. Web. 11 Nov. 2009.

Nancy, Jean-Luc. *The Inoperative Community.* Trans. Christopher Fynsk. Minneapolis: U of MN P, 1991. Print.

Nancy, Jean-Luc, Avital Ronell, and Wolfgang Schirmacher. "Love and Community: A Roundtable Discussion." August 2001. Web. 23 Dec. 2009.

Pachoda, Philip. "Letter from the director: Digital transition." The University of Michigan Press. Web. 2 Nov. 2009.

Scholz, Trebor. "Market Ideology and the Myths of Web 2.0." *First Monday.* 3 Mar. 2008. Web. 28 Dec. 2009.

"The Modern Language Association of America." *Modern Language Association of America Proceedings* 1 (1884): I-Vii. Print.

Ulmer, Gregory. "Reality Tables: Virtual Furniture." *Prefiguring Cyberculture: An Intellectual History.* Eds. Darren Tofts, Annemarie Jonson, and Alessio Cavallaro. Cambridge, MA: MIT P., 110-129. Print.

Video Credits

"3 female avatars go shopping at Armidi in Second Life." Torley. YouTube.com. 5 Mar. 2009. Web. 8 Jan. 2010. http://www.youtube.com/watch?v=72zsNzLs7_o.

"BBC - Digital Revolution (Working Title) - Digital Revolution." BBC - Homepage. Web. 25 Dec. 2009. http://www.bbc.co.uk/digitalrevolution/.

"Emanuel Mangengin in Cameroon on mobile phones in Africa." Sjoerd Sijsma. YouTube.com. 3 June 2009. Web. 24 Dec. 2009. http://www.youtube.com/watch?v=QTh2D5mHH_0.

"The first film ever 'Exiting the Factory' (1895)." AlphaBravoBravoYanke. YouTube.com. 2 Nov. 2007. Web 8 Jan. 2010. http://www.youtube.com/watch?v=OYpKZx090UE

"Free." Airtone. CCMixter. 19 Dec. 2009. Web. 25 Dec. 2009. http://ccmixter.org/files/airtone/24436.

"The Internet as Playground and Factory - Alex Halavais." Voices from the Internet as Play. Vimeo.com. 1 Dec. 2009. Web. 15 Dec. 2009. http://vimeo.com/7954685.

"The Internet as Playground and Factory - Howard Rheingold." Voices from the Internet as Play. Vimeo.com. 1 Dec. 2009. Web. 15 Dec. 2009. http://vimeo.com/7919949.

"The Internet as Playground and Factory - Ken Wark." Voices from the Internet as Play. Vimeo.com. 1 Dec. 2009. Web. 15 Dec. 2009. http://vimeo.com/6428602.

"The Internet as Playground and Factory - Nick Monfort." Voices from the Internet as Play. Vimeo.com. 1 Dec. 2009. Web. 15 Dec. 2009. http://vimeo.com/8204449.

"Intro to Second Life." Giff Constable. YouTube.com. 24 June 2007. Web. 24 Dec. 2009. http://www.youtube.com/watch?v=CaLKFeJLnqI.

"Kevin Kelly on the next 5,000 days of the web." TED.com. July 2008. Web. 21 Dec. 2009. http://www.ted.com/talks/kevin_kelly_on_the_next_5_000_days_of_the_web.html.

"New York City Street Walkers." Steve Garfield. blip.tv. 5 Nov. 2008. Web. 7 Jan. 2010. http://blip.tv/file/1435946?filename=Stevegarfield-NewYorkCityStreetWalkers753.MOV.

"Toyota Camry Hybrid Factory Robots." gizmodoAU. YouTube.com. 30 Aug. 2009. Web. 8 Jan. 2010. http://www.youtube.com/watch?v=82w_r2D1Ooo.

"Trading Floor at New York Stock Exchange (NYSE)" EH11937. YouTube.com. 9 Aug. 2007. Web. 25 Dec. 2009. http://www.youtube.com/watch?v=Q7FdaiPQuDg.

"Transitions II." Soundprank. CCMixter. 29 Nov. 2009. Web. 25 Dec. 2009. http://ccmixter.org/files/soundprank/24074.

"World of Warcraft Gameplay (HD)." Ddrmaster57. YouTube.com. 18 Jan. 2009. Web. 24 Dec. 2009. http://www.youtube.com/watch?v=uDel5XNUIw.

JOURNAL OF SECOND LANGUAGE WRITING

The *Journal of Second Language Writing* is on the Web at http://www.journals.elsevier.com/journal-of-second-language-writing/

The *Journal of Second Language Writing* is devoted to publishing theoretically grounded reports of research and discussions that represent a contribution to current understandings of central issues in second and foreign language writing and writing instruction. Some areas of interest are personal characteristics and attitudes of L2 writers, L2 writers' composing processes, features of L2 writers' texts, readers' responses to L2 writing, assessment/evaluation of L2 writing, contexts (cultural, social, political, institutional) for L2 writing, and any other topic clearly relevant to L2 writing theory, research, or instruction.

"A Biliteracy Agenda for Genre Research" by Guillaume Gentil

We selected Guillaume Gentil's article for this volume because it represents the kind of rich interdisciplinary work that contributes to writing studies very broadly, considering genre knowledge for both first and second language writers and drawing on numerous lines of research in doing so. In addition, the paper is a novel addition to recent theorizing and empirical research on multicompetence, multilingualism, and language use in its application to literacy development.

6 A Biliteracy Agenda for Genre Research

Guillaume Gentil

Abstract

Most research on the development of genre knowledge has focused on genre learning in either a first language (L1) or a second language (L2). This paper highlights the potential of a biliteracy perspective on genre research that combines insights from literacy and bilingualism in order to examine how multilingual writers develop and use genre expertise in more than one language. From a theoretical point of view, the theorization of genre and genre knowledge in composition studies has developed relatively independently from the theorization of language and language proficiency in second language studies. It is argued that conceptually untangling the interrelated nature of genre, writing, and language expertise is a prerequisite for understanding multilingual genre learning. Research on genre learning and genre variation across languages and within multilingual communities is then reviewed to shed further light on the interrelationship between genre and language knowledge empirically. Pedagogical implications for better addressing the needs of multilingual writers are suggested.

Keywords: Biliteracy; Multilingual genre learning; L1/L2 writing development; Writing expertise; Common underlying proficiency; Second language proficiency; Communicative competence

Introduction

A few years ago, the guest editor to this special issue volume offered a state-of-the-art review of 60 empirical studies that have investigated how writers learn genre in a first language (L1) and second language

(L2) (Tardy, 2006). While the review compared L1 and L2 genre learning, it is noteworthy that almost all works cited focused on either L1 writers or L2 writers. Searches of the bibliographical databases with keywords such as "multilingual/bilingual," "writers/writing/written," and "genres" yielded several hits, but in many cases, the descriptor "multilingual writers" was used as a preferred equivalent for L2 or English-as-a-second-language (ESL) writers. While the label "multilingual" may better highlight the research participants' rich linguistic repertoire, it proved somewhat misleading given that the focus of the studies retrieved was primarily on L2 (and mostly ESL) writing development.

The lack of research on multilingual writers who learn genres in more than one language appears to be symptomatic of what Matsuda (1999, 2010) calls a "disciplinary division of labour" between (first language) composition and second language studies. Because the latter did not focus on written language and the former did not concern itself with L2 writers, it became apparent in the 1960s that the needs of ESL writers in American postsecondary institutions were not being served. This prompted the emergence of L2 writing studies at the intersection of, or as a "symbiont of," composition and second language studies (Matsuda, 1999). Efforts have thus been made, or called for, to integrate a second language perspective into rhetoric and composition and vice versa. While L2 writing studies aim to address L2 writers' needs specifically, they still leave out the needs of writers who must write alternatively in two languages or more, often reading (or speaking) in one language and writing in another.

I have argued elsewhere that the division of L1 and L2 language studies results in institutional practices and arrangements that compartmentalize educational resources away from multilingual writers (Gentil, 2005, 2006). In this paper, I argue that such a division also constrains theory building in genre research, and I outline the potential of a biliteracy perspective for understanding genre learning in two languages or more.

The simplest definition of biliteracy is "the conjunction of literacy and bilingualism" (Hornberger, 2003, p. 3). A biliteracy perspective on the study and teaching of genres thus attempts to combine insights from research in literacy and bilingualism in order to shed light on how multilingual writers develop and use genre expertise in more than one language. Literacy is meant to include the linguistic, cognitive, and sociocultural dimensions of reading and writing. Biliteracy is used here to refer to both bilingual and multilingual literacy, even though it may be more accurate to subsume bilingualism under multilingualism rather than the other way around (Jessner, 2006). The term "multiliteracy" is avoided to limit confusion with the pluralized notion of "multiliteracies," a concept introduced by the New London Group (1996) to emphasize multimodality and multiculturalism in the context of (primarily monolingual) English literacy education.

A biliteracy perspective has the potential to shed light on two key questions that may not have received due attention in genre research. The first is pedagogical: How can we help multilingual writers draw on the genre knowledge they have learned in one language when they write in another? The answer to this question hinges on a second, more theoretical question: How does genre knowledge intersect with writing expertise and language knowledge? While the relationship between the development of genre knowledge, writing expertise, and language knowledge need not be of central concern when the focus is monolingual writing, teasing this out is at the core of our understanding of multilingual writing development. This is because the more genre knowledge may be found to be language specific, the more multilingual writers are likely to have to relearn genres in each language. Conversely, the more genre knowledge may be found to be a "common underlying proficiency" (Cummins, 2000), the more it may be acquired in one language and used in another.

To address these questions, this paper will first consider theories of genre knowledge, writing expertise, and language knowledge, and then review research on genre use and genre learning across languages. While few studies have examined multilingual writing development from a genre perspective, research into genre variation across monolingual communities and, more interestingly, within multilingual communities will also be considered to help relate genre and language knowledge. The implications of such research for theory building and pedagogy will be drawn with a view to addressing more effectively the learning needs of multilingual writers.

GENRE KNOWLEDGE AND LANGUAGE KNOWLEDGE: THEORIES

One unintended consequence of the disciplinary division of labour is that the theorization of genre and genre knowledge in composition studies has developed relatively independently from the theorization of language, language proficiency, and communicative competence in second language studies. Tardy's (2009) integrated model of genre knowledge provides a framework for conceptualizing the relationship between genre and language knowledge from the perspective of L2 writing studies. This model will be compared to models of second language proficiency.

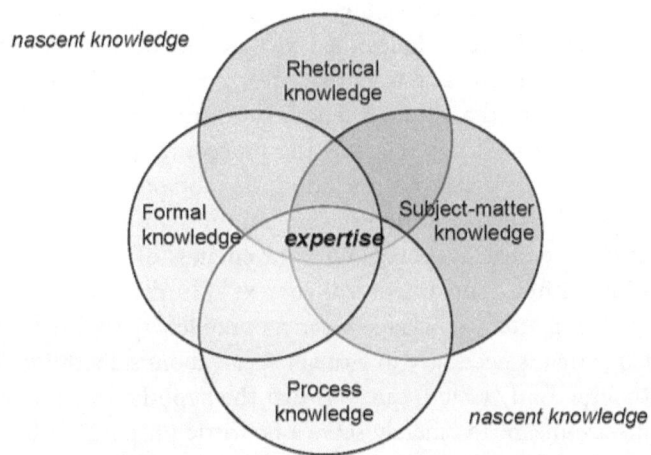

Fig. 1. Integration of genre knowledge. Reprinted from *Building Genre Knowledge* by Christine Tardy. (C) 2009 by Parlor Press. Used by permission.

GENRE KNOWLEDGE: FROM A TEXTUAL TO A SOCIAL VIEW

Traditionally genres were thought of as kinds of texts or text types, such as letters of recommendation, newspaper articles, recipes, and the like. Since the mid-1980s, however, a broader, sociological view of genre as social action has been advocated. In a widely cited essay associated with this view, Miller (1984) defines genres as typified responses to recurring social situations. Text-types, then, are but the by-products of a typification process: They are socially recognized, stabilized-for-now typified forms that result from repeated social practice, and yet they also serve as resources that help structure future social practice. The genre analyst's attention, so the argument goes, should therefore be focused on the action that a genre carries out and the social situation it is part of, rather than on its formal features.

This shift in perspective has major implications for the conceptualization of genre knowledge. As Tardy (2009) points out, if one adopts a "thoroughly rhetorical view" of genre as social action, genre knowledge must include much more than an understanding of text forms. Rather, it must integrate all the kinds of knowledge that are necessary to perform the genre. Specifically, Tardy (2009) identifies four dimensions of genre knowledge: formal, process, rhetorical, and subject-matter knowledge (see Fig. 1).

Formal knowledge includes the lexicogrammatical conventions of the genre, the structural moves that are common to the genre, and the modes and media through which the genre may be communicated. Process knowledge refers to the procedural practices through which a genre is carried out, including the composing processes for written genres. Rhetorical knowledge "captures an understanding of the genre's intended purposes and an awareness of the dynamics of persuasion within a sociorhetorical context" (Tardy, 2009, p. 21). Finally, subject-matter knowledge is the more or less specialized content knowledge that is necessary to write or speak about something.

Although Tardy (2009) cautions that the hypothesized knowledge domains are meant to "merely serve a heuristic purpose" rather than represent "any kind of epistemic reality" (p. 20), there is some indirect empirical evidence for the modular or componential nature of genre knowledge. This evidence is indirect because I am not aware of research that has examined the modularity of genre knowledge specifically. However, several strands of research on bilingualism and biliteracy point to the modularity of mind and language. In a recent review on the subject, Francis (2008) views modularity as the degree to which a complex ability (such as the ability to understand and produce academic discourse) can be broken down into relatively specialized, autonomous, yet interconnected components such as dedicated knowledge structures and processing mechanisms. While Fodor's (1983) early formulation of a modular mental architecture has been subject to debate, the introduction of the basic idea of modularity to the study of bilingualism proved useful, affording opportunities for examining the internal structure of, and interaction between, language and thought.

An influential model of modularity in bilingual education is Cummins' (2000) hypothesized distinction between a common underlying proficiency (CUP) and the language-specific aspects of academic performance. Based on considerable evidence that children in bilingual education programs need not relearn much of the subject-matter knowledge, numeracy skills, and problem-solving and literacy-related abilities they have acquired in one language as they use another language, Cummins (2000) posits that many of the academic and cognitive abilities that underlie academic performance are not language bound. He refers to these underlying abilities as the CUP. Research on exceptional bilingualism and bilingual mental representations further supports the idea that conceptual and linguistic structures are relatively autonomous and yet interact (Bhatia & Ritchie, 2004; Francis, 2008). If this is so, then it is likely that formal knowledge and subject-matter knowledge are relatively independent components of genre knowledge.

In the field of second language writing, research on the interrelationship between L2 proficiency and writing expertise further points to the distinctive natures of process knowledge and formal knowledge. Cumming (1989) showed that the problem-solving behaviours of second language writers are independent of spoken L2 proficiency but relate directly to the writing expertise they have developed in their first language. Specifically, writers assessed to have developed composing expertise in their first language were found to be able to draw on such expertise to the extent that they were not limited by their command of lexicogrammatical resources in a second language (see also Baba, 2009; Manchón, Roca de Larios, & Murphy, 2009; Sasaki, 2002; Sasaki & Hirose, 1996). Within-subject comparisons of summarizing, composing, and revising strategies in two languages further suggest that these strategies are mostly used in similar ways in both languages but vary with people's levels of writing expertise in their mother tongue (Albrechtsen, 2008; Arndt, 1987; Cumming, Rebuffot, & Ledwell, 1989; Hall, 1990; Jones & Tetroe, 1987; Pennington & So, 1993; Schoonen, Snellings, Stevenson, & van Gelderen, 2009; Whalen & Ménard, 1995). Interestingly, relatively advanced bilingual writers have been shown to make strategic use of their L1 for managing some of the more cognitively demanding aspects of composing an

L2 task, such as the planning of the task and the solving of discourse and rhetorical problems, even when their proficiency was high enough to allow relatively fluent formulation directly in the L2 (Manchón et al., 2009). While bilingual writers remain dependent on their formal knowledge of the language of composing for text generation, they may advantageously resort to a stronger language (typically but not necessarily their L1) for handling the more procedural and conceptual dimensions of writing, as this stronger language allows for deeper levels of processing.

Together, these studies suggest that many of the cognitive skills associated with the procedural aspects of writing are part of an underlying composing competence or CUP which, once developed in one language, can be used in another. Although they do not assess process knowledge and formal knowledge as components of genre knowledge specifically, researchers typically ask bilingual writers to undertake different writing tasks. For instance, participants in Cumming's (1989) study were asked to write an informal letter, a summary of a booklet, and an expository argument. Successful performance on each writing task thus assumed familiarity with the corresponding genre both at the process and the formal levels. Writing expertise in the L1 was assessed in part through writers' self-reported familiarity with these genres, and it is likely that the expert writers whose L2 writing performance was deemed superior were able to apply the genre knowledge they had developed in their L1 (French) when composing in the L2 (English).

Writing expertise in Cumming's (1989) study appears to be a global, composite construct that is assessed through self-reported professional writing expertise, holistic rating of L1 compositions, and "self-ratings of abilities to write in French in a variety of common situations" (p. 87). Such a global construct may conflate various aspects of writing expertise which a genre perspective can help tease apart. Indeed, in reviewing research on the linguistic and cognitive demands of foreign language writing, Schoonen et al. (2009) conclude that "one of the major challenges in writing research is the assessment of the core construct itself, 'writing proficiency'" given that "generalizability of scores across tasks is generally low" (p. 96). They add that "task effects," among which they specifically include "genre familiarity," "often contaminate the assessment of a writer's linguistic writing proficiency in research" (p. 78). Perhaps one of the potential contributions of genre-oriented approaches in future L2 writing research is precisely to contribute to more cognitively oriented approaches by shedding light on the nature of writing proficiency and its variability across genre-specific writing tasks. A central question is the extent to which one's writing expertise intersects with one's genre repertoire. Genre repertoire may be defined based on Gumperz's (1971) concept of verbal repertoire as the range of genres that an individual—or a community—owns. Writing expertise may thus be a function of both the depth and the breadth of one's genre knowledge. For some writers, the expected expertise may be a high level of competence in a very small range of specialized genres; for others, it may be a more moderate level of competence in a broader range of genres.

A related question is the extent to which writing expertise can be demonstrated through an unfamiliar genre. In other words, would the expert writers in Cumming's (1989) study have been able to demonstrate their writing expertise in their L2, had they been asked to cope with unfamiliar L2 genres? On the one hand, one could expect that if asked to write in an unfamiliar genre, highly skilled writers might approach it in ways that, in contrast to less skilled writers, do demonstrate their expertise. On the other hand, one could also expect that while highly skilled writers may cope better than less skilled writers with unfamiliar genres, their overall performance is more likely to be less satisfactory than that of skilled (or not so skilled) writers who are familiar with the genre at hand. The underlying issue is how much writing expertise can be abstracted as a cognitive skill from the genres called upon by specific contexts of writing. Arguably, writing expertise may at least in part refer to an underlying cognitive competence that reflects a writer's ability to engage with a novel writing situation. We may call it rhetorical flexibility, resourcefulness, or ingenuity. In many studies and situations, however, writing expertise is assessed against quality expectations for the final product, so a writer's resourcefulness may be little valued. Ultimately, a genre approach to writing expertise may call for a situated perspective that examines how the social recognition and valuation of writing expertise hinges on genre expectations that vary with social, historical, and cultural contexts.

To revisit Cumming's (1989) study from this perspective, the question arises as to whether the so-called expert L1 writers would have been as able to demonstrate their writing expertise in their L2 had expectations with regard to the realization of the genres they were asked to perform been markedly different in their L1-medium and L2-medium discourse communities. In the Canadian context of the study, the genre-related expectations of the French and English raters may well have been similar. However, in other crosslinguistic configurations, greater cultural differences in genre expectations may complicate the evaluation of writing expertise across languages (for a discussion, see Ortega & Carson, 2010). The following analogy, although not perfect, may help illustrate this point: Would the talent of a good French chef be of any use and value in a Thai restaurant? However exquisite it may be, a boeuf bourguignon will not satisfy a customer who ordered a beef curry. That said, if a French chef can adapt her repertoire of culinary techniques and recipes, then she may learn to satisfy expectations for Thai cuisine more quickly than someone with no culinary experience whatsoever. She may even be able to demonstrate a superior culinary expertise that blends the best of Thai and French cuisine in novel ways—on the condition that she can find a restaurant, or market, that celebrates fusion cuisine. Similarly, the extent to which a writer will be able to build on her writing expertise across linguistic and cultural contexts may depend as much on her own ability to transfer, adapt, and innovate with genres crosslinguistically as on her finding a context that will validate what she can do.

To my knowledge, research on the interrelationship between writing expertise and language proficiency, or more specifically, the cognitive and the linguistic dimensions of L1 and L2 composing, has not paid much attention to such complicating factors as the breadth and depth of genre repertoires and cultural variations in the genre expectations against which writing expertise is evaluated. Nor has this line of research examined the modular nature of genre knowledge directly, taking genre as a context rather than an object of study. This research does, however, provide indirect evidence for the relative autonomy of formal and process knowledge within genre knowledge. If to know a genre means to know both which composing strategies and which language resources are most appropriate for it, then one may know the composing strategies in one language but be unable to exploit them without command of the language in which the genre must be realized in a particular context.

As for rhetorical knowledge, the fourth dimension in Fig. 1, Tardy (2009) acknowledges that it has great potential to overlap with both formal and process knowledge (p. 21), and so it is less clear the extent to which its hypothesized nature as a distinct component of genre knowledge can be confirmed empirically. Arguably a potentially more clear-cut distinction is that between knowledge of discourse organization beyond the sentence level and knowledge of lexicogrammar, both of which are part of Tardy's (2009) formal knowledge. The successful realization of a genre requires the knowledge of systemically available, socioculturally preferred, and strategically advisable patterns of lexis, grammar, and discourse organization. Earlier contrastive research inspired by Robert Kaplan (1966) assumed that rhetorical patterns of discourse organization are "unique to each language and culture" (Connor, Nagelhout, & Rozycki, 2008, p. 1) without distinctions being made between linguistic and cultural influences. In a Sapir-Whorfian manner, language was viewed as largely determinative of preferred cultural thought patterns so that ways of writing were believed to be intrinsically linked to the language in which they were expressed. More recent intercultural rhetoric research suggests that the relationship between organizational patterns and language systems is a complex one (see, e.g., Hirose, 2006). Research on parallel genres—genres that develop in response to similar exigencies in two languages or more—suggests that discourse knowledge and lexicogrammatical knowledge may be two relatively independent modules of genre knowledge, a point to which I shall return.

Last, a component of genre knowledge that does not figure prominently in Tardy's (2009) model but that is arguably worth adding is that of metaknowledge—the explicit understanding of specific genres and of genre as a concept. Such metaknowledge has been shown to develop as writers learn to analyze genre exemplars (see, e.g., Cheng, 2007), and it can be hypothesized that such knowledge is equally part of a writer's CUP: Once a writer has acquired the ability to pay attention to generic features and to verbalize her understanding of genre and genre variation in one language, this ability should be available for use while composing or analyzing genres in another language.

In sum, Tardy's (2009) integrated model of genre knowledge provides a useful framework for conceptualizing the relationship between genre knowledge, language proficiency, and writing expertise both theoretically and empirically. To tease out this interrelationship further, Tardy's model will now be compared to models of second language proficiency.

Language Proficiency: From Grammatical to Communicative Competence

Much theorization on the nature of language proficiency has been spurred by language assessment specialists given their need to ground language tests on well-defined constructs. An example of an earlier and influential attempt to assess second language proficiency is provided by Carroll's (1975) large-scale comparative study of the teaching of French as a foreign language in eight countries. Underlying Carroll's test battery is a skills model of language proficiency in which proficiency is for the most part assessed "globally," through performance in the four skills of reading, listening, speaking, and writing, rather than "discretely," through the knowledge of particular items of vocabulary, morphology, or syntax. However, such a skills/component model of L2 proficiency has been criticized for failing to clarify how skills and knowledge are related, and for reducing language knowledge to lexicogrammatical accuracy at the sentence level (Bachman, 1990, p. 82). Hymes's (1972) call to broaden Chomsky's notion of grammatical competence has inspired efforts to reconceptualize L2 proficiency as a communicative competence in a second language. As Harley, Allen, Cummins, and Swain (1990) argue:

> In the area of language teaching . . . the predominant emphasis until recently has been on the teaching of grammar. The implicit conception of language proficiency, as it has been operationalized in second language classrooms, has entailed viewing proficiency as little more than grammar and lexis. The recent movement toward communicative language teaching has been associated with a broader view of language that includes not only its grammatical aspects, but also the ability to use language appropriately in different contexts and the ability to organize one's thoughts through language. (p. 7)

While the need for an expanded conception of language proficiency has generally been agreed upon, exactly what such a communicative competence entails has been subject to various interpretations. In their original framework, Canale and Swain (1980) considered two dimensions in addition to grammatical competence: sociolinguistic competence and strategic competence. Canale (1983) separated out discourse competence (referring to rules of coherence and cohesion) from sociolinguistic competence (referring to sociocultural rules). Bachman (1990) and Bachman and Palmer (1996) have identified slightly different components, and have also re-organized and renamed them over the years. A detailed comparison of these models need not be of concern here. Rather, at issue is where genre knowledge fits within this expanded view of second language proficiency. To examine this, I will focus on Douglas's (2000) model of specific purpose language ability, which itself draws closely on Bachman (1990) and Bachman and Palmer (1996).

Douglas (2000) defines specific purpose language ability as a kind of communicative language ability in a specific context of language use or "target language use (TLU) situation." He hypothesizes that this ability results from the interaction of language knowledge with background knowledge by means of strategic competence (see Fig. 2).

The distinction between strategic competence and language knowledge follows Hymes's (1972) argument that communicative competence is "dependent upon both (tacit) knowledge and (ability for) use" (p. 282). Strategic competence represents the "mental capacity for implementing the components of language knowledge in contextualized communicative language use" (Bachman, 1990, p. 84). Specifically, it includes the ability to assess the communicative situation, to set a goal on how to respond to it, and to plan and monitor this response. It involves choosing, retrieving, and organizing what elements of language knowledge and background knowledge are available and required to reach the established communication goal.

Language knowledge itself is broken down into four components: grammatical knowledge (which includes knowledge of vocabulary and phonology as well), textual knowledge (i.e., knowledge of cohesion rules and of rhetorical or conversational organization), functional knowledge (Bachman's 1990 illocutionary competence or understanding of how language forms relate to language functions), and sociolinguistic knowledge (understanding of appropriate ways to use language in specific contexts).

Where does genre knowledge fit in? In his original formulation, Bachman (1990) does not use the concept of genre but draws on Swales's (1988) earlier conceptualization of "discourse domain" as the conventions that characterize the language used by discourse communities for specific functions, such as "written mail requests for reprints of papers" or "entries in philatelic catalogues." Discourse domain thus

Language knowledge

Grammatical knowledge
  Knowledge of vocabulary
  Knowledge of morphology and syntax
  Knowledge of phonology

Textual knowledge
  Knowledge of cohesion
  Knowledge of rhetorical or conversational organization

Functional knowledge
  Knowledge of ideational functions
  Knowledge of manipulative functions
  Knowledge of heuristic functions
  Knowledge of imaginative functions

Sociolinguistic knowledge
  Knowledge of dialects/varieties
  Knowledge of registers
  Knowledge of idiomatic expressions
  Knowledge of cultural references

Strategic competence

Assessment
  Evaluating communicative situation or test task and engaging an approp discourse domain
  Evaluating the correctness or appropriateness of the response

Goal setting
  Deciding how (and whether) to respond to the communicative situation

Planning
  Deciding what elements from language knowledge and background know are required to reach the established goal

Control of execution
  Retrieving and organizing the appropriate elements of language knowled carry out the plan

Background knowledge

Discourse domains
  Frames of reference based on past experience which we use to make ser

Fig. 2. Components of specific purpose language ability. Reprinted with the permission of Cambridge University Press from *Assessing Languages for Specific Purposes* by Dan Douglas. (C) 1999.

defined appears to be a precursor of Swales's (1990) concept of genre. For Bachman, awareness of such domains is part of the broader category of "sensitivity to differences in register," which itself is part of sociolinguistic competence. Douglas (2000) does not specify the location of genre knowledge within his specific purpose language ability construct. Rather, he identifies genre as an element of the context of communication that must be recognized in order for a test taker or a language user to respond appropriately to the communicative situation (p. 43; pp. 61–62, pp. 89–90). He further defines genres according to Hymes as "categories of communication" such as poems, curses, monologues, lectures, advertisements, and so on (p. 43, p. 61).

However, Tardy's (2009) extended definition of genre provides further insight into the possible location of genre knowledge as part of Douglas's (2000) specific purpose language ability. If one adopts a traditional view of genre as text types and of genre knowledge as understanding of textual form, then it seems logical to place genre knowledge within textual knowledge. Alternatively, in their taxonomy of language knowledge, Grabe and Kaplan (1996) subsume genre knowledge and textual knowledge under what they call "discourse knowledge." However, to do justice to a "thoroughly rhetorical view of genre" as social action and of genre knowledge as integrating all the kinds of knowledge that are necessary to perform the action, genre knowledge must logically integrate all the components of the specific purpose language ability. In fact, what Douglas (2000) calls "language knowledge" and "background knowledge" is very similar to what Tardy calls "formal knowledge" and "subject-matter knowledge" respectively.

As for strategic competence, the ways in which Douglas (2000) and Bachman (1990) define it eerily resemble cognitive models of the writing process such as those of Flower and Hayes (1980) and Hayes (1996). Bachman and Palmer (1996) exclude the four language skills of listening, reading, speaking, and writing from language ability. Rather, they view a skill like writing as "the contextualized realization of the ability to use language in the performance of specific language use tasks" (pp. 75–76). However, research by Cumming (1989) and others suggests that a composing competence exists independently of the linguistic knowledge that is needed to realize it. What distinguishes so called skilled and less-skilled writers is precisely this ability to assess the writing situation, set goals in responding to it, harness language and conceptual resources, and monitor their uses while composing. That is, composing competence appears to be a type of what Bachman and Palmer (1996) call "strategic competence." If this is so, then Tardy's process/rhetorical knowledge equates with Bachman's (1990) and Douglas's (2000) strategic competence.

What emerges from this short genealogy of theory building in composition studies and applied linguistics is that, as researchers in each field have endeavoured to develop expanded views of genre knowledge and language proficiency from more sociological perspectives, they have come up to characterize the two concepts in nearly identical ways. In fact, examples of specific purpose language abilities given by Douglas (2000), such as a teaching assistant's ability to run a chemistry tutorial, are abilities to enact particular genres. While a greater understanding of the relationship between language use and language ability in specific contexts of communication has been gained, such theoretical convergence has made it very difficult indeed to understand, on a theoretical level at least, how multilingual writers develop and apply genre knowledge as they learn and use more than one language.

In an attempt to overcome this theoretical road block, I now turn to a systemic functional linguistic perspective on genre and language.

Genre Knowledge and Language Knowledge: A Systemic Functional Linguistic Perspective

A limitation of the models of L2 ability developed in the wake of work by Hymes (1972), Canale and Swain (1980), and Bachman and Palmer (1996) in North America is that they treat every component of language knowledge on the same level. The systemic functional linguistic (SFL) approach developed by Halliday and followers in Britain and Australia helps to specify the hierarchical structure of language knowledge and the relationship of language to context of use (for a recent formulation, see, e.g., Martin & Rose, 2008). SFL conceives of language as a stratified set of interlocking systems for meaning-making (see Fig. 3). In this stratified model, the phonological patterns (sounds) and graphonological patterns (spellings) are reinterpreted at a higher level of abstraction as lexicogrammar (wordings), which are in turn reinterpreted at the next stratum as discourse semantics (meanings).

To put in another way, discourse semantics is "realized" (encoded, symbolized, or expressed) in lexicogrammar, which in turn is realized in graphophonology. Language is therefore doubly articulated at the level of expression (phonology/graphology) and at two levels of content (the lower level of lexicogrammar and the upper level of discourse semantics).

Together, these interlocking systems constitute resources for meaning making: The meaning potential of the English language system is all that can be meant in English. As people use a language, they realize some of its meaning potential by making linguistic choices among possible options in specific contexts. SFL further proposes a stratified model of context: While a text realizes patterns of social interaction at the level of the context of situation, each situation in turn realizes patterns in a culture (Martin & Rose, 2008, p. 10).

This stratified model of language in context has important implications for the theorization of genre and language knowledge. It allows the conceptualization of each level as relatively independent of the other. For instance, similar discourse meanings may be expressed through the lexicogrammatical resources of two languages or more. From an SFL perspective, genres belong to the level of the context of culture: They "are recurrent configurations of meanings [that] enact the social practices of a given culture" (Martin & Rose, 2008, p. 6). In Hyland's (2007) apt phrase, they are "socially recognisable patterned ways of using language" that are identified by members of a discourse community sharing a common culture (p. 149). While discourse communities using different languages may develop different preferences in responding to similar recurring rhetorical situations, it is quite conceivable that they may also develop similar generic strategies. Halliday and Martin (1993) showed that while scientific English is a kind of English and scientific Chinese a kind of Chinese, both tend to use similar discourse strategies that characterize the scientific register. As scientists ran into similar rhetorical problems regardless of the language(s) they had at their disposal, it is likely that they developed similar research genres as well. In an ongoing study of the genres used in the teaching of mathematics in several countries, Artemeva and Fox (2010) have identified a common chalk-talk genre used by professors to walk students through mathematical reasoning; preliminary findings indicate that this genre exhibits remarkably similar properties in the various languages in which it is realized.

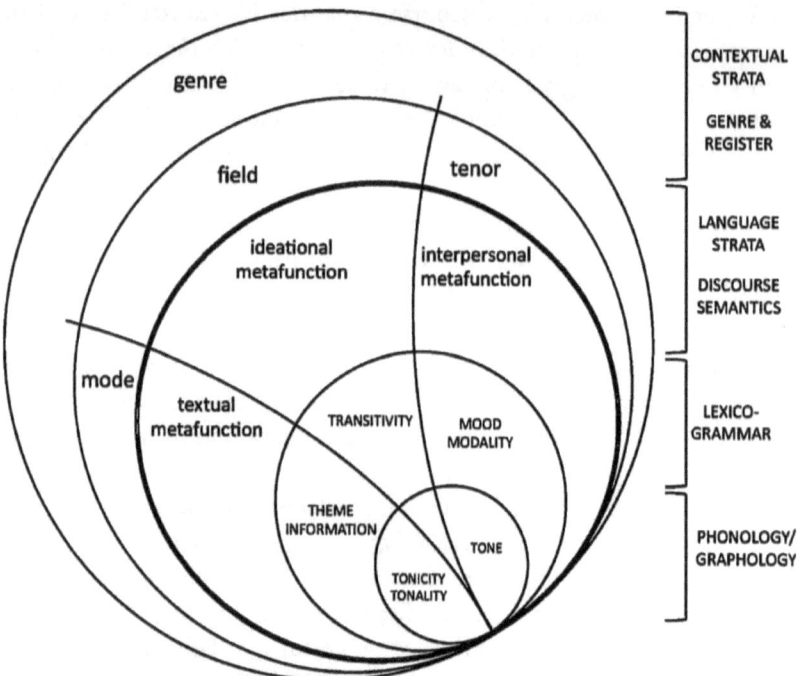

Fig. 3. Stratified model of language and context. Adapted from a figure graciously provided by David Rose.

In the next section, I review research on genre use and genre learning across languages to provide further evidence for the relative independence of discourse semantics, lexicogrammar, and generic strategies. The main underlying argument can be summarized as follows:

- A genre can be realized in different languages.
- Genre expertise is dependent on the knowledge of a language system to be exploitable.
- Once acquired in language A, genre knowledge may be exploitable in language B to the extent that (a) one has the knowledge of language B needed to express it, and (b) the sociocultural expectations regarding the realization of a given genre in language A approximate those of its realization in language B.

Before making this argument, however, it may be useful to revisit Tardy's (2009) model of genre knowledge in light of the above insights. First, a possible weakness in this model is the unclear distinction between genre knowledge and genre competence. Recall that Hymes (1972) views competence as the sum of knowledge and ability for use. If one agrees with this terminology, what Tardy calls "genre knowledge" may be more appropriately named "genre competence" (or genre expertise) given that it appears to include a strategic competence component ("process knowledge" and "rhetorical knowledge"), that is, an ability for use. That said, the term knowledge has also been used in a more encompassing way to refer to both declarative knowledge and procedural knowledge (for a discussion, see Paradis, 2004), in which case genre knowledge may appropriately refer to both explicit knowledge *about* genre and implicit, *how-to*-perform-a-genre knowledge. This terminological distinction aside, the inclusion of process knowledge within genre expertise is a strength of Tardy's model compared to an SFL view of genre. Indeed, a criticism of SFL is that, being a purely linguistic theory, it does not take into account the cognitive aspects of spoken and written language use. Yet the contributions of cognitive approaches to our understanding of composing processes are worth acknowledging. In keeping with the principle of stratification, strategic/composing competence may possibly be located at a higher, more abstract level than lexicogrammar and graphophonology in that it must be realized through a language system and a writing system. Yet as a common underlying proficiency, once acquired in one language, it may be exploitable in another.

If genres are socially recognizable patterned ways of making meaning by means of a language system, then ultimately genre competence can be viewed as the ability to recognize and draw on these regularities by strategically harnessing linguistic, cognitive, and cultural resources. Bakhtin (1986) argues that speech communication would be almost impossible if we did not cast our speech in generic forms and did not recognize the genre of another's speech from the very first words (p. 79). Genre competence must therefore be as central to communicative competence as lexicogrammatical competence. One important difference between the two, however, as Bakhtin reminds us, is that language forms are "stable and compulsory (normative) for the speaker, while generic forms are much more flexible, plastic, and free" (p. 79). The grammars of standardized languages such as English or French have taken centuries to evolve and are entrenched by normative forces such as usage guides, prescriptive grammars, schools, and the French Academy. While the institutionalization of some social practices, such as scientific research, exerts a stabilizing influence on some genres, new technologies, globalization, and changing communication demands can lead to the rapid emergence of new genres—often through the creative recombination of old genres. Genres on the Internet are a good example of this (Giltrow & Stein, 2009).

Genre Knowledge and Language Knowledge: Selected Research

Thus far, the argument has been mostly theoretical, although I have tried to cite empirical evidence for the modularity of Tardy's (2009) hypothesized components of genre knowledge. Empirical evidence for the hypothesized components of L2 communicative competence has been more mixed (for a review, see Bachman, 1990, p. 86), but by and large it does indicate that lexicogrammatical competence is distinct from higher order discourse competence such as the ability to organize text. To further support the claim that the same genres can be realized through different language systems in keeping with the SFL stratified model of language and discourse, I propose to review research that has examined the enactment and learning of genres across language systems. Traditionally, such research has focused on genre variations across monolingual communities. However, I will argue that, for the purpose of teasing out genre competence from language knowledge, it may be more useful to consider genre variations within bilingual or multilingual communities.

Genre Variations Across Monolingual Communities

Because of its focus on the analysis of differences and similarities in writing across languages and cultures, contrastive rhetoric has contributed to our understanding of crosslinguistic genre variation. At the same time, this strand of research has also benefited from developments in genre studies. As noted above, earlier work assumed that rhetorical patterns of discourse organization were unique to each language and culture without much consideration given to variations within cultures. This led to stereotyping rhetorical patterns according to language groups: In his famous 1966 paper, Kaplan concluded that English writing tends to be "linear," Romance writing, "digressive," and Oriental writing, "circular." One criticism of this earlier work was that it did not take into account variations within languages, particularly variations according to genres. Yet there can be more variation between a textbook and a research article by the same writer in English (see, e.g., Hyland, 2000) than between two research articles written in different languages (e.g., Moreno, 1997). In response to such a criticism, contrastive rhetoric—or intercultural rhetoric as it is currently referred to (Connor et al., 2008)—now takes such genre-dependent variation into account and is careful to compare rhetorical preferences across languages within what is assumed to be the same genre. However, the basic underlying premise still is that "any given language is likely to have written texts that are constructed using identifiable discourse features, and these features may differ across languages or be coded using different linguistic configurations" (Connor, 2003, p. 218). This Sapir-Whorfian premise is expressed even more strongly by Moreno (2008), who argues that "the language code is inescapably associated with a writing culture" (p. 34).

To analyze how discourse features vary across languages, intercultural rhetoric research typically compares exemplars of a given genre composed by monolingual writers in Language A and in Language B, and then compares genre exemplars composed by L1 writers and L2 writers in Language B. If the discourse patterns found in the latter texts are deemed to resemble those found in Language A rather than those of Language B, then the writers composing in their second language are assumed to have transferred discourse preferences from Language A (their first language) to Language B (their second language) (see Moreno, 2008, for a step-by-step description of contrastive rhetoric research procedures). If the transferred discourse preferences are further found to be inappropriate for Language B, then negative transfer is supposed to have occurred. A recent example of this line of research is a series of studies by Al-Ali (2004, 2006), who first compared application letters written in English and Arabic by native speakers and then examined application letters written in English by Jordanian Arabic-English bilinguals. As the letters written in English by the Jordanian writers contained rhetorical moves that are not typically used by English native speakers but that can be found in the Arabic letters, it was concluded that the bilingual writers had transferred culture-specific genre knowledge across languages.

This line of research appears to support the contention that discourse communities using different languages tend to develop different genre expectations, and, therefore, the genre knowledge acquired in one language may not be readily applicable in another. However, it should be pointed out that even though rhetorical and stylistic differences can be found in the preferred ways to accomplish similar communicative purposes across languages and cultures, the fact that researchers and non-specialists alike are still able to identify the same or similar genres—the application letter genre in this case—across languages does suggest that discourse communities using different languages may in fact develop similar, though not identical, generic strategies to respond to similar rhetorical situations. If this is the case, then at least some of the genre knowledge acquired in one language may be of use in producing a related genre in another language. Second, this kind of research typically does not examine how the same writers negotiate similar genres across languages. As Canagarajah (2006) argues, to fully appreciate the resourcefulness of multilingual writers one must move away from "inference" or "correlationalist" models of multilingual writing and adopt a "negotiation model." That is, one should study how the same writer composing in multiple languages "shuttles" creatively between discourse communities using different languages. Ideally, he adds, one "should study the author writing relatively the same genre though for different audiences and languages" (p. 591).

Two examples of this line of research are Parks and Maguire (1999) and Parks (2001). Parks focused on how francophone nurses in Quebec learned to negotiate two nursing genres—nursing notes and nursing care plans—first as students in a French-medium university and then as apprentice nurses in an English-speaking hospital. As they were experiencing a dual transition from school to the workplace and from one language community to another, these nurses had to relearn what they thought would be the same genres. Although differences in genre expectations were in part attributed to differences in the nursing approaches adopted in French and English hospitals in Quebec, there was nothing "intrinsically English" in the nursing note genre they had to learn at the hospital; similar genre constraints and affordances could have been adopted in a French-medium hospital too. In many ways, their transition was not unlike that of monolingual graduates who must adapt their genre knowledge to the new rhetorical exigencies of the workplace; the additional challenge for them was to develop enough lexicogrammatical resources in English to be able to instantiate the genre in that language.

Because Parks' (2001) study focused on a transition across two monolingual communities—a French-speaking university and an English-speaking hospital—it makes it difficult to determine whether differences in genre expectations are related to the culture of these discourse communities or to the language in which this culture is expressed. To further untangle linguistic and cultural influences on genre expectations, it is useful to examine how multilinguals negotiate the same or related genres within bilingual or multilingual communities.

Genre Variations within Bilingual or Multilingual Communities

With 11 official languages, South Africa offers an interesting context for studies of genre variations within multilingual communities. Deumert and Masinyana (2008) analyzed instant text messages by the same South African writers in English and isiXhosa. They found that the isiXhosa messages differed markedly from the English messages in that they contained no abbreviated materials, non-standard spellings, or paralinguistic restitutions such as smileys and exclamation marks. The authors explain this finding by pointing out that different sociolinguistic norms are associated with the use of English and isiXhosa in SMS communication. What makes this study particularly noteworthy is that the bilingual participants are not shuttling back and forth between two monolingual discourse communities. Rather, they seem to inhabit one bilingual discourse community whose norms constrain how the same genre is instantiated according to the language in which it is realized. This study suggests that bilingual writers obtain genre knowledge in relation to the particular language in which they learn to use a genre. The extent to which they are inclined and allowed to realize a closely related genre in similar ways in two languages may thus depend on the perceived degree of match in the sociolinguistic norms associated with the use of each language. This is not to say that a linguistic code, in the sense of the formal meaning-making possibilities of a language system such as isiXhosa, itself necessarily constrains how a genre is to be enacted. That abbreviations and exclamations are not socially sanctioned in isiXhosa text messaging does not mean that they are not linguistically possible in that language.

Canagarajah (2006) further sheds light on genre variation by focusing on a multilingual writer shuttling within a bilingual Tamil-English community and an (arguably) monolingual English community. He compares how Professor Sivatamby, a scholar in Sri Lanka, composed three research articles on roughly the same topic in two languages (English L2 and Tamil L1) and three different rhetorical contexts: for local publication in L1, for local publication in L2, and for foreign publication in L2. Focusing on the introduction in the articles, the study shows how this rhetorically savvy writer adapts his rhetorical and discourse strategies in response to perceived differences in the audience preferences. Interestingly, the strategies used for the two texts intended for local publication tend to be more similar— despite being written in two languages—than those used for the foreign publication. Canagarajah (2006) explains this finding by arguing that "both the English-dominant and Tamil-dominant scholars belong to the same community" with related expectations about the research article genre (p. 595). In contrast, the article for foreign publication is intended for an international English-medium discourse community with assumed different rhetorical expectations. Sivatamby appears to adapt to these expectations and yet also to resist them in an attempt to produce a "multivocal discourse that merges the strengths of local scholarly discourse with the dominant conventions of mainstream academic discourse" (p. 598). What this suggests is that far from being conditioned by linguistic codes, multilingual writers may develop superior rhetorical savvy and genre competence as they negotiate rhetorical demands across languages and discourse communities.

A third study looks at a speech genre rather than a written one. Garrett's (2005) examination of a "code-specific" genre in a bilingual Creole-English community illuminates the interplay between linguistic resources and sociocultural norms. The community is a rural village in St. Lucia; the genre is cursing. In this community, English tends to displace Creole for most functions. An exception is cursing. From a very young age, children are shown to be socialized to curse by means of Creole, a language that they are discouraged from using under most other circumstances. Obviously, cursing is linguistically possible in English as well, but in this particular community, strong normative constraints restrict the choice of the language in which this genre is realized. Cursing simply does not have much perlocutionary force in that community when done in English.

What these examples suggest is that the same or similar genres can be realized in different languages, but that discourse communities can have strong preferences regarding which language is used to accomplish a genre and how the genre is to be realized in that language. These normative preferences must thus be part of a multilingual writer's genre knowledge. At the same time, in other bilingual communities, the same genre expectations can hold regardless of the language system used. This is what my own research on bilingual writers in bilingual discourse communities in Canada suggests. A first study (Gentil, 2005) took place in the context of a primarily English-medium university in Quebec allowing the use of English and French for the completion of course assignments and comprehensive exam essays. When Katia, a doctoral student in cultural studies, had figured out her professors' expectations for the comprehensive exam essay after writing the first one in English, she was able to apply much of her genre knowledge when she wrote the second one in French. The only thing that she needed additionally was the French lexicogrammatical resources, and particularly the terminological resources, in order to realize this genre in French, which in her case was problematic, even though French was her native language, because most of her sources were in English.

Similar findings were obtained in another context—the Canadian federal public service—which also allows for English and French to be used as a language of work under certain conditions (Gentil et al., 2008). As part of her tasks, Jill, a librarian and experienced writer in English (her first language), was required to write emails that accompanied the reference search results that she sent in response to specific queries. A comparison of her English and French emails showed that the discourse organization and communicative intent she was trying to achieve was the same in the two languages. The only limiting factor that prevented her from tapping the knowledge of that particular email genre while composing in French was her limited command of French lexicogrammatical resources as appropriate for a professional register.

If I may draw on my personal experience, I currently work in an English-speaking university that allows for use of French in a restricted context—mostly within the Department of French. I recently supervised two master's students in English and French, each writing in her first language. Striking were the similarities in the challenges they encountered in becoming familiar with the thesis genre: learning what information goes where and why, making connections between the data and the literature, and managing information flow between and within paragraphs. In terms of language use, both struggled to master the academic register I expected of them, although from opposite ends as it were. Contrary to stereotypical ideas that may be associated with each language, I encouraged the English student away from a tendency to use needlessly ornate language, while I encouraged the French student away from a tendency to use too informal a register which I deemed more appropriate for spoken use.

I have not yet had the opportunity to supervise the same student in two languages. But again if I may draw on my own experience, writing my second master's thesis in English (in second language education) proved much easier than writing my first master's thesis in French (in plant pathology), even though French was not only my first language but also a language in which I had gained considerable writing experience. In contrast, I had only three years' experience in an English-speaking university context when I composed the second thesis. Lexicogrammatical choices did not, and still do not, come to me as intuitively in English as in French. I believe that part of the reason the second thesis proved easier was that I was able to apply my knowledge of the conventions of the thesis genre I had learned in French, while adapting to the demands of a new institutional and disciplinary context.

The way I set about to write a research article is hardly different in French, say for the *Canadian Modern Language Review*, than in English, say for the *Journal of Second Language Writing*. The language I use is mostly a meditational means for making meaning. This being said, language systems such as English and French are also socially recognized domains of language behaviour. As such, they each function as a "sociolinguistic sign" (Hymes, 1972, p. 291) whose meaning lies in the attitudes, values, identities, and loyalties attached to it. Hence, when I choose to publish in French despite the greater potential return of publishing in English, I am keeping a commitment (Gentil, 2005) to my linguistic community—particularly to the francophone students I see struggling to understand academic literature in English. Further, I must take account of differences in the overlapping yet distinct academic discourse spaces that are mediated by each language: The ongoing conversations, interlocutors, reference points, and interests are not quite the same. Beyond that, perhaps genre expectations are different too, but these differences may be so subtle as to escape notice.

In sum, the research reviewed thus far on crosslinguistic genre variation suggests that genre-related rhetorical and discursive preferences are *not* linguistically determined. The same genre can be realized in quasi-identical ways in two languages if sociocultural norms allow it. This finding is in keeping with the hypothesized modular and stratified structure of genre competence. That said, before drawing pedagogical implications, a qualification is in order. Based on a comparative analysis of four scholarly books in linguistics and anthropology translated from English to French or French to English, Celle (2009) observes that direct questions are much more frequent in her corpus in French than in English. She argues that direct questions are typically avoided by the English authors or translators for pragmatic reasons, because they would increase the intersubjective distance between the author and the reader. While acceptable or expected in French scholarly discourse, such a distance is believed to be at odds with rhetorical expectations in English scholarly discourse. Instead of asking direct questions, English authors/translators resort to other formulations, including embedded questions, which, according to Celle (2009), minimize authorial distance vis-à-vis the reader. Direct questions are grammatically possible in both languages, as evidenced by their rare occurrences in the English corpus. This observation provides further support to the claim that lexicogrammatical systems, and hence lexicogrammatical competence, are relatively independent from discourse expectations about language use. At the same time, however, Celle (2009) notes that English grammar affords more flexibility in the construction of embedded questions than French grammar does, for instance by allowing an embedded question as a complement of a nominalized predicate (*It is an interesting question whether* vs. **C'est une question intéressante si*). Thus, one cannot rule out that crosslinguistic differences in grammatical affordances (e.g., with respect to embedded questions) may influence rhetorical preferences across languages (e.g., with respect to authorial distance). This example highlights the potential of translation studies to uncover subtle crosslinguistic differences in genre expectations.

Genre Knowledge and Language Knowledge: Coda

I opened this paper by asking a theoretical question: How does genre knowledge intersect with writing expertise and language knowledge? Answering this question was presented as a prerequisite to answering a related pedagogical question: How can we help multilingual writers draw on the genre knowledge they have learned in one language when they write in another? Regarding the first question, to make sense of multilingual genre learning, I have proposed adopting a rhetorical view of genre as typified rhetorical action, a cognitive view of writing expertise as a form of strategic (composing) competence, and a stratified, Hallidayan view of a language as an interlocking set of phonographological, lexicogrammatical, and semantic systems that together comprise a meaning potential. Within this perspective, I have attempted to show the following:

- A genre can be realized in different languages.
- Genre expertise is dependent on the knowledge of a language system to be exploitable.
- Discourse communities using *different* languages may develop different preferences in responding to rhetorical situations, but they may also develop similar (generic) strategies to respond to similar (typified) rhetorical situations.
- Discourse communities using *several* languages may privilege one language for specific genres, or not.
- Expert multilingual writers can draw on their whole repertoires of genres and rhetorical strategies across languages strategically.

I hope that these theoretical clarifications can help to better address the learning needs of multilingual writers. As we better understand the components of genre expertise in multilinguals, we should be able to better analyze their needs. The key is to identify what kinds of prior knowledge they bring to the writing situation at hand so as to help them draw upon it as they develop the knowledge domain that they lack to accomplish a genre. For instance, in the case of a mature professional writer such as Jill, spending much instructional time on the procedural or discourse organization aspects of the professional email genres she uses would appear to be a waste of time: She mostly needs the lexicogrammatical resources to realize these genres in French.

If a genre is expressed in, but not tied to, a language system, then the question also arises as to the language in which it may be preferable to help learners develop various aspects of genre knowledge. A corollary of Cummins' (2000) notion of common underlying proficiency is what he calls the "interdependence principle":

> To the extent that instruction in Lx [Language X] is effective in promoting proficiency in Lx, transfer of this proficiency to Ly [Language Y] will occur provided that there is adequate exposure to Ly (either in school or environment) and adequate motivation to learn Ly (p. 38).

Despite the common belief that immigrants to the US or English Canada should be schooled in English as soon as possible, much bilingual education research suggests that it may be advantageous for them to continue education in their first language while they are learning English. The reason is that instruction in English is not likely to be effective in promoting CUPs in English if learners fail to understand the language of instruction. Neither are they likely to transfer whatever CUPs they may have developed from English to their L1 if the L1 is not supported in the academic environment. Conversely, they are more likely to develop CUPs in their L1 and then to transfer these proficiencies from their L1 to English, a language which is strongly supported in the environment. Because many aspects of genre expertise are CUPs, it may thus be preferable for multilingual writers to develop them in their L1 or stronger language first.

This is not to say that transfer cannot occur from a weaker to a stronger language. Early French immersion programs in Canada provide a good example of a context of additive bilingualism in which English-speaking students have been shown to transfer proficiencies, including literacy skills, from French to English. Generally, transfer is more likely to occur from a minority to a majority language because quality of instruction, exposure, and motivation are typically greater for majority languages than for minority languages (for a discussion, see Cummins, 2000). This may partly explain why instances of bidirectional transfer have been reported among bilingual Japanese-English writers in Japan, especially after extended periods of study in English-speaking countries (Rinnert & Kobayashi, 2009). For these writers, Japanese likely remains a dominant language and yet English also has high status as an international language.

Nor is this to say that transfer of genre expertise across languages will necessarily occur or be successful. First, Cummins (2000) has hypothesized that a threshold level of competence in the second language must be obtained for a cognitive proficiency to be transferrable to that language. While Cummins (2000) acknowledges that the threshold hypothesis remains speculative (pp. 37–38, p. 175), several of the studies cited above point to a possible threshold effect in the transfer of writing expertise: L1 writing expertise appears to be useable in the L2 on the condition that L2 proficiency is not limiting (see, e.g., Cumming, 1989; Manchón et al., 2009). Second, as I have also tried to argue, even if L2 proficiency is sufficient, genre knowledge developed in the L1 (or the L2) may be of limited use in the L2 (or the L1) if the sociocultural expectations regarding the realization of a given genre in the two languages differ markedly. The successful crosslinguistic transfer of genre knowledge may therefore be facilitated in an educational context that promotes not only dual language development but also cultural sensitivity with regard to genre performance in each language. Additionally, Cummins (2000) insists on the motivational influence of societal power relations on the likelihood of crosslinguistic transfer. Bilingual writers are more likely to transfer genre knowledge from Language A to Language B if the enactment in Language B of the written genres (or particular features thereof) acquired in Language A is socially authorized and valued. Indeed, Rinnert and Kobayashi (2009) suggest that the bilingual Japanese-English writers in their studies tend to selectively transfer specific patterns of discourse crosslinguistically (and bidirectionally) based on their evaluations of these patterns. For instance, they appear to be more disposed to adopt, in their L1 writing, a particular rhetorical feature (such as making a counterargument in an essay) they were taught in a L2 writing class, if they believe this feature to be of value in a given L1 context of writing.

A last finding from bilingual education research that is worth emphasizing is this: if the educational context allows students to develop age-appropriate competence in two languages, they are likely to benefit from bilingualism cognitively. These cognitive benefits include greater creativity, mental flexibility, communicative sensitivity, selective attention, and metalinguistic awareness (see, e.g., Jessner, 2006, for a review). It thus seems likely that multilingual genre learning should promote genre awareness, rhetorical flexibility, and audience sensitivity, although this remains an empirical question.

Despite the potential value of a biliteracy perspective on genre learning for both theory building and pedagogy, more research is needed in this area. One reason for this dearth of research is the difficulty in finding multilingual writers who are actually writing in more than one language. Most university and workplace contexts in North America have a strong monolingual orientation, and consequently most research on so-called "multilingual" writers focuses on multilinguals who write mostly or exclusively in their second language. Canada's bilingual policies help to create contexts for bilingual writing, but even there, truly bilingual postsecondary or professional contexts are hard to find. Institutional structures and disciplinary divisions of labour between literature, composition and rhetoric, second-language writing studies, and translation studies sequester resources away from multilingual writers (Gentil, 2006). A recent study of two programs promoting academic biliteracy in a US university is encouraging (Skilton-Sylvester, 2007). The more these programs multiply, the more opportunities for biliteracy-oriented genre research will arise.

In the meantime, one may further explore existing contexts of multilingual writing development. As Ortega and Carson (2010) argue, it is "a theoretical imperative to investigate multicompetent writing across a fuller spectrum of contexts where biliteracy is a needed cultural capital" (p. 62). The near exclusive focus of empirical studies on college-level populations in ESL or EFL contexts in L2 writing thus far has hampered theory building in the field. In particular, to better understand the relationship between linguistic expertise and composing ability, one should examine writing development in a variety of populations. One overlooked group identified by Ortega and Carson (2010) includes the large number of child and adult immigrants and refugees and many bilingual indigenous people who are developing writing expertise in an L2 but are non-literate or semi-literate in their L1 (p. 63). However, I would like to add populations representing other configurations of writing expertise and language proficiency as well. These include highly literate writers in their L1 with only incipient oral proficiency in their L2, who may be found among visiting scholars in foreign-language environments, writing professionals who encounter a new language, and so on. Studies that compare first-and foreign-language writing development among secondary and college-level students are useful as well, but as writing expertise then develops along language proficiency, the two are not always easy to differentiate (a point which Manchón et al., 2009, duly acknowledge, p. 117). It is thus useful to consider a variety of trajectories of multilingual writing development, not only across monolingual communities but also between and within multilingual communities.

The genre construct itself has much to contribute to the study of multilingual writing development. As I have tried to show, it adds another layer of complexity to the theorization of writing expertise and language proficiency by raising questions such as: How does writing expertise intersect with a writer's breadth and depth of genre knowledge in a given language? How does it intersect with her awareness of genre(s) and her authoritative power to innovate with genres in a given context? How much can the evaluation of writing expertise be abstracted from sociocultural expectations about genre performance in a language? What are the developmental and sociocultural conditions for the successful transfer of genre knowledge across languages? To what extent is genre performance in a language contingent on the writer's knowledge of the language and on the systemic possibilities for meaning-making afforded by the language? I look forward to future L2 writing research that addresses some of these questions by adopting a biliteracy perspective on genre learning and genre use.

Acknowledgments

I would like to thank Christine Tardy and two anonymous reviewers for their comments on an earlier version of this article. I am also grateful to David Rose for graciously providing a figure, to Cambridge University Press and Parlor Press for allowing me to reproduce figures, and to Stephen Slessor for his editorial comments.

References

Al-Ali, M. (2004). How to get yourself on the door of a job: A cross-cultural contrastive study of Arabic and English job application letters. *Journal of Multilingual and Multicultural Development, 25*, 1–25.

Al-Ali, M. (2006). Genre-pragmatic strategies in English letter-of-application writing of Jordanian Arabic-English Bilinguals. *International Journal of Bilingual Education and Bilingualism, 9*(1), 119–139.

Albrechtsen, D. (2008). Writing in two languages. In D. Albrechtsen, K. Haastrup, & B. Henriksen (Eds.), *Vocabulary and writing in a first and second language* (pp. 112–159). New York: Palgrave Macmillan.

Arndt, V. (1987). Six writers in search of texts: A protocol-based study of L1 and L2 writing. *ELT Journal, 41*, 257–267.

Artemeva, N., & Fox, J. (2010). Chalk Talk: A principal genre of the university mathematics classroom. In H. Graves & R. Graves (Eds.), *Interdisciplinarity: Thinking and writing beyond borders. Proceedings from the 25th Conference of the Canadian Association of Teachers of Technical Writing, 2008* (pp. 167–183). Edmonton: Canadian Association for the Study of Discourse and Writing.

Baba, K. (2009). Aspects of lexical proficiency in writing summaries in a foreign language. *Journal of Second Language Writing, 18*, 191–208.

Bachman, L. (1990). *Fundamental considerations in language testing.* London: Oxford University Press.

Bachman, L., & Palmer, A. (1996). *Language testing in practice.* London: Oxford University Press.

Bakhtin, M. (1986). *Speech genres and other late essays.* Austin: University of Texas Press.

Bhatia, T., & Ritchie, W. (2004). *The handbook of bilingualism.* Oxford: Blackwell.

Canagarajah, S. (2006). Toward a writing pedagogy of shuttling between languages: Learning from multilingual writers. *College English, 68*(6), 589–604.

Canale, M. (1983). From communicative competence to communicative language pedagogy. In J. Richards & R. Schmidt (Eds.), *Language and communication* (pp. 2–27). London: Longman.

Canale, M., & Swain, M. (1980). Theoretical bases of communicative approaches to second language teaching and testing. *Applied Linguistics, 1*,1–47.

Carroll, J. (1975). *The teaching of French as a foreign language in eight countries.* New York: John Wiley & Sons.

Celle, A. (2009). Question, mise en question: la traduction de l'interrogation dans le discours théorique. *Revue française de linguistique appliquée, 14*(1), 39–52.

Cheng, A. (2007). Transferring generic features and recontextualizing genre awareness: Understanding writing performance in the ESP genre-based literacy framework. *English for Specific Purposes, 26*, 287–307.

Connor, U. (2003). Changing currents in contrastive rhetoric. In B. Kroll (Ed.), *Dynamics of second language writing* (pp. 218–241). Cambridge: Cambridge University Press.

Connor, U., Nagelhout, E., & Rozycki, W. (Eds.). (2008). *Contrastive rhetoric: Reaching to intercultural rhetoric.* Amsterdam: John Benjamins.

Cumming, A. (1989). Writing expertise and second-language proficiency. *Language Learning, 39*(1), 81–141.

Cumming, A., Rebuffot, J., & Ledwell, M. (1989). Reading and summarizing challenging texts in first and second languages. *Reading and Writing, 2*, 201–219.

Cummins, J. (2000). *Language, power and pedagogy: Bilingual children in the crossfire.* Toronto: Multilingual Matters.

Deumert, A., & Masinyana, S. (2008). Mobile language choices—The use of English and isXhosa in text messages (SMS): Evidence from a bilingual South African sample. *English World-Wide, 29*(2), 117–147.

Douglas, D. (2000). *Assessing languages for specific purposes.* Cambridge: Cambridge University Press.

Flower, L., & Hayes, J. (1980). The dynamics of composing: Making plans and juggling constraints. In L. Gregg & E. Steinberg (Eds.), *Cognitive processes in writing* (pp. 31–50). Hillsdale, NJ: Lawrence Erlbaum.

Fodor, J. (1983). *Modularity of mind.* Cambridge, MA: MIT Press.

Francis, N. (2008). Modularity in bilingualism as an opportunity for cross-discipline discussion. In Cummins, J., & Hornberger, N. Eds. *Encyclopedia of language and education. Vol. 5* (pp.105–116). Retrieved from SpringerLink.com.

Garrett, P. (2005). What a language is good for: Language socialization, language shift, and the persistence of code-specific genres in St. Lucia. *Language in Society, 34*, 327–361.

Gentil, G. (2005). Commitments to academic biliteracy: Case studies of francophone university writers. *Written Communication, 22*, 421–471.

Gentil, G. (2006). EAP and Technical Writing without borders: The impact of departmentalization on the teaching and learning of academic writing in a first and second language. In P. Matsuda, C. Ortmeier-Hooper, & X. You (Eds.), *The politics of second language writing: In search of the promised land* (pp. 147–167). West Lafayette: Parlor Press.

Gentil, G., Bigras, J., & O'Connor, M. (2008, March). *Process or post-process pedagogies? Insights from a learner needs analysis of second language writers.* Paper presented at the Annual Conference of the American Association for Applied Linguistics, Washington, DC.

Giltrow, J., & Stein, D. (2009). *Genres in the internet: Issues in the theory of genre.* Amsterdam: John Benjamins.

Grabe, W., & Kaplan, R. (1996). *Theory and practice of writing.* London: Longman.

Gumperz, J. (1971). *Language in social groups.* Stanford, CA: Stanford University Press.

Hall, C. (1990). Managing the complexity of revising across languages. *TESOL Quarterly, 24*, 43–60.

Halliday, M., & Martin, J. (1993). *Writing science.* Pittsburgh: University of Pittsburgh Press.

Harley, B., Allen, P., Cummins, J., & Swain, M. (1990). *The development of second language proficiency.* Cambridge: Cambridge University Press.

Hayes, J. (1996). A new framework for understanding cognition and affect in writing. In C. Levy & S. Ransdell (Eds.), *The science of writing* (pp. 1– 28). NJ: Lawrence Erlbaum.

Hirose, K. (2006). Pursuing the complexity of the relationship between L1 and L2 writing. *Journal of Second Language Writing, 15,* 142–146.

Hornberger, N. (Ed.). (2003). *Continua of biliteracy.* Toronto: Multilingual Matters.

Hyland, K. (2000). *Disciplinary discourses.* Harlow: Longman.

Hyland, K. (2007). Genre pedagogy: Language, literacy and L2 writing instruction. *Journal of Second Language Writing, 16,* 148–164.

Hymes, D. (1972). On communicative competence. In J. B. Pride & J. Holmes (Eds.), *Sociolinguistics* (pp. 269–293). Harmondsworth, England: Penguin.

Jessner, U. (2006). *Linguistic awareness in multilinguals.* Edinburgh: Edinburgh University Press.

Jones, C., & Tetroe, J. (1987). Composing in a second language. In A. Matsuhashi (Ed.), *Writing in real time: Modeling the production processes* (pp. 34–57). Norwood, NJ: Ablex.

Kaplan, R. (1966). Cultural thought patterns in inter-cultural education. *Language Learning, 16,* 1–20.

Manchón, R. M., Roca de Larios, J., & Murphy, L. (2009). The temporal dimension and problem-solving nature of foreign language composing processes: Implications for theory. In R. M. Manchón (Ed.), *Writing in foreign language contexts: Learning, teaching, and research* (pp. 102– 129). Bristol, UK: Multilingual Matters.

Martin, J., & Rose, D. (2008). *Genre relations: Mapping culture.* London: Equinox.

Matsuda, P. K. (1999). Situating ESL writing in a cross-disciplinary context. *Written Communication, 15,* 99–121.

Matsuda, P. K. (2010, May). *The disciplinary division of labor: A decade later.* Plenary address given at the 2010 Symposium on Second Language Writing. Spain: University of Murcia.

Miller, C. (1984). Genre as social action. *Quarterly Journal of Speech, 70,* 151–167.

Moreno, A. (1997). Genre constraints across languages: Causal metatext in Spanish and English RAs. *English for Specific Purposes, 16*(3), 179–191.

Moreno, A. (2008). The importance of comparable corpora in contrastive linguistics. In U. Connor, E. Nagelhout, & W. Rozycki (Eds.), *Contrastive rhetoric: Reaching to intercultural rhetoric* (pp. 25–43). Amsterdam: John Benjamins.

New London Group. (1996). A pedagogy of multiliteracies: Designing social futures. *Harvard Educational Review, 66*(1), 60–92.

Ortega, L., & Carson, J. (2010). Multicompetence, social context, and L2 writing research praxis. In T. Silva & P. K. Matsuda (Eds.), *Practicing theory in second language writing* (pp. 48–71). West Lafayette, IN: Parlor Press.

Paradis, M. (2004). *A neurolinguistic theory of bilingualism*. Amsterdam: John Benjamins.

Parks, S. (2001). Moving from school to workplace: Disciplinary innovation, border crossings, and the reshaping of a written genre. *Applied Linguistics, 22*(4), 405–438.

Parks, S., & Maguire, M. (1999). Coping with on-the-job writing in ESL: A constructivist-semiotic perspective. *Language Learning, 49*(1), 143–175.

Pennington, M., & So, S. (1993). Comparing writing process and product across two languages: A study of 6 Singaporean university student writers. *Journal of Second Language Writing, 2*, 41–63.

Rinnert, C., & Kobayashi, H. (2009). Situated writing practices in foreign language settings: The role of previous experience and instruction. In R. M. Manchón (Ed.), *Writing in foreign language contexts: Learning, teaching, and research* (pp. 23–48). Bristol, UK: Multilingual Matters.

Sasaki, M. (2002). Building an empirically-based model of EFL learners' writing processes. In S. Ransdell M.-L. Barbier (Eds.), *New directions for research in L2 writing* (pp. 49–80). Dordrecht, Netherlands: Kluwer Academic Publishers.

Sasaki, M., & Hirose, K. (1996). Explanatory variables for EFL students' expository writing. *Language Learning, 46*, 137–174.

Schoonen, R., Snellings, P., Stevenson, M., & van Gelderen, A. (2009). Towards a blueprint of the foreign language writer: The linguistic and cognitive demands of foreign languagewriting. In R. M. Manchón (Ed.), *Writing in foreign language contexts: Learning, teaching, and research* (pp. 77–101). Bristol, UK: Multilingual Matters.

Skilton-Sylvester, E. (2007). Academic biliteracies for adults in the United States. In K. Riviera K. & A. Huerta-Macias (Eds.), *Adult biliteracy: Sociocultural and programmatic responses* (pp. 131–154). London: Routledge.

Swales, J. M. (1988). Discourse communities, genres and the teaching of English as an international language. *World Englishes, 7*, 211–220.

Swales, J. M. (1990). *Genre analysis*. Cambridge: Cambridge University Press.

Tardy, C. M. (2006). Researching first and second language genre learning: A comparative review and a look ahead. *Journal of Second Language Writing, 15*, 79–101.

Tardy, C. M. (2009). *Building genre knowledge*. West Lafayette, IN: Parlor Press.

Whalen, K., & Ménard, N. (1995). L1 and L2 writers' strategic and linguistic knowledge: A model of multiple-level discourse processing. *Language Learning, 45*(3), 381–418.

THE JOURNAL OF TEACHING WRITING

The *Journal of Teaching Writing* is on the Web at http://www.iupui.edu/~jtw/. Deborah Rossen Knill's essay appears in volume 26, number 1

The Journal of Teaching Writing is devoted to the teaching of writing at all academic levels, from pre-school to university, and in all subject areas of the curriculum. Our mission is to publish refereed articles that address the practices and theories that bear on our knowledge of how people learn and communicate through writing. Articles range in length from short descriptions (ten to fifteen pages) of principles or practices that offer helpful insights to longer pieces (sixteen to twenty pages) that explore topics in greater details. We ask our contributors to show a clear philosophical or theoretical basis for their ideas. An important part of our mission is to demystify the editorial review process for our contributors and to model the teaching of writing as a process of reflection and revision. Our aim is to produce the very best scholarship in writing pedagogy for our readers.

"Flow and the Principle of Relevance: Bringing our Dynamic Speaking Knowledge to Writing" by Deborah Rossen Knill

This essay was chosen because it models the kind of article that *The Journal of Teaching Writing* publishes and that our readers find particularly useful. Rossen-Knill provides a discussion of theory—i.e., the principle of relevance—and then demonstrates its practical value for teachers and students. While the theoretical discussion is clear and engaging, the emphasis of the article is on the application of relevance theory to problems of flow in written texts. I particularly liked how she draws on our linguistic abilities as speakers in presenting her approach to revising problems of flow in written texts.

7 Flow and the Principle of Relevance: Bringing Our Dynamic Speaking Knowledge to Writing

Deborah Rossen-Knill

Flow—the natural forward movement that carries the reader through the text. Readers have a strong intuitive sense of paragraph flow, and perhaps an even stronger intuitive reaction to flow interrupted. Unfortunately, our current teaching strategies around flow fall short of our intuitions because they are too static, vague, or incomplete. With the intent of complementing—not replacing—current strategies to improve paragraph flow, I offer an instructional method that is grounded in a central principle of cooperative conversation, the principle of relevance (Grice; Sperber and Wilson). The principle of relevance, most simply put, states that an utterance should be and is expected to be relevant to the surrounding conversation and to the conversants. On the surface, this principle seems obvious and unremarkable, but when operationalized and applied by students to their own and their peers' writing, it becomes an effective revision tool that draws on students' implicit knowledge of language. Grounded in how communication works in everyday conversation, the principle of relevance, once operationalized in writing, makes the dynamic process between the text and the reader visible to the writer. With their choices and the effects of their choices made visible, students can begin to shape their paragraphs in ways that are responsive both to their communicative intentions and the readers' expectations.

In addition to enhancing flow, applying the principle of relevance demonstrates for students how peers who may not be strong writers may be exceptionally helpful readers. An equalizing force in the classroom, this approach extends the notion of expertise beyond those who are considered the strongest writers to include all those who use language successfully in their daily conversation. As I hope to make clear in this paper, if students can manage everyday conversations, then they already know a great deal about language to help themselves and their peers improve text flow.

Current approaches for addressing problematic flow grow out of an attempt to match text to readers' expectations, but these approaches typically lack either sensitivity to the nuance of making meaning in writing or, borrowing a phrase from Harris, "useful specificity." Based on the idea that flow results from maintaining expected patterns, one approach encourages students to revise a paragraph or essay according to a particular rhetorical mode, such as problem-solution, cause-effect, etc. (Flower 248-49). Another common approach focuses on transition words and phrases (always a key section in handbooks) as a solution to sentence-to-sentence disfluencies. While these suggestions correspond to visible patterns we see in well-crafted writing, they are static solutions that may result in imposing a structure on a set of ideas rather than developing a structure that is integral to the writer's intended meaning. A more dynamic solution, which would no doubt draw on rhetorical patterns and transition phrases, would foreground ideas and the rewriting of ideas (Harris) in a way that responds to writing as an *act* of communication (Austin; Grice; Harris; Searle, *Speech Acts, Expresssion and Meaning*).

A less static and less structural solution to improving paragraph flow involves performing the text, that is, encouraging the writer to listen to herself or others read the text aloud and revise by ear, with or without direct input from peers (Elbow and Belanoff). The challenge here is two-fold. For the student without a "good ear," this approach lacks sufficient direction, the "useful specificity" Harris aims for in *Rewriting: How to Do Things with Texts*. The second challenge for all novice writers is learning how to manage the paradox, "The reader is always right; the writer is always right" (Elbow and Belanoff 62), particularly when there is a mismatch between the writer's and the reader's interpretation of a text. While intonation patterns are critical to making meaning in language, work in functional and rhetorical grammar is only beginning to address the sound-meaning relationship in ways that help the writing instructor and student (Hancock). Again, for teaching writing and learning to write, the immediate issue is still one of "useful specificity."

Another approach to improving paragraph flow, one which offers tremendous specificity, involves using linguistic knowledge about cohesion in spoken discourse. Based on work in linguistics (Clark and Haviland; Prince) and functional and rhetorical grammar (Gopen and Swan; Halliday, *An Introduction*; Hancock; Kolln; Noguchi; Vande Kopple; Williams), this approach includes such strategies as locating known information before new information, and placing the most important information at the end. These strategies provide powerful solutions to problematic flow, solutions that are based on easily understood and easily applied structural knowledge of reader expectations. Although these structural methods address one component of flow, the sentence-to-sentence relationship that is central to cohesion, they do not, as Williams observes, address another important component of flow, the relationships among sentences that create the sense of unity referred to as coherence. To address paragraph coherence, Williams briefly considers Grice's principle of relevance: he notes that the sentences in a paragraph must be relevant to a central point and identifies several ways in which sentences may be relevant, such as by providing "background or context," "reasons supporting a point," "evidence, facts, or data supporting a reason," and "explanation" (206-207). Ultimately, however, Williams apologizes for not being able to offer "a simple way to judge relevance, because it's so abstract a quality" (206). In fact, as I hope to illustrate in this paper, there is a productive and fairly simple way to operationalize relevance theory as articulated by Sperber and Wilson in order to test and enhance sentence connections in a way that strengthens a paragraph's idea relationships.

In developing and using an *explicit knowledge* of relevance, students can gain a working sense of how readers make meaning out of their texts and how writers can use this knowledge to enhance communication of their intended meaning(s). With both writing teachers and students in mind, I introduce relevance theory (Grice; Sperber and Wilson) as a productive means to teach meaningful and dynamic paragraph revision while offering critical insight into how communication works. To illustrate the worth of relevance theory to writing instruction, I include examples and exercises that help instructors and students draw on their implicit knowledge as speakers to test and enhance paragraph flow. The sequence of examples and exercises begins by introducing students to the idea that miscommunication is a *natural* part of communication. For students, this is a new and fundamental concept that they must understand if they are to use the relevance-based exercises effectively.

COMMUNICATION AND MISCOMMUNICATION: TWO NATURAL RESULTS OF ANY UTTERANCE

Students typically come to my college writing classes viewing miscommunication as a mistake, as communication gone wrong. Only a brief look at how people make sense of an utterance dispels this myth. Consider the following statement:

(1) The dog is up.

What might *The dog is up* mean? Without too much interpretive effort, the hearer might think it means that the dog has just stood up or has woken up. If the conversation is taking place in the living room and the speaker and hearer see the dog going toward the front door, the hearer might take (1) to mean that someone is at the door or that the dog wants to go out. Now consider another context: the speaker and hearer are still in the living room, but this time the speaker's son Billy enters the room with his fifth Teddy-Bear hamster on his shoulder, the other four having been eaten by the dog. In these circumstances, the hearer might rightly take *The dog is up* as a warning to Billy, or even as a directive that urges him to get the hamster out of the room. For one final example, consider that the speaker and hearer are once more in the speaker's living room and that the hearer is very familiar with the speaker's husband, who has a habit of going out drinking and fighting each night. Imagine that we hear from the kitchen the click of a beer can being opened, after which the speaker says, "The dog is up." It would be hard to miss the communicated insult. The important point here is that language has tremendous meaning potential (Halliday, *Explorations*), and that spoken and written utterances have the potential to mean many things (Grice; Sperber and Wilson)—including meanings that speakers and writers do not anticipate. Accordingly, the hearer/reader will always have the possibility of selecting an interpretation not intended by the speaker/writer, and the speaker/writer will always have the possibility of discovering new meanings through the effects of her writing on hearers/readers.

The interpretive possibilities of an utterance may not be in students' minds when they write. As a result, students may react to miscommunications as if they were the fault of the reader, who must have made the mistake of missing the intended meaning. This reaction relates to the mistaken belief that in communication *saying* and *meaning* are the same thing. In fact, human communication is not a coding system: it does not simply involve a speaker who codes a thought into an utterance and a hearer who decodes that utterance back into the equivalent initiating thought. Rather, human communication is a complex interpretive system (Grice; Sperber and Wilson).

The interpretative nature of communication may be quite counter intuitive to students–to all people–as speakers and hearers depend on their ability to use language quickly and habitually. If speakers stopped to reflect on how each utterance might be received, they might never get further than wondering how to best order a cup of coffee, and if hearers stopped to work out all possible meanings, it would be an awfully long wait for that coffee. As naturally non-reflective language users, students need several examples to develop a working understanding of how utterances can mean many things. After working through an example similar to *The dog is up,* I typically ask students to work through two additional examples. The first addresses the *say = mean* myth: I write the word *green* on the board and ask each student to privately write down the name of an object in the world that corresponds to this color. Typical responses include grass, pea soup, seawater, etc. Students and I then discuss how differently we each imagine this one simple color and how difficult it is to create in another's mind the precise thought in our own minds.

The second exercise that teaches how communication works asks students to generate possible interpretations of an utterance similar to *The dog is up.* I stipulate a kind of generic room as the context and offer the utterance *It's cold in here,* but any utterance with an obvious explicit interpretation will do. I then ask each student to make a private note of what this text might mean. By now, they understand the concept and begin to have fun. In addition to offering up such possibilities as the literal meaning and requests to turn up the heat or close windows or doors, they imagine that it might be a spurned woman's response to a man or an indirect request for intimacy. Most importantly, they look to each other for the novel interpretations because they have now internalized the idea that what they say will have not only expected, but also unexpected interpretations. My goal, ultimately, is to help students see that communicating effectively is truly an exciting and interesting problem.

Understanding that every utterance has the potential to mean many things shapes one's understanding of miscommunication: miscommunication is a *natural* and *expected* part of communication–*not* a mistake that can be done away with (Dascal). Consequently, the job of the communicator is not to simply do away with mistakes, not simply to correct a text, but something more complicated, more interesting. The communicator's job is to maximize the possibility of successful interpretation and minimize the possibility of misinterpretation. With respect to *The dog is up*, this means that the speaker must do her best to control the communication so that her intended interpretation matches the hearer's first interpretation. She and the hearer must, as much as possible, *expect* the same interpretation. To this end, the writer would work to control the likelihood of the hearer picking out–among the many possible interpretations–the most *relevant* interpretation(s), what we may think of as the "primary intention" of the speaker (Grice 221).

Relevance

In daily conversations, communicators regularly produce and identify the *relevant* interpretation necessary to productive conversations, and without any apparent effort they sense problems with relevance. In fact, people are enormously sensitive to relevance in speaking, and work hard to maintain it. Consider this next example, which also forms the basis of a classroom exercise.

(2) Student: I'd love a cup of coffee.

Teacher: It's raining outside.

To introduce the idea of relevance, I ask a student to say to me, *I'd love a cup of coffee*, after which I reply, *It's raining outside*. I then ask the students what my response means. They offer such interpretations as *It'll be hard to get a cup of coffee because getting the coffee requires going outside and it's raining outside*. It is not trivial that the students can come up with an interpretation, that they have in fact worked out a way to make my response to *I'd love a cup of coffee* relevant. This ability raises several questions: Why do communicators work to identify the relevant interpretation? How does one define relevance, and how do hearers come to the relevant interpretation? Most important to the writing classroom, how does one tap into this conversational ability to help students enhance relatedness (and therefore connectedness) between sentences? Grice's and Sperber and Wilson's discussions of relevance offer some productive answers to each of these questions.

Why do communicators work so hard to identify the relevant information?

Relevance is a fundamental expectation in communication between two rational people (Grice; Sperber and Wilson). Communicators work hard to identify relevant information because they expect to find relevance. Although speakers and hearers generally interact without any conscious awareness of the principle of relevance, they quickly feel its power when they struggle to understand something that at first seems puzzling. Imagine, for example, encountering a friend who is apparently babbling. Unless you decide that your friend is irrational, you work hard to figure out what she has to say because you *presume* that she is trying to convey some relevant message. The presumption of relevance also underlies the ability to work out jokes, such as the following: "How do we know that the Earth won't come to an end? Because it's round! ("Clean Jokes") In fact, jokes not only offer a genre-based demonstration of how hearers work hard to find relevance, but also show that making it difficult for hearers to work out relevance can meet communicative goals and result in enjoyable and productive interactions.

To help students understand the expectation of relevance in written communication, I recommend the following exercise: secretly ask half of the students to each write a short meaningless poem and then present these poems to the other half for interpretation. Typically, students find meaning. In fact, it's quite difficult to avoid finding meaning, an observation that leads the class to consider why one can work out a meaningful message even when none is intended. Through such exercises, as well as examples of jokes and metaphors, students discover that hearers can't help but search for relevance, that in communication, people presume relevance (Sperber and Wilson). The presumption of relevance results from the nature of communication itself. In communication, the speaker intends to produce some effect in the hearer by uttering something, such as when *Please close the window* is used to get someone to close a window. In communication, the speaker also intends for the hearer to recognize the intent to communicate, that is, to recognize that the utterance is not, for example, mere noise, but rather something meant to be attended to by the hearer. In addition, the speaker intends for the utterance to contribute to creating the desired effect in the hearer (Sperber and Wilson, 23, 156). As a result of these communicative intentions, the hearer, who has experience as a speaker and a hearer and so understands these communicative intentions, infers that when a speaker says something, it is purposeful. Sperber and Wilson further suggest that the hearer would believe that the communication is not only purposeful, but potentially useful to the speaker, hearer, or both (155). Thus, hearers infer that an act of communication directed at them will be somehow relevant to them. More generally, this presumption of relevance may perhaps be explained as a reflection of the social nature of human beings, and by extension, the social function of language for humans (Halliday, *Explorations*) and the idea that communication is motivated and directed by interactants' goals, whether these be shared goals (Grice) or distinct individual goals (Rossen-Knill; Sperber and Wilson 161-62).

What is relevance?

Sperber and Wilson formalize relevance as a balance between the cognitive gain and the processing effort involved in interpreting an utterance. They offer the following comparative definition:

> Relevance to an individual
>
> *Extant condition 1*: An assumption is relevant to an individual to the extent that the positive cognitive effects achieved when it is optimally processed are large.
>
> *Extant condition 2*: An assumption is relevant to an individual to the extent that the effort required to achieve these positive cognitive effects is small. (265)

Essentially, the *greater* the worth of the interpretation to the hearer, the *stronger* the relevance; the *smaller* the processing effort, the *stronger* the relevance. As this comparative definition indicates, all utterances have *degrees* of relevance in communication, degrees that depend on the cognitive effect on the hearer, as well as on the amount of effort required to understand the communication. For a communication to be relevant, it must produce "cognitive gains" in the reader, that is, changes in the reader's beliefs that "contribut[e] positively to the fulfillment of [his/her] cognitive functions or goals" (Sperber and Wilson 265). As Pilkington explains, these changes occur when new information in the text interacts with the reader's current beliefs "by causing a relatively weakly held existing assumption to be strengthened, by contradicting and eliminating an existing assumption, or by combining with an existing assumption to yield a contextual implication" (158). The concept of cognitive gain has particular significance for writers and writing instructors, as it suggests that the effectiveness of writing that is meant to function as an act of communication must be measured at least in part by the extent to which it changes the reader's beliefs.

The comparative definition of relevance also helps one understand why flow matters: a high degree of flow minimizes processing effort, whereas a low degree of flow increases processing effort. Consider these next examples, in which processing effort varies. For each example, the accessible contexts for interpretation and the intended message are as equal as possible.

(3) John: Dinner will be ready at 6.

Sue: Sally won't make it to dinner because she's at soccer practice, and soccer practice continues through our dinnertime, and she will stay until the end of soccer practice.

(4) John: Dinner will be ready at 6.

Sue: Sally is at soccer.

In (3), to communicate that Sally will not be at dinner, Sue offers a lengthy response that is highly informative in an explicit way. In (4), to communicate the same message, Sue offers a relatively brief utterance. Which utterance has the higher degree of relevance depends on how much information John needs to easily receive the message that Sally will not be home for dinner. If John can quickly and easily infer the intended message from (4), then the lengthy response in (3) will require excessive effort and thus have the lower degree of relevance. If, however, John doesn't easily understand what Sally's being at soccer before dinner has to do with her being home during dinner, then (4) will require more effort for him to work out than (3), in which case (4) would have the lower degree of relevance. Ultimately, a speaker's (and writer's) structural and informational choices influence how hard the hearer (and reader) must work to figure out the relevance of an utterance. Working out the degree of relevance requires working through the text's actual effect on the receiver—hence the need for readers during the writing process.

As (3) and (4) illustrate, one cannot measure an isolated text's relevance, nor can one assign an abstract or absolute relevance value to a text. By definition, a text's relevance depends on how it is received in communication, on the balance between processing effort and cognitive gain for the hearer/reader. This accounts for the possibility of strong relevance for texts whose interpretations require quite different degrees of effort to understand. On the one hand, a newspaper article might be judged highly relevant because it required minimal processing effort from a reader and led to significant cognitive gains by providing substantial new information about an event of concern to the reader. On the other hand, a text such as a poem, a joke, or, for an extreme example, Joyce's *Ulysses* might require a relatively high degree of effort but still be judged highly relevant because the cognitive gain is exceptionally high. Even though a reader might, for example, find it frustratingly difficult to work out the meaning of a poem on death, he or she may ultimately work out multiple possible meanings that together offer a particularly rich interpretation. In such cases the high degree of cognitive gain may significantly offset the processing effort. Thus, despite the high degree of effort, the poem may be judged to have a high degree of relevance. To offer another example of the way in which the balance between effort and gain determines the degree of relevance, consider an easily understood text that is laden with repetition that does not lead to cognitive gain. Even though the text requires little effort to understand, it would be judged irrelevant because it provided no cognitive gain. As these examples suggest, maximizing relevance is not simply a matter of making the text as explicit and transparent as possible; nor is it simply a matter of incorporating content that is highly worthwhile to the reader. The principle of relevance reinforces the idea that form and meaning work together to bring about a relevant message. Furthermore, it is not the case that any degree of relevance is sufficient. Rather, the hearer or reader expects that the received message will be worth the processing effort, that the speaker or writer has done her best to reach the highest level of relevance (270-271). When students realize that readers expect optimally relevant texts, and that "optimally relevant" will vary with audience, then they will have a reader-based reason to revise.

How do we come to a relevant interpretation?

The process of identifying the relevant interpretation depends on the assumption that people have intuitions about the worth of one interpretation or another. In accordance with minimizing processing effort, hearers select the first relevant interpretation that comes to mind.

An example and discussion from Sperber and Wilson illustrate this point (163-70):

> (5) George has a big cat. (168)

The utterance in (5) prompts the hearer to make a hypothesis about the likely interpretation based on information in the utterance itself and related inferences, as well as encyclopedic knowledge and related inferences. For (5), a first interpretation might be something like, "'George owns a large house cat.'" If the interpretive hypothesis seems to be the "optimally relevant" message from the speaker, then the hearer assumes that this is the intended relevant interpretation and does not pursue other interpretations. If a first interpretation does not seem appropriate or sufficient, then the hearer repeats the process, expending more effort, and formulates the next available interpretation. A second order interpretation might be something like, "George has a tiger, a lion, a jaguar, etc." (168).[1] The critical point for the student is that a hearer or reader does not immediately and indiscriminately generate many interpretations. Imagine how impossible communication would be under such circumstances! Rather, she selects and limits interpretations according to the principle of relevance.

In fact, the hearer begins to formulate interpretations and expectations for subsequent utterances *while she is receiving* an utterance, as the following exercise demonstrates (based on example from Sperber and Wilson (190)). For this exercise, give half of the class statement 1 and half statement 2. Do not let each group know the other group's statement or that more than one statement was distributed.

> Statement 1. Your team is disqualified from the baseball game.
> Statement 2. We have chosen John's mouse for the breeding experiment.

Next, ask each group to write down what object "bat" refers to in the statement, "Peter's bat is too grey." Also ask students to briefly describe or draw the "bat" (what does it feel like? look like?). Alternatively, students can draw a picture of the bat. Finally, let each group present its answers to the other group. Students are typically surprised to discover that there are two kinds of bats: one furry and grey, the other made of wood or aluminum. The important point for discussion is that the moment a speaker produces an utterance, the hearer begins forming assumptions about the meaning of that utterance and what will come next. Transferring this observation to writing can help our students view a paragraph as dialogue involving sentences. As such, each sentence is in dialogue with the subsequent sentence and with the reader. Each sentence causes the reader to develop expectations about relevant information in the subsequent sentence.

How can we tap into our conversational ability to identify relevance in order to help students improve the flow of their writing?

Students' conversational sense of relevance may be activated in written contexts if a written text is presented to them as a kind of conversation. In written text, the sentence may be viewed as the counterpart to the utterance. Accordingly, each sentence in a paragraph is in dialogue with the subsequent sentence, by virtue of their structural proximity. In addition, each sentence is in dialogue with the reader. As is true with two utterances constituting a dialogue, each sentence creates in the reader expectations for relevance, which the subsequent sentence is expected to fulfill. This model may be operationalized with the help of two observations: "A statement often raises a relevant question," and "[A] relevant question is a question the answer to which is certain or likely to be relevant" (Sperber and Wilson 207). I explain it this way to students: according to the principle of relevance, a writer (producing a sentence with the intention to communicate) aims to convey a message that the reader considers worthwhile, given the effort the reader must expend in order to understand it as intended by the writer. The reader, based on her comprehension of the sentence, is primed for a highly relevant subsequent sentence and can anticipate what will likely fulfill this relevance expectation. The moment a reader receives the writer's text, he begins formulating relevance expectations–assumptions, often question-based assumptions, about what will come next. The better the writer's text meets the reader's relevance expectations, the better the text's flow.

Relevance Exercises for the Classroom

Ultimately, students must experience the effect of relevance in writing in order to understand it and use it in their own revision process. The next sequence of exercises is designed to show students the role of relevance in a well-written text, in a problematic text, and finally, in their own texts and revision process.

1. Read aloud the first sentence of a well-written body paragraph. Ask students to jot down the first questions that come to mind, or if it's easier for them, a statement about what they expect the next sentence will be about.
2. Read aloud the second sentence (what might be called the *responding sentence*) of the well-written paragraph. It should answer or come close to answering the students' jotted-down questions, or come close to matching students' statements about what will come next.
3. Repeat the process in steps 1 and 2, beginning this time with the last sentence discussed, that is, using the responding sentence as the initiating sentence.

For comparison's sake, repeat this exercise with a text that does not have a sense of flow or connectedness. In this case, some of the responding sentences will probably fail to meet the expectations generated in readers by the initiating sentences.

Importantly, students should not look for an exact match between the reader's expectation and the writer's text, and they should discuss why an exact match is not predicted: communication is an inference-based system, making it probable that readers will work out different meanings. Success in communication is a relative measure, with our primary goal being to control as well as we can the match between the intended message and the received message. With this probabilistic view of communication, students can feel successful when the writer's second sentence is a close match to the reader's expectations for relevance.

Once students have grasped how to bring their speaking knowledge of relevance to their writing, they can work through the last in this sequence of exercises on relevance. This exercise enables them to see how their writing matches the relevance expectations of their readers, thus supporting the central classroom-based peer response goal of making the audience a real and purposeful presence for writers (Gere).

Using Implicit Knowledge of Relevance in Peer Review Groups

This exercise works best with groups of three or four. With a group of four, the writer can learn how often and how easily her text meets the readers' expectations for relevance.

1. The writer reads or shows only the first sentence of a body paragraph to group members (don't let group members see sen-

tences other than sentence 1). The writer asks group members to jot down a question that quickly comes to mind (or a statement about what will come next).

2. The writer shares sentence 2, and the group considers if this second sentence meets the readers' expectations: does it answer the question (measure of worth)? Can the reader easily find the answer to her question (measure of effort)? The goal is not to look for an exact match, but to consider if the writer's second sentence generally matches the readers' sense of what the sentence is likely to be about.

   a. If the answers to the questions in step 2 are "yes," move on by repeating step 1, now with the writer reading sentence 2 aloud and the readers/listeners jotting down their first expectations for sentence 3 (and so on).

   b. If the answers to the questions in 2 are "no," circle the unexpected, and underline the expected (if present). Then revise. Sometimes I simply let my students try to fix this on their own, suggesting only that they begin by considering three very general structural changes: revise or delete sentence 1; revise or delete sentence 2; or insert sentence(s) between sentence 1 and 2. Alternatively, one might provide additional suggestions of the kind in the Appendix, but the danger here is that students will use the suggestions too prescriptively, inadvertently ignoring the writer's purpose and interest in her project.

While I present this last relevance exercise as a peer-response activity, I often use it in conferences with my students. To demonstrate how the relevance exercise works in a real situation, I offer as an example Ian Stanley's experience.[2] Ian Stanley, a past student in my "Advanced Writing and Peer Tutoring" course, met with me to discuss an early draft of his essay, "On the Importance of Personal Pronouns," which relates how he overcame the harmful effect of pre-college writing assignments that prohibited the use of personal pronouns. During this conference, we went through the relevance exercise for the following excerpt (for reference, I've labeled each sentence in bold: S1, S2, etc.; comments in italics are Ian's notes to himself that were inserted after our conference.):

   S1 "Avoid and ignore absolutes," Valerie suggested as I had failed time and again at articulating direction in my essays. **S2** Baffled by the philosophical nature of Valerie's statement, I initially ignored its potential value to myself as both a writer and orator. S3 Eventually, however, I came to terms that my writing is weak, and that, more importantly, there will always—even if I attain advanced degrees in composition or related fields—be room for improvement. *Does this link nicely???* S4 If ideas are not modifiable, the potential worth of ideas would be ignored, and inventions that stem from previous ideas may not have come into being. S5 If the light bulb were not able to be modified from its original usage, would we have LCD televisions? S6 If the invention of the typewriter prevented the introduction of any other word processing machine into society, would we have the computer as we now know it? S7 Written ideas are no different: Jung's theory on child development would be nonexistent if Freud's theory (from which Jung based a lot of his initial claims) was set in stone.

S8 A launching pad for completing my first college research paper was formed when I came to realize this "family tree" structure of academia. S9 More importantly, however, modifiability of thoughts illuminated that what I have to say does indeed matter, whether or not I use a first, second, or third person perspective. Writing should not merely be about regurgitating answers within strict boundaries. Instead, writing is about modifying previous ideas and offering one's own interpretation or suggestion for improvement of an idea. This realization became lucid as I was faced with the challenge of completing my first college research paper.

In keeping with the exercise Instructions, Ian read one sentence at a time without seeing the subsequent sentence. After reading S1, Ian said that he might expect "more about a specific essay," "elaborat[ion] on the advice 'avoid and ignore absolutes,' or some discussion of 'how I integrated the advice into essays.'"[3] Ian and I then read S2 and observed that it did respond to the expectation about integrating advice into his essays. Specifically, S2 indicates that he did not use this advice because he was "baffled" by it. Ian then read S2 again and noted that it led him to expect a specific example of what his writing was like before and after receiving his stepmother's advice. S3 did not meet his exact expectation, but rather addressed it very generally. We then moved onto reading S3 to see what it led us to expect in S4. In this case, there was a serious mismatch—one that warranted a significant revision. After Ian read S3, he said, "Now that I've come to terms that my writing is weak, I wonder what will happen next with my writing."

S4 did not fulfill Ian's (or my) expectations for continuing the conversation; instead, it shifted to a discussion about ideas being modifiable.

As we continued working through the paragraph to discover how relevant one sentence's response was to the preceding sentence, Ian discovered another serious coherence problem between S8 and S9. After reading S8, he wondered, "what's this family tree structure?" and indicated that he might want "more about the first college research paper." Instead, he encountered a sentence about the modifiability of ideas—clearly an important theme in the essay, but one that was not integrated coherently into this paragraph.

In addition to discovering sentence-to-sentence problems, as his italicized comments to himself indicate, Ian discovered a paragraph-to-paragraph problem. The first sentence of the second paragraph failed to meet the expectations set up by the end of paragraph one. As he explained after reading S7, he expected something about "experience being set in stone and relating that to my experience," although he added that he wasn't sure about this. In this case, he not only felt that his expectations were not met, but also that they were not clearly established. Because his sentences and paragraphs did not relate sufficiently well to one another, they did not create a coherent dialogue.

At this point in the conference, I left these paragraphs for Ian to rewrite on his own. To revise for enhanced flow, Ian had several possible approaches, as explained generally in the Appendix and exemplified here with reference to S3 and S4. Specifically, he could revise S3 (and possibly preceding sentences) so that it led readers to expect S4; he could alter S4 (and perhaps subsequent sentences) if he felt that he wanted to fulfill the expectations originally established in S3; or he could see if deleting either of these sentences would address the problem (is S5 a momentary tangent, or does it lead the paragraph into a new focus, a new conversation?). Alternatively, if Ian felt that there were an unstated connection between S3 and S4, he could develop and articulate this connection and insert new text between S3 and S4.

Ian tried a few different approaches. He first revised the paragraph by inserting a new sentence between S3 and S4, resulting in the following three-sentence sequence:

S3 Eventually, however, I came to terms that my writing is weak, and that, more importantly, there will always—even if I attain advanced degrees in composition or related fields—be room for improvement. S3A Avoiding absolutes is important because absolutes reject the modifiability of ideas. S4 If ideas are not modifiable, the potential worth of ideas would be ignored, and inventions that stem from previous ideas may not come into being.

The new sentence's "Avoiding absolutes" did echo S1's "'Avoid and ignore absolutes'" and so build on the expectation to explain this phrase; however, S3 and S3A were not interacting with optimal relevance. S3A still failed to meet the question S3 raised for Ian: what happened next with Ian's writing? Two themes (a discussion of Ian's writing, and a discussion of the nature of ideas) continued to compete for this paragraph's focus and so disrupted the paragraph's flow.

Ian recognized that a disconnect still remained and revised again, this time by deleting S3 and the associated S2, fleshing out the ideas in S3A and S4, and then relating the discussion of ideas to writing an essay:

> As I failed time and again at formulating direction in an essay during my freshman year of college, my stepmother, Valerie, offered me this ironic advice: "Avoid and ignore absolutes". Avoiding absolutes is important because absolutes reject the modifiability of ideas. If ideas are not modifiable, the potential worth of ideas would be ignored, and inventions that stem from previous ideas may not come into being. If the light bulb were not able to be modified from its original usage, would we have LCD televisions? If the invention of the typewriter prevented the introduction of any other word processing machine into society, would we have the computer as we now know it? Written ideas are no different: Jung's theory on child development would be nonexistent if Freud's theory (from which Jung based a lot of his initial claims) was set in stone. The fact that ideas branch off of one another, and that ideas are malleable, highlights how one can infuse one's own ideas into preexisting ideas. Essays, then, are generally not about regurgitating a previous answer; rather, they are about positing a new question, and attempting to answer that question. This realization became lucid as I was faced with the challenge of completing my first college research paper.
>
> I chose to research the implications of anonymity on the recovery movement. Initially, I had suspected I would conform to the mainstream view that anonymity is essential to the success of the recovery movement, and that, although public funding is necessary to advance health care for re-

covering addicts, it must be achieved without putting a face on the recovery movement. Through a reassessment of my stance, and hence my thesis, emerged a paper that came to be titled: *The Necessities of Surmounting Anonymity in Drug and Alcohol Recovery Programs.* This reassessment is testament to the influence that Valerie's mantra to "avoid and ignore absolutes" had on my writing. Had I not come to understand the modifiability of ideas, I may not have come to challenge mainstream views.

As evidenced by the above excerpt, Ian also addressed the coherence problems between paragraphs and within paragraph two. Importantly, to complete the revision, Ian did not rely only on the relevance exercise. Once he revised so that sentences were relevant to one another, he revised again for cohesion using the given-new expectation (Clark and Haviland; Gopen and Swan; Halliday, *An Introduction*; Hancock; Kolln; Noguchi; Prince; Vande Kopple; Williams).

From this interactive relevance exercise, the writer ideally experiences the reader (who can be the writer him/herself) as a thinking individual who continuously processes information and formulates expectations about what will come next in a text. In the example with Ian, the relevance exercise enabled the writer himself to experience his own paper as a reader.

While the reader has an active role in the writer/reader communication, much of the onus for successful communication rests on the writer, who must maximize the possibility that the reader will receive her intended message as optimally relevant. Such control requires that the writer be aware of the unfolding potential meanings (intended and unintended) of her text and anticipate the readers' expectations for relevance. This "writer-responsible" model of written communication is, however, a cultural construct: across cultures, rhetorical patterns and expectations vary according to how much responsibility they locate with the writer and reader (Leki 90). Relevance theory has the potential to reveal such differences in how people construct meaning in and from texts. In addition, because the relevance exercise is based on what all proficient speakers implicitly know, it has the potential to be an equalizing force in the classroom.

The large majority of students communicate successfully in their day-to-day lives. Drawing on their implicit knowledge as speakers and hearers, they can build on their strengths as speakers and hearers, on their established expertise as language users. While students may express concerns about their peers' ability to "correct their writing"—a teacher's job, some will say—they do not typically criticize their peers' ability to hold an everyday conversation. And it is precisely this ability to converse successfully—not the ability to write—that serves as the knowledge base for the successful peer review. However, even though speakers and hearers share an implicit understanding of the principle of relevance, their diverse language backgrounds, their particular language and cultural histories (Toolan 162), may lead to unanticipated differences in relevance expectations among readers or between the writer and reader. If these differences are welcomed and considered in the classroom, then all students are offered an opportunity to gain a culturally-sensitive understanding of how audience expectations interact with the writer's text to create meaning.

In discussing how different language backgrounds affect expectations for textual coherence, Leki explains,

> In reading any text, the reader is to some extent called upon to make inferential bridges among the propositions of the text based on the reader's own knowledge of the world. . . . To the extent that members of different cultures do not share the same collective knowledge and experience, the non-native writer may miscalculate the ability of the native reader to construct these inferential bridges.[4] (Leki 93)

Leki offers examples of how student writers experience these different cultural expectations around producing writing that asks for the appropriate amount of inferencing from the reader. One graduate student from the People's Republic of China says, "'It seems that we need a conclusion in English, but we often leave it [off] to let people think when we write in Chinese. We must explain things more clearly and exactly for Americans'" (Matalene qtd. in Leki, 96). Such a writer, who may understand the abstract suggestion to be more explicit, might benefit from concrete feedback that reveals precisely what questions or expectations his/her text raises for a set of readers. Describing other cultural perspectives on writing, Leki observes that "Arabic rhetoric encourages the ability to find another way to say the same thing" (99-100), a tendency that would likely be viewed by those from some other cultures as "exaggerated and excessively assertive" (100). Revealing these differences can have a positive outcome, with two qualifications. First, writing instructors must be committed to inclusive classroom discussions.[5] Specifically, instructors and students might discuss mismatches in expectations and explicitly work out how a particular sentence might yield different responses from audiences with different backgrounds. Such a discussion might emphasize for writers the need to identify and then work out how to write to a specified audience. Without such discussions, the "different" expectations might be ignored, or worse, "corrected." Second, both the writer and reader must proceed with the following paradox in the foreground: "The reader is always right; the writer is always right" (Elbow and Belanoff 62). Within an inclusive classroom and guided by Elbow and Belanoff's paradox, students can use unexpected misalignments in writers' and readers' expectations as an opportunity to discuss how differences in language-background affect how we create meaning in and from texts,[6] and how these differences shape our decisions as writers. Such dialogue supports writing instructors' goals of helping students make informed decisions about how to revise their texts for particular audiences in our increasingly global and diverse communication contexts.

While this paper grows out of work in language philosophy (Grice) and cognitive science (Sperber and Wilson), the resulting strategy–an operationalized principle of relevance–is easy to implement and is based in what students already know. Students know "[h]ow to do things with words" (Austin) quite intuitively from their daily experience as speakers, regularly making choices at all levels of language use to bring about desired ends, whether this be to borrow a car, convince a friend to go to the movies, or get help from a professor. This is not to suggest that all aspects of speaking and listening transfer productively to writing and reading, nor that the principle of relevance can account fully (or even in good part) for a well-crafted paragraph. However, students can make great progress in writing by using their implicit knowledge of relevance to test and enhance paragraph flow. Bringing their implicit knowledge of relevance to explicit awareness further helps them understand that writing is an interesting problem, one that changes with each text and each intended audience. Students can draw on the principle of relevance to make choices about their writing based not only on their intended meaning, but also on how well their particular choices meet readers' expectation for relevance. Ultimately, whichever structure or piece of information a writer chooses, however the writer orders constituents, the parts work together to communicate an idea that requires *more or less effort* to interpret and has *more or less* positive effect on the reader. While focused on the reader, however, the writer must never lose sight of her reason for writing or her intended message. Throughout the peer review process, the writer's intended purpose must figure centrally in the discussion about how to align the writer's intended message with reader expectations. Otherwise, the resulting paragraph will fail to communicate the writer's intentions, and thus fail as a communicative text. A conscious awareness of relevance provides students with a real working sense of how readers make meaning out of their words, and how writers can use this knowledge to enhance communication of their intended meaning. Thus, by managing and maintaining relevance, students begin to manage and maintain paragraph flow.

NOTES

1 Sperber and Wilson further explain that the indeterminacy of this statement (is it a tiger, lion, jaguar, some other big cat?) may, depending on the context, require excessive processing effort (168). If the hearer did not know the type of cat and the speaker did, a more relevant utterance might have specified the type of big cat (168).

2 Special thanks to Ian Stanley for allowing me to use excerpts from his drafts and our conversations.

3 Ian's comments are from a conference that sought to recreate our first conference, nearly a year ago, on this same draft. While Ian's drafts included notes based on our conferences, I did not have transcripts from these conferences and did not want to construct his responses based only on his notes and our memories. For this reason, Ian and I went through the relevance exercise again on an unmarked early draft so that I could present his account of what his sentences led him to expect. His responses resulted in his identifying the same flow problems that he had identified during our first conference.

4 And vice versa: similarly, the native speaker may well miscalculate the non-native speaker's expectations around constructing inferences.

5 For language-diversity pedagogies and related classroom practices, see the *Journal of Teaching Writing*, Volume 21.1 & 2.

6 See, for example, Anne Johns's article, which draws on schema theory to explain how ESOL students come to the revision process with quite different expectations than those of their English-speaking counterparts.

WORKS CITED

Austin, J.L. *How to Do Things with Words*. Ed. J. O. Urmson and Marina Sbisa. 2nd ed. Cambridge, MA: Harvard UP, 1975. Print.

Clark, Herbert H., and Susan E. Haviland. "Comprehension and the Given-New Contract." *Discourse Production and Comprehension*. Ed. Roy O. Freedle. Norwood: Ablex, 1977. 1-40. Print.

"Clean Jokes: Silly Collection 02." *AhaJokes.com*. Aha! Jokes LLC, 2010. Web. 15 Feb. 2011.

Dascal, Marcelo. "Searle on Conversation and Structure." *(On) Searle on Conversation*. Amsterdam: Benjamins, 1992. 35-56. Print.
Elbow, Peter, and Pat Belanoff. *Sharing and Responding*. New York: Random House, 1989. Print.
Flower, Linda. *Problem Solving Strategies for Writing*. 3rd ed. San Diego: Harcourt, 1981. Print.
Gere, Anne Ruggles. *Writing Groups: History, Theory, and Impications*. Carbondale: Southern Illinois UP, 1987. Print.
Gopen, George D., and Judith A. Swan. "The Science of Scientific Writing." *American Scientist* 78 (1990): 550-558. Print.
Grice, Paul. *Studies in the Way of Words*. vols. Cambridge: Harvard UP, 1989. 22-40, 117-137. Print.
Halliday, M.A.K., and Christian M. I. M. Matthiessen. *An Introduction to Functional Grammar*. London: Arnold, 1985. Print.
—. *Explorations in the Functions of Language*. New York: Elsevier, 1977. Print.
Hancock, Craig. *Meaning-Centered Grammar: An Introductory Text*. London: Equinox, 2005. Print.
Harris, Joseph. *Rewriting: How to Do Things with Texts*. Logan: Utah State UP, 2006. Print.
Johns, Anne. "The ESL Student and the Revision Process: Some Insights from Schema Theory." *Journal of Basic Writing* 5.2 (Fall 1986): 70-80. Print.
Kolln, Martha. *Rhetorical Grammar: Grammatical Choices, Rhetorical Effects*. 5th ed. New York: Pearson, 2007. Print.
Leki, Ilona. "Contrastive Rhetoric." *Undestanding ESL Writers: A Guide for Teachers*. Portsmouth: Boynton/Cook, 1992. 88-104. Print.
Noguchi, Rei R. *Grammar and the Teaching of Writing: Limits and Possibilities*. Urbana: NCTE, 1991. Print.
Pilkington, Adrian. "Introduction: Relevance Theory and Literary Style." *Language and Literature* 5.3 (1996): 157-162. Print.
Prince, Ellen. "Toward a Taxonomy of Given-New Information." *Radical Pragmatics*. Ed. Peter Cole. New York: Academic Press, 1981. 223-55. Print.
Searle, John R. *Expresssion and Meaning: Studies in the Theory of Speech Acts*. Cambridge: Cambridge UP, 1979. Print.
—. *Speech Acts*. Cambridge: Cambridge UP, 1969. Print.
Sperber, Dan, and Diedre Wilson. *Relevance: Communication and Cognition*. 2nd ed. Malden, MA: Blackwell, 1995. Print.
Toolan, Michael. "On Relevance Theory." *New Departures in Linguistics*. Ed. George Wolf. New York: Garland Publishing, 1992. 146-62. Print.
Vande Kopple, William. *Clear and Coherent Prose*. Glenview: Scott, Foresman and Company, 1989. Print.
Williams, Joseph M. *Style: Ten Lessons in Clarity and Grace*. 8th ed. New York: Longman, 2005. Print.

Appendix: Trouble-Shooting for Relevance Problems

Some Possible Problems Suggested by Sperber and Wilson (143), along with Some Solutions

Problem: sentence 2 doesn't add anything for the reader, either in terms of information or attitude.
Solutions: delete sentence 1 or 2.

Problem: reader can work out the relevance to sentence 1, but has to work very hard.
Solutions:
    a. decide that the effort is meaningful and purposeful and that there is not a better way to communicate the intended meaning.
    b. revise sentence 1 and/or 2; add extra sentences before or after sentence 1. Consider changes in structure (e.g., location of given, new, and important information); reduce set of possible interpretations by using more precise words or enlarge possible set by using more general terms; delete misleading information in sentence 1 or unexpected information in sentence 2; locate primary information in main clauses rather than phrases.

Problem: reader can't work out relevance to sentence 1; but writer believes it exists.
Solutions: have writer explain the connection, and then consider the following possibilities:
    a. make inference chain between sentence 1 and 2 explicit (this may involve, for example, including critical background information, articulating assumptions or definitions, explicitly stating an implied idea in sentence 1; Williams's list of ways in which ideas may relate to one another may prove helpful in argumentative writing (206-207).
    b. relocate sentence 1 or 2 to another place in the paper; or
    c. delete sentence 1 or 2.

JOURNAL OF WRITING RESEARCH

The *Journal of Writing Research* is on the Web at http://jowr.org/

The *Journal of Writing Research* is an international peer reviewed journal that publishes high quality theoretical, empirical, and review papers covering the broad spectrum of writing research. The journal is inherently cross-disciplinary, publishing original research in the different domains of writing research. We aim to report state-of-the art research and to provide a forum for both established experts and emerging talent. The Journal of Writing Research is concerned with multiple perspectives on writing and acts as a reference for all those interested in the basics of writing processes and knowledge of written composition.

Writing in Natural Sciences: Understanding the Effects of Different Types of Reviewers on the Writing Process by Melissa M. Patchan, Christian D. Schunn, and Russell J. Clark. *Journal of Writing Research* 2(3), 365-393

JoWR publishes both basic and more applied research, always with a strong emphasis on the processes by which text is produced and on methodological rigour in how these processes are explored. This paper addresses a question that has direct application to writing instruction – what difference does it make whether students write reports for peers or for teaching assistants – and sets about answering it by means of robust experimental methods and measures. The authors present a well-evidenced, detailed and nuanced account of the interaction between perceived audience for a text and the processes by which it is produced.

8 Writing in Natural Sciences: Understanding the Effects of Different Types of Reviewers on the Writing Process

Melissa M. Patchan, Christian D. Schunn, and Russell J. Clark

During the 1960s, academics began to see the importance of writing as pedagogy for enhancing learning, which developed into the Writing Across the Curriculum (WAC) and Writing in the Discipline (WID) movements (for a review, see Ochsner & Fowler, 2004). WAC aimed at students in their first two years of college with a focus on enhancing students' general knowledge. By contrast, WID aimed at students in their final two years and to refine their disciplinary knowledge—that is, the knowledge of how to read and write within their discipline. This disciplinary knowledge comprises subject matter knowledge as well as genre knowledge (Bazerman, 2008; Prior, 2006). The current study questions how well the typical WID environment supports its writing learning goals.

In a number of countries, including the US, two methods are frequently used for evaluating writing in undergraduate natural science courses: either a graduate student teaching assistant (TA) assigned to teach the course provides feedback on writing or a peer-review process is used in which the students grade and provide feedback to one another. We chose a context (i.e., large undergraduate introductory physics course) that typifies the common problem of incorporating writing in courses with high enrollment numbers and overloaded TAs. The contrasting methods for feedback in this setting are especially interesting because each method appears to emphasize different types of knowledge that are both necessary for writing. Across these methods, it is important to examine whether students are receiving sufficient writing instruction that balances the various core types of knowledge critical for writing success.

Several types of knowledge critical to effective writing have been identified—including discourse community knowledge, subject matter knowledge, genre knowledge, rhetorical knowledge, and writing process knowledge (Beaufort, 2004). Further, as Beaufort noted, each type of knowledge is likely to overlap with the other types of knowledge. Thus, there is no clear demarcation between what demonstrates subject matter knowledge and what demonstrates genre knowledge. That is, it is very hard to examine all writing moves or pieces of feedback on writing and categorize each clearly and uniquely in a single type of knowledge. However, the lack of clear lines of demarcation does not mean these distinctions are meaningless. Individuals receive training that focus on different types of knowledge, which produces different skill levels and possibly different values being placed on the relative importance of the types of knowledge.

For example, graduate students in physics would have developed considerable knowledge of physics content (e.g., which questions are important, how experiments are setup, how analyses are done) and some genre knowledge specific to writing in physics (e.g., from reading articles). In contrast, they would have relatively little rhetorical knowledge and knowledge about the writing process because they likely received little writing instruction and few opportunities to practice as writers. Further, they might have received feedback on writing that focused primarily in factual errors of the subject matter. For many of natural science courses, the TAs are non-native English speaking graduate students. As a result, these differences in training are further amplified (Braine, 2002; Reinhardt, 2007). These TAs are likely to be even less proficient in their rhetorical knowledge and writing process knowledge, which is likely to reflect in their commenting practices.

Peers, on the other hand, are just beginning to develop content knowledge and may have only a shallow understanding of the concepts. In addition, they will have very little experience with the genre of writing in physics (e.g., examples of scientific writing, outlines of what is expected in each section). Instead, they will have had relatively more training about rhetorical situations and the writing process from their high school English classes and freshman composition courses. Furthermore, the feedback on their writing will likely have focused on the ways in which their arguments were expressed in addition to issues of factual correctness.

These differences between the two possible evaluators are likely to affect multiple aspects of the writing process. In this context, the writing process refers to all of the steps of a multi-draft writing assignment: writing a first draft, the evaluation of the first draft, and revising the first draft based on feedback received. First, the evaluator becomes the apparent audience of the paper and therefore could affect how the first draft is written. Second, the differences in prior experiences will likely influence what kinds of problems are detected, how they are valued, and thus what kinds of comments are provided. Third, the different kinds of comments could in turn affect the types of revisions made by the student and the resulting quality of the final draft. Therefore, how TAs and undergraduate students differentially impact each of these steps should be considered. The next three sections will address the expectations for each.

HOW DO THE TWO TYPES OF EVALUATORS INFLUENCE QUALITY OF THE FIRST DRAFT?

Writing is supposed to be communicative; therefore, to whom the text is communicating (i.e., audience) should influence the writing process. Early writing research has shown that expert writers frequently consider the intended audience during the writing process in order to make decisions about which content to include and how to organize that content (Berkenkotter, 1981; Flower & Hayes, 1980). Interestingly, while novice writers have demonstrated the ability to adapt their texts for different audiences, the highest quality text was not always the one being evaluated for a grade.

Several researchers compared texts written for instructors (for a grade) to texts written for peers (not for a grade) and found that the texts written for the peers was more organized, contained richer content, and use clearer language; these texts were noticeably higher quality (Cohen & Riel, 1989; Gallini & Helman, 1995; Ward, 2009). Sato and Matsushima (2006) compared texts written to be as accurate as possible to texts written so a reader could accurately recreate an abstract object. The participants who wrote texts for a reader spent more time planning and writing. In addition, the texts had shorter sentences, more subsidiary and meta descriptions, and were considered to be higher quality.

In each of the instances where the text was written for evaluation, the intended audience was someone with greater subject matter knowledge. This situation is common in written instruction; throughout elementary school, secondary school, and university, students frequently write only for their instructor, who has greater subject matter knowledge (Ede, 1979). However, this type of audience is especially awkward because it violates a major social norm. According to Gricean's Maxim of Quantity, "Do not make your contribution more informative than is required," a writer should not communicate information that the reader already knows (Grice, 1975, p. 45). In struggling with providing enough information to be considered accurate but also not providing information that the reader already knows, it may not be too surprising that the texts written for instructors were less coherent and did not contain as rich content.

In the current study, we sought to demonstrate that the lower quality texts are not resulting from the presence of evaluation, but rather the level of familiarity with the content being written about would affect the quality of the writing. Therefore, students were either evaluated by their TA or evaluated by a small group of peers. Because the TA had more subject matter knowledge and deeper knowledge of the particular assignment that was to be described in the paper than the peers, the first drafts that were written for peers were expected to be of higher quality than those written for their TA.

How do the two types of evaluators affect the type of feedback provided?

The varying levels of expertise for the two types of evaluators would likely affect the amount of feedback provided and on what that feedback focused. First, there would be a large difference in the workload for the evaluator. As the instructor, the TA would need to grade all of the students' papers. This amount is frequently as much as 20–25 papers, but sometimes can be well over 50 papers. In comparison, students are typically only assigned a small subset of the papers (e.g., 1 to

5 papers). Thinking about this large difference in workload, one may come to the conclusion that peers would be able to spend more time per paper than the instructor, which would result in more feedback. However, in prior research, undergraduate students either provided less feedback (Cho, Schunn, & Charney, 2006) or the same amount of feedback (Patchan, Charney, & Schunn, 2009) as instructors.

Several subject variables could explain this unexpected result. One important factor is how much the evaluator values providing feedback. There are some dedicated instructors who spend a lot of time per paper regardless of the number of papers to be evaluated, and there are some instructors who do not feel strongly about teaching writing that might spend a minimal amount of time on each paper. The same variability is likely to be seen with students as evaluators. Another important factor is experience with evaluation. Most instructors have evaluated many papers, which would allow them to provide feedback more efficiently (i.e., they could grade more papers in a shorter amount of time). By contrast, students have very little experience evaluating writing, so they would likely need more time per paper in their evaluations. Because of these additional variables, it is unclear which type of evaluator would be able to provide more feedback on a one-to-one comparison.

Despite the possible variability in one student review to one TA review comparisons, the number of evaluators for each paper would most likely affect how much feedback is provided. If an instructor was the only evaluator of student writing, then the students would receive feedback from only one source. In peer-review, a small group of students could be used to evaluate each paper. Therefore, the amount of feedback provided is multiplied by the size of the group. In previous pilot work, each student's review frequently commented on different problems (almost 75% of the comments are unique problems). Thus, there would be no question that the overall number of problems being detected by a group of peers would be greater than the amount detected by a single instructor. In addition, when multiple students comment on the same problem, students would be less able to rationalize that the problem was just a quirky personal preference ignoring and resulting in fewer problems being ignored.

Finally, as mentioned previously, the prior experiences of the non-native English speaking TAs are likely to result in strong content matter knowledge, moderate genre knowledge, and weak rhetorical and writing process knowledge. In contrast, the undergraduate students are likely to have weak content matter and genre knowledge and moderate rhetorical and writing process knowledge. These relative differences in knowledge will likely influence what kinds of problems in written documents are detected, how they are valued, and thus what kinds of comments are provided to students. Of course, there will be many issues that sit at the intersection of these types of knowledge and may be detected through multiple routes (e.g., as a violation of the genre and rhetorical issues); other problems may be detected with only basic levels of knowledge that are shared across the two different groups. Therefore, there might also be considerable overlap across problems detected and comments provided.

Several studies have specifically examined the focus of feedback provided by content instructors and undergraduate students. Feedback provided by engineering instructors focused primarily on the accuracy of the content in the text and sometimes the conventions of the disciplinary genre (Smith, 2003a, 2003b). While the undergraduates provided more solutions overall, the history instructor's solutions were more likely to focus on the subject matter issues (Patchan et al., 2009). This evidence would support the hypothesis that the focus of the feedback would depend on the types of expertise of the evaluator.

In the current study, the TAs were expected to focus less on rhetorical and writing process issues than the peers because the TAs would likely feel that it is not their job to do so. In addition, the TAs were expected to focus more on subject matter issues than the peers because the TAs would feel more confident in their diagnoses.

How do the Two Types of Evaluators Affect the Revisions?

Many researchers have examined how writers of varying expertise revise their work, but in these contexts, the writer revised without the aid of feedback (e.g., Flower, Hayes, Carey, Schriver, & Stratman, 1986; Myhill & Jones, 2007). Without any guidance, students typically edit their papers rather than revise their text (e.g., correcting typos, misspelled words, grammatical errors, and maybe reword some sentences). These low-level revisions are not likely to result in significant draft quality differences. However, with very little training, students are able to change how they revise. After just eight minutes of training on how to make global revisions, students were able to make more global revisions and their papers' quality improved more so than students who were just asked to revise text without receiving the same training (Wallace & Hayes, 1991). This finding supports Fitzgerald's (1987) conclusion that feedback seemed to improve the quality of revisions.

As previously mentioned, instructors and peers are likely to comment in different ways. These differences are especially important because certain types of feedback seem to be more useful than others. Writers benefited the most from feedback that was general and focused on global issues (Cho & MacArthur, 2010; Strijbos, Narciss, & Dunnerbier, 2010). Furthermore, the accuracy of the criticisms and the justifications for the suggested revisions had an impact on the quality of the revisions being made (Gielen, Peeters, Dochy, Onghena, & Struyven, 2010). While these features of feedback seem to impact revision, no studies have examined how feedback focused on subject matter versus rhetorical issues affect the types of revisions.

Several studies have examined at a more general level whether the type of the evaluator affected students' revisions. Writers revised more successfully after reflecting on a particular audience (Jucks, Schulte-Lobbert, & Bromme, 2007; Midgette, Haria, & MacArthur, 2008). While students were more likely to use feedback provided by instructors, their revisions were more successful when implementing peer feedback (Miao, Badger, & Zhen, 2006).

In the current study, the types of revisions were expected to reflect the types of feedback that was provided in a straightforward fashion: if the comments focused on the content, then the students are likely to make changes regarding the content, and if comments focused on the prose, then the students are likely to make changes regarding the prose. Because the TAs were expected to comment more on the content, students who received feedback from their TA were expected to make more content revisions. Because the peers were expected to comment more on the prose, students who received feedback from their peers were expected to make more prose changes.

Hypotheses

In the current study, we examined the relative efficacy of two common, pragmatic choices for providing feedback on writing (i.e., non-native English TAs or peer-review) by looking at the influences of the two choices on the writing process. In an introductory physics lab course, students wrote lab reports to be graded either by their non-native English TA or a group of their peers. Several expectations about each of the steps of a multi-draft writing assignment have been identified regarding the general difference between groups:

1. The quality of the first draft was expected to be higher when writing for their peers than when writing for their TA.
2. Students were expected to focus more on prose issues than TAs.
3. TAs were expected to focus more on physics issues than students.
4. Students, who received feedback from their peers, were expected to make more prose changes.
5. Students, who received feedback from their TA, were expected to make more physics changes.
6. As a result of these expectations, students who initially wrote to their peers were expected to produce final drafts of higher quality than those who initially wrote to their TA.

There are likely to be differences across individuals within each group, but these individual differences are not the focus of this paper.

METHOD

Overview

In this study, we experimentally manipulated the type of evaluators of students' writing in order to draw some conclusions about the effects of different audiences on the writing process. More specifically, we examined the writing quality of first and second drafts of two reports, the feedback provided by students and TAs, and the changes made between first and second drafts.

General Method

Course context & participants. The participants in this experiment included 211 students who were enrolled in an Introduction to Laboratory Physics course and 11 TAs who taught the lab sessions. The course included a diverse student population, with many different majors represented (e.g., biology, chemistry, nursing, pharmacy, and pre-medicine). Almost 60% of the students were female, and less than 3% were not native-English speakers. Most of the students were sophomores (33%), juniors (43%), or seniors (17%). While none of the TAs were native English speakers (primarily Cantonese or Mandarin native speakers), all of the TAs were sufficiently fluid in written and spoken English to meet university guidelines for TAs responsible for face-to-face instruction.

The course was designed to expose students to the experimental process in physics by obtaining, analyzing, and presenting their own experimental results. One form of presenting results involved writing formal lab reports, which included five sections: abstract, introduction and theory, experimental setup, data analysis, and conclusion (see Appendix A for details). Each student was required to write two formal lab reports: one on ballistic motion and one on the charge to mass ratio (e/m) of the electron. For each report, the first draft was graded and commented upon by either the TA or four peers (see Appendix B for reviewing guidelines). Then the students were expected to revise their report based on the feedback they received. The TA graded all of the final drafts. The first draft, reviewing activities, and the final draft of both reports were collectively worth 30% of their final grade.

Design. Each lab section was randomly assigned to one of two conditions: peer-first and TA-first. In the peer-first condition, four peers were assigned to review each of the first reports using an online peer-review system. In the TA-first condition, the students' TA would review their paper. The source of feedback was then counterbalanced for the second report (i.e., the TA reviewed the second report in the peer-first condition, and four peers reviewed the second report in the TA-first condition).

Review support structures. Students had one week to write their first draft, and they were required to submit them electronically. Where they submitted their papers depended on who would be reviewing them. Therefore, students were aware of who their audience was. Students, whose papers were to be reviewed by other peers, submitted their first draft through the SWoRD (Scaffolded Writing and Rewriting in the Discipline) system, an anonymous web-based reciprocal peer-review system. Students, whose papers were to be reviewed by their TA, turned their papers in through the university's *Blackboard* system. While there were minor interface differences in how students submitted their papers to their peers or TA, both interfaces were basically a simple document-upload interface. Thus this difference would be highly unlikely to affect the quality of the paper, which would be completed by the time the document upload step began.

The SWoRD system was used to facilitate the process of distributing documents and reviews to peers (Cho & Schunn, 2007), while the more straightforward distribution of documents to and feedback from TAs was handled by Blackboard. Different systems were used for both generalization and pragmatic considerations. In terms of generalization, multiple peer review requires some kind of method to support that process (whether face-to-face or online), and TA feedback would typically involve a different method. Pragmatically, SWoRD did not have a facility for distributing all papers to TAs and Blackboard did not have a facility for distributing papers to a fixed number of peers. Critical to the internal validity of the experiment, instructions for the rating dimensions and providing comments were exactly the same between peers and TAs. Further, the basic process was the same between the two interfaces: authors upload papers, reviewers download papers, reviewers upload comments, authors view comments, authors revise documents, and authors upload final drafts.

After the first draft deadline, the students and TAs had one week to review the papers assigned to them. The TAs reviewed all of the papers in their lab (ranging from 11 to 18 students), and each peer reviewed four papers. Both students and TAs provided feedback and a rating from a 7-point scale on three different dimensions; they received detailed instructions about how to review papers. Two of the dimensions (i.e., Introduction, Theory and Experimental Setup; Abstract, Conclusion, and References) focused on the prose aspects of the report, and one of the dimensions (i.e., Data Analysis and Results) focused on the physics aspect of the report.

For the reports to be reviewed by students, the SWoRD system automatically distributed each paper to four peers. The pool of students used to randomly assign reviewers was the whole class (i.e., all 211 students), not just students from the same lab. Therefore, it would be nearly impossible for the students to identify the author or reviewer unless the student included it (which they were instructed not to).

After receiving their feedback, the students then revised their reports using that feedback. The TAs graded their students' final drafts for both reports. They did not have access to the peers' comments, so the peer evaluations would not influence the final quality marks.

Data Analysis. We had several expectations about each of the steps of a multi-draft writing assignment have been identified. In order to test all of our hypotheses, several different samples of the data were necessary. Therefore, each step of the writing assignment will be discussed as if it was its own study.

Study 1A: Initial Draft Quality

First, we wanted to know how the two types of evaluators influenced the quality of the first draft. That is, do peers write differently when the apparent audience is their peers versus their TA? The quality of the first draft was expected to be higher when writing for their peers than when writing for their TA. To eliminate bias in ratings, expert ratings were used to compare the quality of the students' first draft.

Method

Sample. Of the 211 students, a sample of 50 students, sufficiently large for statistical analysis, was randomly selected. Half of the students were from the peer-first condition and half from the TA-first condition. In order to use a representative sample, the number of students selected from each section was based on how many students there were in that section.

Coding. The ratings of two outside experts (i.e., a writing expert and a content expert) were used instead of the students and TAs ratings to obtain fully comparable and face-valid evaluations. The writing expert was a full-time faculty member from the university writing center, and the content expert was a native English physics graduate student who had prior experience with teaching this particular lab. These experts were specifically chosen for high face-validity, which should reduce the likelihood that important aspects of the writing would be missed. In addition, both experts were given the same rubric as the students to guide their attention to criticism factors of writing in these documents. The two experts rated the quality of the 50 students' first and second drafts of both reports—a total of 200 papers. The writing expert rated the first and third dimension because these focused more on prose aspects of the lab report, and the writing expert would thus provide the highest validity judgments for those dimensions. No content knowledge was necessary to evaluate the prose in these sections. The content expert rated the second dimension, which focused on the domain knowledge of the report, and thus a content expert was necessary for evaluation of that dimension. Experts were blind to condition and draft. Correlations between first and second drafts (by dimension) indicated that the experts were able to produce reliable ratings (writing expert: $r(164) = .86$, $p < .001$; content expert $r(94) = .64$, $p < .001$).

Results & Discussion

The dependent measure of interest was the quality of the first draft, which was measured by combining the expert ratings into one composite score (out of 21 possible points). The quality was then compared across the two types of audience (i.e., peers versus non-native English TAs). Students wrote better papers for their peers than they did for their TA (see Figure 1), $t(83) = 2.24$, $p = .03$.

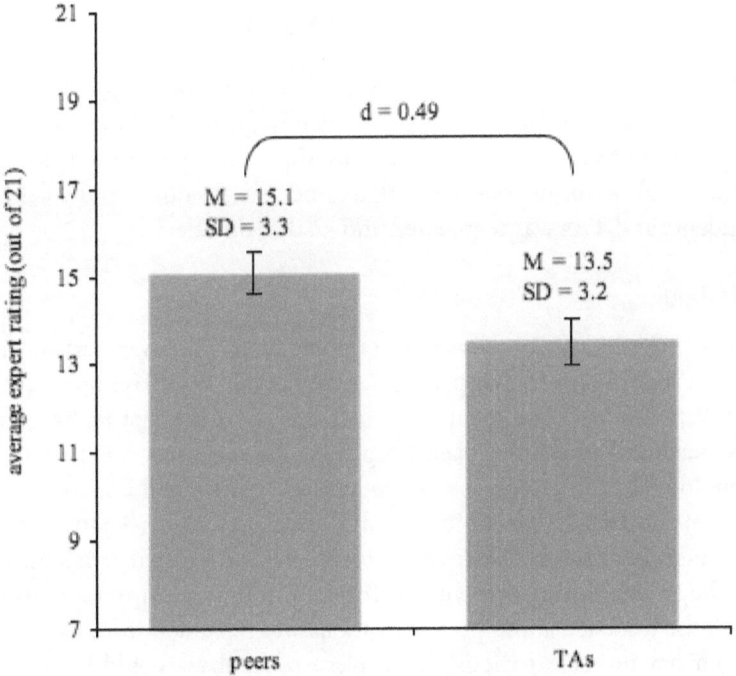

Figure 1: Average total score of first draft by initial evaluator (with SE bars)

One may wonder whether this audience effect generalizes across all reviewing dimensions, especially since the focus of the dimensions vary from prose features to physics features. The expert ratings for each dimension were analyzed as within-subjects variables. None of the interactions involving dimension were significant: the first draft ratings for all three dimensions were higher when the audience was their peers rather than their TA (see Table 1).

Table 1: Means and standard deviations of first draft by reviewing dimension for peer evaluators and TA evaluators

	Peers		>	TAs
	M	SD	M	SD
Introduction, Theory, and Experimental Setup	5.3	1.3	4.7	1.6
Data Analysis and Results	5.0	1.8	4.3	1.6
Abstract, Conclusion, and References	5.0	1.1	4.6	1.4

Study 1B: Feedback Features

Next we wanted to know how feedback differed when provided by undergraduate students versus non-native English TAs. Students were expected to focus more on prose issues than TAs. TAs were expected to focus more on physics issues than students. Feedback provided by students and TAs was segmented and analyzed in detail.

Method

Sample. A total of 29 peers were sampled from the seven sections in which the first report was peer-reviewed, and all of the five non-native English TAs who commented on first drafts for the first report were included. All of the feedback from these 34 reviewers was first broken down by dimension (i.e., Introduction, Theory and Experimental Setup; Abstract, Conclusion, and References, Data Analysis and Results). Because feedback could focus on many different issues, all of the feedback was segmented using idea unit as the unit of analysis (i.e., the feedback about poor transitions was separated from feedback about having a clear thesis). Each piece of feedback could have anywhere from 3 to 37 segments. A total of 796 feedback segments were analyzed.

Coding. The comments of interest were the criticism comments (i.e., feedback that describes a problem and/or solution rather than praise or summary statements). Therefore, the comments were first categorized as criticism or not (102 segments were double-coded with 100% agreement). Each piece of criticism was then categorized as either focusing on physics (e.g., calculations, data, equations, interpretations, theory) or focusing on prose (e.g., audience, content, flow, length). Some of the criticism comments were too vague to be labeled as physics or prose, so they were just labeled as nonspecific. For example, it was unclear whether a comment like "This section needs a lot of work!" is referring to physics or the prose aspect of the paper. Less than 5% of the segments were labeled nonspecific. The reliability of coding was checked by two research assistants who independently code a subset of the segments; 102 segments were double-coded with moderate reliability (Kappa = .74), well above the typical threshold of .41 for acceptable reliability (Landis & Koch, 1977).

Results & Discussion

The first dependent variable of interest was length (i.e., number of words in all of the comments provided by one reviewer). The length of the comments was examined across the two types of reviewers (i.e., peers vs. non-native English TAs). Analyses compared the average peer (single review) to the average TA (single review). Individual peers provided longer reviews than the TAs (see Figure 2), $t(32) = 2.43, p < .001$. This result replicated for each reviewing dimension. Further, taken from a writer's perspective, the four peers assigned to provide feedback would provide comments almost ten times longer than a TA's comments.

The second dependent variable of interest, orthogonal to length of comment, was type of comments (i.e., focusing on physics or focusing on prose). This variable was also compared across the two types of reviewers (i.e., the average peer compared to the average TA). Overall, individual peers comment on marginally more issues than individual TAs (see Figure 3), $t(32) = 1.98, p = .06$. As expected, peers focused more on prose issues than the TAs, $t(32) = 2.43, p = .02$. Interestingly, peers focused on physics issues just as frequently as the TAs, $t(32) = 1.28, p = .21$. However, from a writer's perspective, peers would comment on almost seven times as many ideas overall than the TA—11 times as many prose issues and six times as many physics issues.

STUDY 1C: REVISIONS

Next, we wanted to know how revisions differed when students received different amounts and types of feedback. Students, who received feedback from their peers, were expected to make more prose changes. Students, who received feedback from their TA, were expected to make more physics changes. To test this prediction, the revisions students made between their first and second drafts were analyzed.

Method

Sample. The same sample of 50 students used to test the audience effect was also used to examine the effect of feedback on revisions. A list of students' revisions was created using the compare documents function in Microsoft Word 2003. On average students made 32 changes between the first draft and second draft. However, some students did not make any changes, and some students made over 100 changes (even up to 195 changes). A total of 3,165 revisions were coded.

Coding. The revisions were first categorized as either focusing primarily on physics or prose issues. Some revision types were obviously physics (e.g., changing data reported), and some revisions were obviously prose (e.g., changing verb tense). However, some revision types, such as changing wording, could be labeled either as physics or prose. To determine which label was most appropriate, the rule "could someone without any physics knowledge make this change?" was used to label all revisions. All of the prose revisions were further categorized as either low prose or high prose. This determination was based on length of the change. Revisions that involved more than one sentence were considered to be a high prose revision, and revisions that were contained within a sentence were considered to be a low prose revision. The reliability of coding was checked by two research assistants who independently code a subset of the segments. For the type of change (i.e., physics or prose), 202 revisions were double-coded with a resulting moderate reliability (Kappa = .55). For type of prose change (i.e., low prose or high prose), 85 prose revisions (found in the set of 202 double-coded revisions) were double-coded, also with a resulting moderate reliability (Kappa = .71).

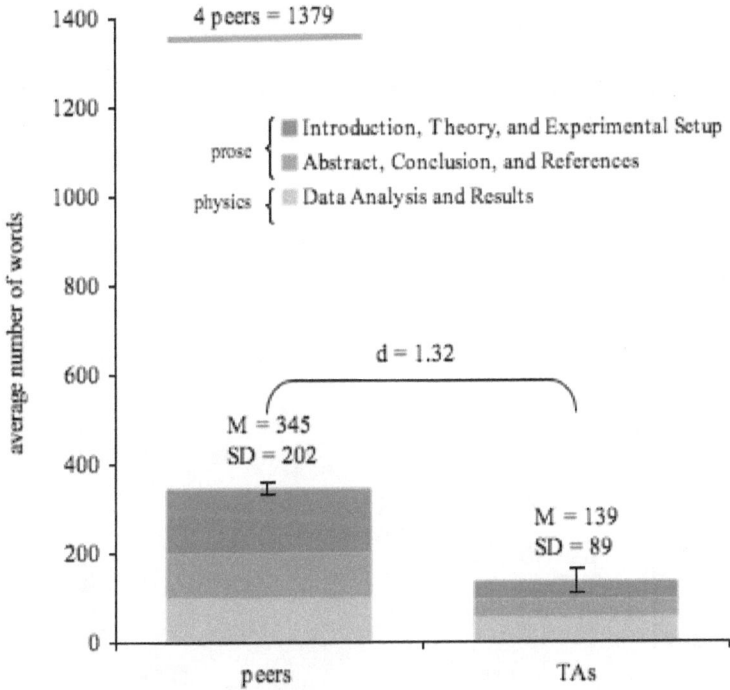

Figure 2: Average number of words per review by reviewing dimension and by type of evaluator (with SE bars)

Results & Discussion

The dependent variable of interest is the average number of revisions made by the students. Again, this variable was compared across the two types of reviewers (i.e., peers vs. non-native English TAs). Overall, students made more changes when feedback came from peers than when feedback came from TAs, $t(81) = 3.82, p < .001$.

There were several types of changes one could make (i.e., a change focused on physics issues, a changes focused on high-level prose issues, or a change focused on low-level prose issues). The number of physics changes did not differ by who provided feedback, but students who received feedback from peers made more prose changes than those who received feedback from TAs (see Figure 4), $t(81) = 4.67, p < .001$. This result replicated for both low-level changes and high-level changes. Overall more low-level changes were made than high-level changes, $t(162) = 7.96, p < .001$.

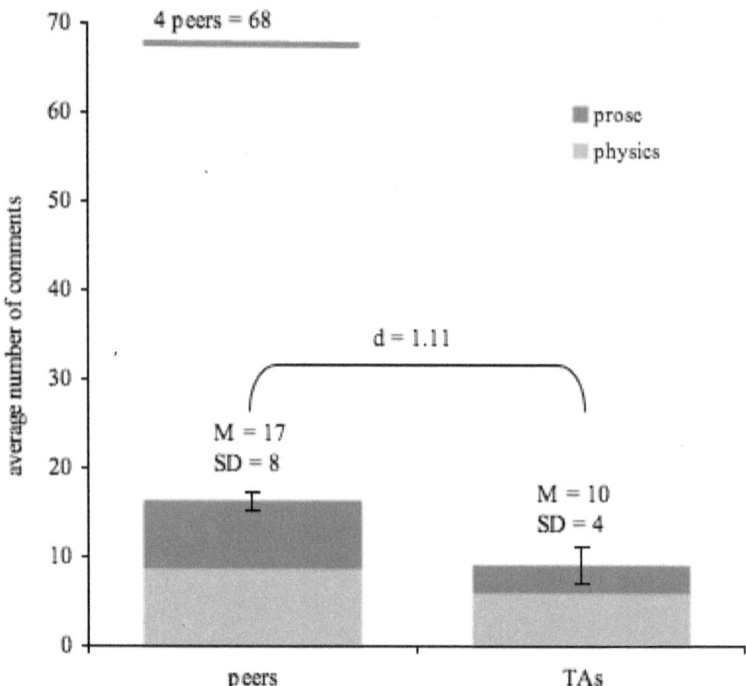

Figure 3: Average number of comments by comment type and by type of evaluator (with SE bars)

GENERAL DISCUSSION

Summary of Results

First, there was a significant audience effect: the quality of students' first draft was greater when they were writing for their peers than when they were writing for their TA. This audience effect generalized across all reviewing dimensions (i.e., when focusing on prose or physics issues).

In regards to commenting, students provided longer comments than TAs. They also discussed more ideas. While not completely surprising, this finding was not what was predicted. In previous research, instructors' comments were longer than students' comments (Cho et al., 2006; Patchan et al., 2009). One reason for the difference could be that the non-native English graduate students in the current study

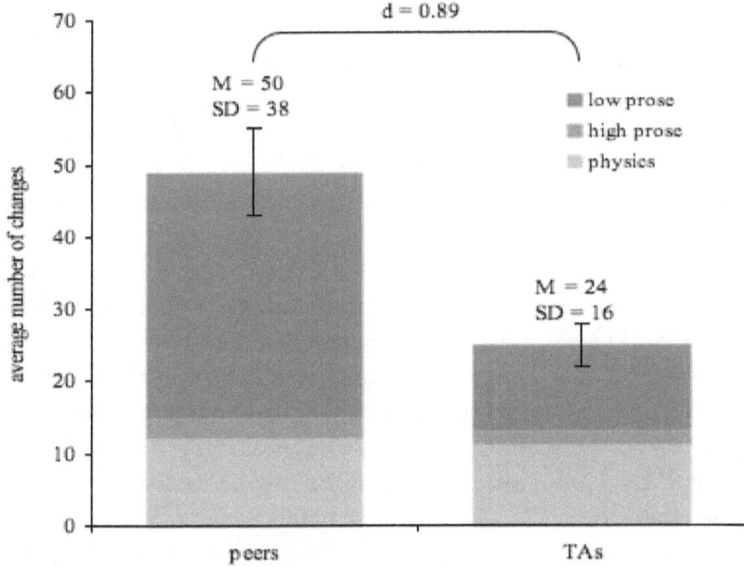

Figure 5: Average total score of final draft by initial evaluator (with SE bars)

may have found the task of commenting more difficult due to their relatively weaker language proficiency and therefore commented less.

From a writer's perspective, the difference between the length of a peer's review and a TA's review was amplified because students receive feedback from four of their peers. Therefore, on average a student would receive almost 1400 words of feedback from their peers but only a little more than 100 words from their TA (as indicated in Figure 2). These large differences could be quite important. Due to the large amount of feedback provided by peers, the writer should have a number of high quality comments to help with revision, even though not all students are experts in writing or providing feedback. On the other hand, the students would need to sift through a lot more feedback to determine which comments were the most appropriate or useful. Students could become overwhelmed with the need to sift through so much feedback, but the sifting-through-feedback task could also be beneficial to the student. That is, it could help the student better understand the writing process (i.e., what works and what does not) and the reviewing process (i.e., what makes for good feedback).

While there were no differences overall in the amount of physics versus prose comments, students commented about prose more than the TAs. Surprisingly, there were no differences between students and TAs on the amount of physics comments. The TAs were expected to comment more about physics problems than the students because this area would fall within their expertise. Perhaps difficulties with English prevented the TAs from being able to create comments focusing on physics.

Several differences in revisions occurred, which likely resulted from the differences in comments received. Overall, students made more changes after receiving comments from their peers, which is not surprising because they received more feedback from their peers. In addition, more prose changes were made based on feedback from peers rather than in response to the TA. More specifically, students made a lot more low-level prose revisions after receiving feedback from peers rather than their TA. On the other hand, there were no differences in the number of physics changes. This finding partially supports the expectation that revisions would correspond with the content of the feedback. Students provided more prose changes than the TAs, so more prose revisions would be expected when feedback came from peers. However, the group of peers provided about six times as much physics feedback as the TA alone.

There were several possible explanations for this surprising null effect on the number of physics revisions. First, there may have been redundancy among peer comments. Therefore, the number of unique physics suggestions provided by the group of peers may have been equivalent to the number provided by the TA. This explanation seems unlikely. In previous studies, we have examined how often students comment on the same issues and found that a majority of student comments in a set of four or five peer comments on a paper involve unique issues (i.e., each peer finds additional errors not noted by other peers). Another explanation could be that the TAs would be considered the authority on content issues, and thus students would likely implement all of the TAs suggestions but only some of the peer comments (given some skepticism of their peers' ability to comment on the physics content). Therefore, they may be more selective in which comments they actually implement.

Even though there were differences across conditions in first draft quality, comments received, and revisions made, there was only a moderate difference on final draft quality. Why was the condition effect not larger for second drafts? One possibility is that the shift from peer grader to TA grader undercut the forcefulness of peer grades (i.e., comments could be more safely ignored when the evaluator changed). However, this explanation would have predicted fewer revisions rather than more revisions in the peer feedback condition. A more likely explanation involves differences in the quality of feedback—the TAs' comments may have been better than the peers' comments. Covariate analyses, if all comments to each author had been coded, would provide some data to this point. In addition, comparing the quality of comments becomes further complicated when considering the students' ability to comprehend the comments. Experts could rate whether the comments, if acted upon, could improve the content of the paper. In doing so, we may see that the TAs appeared to provide higher quality comments than the students. However, it would be unclear whether the students who read the comments would understand them enough to be able to successfully revise their paper. For example, Cho and colleagues (2006) found that instructors thought other instructors comments were more accurate and useful than peer comments while peers saw instructor and peer comments as equally accurate and useful. This complex issue should be examined in future research.

Implications

The current study provides additional support for the validity of using peer-review to evaluate student writing. Most studies that examine the validity of peer-review focus on the validity of the ratings (Cho et al., 2006; Cho, Schunn, & Wilson, 2006). Few studies have compared the comments provided by students to comments that would have been provided by an instructor (Cho et al., 2006; Patchan et al., 2009). While these studies have shown that students are able to provide comments that are similar to instructors, many individuals (both instructors and students) are still skeptical about the effectiveness of peer comments. The results of the current study show that the peer-review process can have benefits on a multitude of levels. First, students who write for their peers create first drafts of better quality than when writing for an instructor. Second, students can receive more feedback about their draft from their peers than they would from their instructor—especially more feedback focusing on how to improve the prose.

Finally, when students receive feedback from their peers, they are likely to make more revisions—again, these changes tend to focus on the prose. While there seem to be a lot of benefits to the students, the final draft quality is not that much different when initially written for peers. At the very least, this result does support the use of peer-review as acceptable practice, in that it could produce outcomes for student authors that would be, at minimum, equivalent to what they would get if an instructor evaluated their work.

We are not advocating for replacing TA feedback entirely with peer feedback. Faculty, TAs, and students are likely to find that situation very controversial. Instead, we are arguing that peer feedback may be just as effective as TA feedback for first drafts. TA workload (which is often quite high in lab contexts with significant writing components) may be reduced, or shifted to other feedback tasks by having peers provide feedback on first drafts. Alternatively, peer feedback may be added to TA feedback on first drafts, perhaps providing an optimal balance of audiences and prose/content knowledge oriented feedback. We also note that peers are likely to be obtaining some benefits from providing feedback to peers (Wooley, 2007; Wooley, Was, Schunn, & Dalton, 2008), although we did not examine such effects in this study.

Caveats

There are several caveats to these finding that must be taken under consideration. First, the focus of the current study was to examine whether students are receiving sufficient writing instruction in natural science contexts that balances the various core types of knowledge (i.e., subject matter knowledge, rhetorical knowledge, writing process knowledge) critical for writing success. This distinction is very important because the two most common evaluators of student writing are peers and graduate students. In many physics courses offered at universities in the US, the graduate students teaching the courses with the high writing components (i.e., labs) tend to be non-native English speaking. This language distinction is most prominent in physics courses and not as strong in other natural science disciplines, such as biology. Therefore, our results regarding the effects of TAs on student writing may only generalize to settings in which the TA is a non-native English speaker. On the other hand, the physics context is very similar to other natural science disciplines in that the instructors have a much deeper understanding of the domain than the peers. If this content knowledge difference is what drives the current findings, rather than the language proficiency difference, then the results of the current study may generalize to all natural science disciplines.

A second caveat involves the nature of the peers. Although coming from a variety of disciplinary backgrounds, one might wonder how the TA versus peer results would have changed if the students had all been significantly stronger writers (e.g., at more selective universities/colleges than the currently studied setting, or in honors/advanced sections), or significantly worse writers (e.g., as occurs at less selective universities/colleges than the currently studied setting). A related dimension involves student motivation levels, which has several elements: 1) do the students perceive grades in the given course as important and thus worth significant effort overall, and 2) do the students more specifically perceive the peer review task as important and thus worth significant effort? Future research should examine these variables more carefully.

The third caveat to be considered is the structure of the reviewing task in the current study. Very detailed guidelines were provided to both the students and the TAs about how to review a paper. These guidelines not only offered structure to the type of feedback that should be provided, but the guidelines also set specific expectations for what should be considered important in writing a formal laboratory report. Previous research has shown that just a little guidance could greatly affect one's writing behaviors (Wallace & Hayes, 1991). Therefore, these results may only generalize to those instances where specific guidelines for reviewing are provided. Peers are quite likely to be influenced by reviewing guidelines. If students are only told to point out problems with their peer's writing, they are likely to just edit the paper. Instead of using broad instructions, students are providing specific prompts to help them focus on important prose and content issues. For example, one comment prompt requested reviewers to "describe any problems in understanding how the final results relate to the theoretical predictions." Once prompted, students were capable of formulating comments regarding more sophisticated issues that would otherwise have been overlooked. TAs are also very influenced by reviewing guidelines (Smith Taylor, 2007), but perhaps in a different way. Interestingly given the same prompts, the TAs from our study did not provide as much prose comments as the peers. For example, one comment prompt asked "Was the writing appropriate for the target audience (your fellow classmates)? If not, then explain why." Despite these specific prompts, the TAs continued to focus more on the content issues. From our study, we do not know how the reviews from each group would compare when 'unstructured', although prior research would suggest that both peer and TA comment quality would significantly suffer.

Future Research

One possible direction for future research could be to compare the effects of non-native English graduate student TAs versus native English graduate student TAs, again looking separately at the different steps in the writing-commenting-revision process. Would the students perceive these two groups as different audiences? How does the feedback provided by the TAs differ? The results could help determine whether the current study's findings generalize to all graduate-student TAs. It would also be useful to know whether these results are specific to science writing or could they generalize to other domains.

Summary/Conclusion

In the current study, students wrote better first drafts when they expected their peers to grade that draft rather than their TA. Students provided longer comments and more comments about prose problems than the TAs. As a result, students made more revisions after receiving feedback from peers than from their TA. Interestingly, these differences did not seem to have a large impact on the final draft score, indicating that students may need additional training on how to provide higher quality feedback. Based on these results, peer feedback should be used to supplement (not replace) the TA feedback—peers can focus on the writing aspects of the paper, while the TA focuses on the physics/domain aspect of the paper.

REFERENCES

Bazerman, C. (2008, November). *US Writing Across the Curriculum and Writing in the Disciplines in Context.* Paper presented at the Proceedings of the International Conference « de la France au Québec : l'Ecriture dans tous ses états », Poitiers, France.

Beaufort, A. (2004). Developmental Gains of a History Major: A Case for Building a Theory of Disciplinary Writing Expertise. *Research in the Teaching of English, 39*(2), 136-185.

Berkenkotter, C. (1981). Understanding a Writer's Awareness of Audience. *College Composition and Communication, 32*(4), 388-399.

Braine, G. (2002). Academic literacy and the nonnative speaker graduate student. *Journal of English for Academic Purposes, 1*(1), 59-68.

Cho, K., & MacArthur, C. (2010). Student revision with peer and expert reviewing. *Learning and Instruction, 20*(4), 328-338.

Cho, K., & Schunn, C. D. (2007). Scaffolded writing and rewriting in the discipline: A web-based reciprocal peer review system. *Computers & Education, 48*(3), 409-426.

Cho, K., Schunn, C. D., & Charney, D. (2006). Commenting on writing - Typology and perceived helpfulness of comments from novice peer reviewers and subject matter experts. *Written Communication, 23*(3), 260-294.

Cho, K., Schunn, C. D., & Wilson, R. W. (2006). Validity and reliability of scaffolded peer assessment of writing from instructor and student perspectives. *Journal of Educational Psychology, 98*(4), 891-901.

Cohen, M., & Riel, M. (1989). The effect of distant audiences on students' writing. *American Educational Research Journal, 26*(2), 143-159.

Ede, L. S. (1979). On Audience and Composition. *College Composition and Communication, 30*(3), 291-295.

Fitzgerald, J. (1987). Research on Revision in Writing. *Review of Educational Research, 57*(4), 481-506.

Flower, L., & Hayes, J. R. (1980). The Cognition of Discovery: Defining a Rhetorical Problem. *31*(1), 21-32.

Flower, L., Hayes, J. R., Carey, L., Schriver, K., & Stratman, J. (1986). Detection, Diagnosis, and the Strategies of Revision. *College Composition and Communication, 37*(1), 16-55.

Gallini, J. K., & Helman, N. (1995). Audience awareness in technology-mediated environments. *Journal of Educational Computing Research, 13*(3), 245-261.

Gielen, S., Peeters, E., Dochy, F., Onghena, P., & Struyven, K. (2010). Improving the effectiveness of peer feedback for learning. *Learning and Instruction, 20*(4), 304-315.

Grice, H. P. (1975). Logic and conversation. In R. Cole & J. Morgan (Eds.), *Syntax and semantics: Vol.3, Speech acts* (pp. 41-58). New York: Academic Press.

Jucks, R., Schulte-Lobbert, P., & Bromme, R. (2007). Supporting experts' written knowledge communication through reflective prompts on the use of specialist concepts. *Zeitschrift Fur Psychologie [Journal of Psychology], 215*(4), 237-247.

Landis, J. R., & Koch, G. G. (1977). The measurement of observer agreement for categorical data. *Biometrics, 31*(1), 159-174.

Miao, Y., Badger, R., & Zhen, Y. (2006). A comparative study of peer and teacher feedback in a Chinese EFL writing class. *Journal of Second Language Writing, 15*(3), 179-200.

Midgette, E., Haria, P., & MacArthur, C. (2008). The effects of content and audience awareness goals for revision on the persuasive essays of fifth- and eighth-grade students. *Reading and Writing, 21*(1-2), 131-151.

Myhill, D., & Jones, S. (2007). More than just error correction - Students' perspectives on their revision processes during writing. *Written Communication, 24*(4), 323-343.

Ochsner, R., & Fowler, J. (2004). Playing devil's advocate: Evaluating the literature of the WAC/WID movement. *Review of Educational Research, 74*(2), 117-140.

Patchan, M. M., Charney, D., & Schunn, C. D. (2009). A validation study of students' end comments: Comparing comments by students, a writing instructor, and a content instructor. *Journal of Writing Research, 1*(2), 124-152.

Prior, P. (2006). A sociocultural theory of writing. *Handbook of writing research*, 54-66.

Reinhardt, J. (2007). *Directives usage by ITAs: An applied learner corpus analysis.* Unpublished Doctoral Dissertation, The Pennsylvania State University.

Sato, K., & Matsushima, K. (2006). Effects of audience awareness on procedural text writing. *Psychological Reports, 99*(1), 51-73.

Smith, S. (2003a). The role of technical expertise in engineering and writing teachers' evaluations of students' writing. *Written Communication, 20*(1), 37-80.

Smith, S. (2003b). What is "Good" Technical Communication? A Comparison of the Standards of Writing and Engineering Instructors. *Technical Communication Quarterly, 12*(1), 7 - 24.

Smith Taylor, S. (2007). Comments on lab reports by mechanical engineering teaching assistants: Typical practices and effects of using a grading rubric. *Journal of Business and Technical Communication, 21*(4), 402-424.

Strijbos, J. W., Narciss, S., & Dunnebier, K. (2010). Peer feedback content and sender's competence level in academic writing revision tasks: Are they critical for feedback perceptions and efficiency? *Learning and Instruction, 20*(4), 291-303.

Wallace, D. L., & Hayes, J. R. (1991). Redefining Revision for Freshmen. *Research in the Teaching of English, 25*(1), 54-66.

Ward, M. (2009). Squaring the Learning Circle Cross-Classroom Collaborations and the Impact of Audience on Student Outcomes in Professional Writing. *Journal of Business and Technical Communication, 23*(1), 61-82.

Wooley, R. S. (2007). *The Effects of Web-Based Peer Review on Student Writing.* Unpublished Empirical, Kent State University.

Wooley, R. S., Was, C., Schunn, C. D., & Dalton, D. (2008). *The effects of feedback elaboration on the giver of feedback.* Paper presented at the Cognitive Science.

Appendix A

Formal Lab Report Contents

1. Abstract - This is a one paragraph complete summary of the experiment and your results.
2. Introduction and Theory - Here you should describe the basic physical theory behind the experiment and how the experiment tests the theory. Include all the relevant formulas and how they are used. Write in your own words; do not copy text from the lab manual. You are allowed to use figures from the lab manual provided you reference them in the report
3. Experimental Setup - Explain the experimental procedure and how the data was collected. Your report should include enough information that anyone reading it could reproduce your experiment. Be specific about the equipment used and the experimental procedure. If necessary, include labeled diagrams of the equipment. You may copy and reference figures from the manual, but do not copy the written material.
4. Data, Analysis and Questions - Include your data in tables with labels and captions. Likewise, show the results of your analysis in tables and plots with labels and captions. Your results here should support your conclusions in the next section. You should also include the answers to all questions asked in the lab manual.
5. Conclusion - The conclusion should be a summary of the whole experiment but it should focus on the final results. Include your own observations and comments regarding the experiment and suggest ways to improve the results. Explain how your data and analysis support the theory behind the experiment. If they do not support the theory, then explain why not.
6. References – A list of references you used in writing the report.

Appendix B

Formal Lab Report Review Form

When you review, there are two very important parts to giving good feedback.
1. Give very specific comments rather than vague comments: Point to exact page numbers and paragraphs that were problematic; give examples of general problems that you found; be clear about what exactly the problem was; explain why it was a problem, etc.
2. Make your comments helpful. The goal is not to punish the author for making mistakes. Instead your goal is to help the author improve his or her paper. You should point out problems where they occur. But don't stop there. Explain why they are problems and give some clear advice on how to fix the problems. Also keep your tone professional. No personal attacks. Everyone makes mistakes. Everyone can improve writing.

This evaluation form is divided into three parts:

1. Introduction, Theory and Experimental Setup
2. Data Analysis and Results
3. Abstract, Conclusion and References

For each part you will provide written comments for the author and a numerical score from 1 to 7, where 7 means excellent. There are guides below for how to assign the numerical values, but ultimately you should use your best judgment.

If you are using the SWoRD system (peer reviews) note that this form DOES NOT automatically submit your reviews to the system. After you are done, you need to access SWoRD, enter your numerical scores and copy and paste your review comments into the online form.

Introduction, Theory and Experimental Setup

Did the writing flow smoothly so you could understand the theory as it was tested with the experimental setup? This dimension is not about low level writing problems, like typos and simple grammar problems, unless those problems are so bad that it makes it hard to understand the text. Instead this dimension is about whether the author adequately explained the theory and the experimental setup used to test the theory. Is the purpose of the experiment clear? Is the experimental procedure described in sufficient detail? Are the transitions from one section to the next harsh, or do they transition naturally?

Your Comments

First summarize what you perceived as the purpose of the experiment and what it was testing so that the author can see whether the readers understood the writing in this section.

1. Describe any problems to understanding the theory as presented by the author.
2. Was the writing appropriate for the target audience (your fellow classmates)? If not, then explain why.
3. Describe any problems in understanding how the experimental setup tested the theory and avoided any likely experimental uncertainties.
4. If you thought some aspect of this section was done well, mention what was good about it. Be sure to give specific advice for how to fix any problems and praise-oriented advice for strengths that made the writing good.

Your Rating

1. Excellent — The written explanation of the theory and the experimental method is clear and very easy to understand.
2. Very Good — The written explanation of the theory and the experimental method is clear and somewhat easy to understand.
3. Good — The written explanation of the theory and the experimental method could be made a little clearer.
4. Average — The written explanation of the theory and the experimental method could be made a lot clearer.
5. Poor — It is somewhat difficult to understand either the theory or the experimental method used from the writing.
6. Very Poor — It is very difficult to understand either the theory or the experimental method used from the writing.
7. Disastrous — Cannot understand either the theory or the experimental method used from the writing.

Data Analysis and Results

This dimension is about how the theoretical predictions compare to the experimental results. Are the theoretical predictions accurate; in other words did the author apply the theory to the experimental setup correctly so as to produce an accurate prediction? Did the author collect a good sample of data and was the analysis of the data performed correctly? Finally, did the final results agree with the theory within the experimental uncertainties and if not, did the author provide an adequate explanation for the discrepancy?

Your Comments

1. Describe any problems in understanding how the theoretical predictions were calculated.
2. Describe any problems in understanding how the data analysis calculations were performed.
3. Describe any problems in understanding how the final results relate to the theoretical predictions.
4. Describe whether significant deviations from the theoretical prediction (if any) are explained.
5. If you thought some aspect of the Data Analysis and Results section was well done then mention what was good about it.

Your Rating

1. Excellent — The calculations are clear and complete. The results are consistent with theory and any unusual deviations are clearly explained.
2. Very Good — The calculations are clear and complete. The results are reasonably consistent with theory and any unusual deviations are clearly explained.
3. Good — The calculations are clear and complete. The results are somewhat consistent with theory and any unusual deviations are adequately explained.
4. Average — The calculations are not clear or complete. The results are somewhat consistent with theory and any unusual deviations are adequately explained.
5. Poor — Calculations are incomplete or unclear. The results are somewhat inconsistent with the theory and only a poor explanation for the disagreement is given.
6. Very Poor — Calculations are incomplete or unclear. The results are inconsistent with the theory and only a poor explanation for the disagreement is given.
7. Disastrous — Calculations are incomplete and unclear. The results are wildly inconsistent with the theory and no adequate explanation for the disagreement is given.

Abstract, Conclusion and References

This dimension concerns the content of the abstract and the conclusion. The abstract should be a short (one paragraph) summary of the whole report including the final results. The conclusion should also be a brief summary of the whole report but it should focus more on the final results and on the comparison of those results to the theoretical predictions. The conclusion may be longer than one paragraph.

Your Comments
1. Describe any problems with the abstract or conclusion length.
2. Describe any main ideas or results missing from the abstract.
3. Describe whether the conclusion focuses on the main results and any problems in explaining how the results relate to the theory.
4. Were references properly cited for materials (ideas, figures or text) that were included from external sources?
5. If you thought some aspect of the abstract or conclusion was well done, mention what was good about it.

Your Rating
1. Excellent — The abstract briefly captures the main ideas of the whole report including the results. The conclusion briefly summarizes the whole report but focuses on the main results and how they relate to the theory. References were properly cited for all materials included from outside sources.
2. Very Good — The abstract captures the main ideas of the whole report including the results but is a little too long. The conclusion briefly summarizes the whole report and focuses somewhat on the main results and how they relate to the theory. References were properly cited for all materials included from outside sources.
3. Good — The abstract captures most of the main ideas of the whole report including the results but is a little too long. The conclusion briefly summarizes the whole report and only adequately focuses on the main results and how they relate to the theory. References were properly cited for all materials included from outside sources.
4. Average — The abstract captures some of the main ideas of the whole report including the results but is too long. The conclusion briefly summarizes the whole report but does not adequately focus on the main results and how they relate to the theory. Some references were omitted for materials included from outside sources.
5. Poor — The abstract misses some of the main ideas of the whole report and is a little too long. The conclusion summarizes most of the report and does not adequately discuss the main results and how they relate to the theory. Some references were omitted for materials included from outside sources.
6. Very Poor — The abstract misses most of the main ideas of the whole report and is too long. The conclusion summarizes only some of the report and does not adequately discuss the main results and how they relate to the theory. Many references were omitted for materials included from outside sources.
7. Disastrous — The abstract misses the main ideas of the whole report and is much too long. The conclusion fails to summarize the majority of the report and fails to discuss the main results and how they relate to the theory. No references were provided for materials included from outside sources.

KAIROS

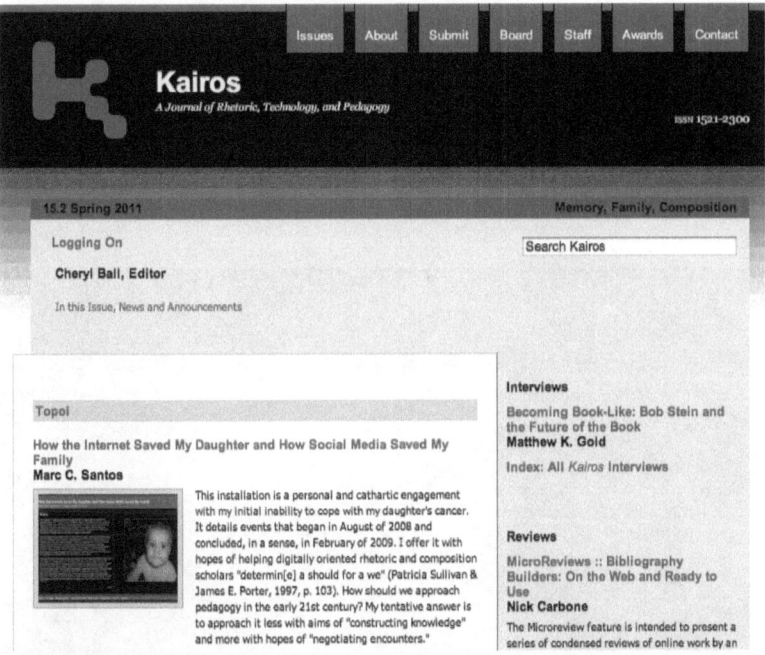

Published in *Kairos: A Journal of Rhetoric, Technology, and Pedagogy* 15.2 (Spring 2011). http://kairos.technorhetoric.net/15.2/topoi/santos/index.html

Kairos has always been an online-only publication, first publishing in 1996. It has always been an independent, open-access publication and has run, thanks to server space gifted from 1996-2006 by Texas Tech and from 2006-present by Michigan State. Despite this in-kind service, the journal is not directly affiliated with those or any institution or organization and runs completely on volunteer editorial and technical labor.

"How the Internet Saved My Daughter and How Social Media Saved My Family" by Marc Santos. *Kairos* 15.2 (2011).

This piece received far and wide praise in rhetoric and composition circles immediately after its publication in the January 2011 issue of *Kairos*. The powerful, personal, researched essay on the discovery and (hopeful) eradication of Santos' infant daughter's eye cancer—aided in large part to the watchful audience of social media readers Santos had—touched on deep rhetorical and familial issues that rhet/comp scholarship is only beginning to address with any sincerity.

9 How the Internet Saved My Daughter and How Social Media Saved My Family

Marc C. Santos

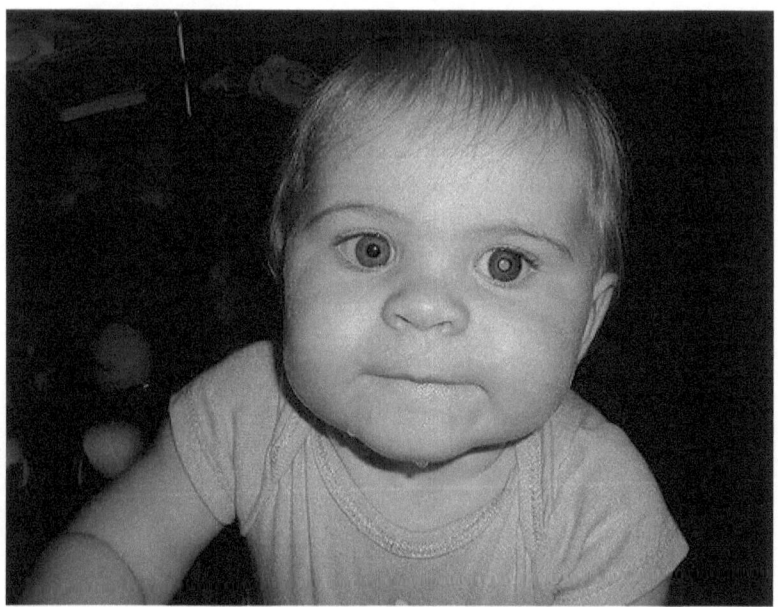

PREFACE

This installation is a personal and cathartic engagement with my initial inability to cope with my daughter's cancer.* It details events that began in August of 2008 and concluded, in a sense, in February of 2009. I offer it with hopes of helping digitally oriented rhetoric and composition scholars "determin[e] a 'should' for a 'we'" (Patricia Sullivan & James E. Porter, 1997, p.103). How should we approach pedagogy in the early 21st century? My tentative answer is to approach it less with aims of "constructing knowledge" and more with hopes of "negotiating encounters."

Given my suspicion toward traditional forms of rationality, this project, I hope, represents what Sullivan and Porter describe as feminist research in *Opening Spaces*. This is my first extended attempt to think through my own experiences and transformation. I share this engagement with you because I think it helps me theorize a dimension of rhetorical encounter preceding consciousness or knowledge production. Later in the project, I term this dimension *rhetorical support*—implicitly echoing Burke's paradox of substance—as the dimension upon which Being (be it identity, community, ideology, narrative) emerges. A digital-pedagogic practice dedicated to rhetorical support would place the quest for knowledge equally alongside values such as humility, courage, and risk.

I draw upon the work of Jim Corder and, to a lesser extent, Emmanuel Levinas and Alphonso Lingis. Such works speak to the dialogic potential of 21st century technologies, offering us robust theories that emphasize the human need for, and potential disruption caused by, others and their narratives. I want to use these theories and my own traumatic experiences—what Corder will identify as challenges to my narrative—to question what is fast becoming a commonplace among digital humanists: that social media sites, particularly Facebook, are fueled by and further fuel humanity's worst narcissistic tendencies. Where this critique locates narcissism as a cause, I will instead argue that digital technologies might awaken desire for something missing from atomistic modern life; they rekindle a desire for others. What might appear as narcissism could be attending to the abyss, and a new, distributed form of loquacious huddling.

Our Story

August 8, 2008. I remember spending most of the morning deliberating what kind of shoes to buy. My wife Megan, one-year-old daughter Rowan, and I had just moved to Tampa, Florida. As I was preparing to start my new job with the University of South Florida, I considered new shoes an important part of my pending professional preparatory process. My quiet time with coffee, computer, and images of shoes (and, after shoes, ice cream, for Rowan's sake, of course), was interrupted by my wife hysterically running at me, shaking her computer and yelling "LOOK AT THIS!!!"

"This" was a link to a website on retinoblastoma, including a picture of white eye reflex.

Some backstory here: For a little more than a week Meg had noticed that Rowan's left eye was slightly changing color from a light blue to a sea green. As first-time parents, we weren't sure if this was normal (it wasn't covered in the manual), so Meg posted a question to her Babyfit.com group, a social network putting parents-to-be in contact with other expectant parents with a similar due date. It seemed that other parents had not experienced spontaneous eye color change and requested a picture. As you can see, what is distinctive about the photograph is the "white eye reflex" instead of the more typical red eye reflex. Meg and I had noticed this once or twice before in Rowan's pictures, but dismissed it as an odd reflection (and the internet will tell you it is an odd reflection about 99% of the time). One mom, Madeline Robb from Manchester, England, noticed the picture and remembered an acquaintance's ordeal years earlier. Specifically, she remembered how white eye reflex can be, in rare cases, a sign of a serious medical problem. She did an internet search and reluctantly sent us the email and link appearing on the next screen.

> SUBJ: Hey
>
> "Hey Megan
>
> It must be so hot there right now! I've spent two full summers in that Florida heat and humidity.. ah!
>
> How is the process of settling in going?
>
> You and Rowan are looking great!
>
> I just noticed something – Rowan's left eye is reflecting in some of her pictures (esp the ones where she's in her pink t-shirt).
>
> The reason I'm writing this is because an acquaintance of ours noticed the same thing in the pictures of their child and it was found to be serious.
>
> Don't panic, I just wanted to suggest that you have her checked by an optometrist from the experience our acquaintances had with their child.
>
> I'm not saying it definitely IS anything but she's such a precious girl I had to mention it.
>
> Here is a link to something – but before you look – I'm not trying to scare you.
> tinyurl.com/yg4pld
>
> Keep me posted!
>
> Maddie x"

What is interesting here, particularly in light of where this presentation will end, is Madeline's hesitancy to send the link. She didn't really know us at all, and she was sincerely concerned with causing us undue panic. In interviews with *Inside Edition*, *Reader's Digest*, *USA Today* and other publications, Madeline consistently references the difficulty she faced in composing this email.[1] We can read it, too. The phatic and tense introductory lines seeking to form some trace of identification, the awkward and impossible transition, the repeated avoidance of certitude. But, fortunately, courageously, miraculously she did send the link.

Which brings us back to the grumpy husband, the hysterical wife, and the shaking laptop.

My immediate response (likely ironic to anyone familiar with my research agenda) was, "Are you going to trust everything you read on the internet?" I was annoyed. Not because my daughter might have some long, impossible-to-pronounce disease. I knew my daughter was fine. I was annoyed because I knew my morning of shoes and ice cream was about to be suffocated by an unnecessary trip to the doctor's office.

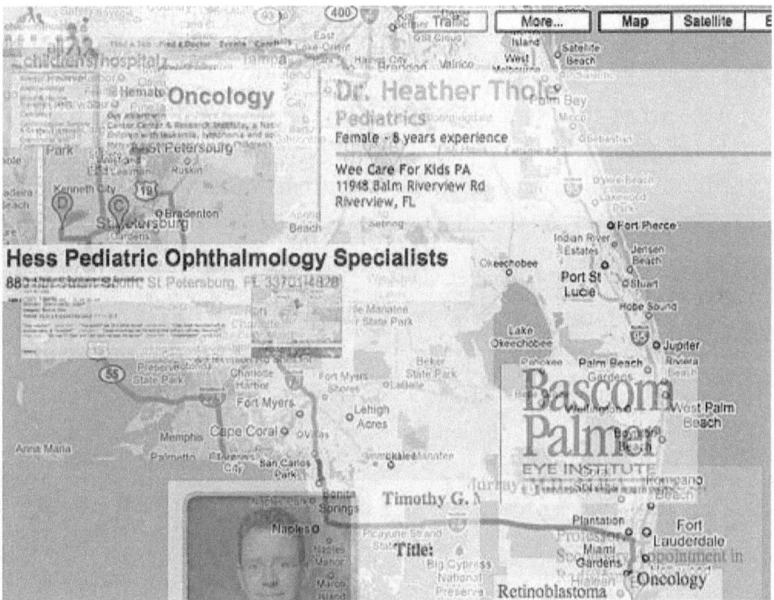

I WAS WRONG

100 miles, 13 hours, three doctors, one MRI and one CAT scan later, we learned that our daughter had retinoblastoma, an extremely aggressive and dangerous form of eye cancer. Three days, 300 miles, one hurricane, and one exam under anesthesia later, we learned that we were very fortunate that her cancer was unilateral rather than bilateral. We learned that she would likely never again see out of her left eye. We learned that we would have to decide whether to subject her to radiation treatment in an attempt to save the eye. We learned that she would have to undergo six months of extensive chemotherapy. We learned that, even if she beat retinoblastoma, she would be at an extremely high risk to develop another form of cancer in childhood or adolescence. We learned that the tumor, undiagnosed at her three-, six-, and nine-month pediatric checkups was likely present since birth and had grown to occupy almost 80% of her eye. We learned that retinoblastoma almost exclusively affects children. We learned that, because retinoblastoma affects so few children every year, most pediatricians do not bother to actually check eyes in a dark room (the only method of early detection).

We learned that, had we waited another two months until her 12-month checkup, Rowan's tumor would have in all probability spread to cells outside of her eye, onto her brainstem, and into her brain. Had those cells spread, she would have most certainly died.

Literally, the internet saved my daughter's life.

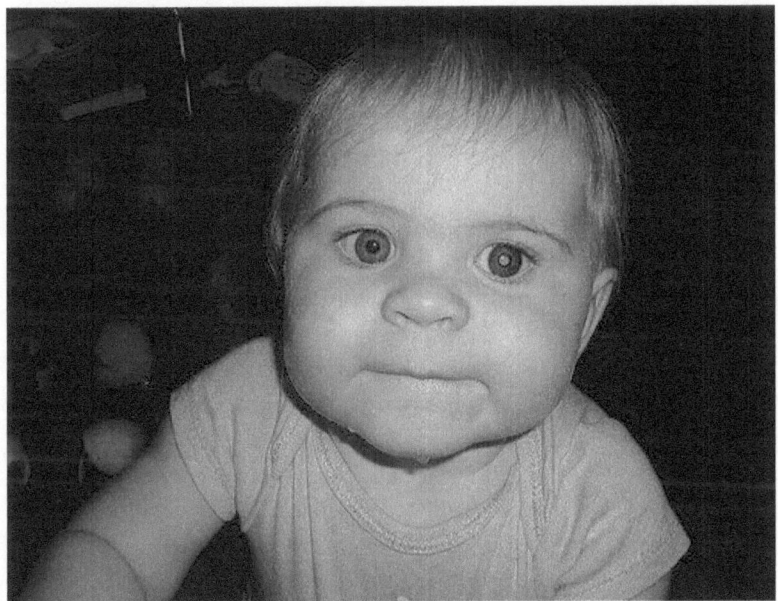

RHETORICAL SUPPORT

As my title suggests, when I first began reflecting on my family's story, I could only think of it in terms of providing the internet some good press. This is how our story was packaged and dispensed across mainstream and internet news outlets (and it still gets some attention—*Reader's Digest Canada* ran the story in June of 2010—almost two full years later). Given that the Web 2.0 honeymoon is pretty much over (both in the mainstream and in academia), I felt the ol' internets could use some good press.

When I say that the honeymoon is over, I am thinking of three primary assaults on Web 2.0/social media/the ol' internets. First, there is the Foucault/Hardt and Negri inspired work of theorists such as David Golumbia (in *The Cultural Logic of Computation*) or Alexander Galloway and Eugene Thacker (in *The Exploit*). These theorists position network technologies as radically extending and diffusing forms of hierarchy and control and thus further entrench capitalist and conservative values. Rather than producing democracy, such diffusion and entrenching actually hinder the possibility for resistance. Second, there is the work of Nicholas Carr (2008), who intelligently extends the early hyperbolic rantings of Andrew Keen. Summarized bluntly, Carr argues that the internet makes us stupider by eroding attention span and overwhelming memory. Third, there is the work of Jean M. Twenge and W. Keith Campbell, William Deresiewicz, and others on the internet's amplification of narcissism, particularly among young adults. I believe such critical work is important; all three remind us that the internet is not a ubiquitous good. While I think my story suggests a response to all three of these dispositions, I by and large will limit myself in this work to confronting the third (though I will address Carr briefly; given the sophistication of their work, I will not attempt a direct response at Golumbia, Galloway, or Thacker here). I will urge rhetoric and composition scholars (a we) to take an investment in determining how these new technologies will determine us (a should).

My thesis might be reduced to the following: Because social media technologies expose and facilitate intersubjective relationships, we should invest ourselves in fostering relationships, rather than with persuading audiences or constructing knowledges. This means encouraging participation rather than merely encouraging knowing, thinking, or even—as many theories of new media do—producing.

> **Thomas Friedman, *The World is Flat***
>
> That tipping point was reached sometime around the year 2000, when the flatteners converged on such a scale and with such intensity that millions of people on different continents suddenly started to feel that something...something...was new. They couldn't always quite describe what was happening, but by 2000 they sensed that they were in touch with people they'd never been in touch with before, were being challenged by people who had never challenged them before, were competing with people with whom they had never competed before, were collaborating with people with whom they had never collaborated before, and were doing things AS INDIVIDUALS they had never dreamnt of doing before.
>
> What they were feeling was the flattening of the world (p.204).

As a coda to Rowan's story, I would point out that at least three other children have been diagnosed thanks to our story's mass broadcast. The internet makes it easier to pay it forward.

Certainly our story lends credence to what terms such as "noble amateur" or "flattened infoscape" really mean. Few are arguing that social media are going to allow Madeline, the stay-at-home mom, to epistemically contribute to the cure for cancer. Research of that nature will continue to be conducted by an exclusive, well-supported, institutionally validated few. But social media do exponentially engage many in sharing the products of those elite few. Anyone familiar with Steven Johnson or Clay Shirky understands that this is what we mean by an increasingly smarter 21st century American populace. Knowledge construction might not be necessarily more egalitarian or democratic, but knowledge distribution certainly is.

In regards to Carr's arguments, I would note that he relies on particular, individualistic measures of intelligence—and he treats these measures as universally good. I would assert that Carr worries over individuals getting stupider because he doesn't have the disciplinary apparatus necessary to acknowledge that a body can be smart. Nor does he seem open to the idea that the forms of intelligence he chooses to highlight might in fact be a production of literacy and print mediums, and quite inessential (in every sense of the word) to human progress or happiness.

In some ways, then, Carr's criticisms remind me of rhetoric's ancient battle—it is Socrates and Callicles all over again; one emphasizes the intellect of the individual [mind], one speaks to necessity of the mass [body].[2] In articulating a theory of participation for 21st century digital rhetoric and composition, I am looking to intertwine these two positions—to make the individual mind a responsible (and responsive) agent embedded within the social body.

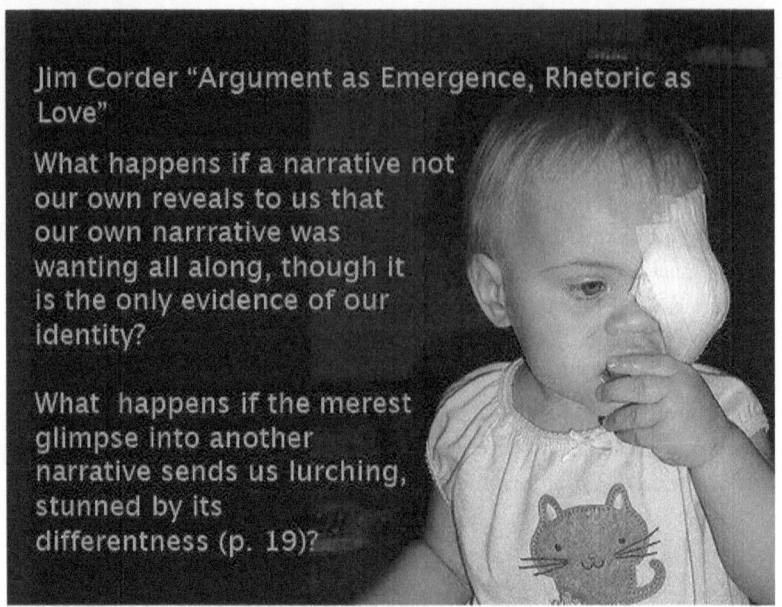

Jim Corder "Argument as Emergence, Rhetoric as Love"

What happens if a narrative not our own reveals to us that our own narrrative was wanting all along, though it is the only evidence of our identity?

What happens if the merest glimpse into another narrative sends us lurching, stunned by its differentness (p. 19)?

The impact social media had upon my family doesn't necessarily end with diagnosing Rowan's cancer; it is not exhausted in the *knowing* about the cancer. It extends to how it provided us with emotional, and what I want to term rhetorical, support. My story suggests how one particular techno-social internet practice, social media and social networking, is transforming both the ways in which our stories shape us (emphasis on the quantity of the "our") and the ways in which our mass presence transforms our psycho-social reliance on stories. The definition of rhetorical support worked out here will draw upon and extend Jim Corder's (1985) exploration of narrative in his essay "Argument as Emergence, Rhetoric as Love" through a (albeit brief) discussion of Emmanuel Levinas's notion of asymmetrical intersubjectivity.

For Corder, all individuals "narrate" a story that locates them within the fabric of space and time. Rhetoric supports and facilitates consciousness; rhetorical narratives provide a frame of reference for understanding and navigating the world. The interruption of one's narrative disorients the subject, and requires revision. Rhetoric, for Corder, becomes a willingness to change one's narrative; when confronted by a distressing narrative, a rhetorical subject learns to turn inward ("Why don't I believe that?") rather than outward ("How can you believe that?"). How do we resist the innate and powerful urge to turn into a defensive jerk?

Here I would point to Julia Kristeva's (1991) conclusion in her recent *Strangers to Ourselves*: "To worry or to smile, such is the choice when we are assailed by the strange; our decision depends on how familiar we are with our own ghosts" (p. 191). Levinas' asymmetrical intersubjective ethics suggest that Corder's narration is not necessarily a conscious operation; rather it is extra-conscious activity that lays the ground from which consciousness emerges. Furthermore, I would argue that social media mean that we no longer individually narrate stories. Today's technology allows for a sense of self emanating from our networked existence with others: The linear plot is replaced by the matrixed assemblage (in that our lives come to be understood less in terms of a "where-have-I-been-and-where-will-I-go?" and more in terms of "who-am-I-[with]"). These are not mutually exclusive.

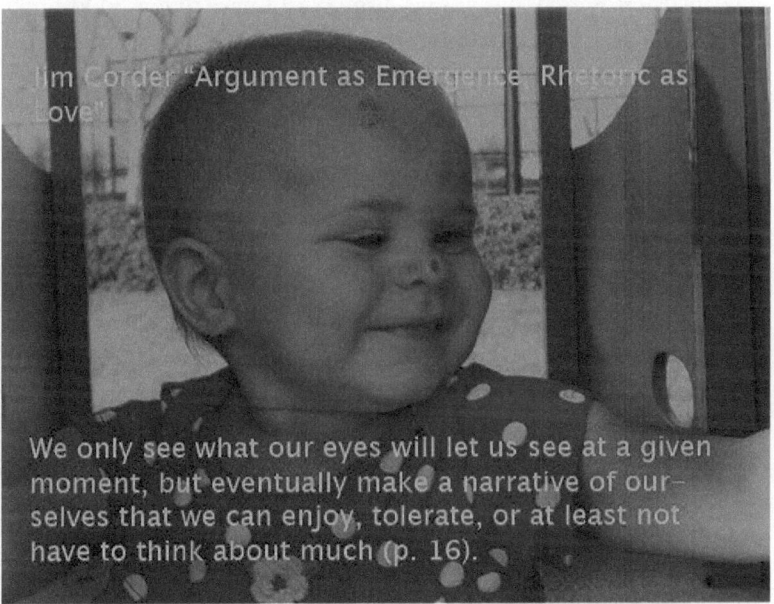

Jim Corder "Argument as Emergence, Rhetoric as Love"

We only see what our eyes will let us see at a given moment, but eventually make a narrative of ourselves that we can enjoy, tolerate, or at least not have to think about much (p. 16).

I am advocating an approach to digital rhetoric not framed strictly as consciously directed, linear transference of episteme between two autonomous and fully formed subjects. Rather, I urge that we attend to how particular social media encounters, always affective and epistemic, contribute to and complicate subject formation and social relations. Living with others is hard work. There is no reason why it can't be hard scholarly work.

In Corder's terms, I am approaching rhetoric as a willingness to revise one's own orientation rather than as a preoccupation with manipulating an other's narrative. The former approach conjures monikers such as "persuasion, argument, and antagonism." The latter I would associate with terms such as preontological, ethical, and agonism.

In theorizing rhetorical support, I am looking to extend Corder's conscious disposition toward change into a theory of a kind of change that precedes consciousness. I am reading Corder's work through the phenomenological, metaphysical ethics of Emmanuel Levinas (1969) and Alphonso Lingis (1994). In short, Levinas's ethics stress our debt to alterity for the very formation of our existence; this debt charges us with an infinite responsibility for others. These intersubjective ethics are asymmetrical because I cannot assume that I construct the other as she constructs me—I always owe more than I have to give. The other changes me before a (conscious, thinking, responsive) "I" ever emerges on the scene to make any kind of "sense." Lingis works from this proposition to speak to the importance of "being-there" (as a *saying* entity) over the concern for the content of what might be said.

I am born from an irrecoverable affective engagement with others. That the relation is irrecoverable is why, like Burke's abyss, it potentially haunts me. Thus, Levinas asks us to attend to all others rather than to bury ourselves deeper into our symbol systems. In terms more familiar to rhetoric, to welcome them rather than persuade them (or, as Victor Vitanza might write, to ontologize, categorize, and hence "kNOw them"). I hope those familiar with D. Diane Davis' project for a "non-appropriative rhetoric" will see connections here since, like Davis, I am interested in tracking down a dimension of rhetoric not immediately reducible to meaning-making (Davis, 2005, pp. 191-192), or, in light of Vitanza, reducing others to categorical meanings.

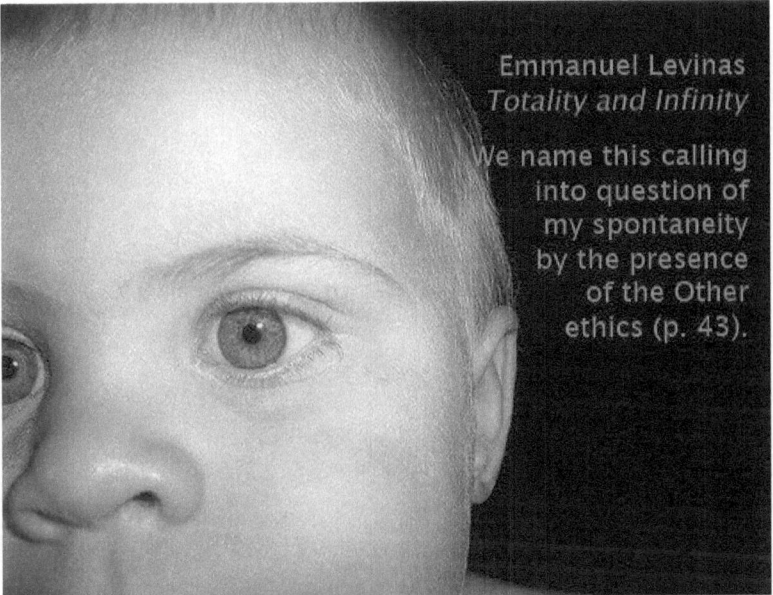

> Emmanuel Levinas
> *Totality and Infinity*
>
> We name this calling into question of my spontaneity by the presence of the Other ethics (p. 43).

My experiences with my daughter's cancer and with social media have oriented me away from a primary interest in what a consciousness does with rhetoric and toward an interest in what rhetoric does with consciousness. It is on the basis of this change in interest that I advocate for a rhetorical-ethics more attuned to attending to others than to explicitly (or intentionally) changing them. Building off of Levinas, we cannot help, by our very presence, to disturb and thus change an other. We can, however, develop a rhetorical-digital-compositional-ethical practice that takes such change into account. Drawn from Madeline's email, my theory of rhetorical support aims to suggest a praxis informed by a delicate balance between courage, humility, and knowledge. We can think here of Wikipedia's contradictory mantra: "Be bold . . . but please be careful."

Intersubjectivist ethics go beyond notions of discourse community. It's not just about people getting together to construct knowledge. It is a further recognition that getting together (re)produces identity or challenges it, depending on the scene and the tenor of the interlocutors. Before we make knowledge, we have to make each other. And, I'll suggest, the willingness to contact an *other* requires a very particular courage.[3]

Cancer, Loss, Change

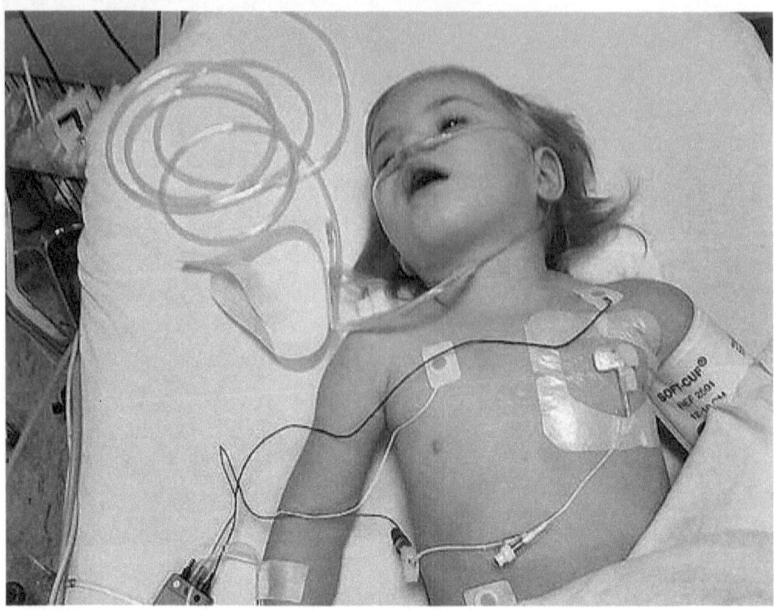

I frankly admit that I haven't done any traditional research into coping with cancer. I hope that my experiences here are fairly representative. Cancer infects every aspect of one's life. While dealing with Rowan's cancer, even everyday tasks became difficult. I never knew when the cancer would find me. I remember standing in a grocery store in Miami looking for string cheese and just losing it in the dairy aisle. Of course, I wasn't simply losing it. I was losing me. Because, especially in those early months when we couldn't know whether the cancer would spread out of Rowan's eye, nothing felt normal and we never felt ourselves. Of course, one can point to the context and rightly say that nothing was normal. But more than that, I would theorize that we were no longer ourselves. Cancer, and its specter of impending death, forced upon us the need for a completely new narrative and hence had engendered the emergence of new people. I am still getting to know me. To this day my wife will often say "I still don't feel myself." I know the feeling. It is likely tied to a resistance to accept what we have become even as we know we are transforming.

In *Breaking Up (at) Totality*, D. Diane Davis (2005) points toward kairotic laughter as an indication of the beyond-consciousness underlying our self-knowledge (see particularly pp. 21-24). Recalling an inability to stop laughing in church, Davis writes:

My whole Being wants desperately **NOT** to laugh, and yet it's clear to me that my will is not in control. [...] I fight desperately for control. But to no avail. My body has been *possessed* by the force of laughter: Despite my reason and my will, laughter BURSTS out. The battle is over: "I" have been conquered (p. 22).

I would contribute to this theory by noting that affective displacement can emerge as a laugh or tears. Davis describes a singular kairotic moment in which we temporarily lose ourselves. I hope, in this section, to describe something of a different duration.

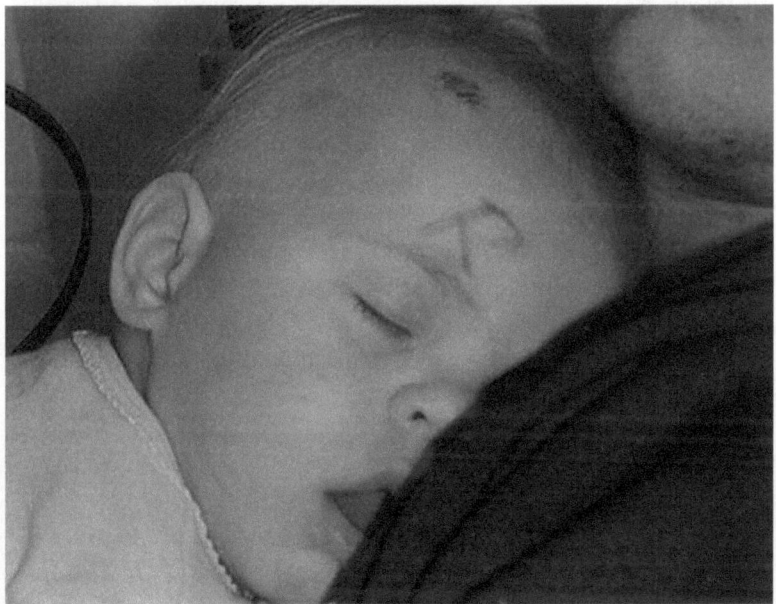

My experience confirms my inclinations toward fluid notions of identity. Cancer isn't something that happens to a self; it's something that transforms it. For evidence of the extent to which cancer forms a "new" person, I would turn to the divorce rate among retinoblastoma families. One of the first things you are told after diagnosis is that couples enduring a child with retinoblastoma have an 80% divorce rate. No doubt much of this can be attributed to the situation's high emotional stakes and the illness's high mortality rate. But also, I would suggest, it is because after a trauma of this magnitude the person you are isn't any longer the person your spouse chose to marry. And all that trauma, emotion, and loss don't make for the best conditions for a new courtship.

First-time parents are likely familiar with a degree of this *unheimlich*: this feeling of displacement, this interruption. But from the moment of our birth, culture, family, and institutions prepare us for and supply us with material to support such a "normal" transformation. There is no such support for childhood cancer. Hence my and my wife's extreme *unheimlich*—we were/are an other to ourselves—an extended experience of Davis' laughing body facing an impotent mind. As a successful white male, this is my first experience as really being anything other than "normal."

The difficulty of dealing with cancer's transformations is caught up in our expectations for particular cultural, familial, and institutional narratives— in our case, the anticipation of what should have been the narrative of Rowan's life. Even though, over one year removed from her last chemotherapy session, her cancer is in complete remission and her right eye shows no seeds, we still live in constant fear. Rowan's future will include a steady diet of exams under anesthesia and MRIs. Furthermore, retinoblastoma is an indicator of a disposition toward cancer. We will spend the rest of her life, in essence, waiting for cancer to return. The traditional narratives of driving her first car, graduating high school, going off to college, getting married, and having children are/will be/will-have-been haunted by the most horrible of possibilities and memories.

Fortunately, this is not a transformation that Rowan has to endure, although her childhood will certainly involve different narratives than those of the children around her. Her story promises to be more of difference than of loss. Not so for my wife and I. We lost our "normalcy." We lost the comfort of rhetorical support. We lost our selves.[4]

Thanks to social media, my wife and I did not, and do not, have to undergo this transformation alone. In addition to a supportive family and good friends, the few face-to-face encounters we had during treatments with other parents, and Meg and Rowan's Tuesday visits to Tampa's exemplary Children's Cancer Center, had social media putting us in contact with other families coping with retinoblastoma, childhood cancer, and the terrible transformations they engender. In the face of such uncertainty, we wanted others to help validate and construct our new life's narrative. In the process, the narrative of our lives (and the specter of bleak endings) becomes enmeshed in a network of altered narratives, to the extent that being-in-network operates alongside (and perhaps overrides) the linear-teleologic imagining of coming-to-be. It is alongside this that I began to sense that perhaps we didn't need to craft a new narrative as much as we needed to find a new network. In all likelihood it's both: a new narrative within a new network. Social media helped facilitate both.

Social media offered rhetorical support by providing us with material to remix into our new story. It also provided us with people to affirm this story. It provided a venue for sharing: complaints about doctors, hospital bureaucracy, fears, frustrations (particularly about meeting a child just in time to learn they will die), loss, the difficulty of rotating a prosthetic eye (my wife and I can actually "one-time" this problem now—talk about the abject transforming into the mundane), hope, hopelessness, detachment, victories, remissions, celebrations, and milestones.

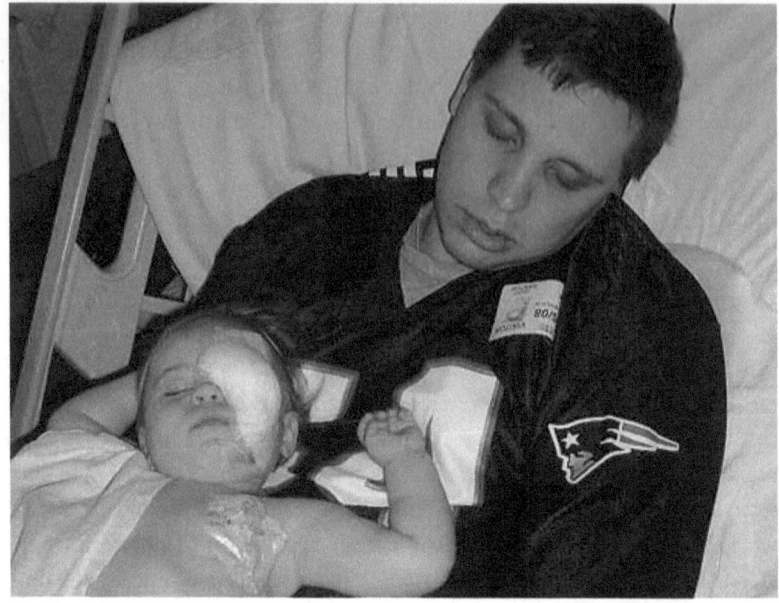

More important than the content of our sharing, it also let us share ears; it let us simply be there to "say." In *The Community of Those Who Have Nothing in Common*, Alphonso Lingis (1994) speaks to the impossibility of visiting the bedside of a dying parent. Particularly, playing with echoes of Levinas' distinction between the said and the saying (in Levinasian terms, the ontological and the ethical, which might be conceptualized as being and becoming), Lingis notes that we often come to find ourselves, in this moment-before-death-that-calls-for-something-to-be-said, with absolutely nothing to say. But, he argues, "What is imperative is that you be there and speak; what you say, in the end, hardly matters" (p. 108).

So, too, with the retinoblastoma community. Social media provide(d) us, as parents, with the ability to say. Another sharing amongst this community is the commonplace discussion of friendship—every parent has the story of good friends who simply disappear after the diagnosis: The disappearance of many friends who simply could not imagine what could be said and therefore offered no saying. Of course, there is also the rise of other acquaintances into friends, who perhaps understood the futility of whatever they said but also recognized the importance of an attending ear. Those people know who they are. We thank them.

To recognize the difference between the saying and the said is to unsettle our (and I mean this broadly to include most who dwell within institutions of higher learning) disposition toward content/knowledge. The said falls within the realms of the ontological, the hermeneutic, the epistemological. The saying, however, attempts to capture something more primal and elusive. In place of the (said) content of a communicative utterance, attention to the saying seeks to interpret the significance of the unsignified performance of an utterance. It is through saying, I believe, that we nourish our sense of place within the infinity of space. And new ways of saying (e.g., new technologies) likely reveal to us other orientations toward things-said and highlight the peculiarities of our ways of saying.

I wouldn't argue that such support is necessarily "consensus" and later in this installation I will address a particularly charged conflict within the community. Nor am I speaking for the internet here as a mass many-to-many communicative technology as much as I am speaking of social media, which I would like to frame as a particular one-to-group-and-back-again communicative technology. It's not *here comes everybody all at once*. Social media are not groups of everybody; rather they enable groups of particular people. One of social media's most unique properties is its ability to put us into proximity with others—to allow both patient thinking and immediate response.⁵

Nor would I argue that all rhetorical support is necessarily good in a strictly moral sense. As many recent critics of social media have pointed out, these technologies and practices can just as easily support terrorism, fascism, oppression, or hate as they can justice, democracy, liberation, or love. But I would argue that such technologies open the possibility for "goodness" and ethics in a pre-moral, ontological, ethical, rhetorically supportive sense. At least they're hating together. My precise interest isn't in the hate of course, but in the potential to come together in new ways, if only because coming into contact, coming together, has the potential to help break us apart. Recalling Kristeva, the reaction to breaking apart can be humility or anger, love or hate. We, as instructors in rhetoric and composition and communication—as scholars across the humanities—have to invest our time, passion, and energy into helping determine how our technologies will determine us.

I want to suggest that social media isn't necessarily bound to the binaries informing Walter Ong's (1986) secondary orality; it is not simply a matter of either the ear or the eye. To a culture so grounded in the ontological distance instigated by Ong/McLuhan's literacy/print (the eye), it might initially seem that this is a reincorporation of the values Ong, Havelock, and others have associated with cultures of the ear. I want to go a step farther, however, and propose that—especially given the "distance" amplified by literacy and print, the primary sensibility of social media is *touch*. Sensibility here is Levinas's term and I use it to suggests an affective, bodily thinking that precedes conscious thought. In proximity to an other's response, we feel them. Their difference touches us at a level "below" the skin and under-our-thought. Rhetorical support is an acknowledgement that words are a pathetic extension of our hands; they can approach as fists (Kenneth Burke, 1984, *Permanence and Change*, pp. 191-192) or in the form of caress (Levinas, 1969, *Totality and Infinity*, pp. 257-258). While they always threaten with violence, we can temper that threat through a willingness to re-orient the self rather than change the other. This is particularly the kind of determinism I believe rhetoric and composition scholars can encourage for technology. Once again: courage, humility, knowledge, and, as Madeline's email emphasizes, risk.

I want to posit my experience with cancer as a hyper-amplification of a basic human condition: a need for others in the face of others. Others as the medium for a sense of belonging and home. Others as the catalyst for first thinking and recognizing ourselves. To manipulate Bill Readings: "Others [and not thought] necessarily as an addiction from which we never get free" (see *University in Ruins*, p. 128). Incorporating touching others to the thinking of thought. Others as a catalyst for thought and thinking; especially a rethinking of the self (as foundational Western concept) by a self (a collection of thoughts put in motion by the stirring of an other). In my particular case, being-with-death might have been the catalyst for a subjective reformation, but others were an indispensible part of the reconstitution responsible for the new me. And it is the technological and social transformations opened up by social media that facilitated this transformation.

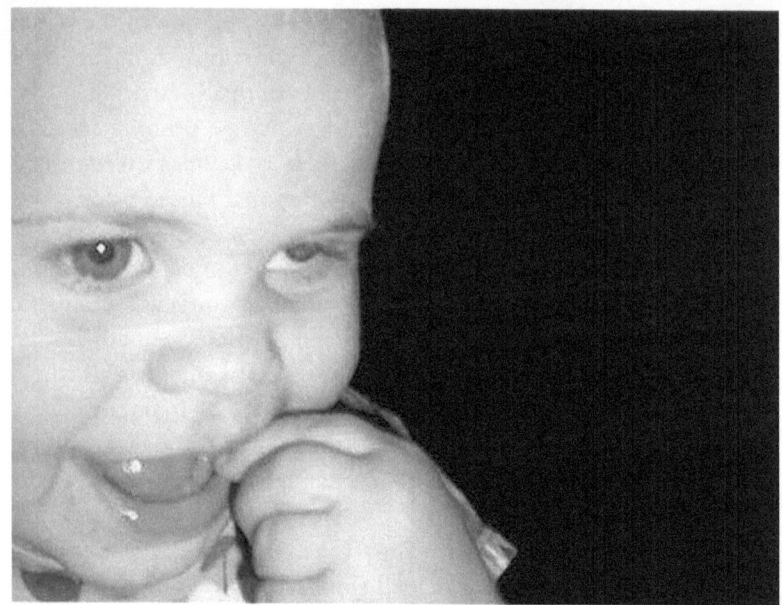

Baseball Cards

It is precisely how social media intensify the addiction to others that some find so troubling, particularly those whose ontological-subjective narrative comes from traditional liberal humanist senses shaped (dare I say determined) by literate and print narratives (especially the Great Canonical ones).[6] I offer as an example William Deresiewicz's (2009) recent Chronicle essay "Faux Friendship," which laments how Facebook displays the disfigured "fluid and flexible" (and thus empty and meaningless) state of contemporary friendship (and, by extension, postmodern subjectivity). He writes of his quantified friend list: "They're simulacra of my friends, little dehydrated packets of images and information, no more my friends than a set of baseball cards is the New York Mets."

The metaphor of childish toys (and childish relationships) also operates in his conclusion that:

> Friendship is devolving, in other words, from a relationship to a feeling, from something people share to something each of us hugs privately to ourselves in the loneliness of our electronic caves, rearranging the tokens of connection like a lonely child playing with dolls.

My first, tongue-in-cheek response here is to remind Deresiewicz that Plato and Aristotle, Byron and Emerson, can be baseball cards too: symbols frozen in time that, through their very distance from the present place and time, offer notions of a better, richer world. This once again rehashes the ancient debates between idealism and sophistry, conjuring the ghosts of Socrates and Callicles. Such is not my explicit purpose here.

Instead, let me agree with Deresiewicz that we do turn to social media for subjective affirmation, that we are in his words "hoping that someone, anyone, will confirm our existence by answering back." But let's not sound too quickly the battle cry of narcissism. Let me argue that answering back—one to group and back again—is the unique power of social media. And let me argue that it both intensifies the call for and makes possible the realization of confirmation impossible in an atomistic, modern age. Further, all that chattering predisposes us to the tentative nature of the narratives upon which we emerge(d) and through which we are sustained. Sharing the ephemeral—our edges— is what helps define us to each other and, more importantly, to ourselves. There's an underlying psycho-social reason why many of us feel the need to share intimate details with groups of friends—reasons that don't amount to self-infatuation. Status posts describing coffee grinds in the fridge, remarking on the tea in Kentucky, exploring "what Lost character am I?," critiquing the sexist speech of telemarketers, or hailing the rediscovery of AC/DC aren't necessarily extensions of a childhood verse "I am special. Look at me" (to quote off the flap of Twenge and Campbell's hyperbolic *The Narcissism Epidemic*). Perhaps they are really a lone sonar ping searching, hoping, for confirmation.

Recognizing what was once considered foundational as perhaps only chatter tends to ramp up disequilibrium. As Deresiewicz himself notes, echoing Foucault, the institutions of the 19th and 20th century—church, state, school—so central not only to subject formation but also to subjects maintaining (after all subjectivity is not an isolated event but rather enacted patterns of performativity) have lost much of their cultural hegemony. Add to this the list of emaciated discursive institutions the literary canon and even the television network (Oh Andy Griffith, oh Cosbys, oh Simpsons, where have you all gone?). Today, I choose my identity from more than three channels. Given both the volume and diversity of the cultural cacophony, we are left evermore loquacious over a seemingly expanding abyss. We can talk ourselves both to *and* from its edge. It's a matter of choice and perspective. I think my story has likely cemented both for me. How about you?

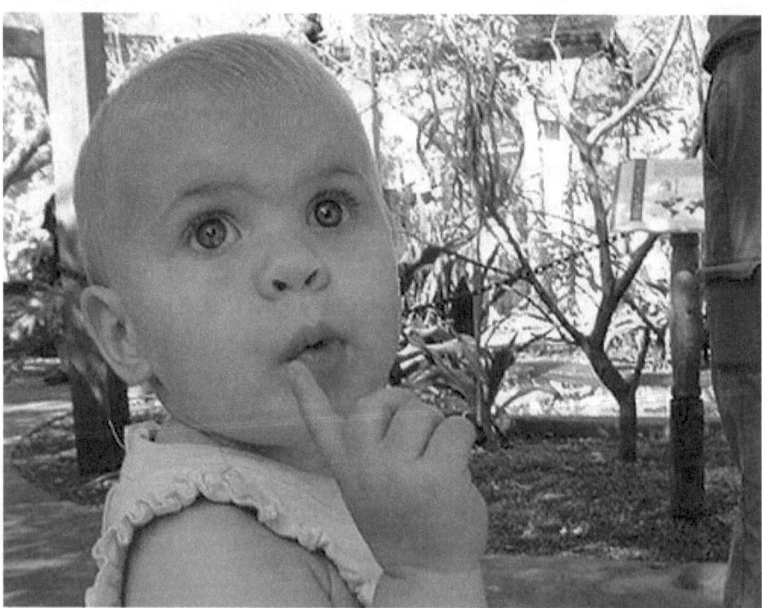

For one doesn't have to have coped with a child's cancer to see the foundations of the self, instituted by thousands of years of literacy and print, coming to be questioned through new media practices.

I am reminded of Michael Feehan's (1985) anecdote from Kenneth Burke's visit to the University of Texas, Arlington:

> KB to The Scholar (offhandedly): What do you believe in?
> The Scholar to KB (leaning forward): What do you believe in?
> KB to The Scholar (impishly grinning): I believe in asking people what they believe in (p. 148).

Perhaps it would be better to ask *who* we believe in. Perhaps more than asking others to expose themselves, we should seek others as a way of asking and exposing our self. And these subtle differences might best express the difference between Burke and Levinas' projects. Both, however, call upon us to dialogically engage the other from a position of ethical weakness (it's ~~turtles~~ others all the way down, after all) rather than ontological, epistemological, or canonical strength.

Our baseball cards form the house of cards (the institution, Foucault might say) from within which we think, work, and live. They trace the line of others (or lead to others, if we think in terms of disciplinary associations) that sketch the boundaries of my self. I think this installation makes it clear who I identify as my house of cards—Burke and Levinas, Corder and Davis, Sullivan and Porter. No doubt I have forgotten others. But to accept intersubjective ethics is to attempt to articulate to whom you are indebted and to invite others to show you how you might be indebted otherwise.

Against Deresiewicz and his liberal humanist baseball cards, I would assert that the need for validation is not new—even if since Socrates the need for validation has been castigated as weakness. What is new are the tools and sources for validation. What to the liberal humanist will always appear as narcissism and exhibitionism, I offer as a manifestation of social uncertainty and the need for others, in the face of such uncertainty, to confirm our existence. I understand my own experiences with cancer as an intensification of the 21st century condition, in which the legitimation crisis has spread from social institutions to the members of society. Such an amplification should not be described either euphorically or fatalistically (and I recognize that I often border on euphoria; I read, listen, and face people such as Deresiewicz, Carr, Golumbia, Thacker, and Galloway precisely in an effort to temper my enthusiasm). I would encourage eschewing dramatic optimism or pessimism. It is transformative. It is change. It is disorienting. It calls for a rhetoric of cooperation, one that aims to change the self and help the other (rather than helping the self by changing the other).

A rhetoric of cooperation is predicated on the necessity, for each subject, of rhetorical support. This is not mourning a loss of autonomy as much as an encouraging of togetherness. My theory: We tend to be more cooperative once we recognize that we need support.

COMING HOME (TO A HOUSE OF CARDS)

I opened this installation with a narrative and, given my investment in the ways social media promote, incite, encourage, and challenge subjective narrativity, and my attachment of Sullivan and Porter's feminist ethics, I feel compelled to close with another.

As I mention earlier, the uniqueness of my family's story led to its mass broadcast; we were featured in countless print, television, and internet news stories and effectively achieved our 15 minutes of fame. Given this, it wasn't unusual for us to get phone calls from people all over the country. One phone call in particular struck me. A mother, likely in her late forties or early fifties from the sound of her voice, called to reassure us regarding our decision to enucleate. She wanted to let us know that Rowan could live to have a healthy, normal life. She had made the same decision over 20 years ago, and her daughter, now 25, had enjoyed a normal childhood. She was particularly proud that she was a soccer player.

I should break here for some context: As I mentioned earlier, the retinoblastoma community is not a homogenized collective. Like any group, its contours flow around its internal controversies. In retinoblastoma groups, one of the most intense controversies concerns how aggressively to fight to save an eye. Such a decision concerns a number of factors: the location of the tumor, whether the cancer has presented unilaterally or bilaterally, whether to use dangerous but often effective localized radiation treatments. Given the extent of Rowan's tumor, this really wasn't a question for Meg and I—we both immediately agreed that the eye had to go. Just hearing about different kinds of treatment can lead to passionate arguments or cause people to leave the group. No one is comfortable questioning their child's care. But many cases are not so clear. And many parents struggle with the body-issue decision to de-normalize their child.

I don't know the particular circumstances that surround the mother who talked with me on the phone that day. But I realized, as she fought through tears to affirm our decision and to tell me her story, that she really wasn't talking to me. She was addressing her daughter, and perhaps more significantly, herself. She was reflecting on a terrible choice she was forced to make so long ago.

I remember her twice saying "I know you feel alone." And that was it, really. We had never felt alone. We had felt many things, but never alone. I came to wonder if she had ever had this conversation with anyone.

Ever.

And, reflecting back, I wonder if, unlike my wife and I who had the benefit of contact with so many parents coping with retinoblastoma, without social media, would this woman simply lacked the technology to communicate with other parents. I wonder if that very technology doesn't also create a disposition, easily misidentified as narcissism, to share the self. To have the courage to contact a stranger. To have the strength to expose oneself. To dance with one's ghosts.

Because that's what I want, I think, if I can claim to know my new self so well. That's want I want my story to signify: that although I could not necessarily control it, I can help others to help me to become otherwise.

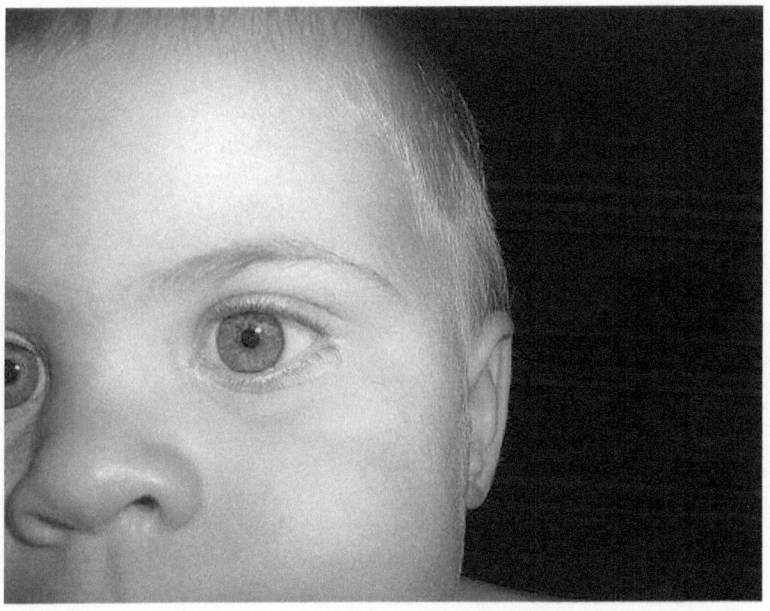

References

Burke, Kenneth. (1984). *Permanence and change*. Berkeley, CA: University of California Publishing.

Carr, Nicholas. (2008, July/August). Is Google making us stupid? What the Internet is doing to our brains. *Atlantic Magazine*. Retrieved from http://www.theatlantic.com/magazine/archive/2008/07/is-google-making-us-stupid/6868/

Carr, Nicholas. (2010, May 24) The Web shatters focus, rewires brains. *Wired.com*. Retrieved from http://www.wired.com/magazine/2010/05/ff_nicholas_carr/2/

Considine, Bob. (2008, August 28). Woman spots baby's eye cancer online. Todayshow.com. *msnbc.com*. Retrieved from http://today.msnbc.msn.com/id/26437081/ns/today-today_health/

Corder, Jim. (1985). Argument as emergence, rhetoric as love. *Rhetoric Review, 4*(1).

Davis, Diane D. (2005). Addressing alterity: Rhetoric, hermeneutics, and the nonappropriative relation. *Philosophy and Rhetoric, 38*(3), 191-212.

Davis, Diane D. (2000). *Breaking up (at) totality: A rhetoric of laughter*. Carbondale, IL: Southern Illinois University Press.

Deresiewicz, William. (2009, December 6). Faux friendship. *The Chronicle of Higher Education*. Retrieved from http://chronicle.com/article/Faux-Friendship/49308/

Feehan, Michael. (1985, Fall/Winter). 3 Days and 3 terms with KB. *Pre/Text, 6*(3-4), 143-148.

Friedman, Thomas L. (2005). *The world is flat: A brief history of the 21st Century*. New York, NY: Farrar, Straus, and Giroux Press.

Gallaway, Alexander, & Thacker, Eugene. (2007). *The exploit*. Minneapolis, MN: University of Minnesota Press.

Golumbia, David. (2009). *The cultural logic of computation*. Cambridge, MA: Harvard University Press.

Kristeva, Julia. (1991). *Strangers to ourselves*. Trans. Leon S. Roudiez. New York, NY: Columbia University Press.

Latour, Bruno. (1999). *Pandora's hope: Essays on the reality of science study*. Cambridge, MA: Harvard University Press.

Levinas, Emmanuel. (1969). *Totality and infinity: An essay on exteriority*. Pittsburgh, PA: Duquesne University Press.

Lingis, Alphonso. (1994). *The community of those who have nothing in common*. Bloomington, IN: Indiana University Press.

Ong, Walter J. (1986). Writing is a technology that restructures thought. In Gerd Baumann (Ed.), *The written word* (pp. 23-50). Oxford, UK: Clarendon Press.

Readings, Bill. (1997). *The university in ruins*. Cambridge, MA: Harvard University Press.

Sullivan, Patricia, & Porter, James E. (1997). *Opening spaces: Writing technologies and critical research practices*. Greenwich, CT: Ablex Publishing Company.

Twenge, Jean M. & Campbell, W. Keith. (2010). *The narcissism epidemic.* New York, NY: Free Press Publishers.

Vitanza, Victor J. (1996). *Negation, subjectivity, and the history of rhetoric.* Albany, NY: State University of New York Press.

Notes

* This installation was initially delivered accompanied by a Prezi at the 2010 Computers and Writing Conference. To maximize accessibility, I forewent transforming it into Flash and have instead used standards-compliant XHTML and CSS. In doing so, I fear I have lost some of the affective movement of the original presentation (unexpected transitions and zooms keyed to particular words and ideas). Such a fear was confirmed by my attentive reviewers, and I appreciate their feedback. Ultimately, my disdain for Flash's accessibility issues, concerns over bitrot, and the time restraints of academic publication led me to keep the project in standards compliant XHTML and CSS. I hope that the chronological progression of images helps relate my experience, both trying and joyous, that I cannot reduce to mere words.

1. From an interview with *USA Today*:

> It wasn't easy for Madeleine Robb to send an e-mail to another mom warning that her baby might have a deadly form of eye cancer. But she's glad she did it - and so is the mother of 1-year-old Rowan Santos.

"I didn't want to scare her," Robb told TODAY co-host Meredith Vieira from London on Thursday. "But then I weighed out the options. If something wasn't wrong, then no real harm was done. If something was wrong, I really had no option, so obviously I had to tell her" (Considine, 2008).

2. Again, I would suggest that Carr's perspective on intelligence is overly determined by literacy and print. Thus, he feels comfortable reducing intelligence to the filtration of information between short and long-term memory (see Carr, 2010). His arguments on sensory overload are predicated on this reduction. Other scholars in digital studies in rhetoric and composition—I am thinking particularly of Gregory Ulmer—might look at the neurological evidence cited by Carr without lamentation; they might interpret it not as the "loss of intelligence" but rather as the transformation of intelligence that calls less for linear rationality (and memory) and more for a logic of assemblage. In fact, one of the assumptions of Steven Johnson's (2010) newest work, *Where Good Ideas Come From*, is that interaction and hyper-activity (my term, not Johnson's) helps stimulate invention, rather than cloud or overwhelm it.

3. As so often happens, Madeline's particular courage reminds me of another project I am working on—one examining the relationship between

Bruno Latour's interpretation of Callicles in Plato's *Gorgias* dialogue and Levinas's suspicions toward ontology. Latour highlights how Callicles' rejection of Socratic rationalism depends upon courage before the masses:

> The *superior* people I mean aren't shoemakers or cooks: above all, I'm thinking of a people who've applied their *cleverness* to politics and thought about how to run their community *well*. But cleverness is only part of it; they also have *courage*, which enables them *to see their policies through to the finish without losing their nerve* and giving up (491a-b, qtd. in Latour, 1999, p. 239). (emphasis Latour's)

In simple terms, I would suggest that courage is as important, if not more important, than critical thinking.

4. It might be interesting here for me to contrast my own difficulties coping with Rowan's cancer to my parents' experiences. Before I was born my parents lost their first child, Benilda, to infant leukemia (a curable condition were she born today). In some ways, they feel as if their loss contributed to the development of medical science—contributed to saving Rowan's life. So, while they have been very supportive and empathetic to our plight, they also perceive Rowan's survival as a kind of validation of their own daughter's death. Thankfully, my parents' story is not solely one of loss. I am learning to appreciate my story as something other than loss as well.

5. In researching my own story, I have come across a number of websites that ridicule Megan and me for not realizing that something was wrong. I find a thread on Williamsboard.com revealing. As one of the interlocutors suggests, Rowan's eye looked perfectly normal except in particular photographs. The fact that Megan and I did not attend to these photographs earlier likely supports theories that we only see what we can handle seeing.

But I note the Williamsboard.com thread for another reason. The internet is a mass landscape. It does not necessarily promote ethical proximity. The people on Williamsboard were not in proximity with us (so they thought), and such distance encourages humor. Sure, it's insensitive, but funny too (who doesn't like laser beams shooting out of a squirrel's eyes?).

Social media, however, as I am attempting to use the term, speaks to localized groups engaged in particular ethical practices encouraged and facilitated by dialogic technologies.

6. Here I would address the potential irony of critiquing literate-print dependencies on narratives in what amounts to be, despite its hypertextual mediation, a linear narrative. What I hope saves me from complete hypocrisy is the tenor of my narrative; it is not meant to be certain of itself and foreclose questioning; but rather, through the tentative and conditional nature of its speculations, welcoming of other responses, angles, and stories. Please send those stories to marcsantos at usf dot edu, or share them on my blog at http://insignificantwrangler.blogspot.com/2011/1/rowans-story.html

PEDAGOGY

Pedagogy: Critical Approaches to Teaching Literature, Language, Composition, and Culture is on the Web at http://www.dukeupress.edu/Catalog/ViewProduct.php?productid=45624

Pedagogy seeks to create a new discourse surrounding teaching in English studies by fusing theoretical approaches and practical realities. As a journal dealing exclusively with pedagogical issues, it is intended as a forum for critical reflection and as a site for spirited and informed debate from a multiplicity of positions and perspectives. It strives to reverse the long-standing marginalization of teaching and the scholarship produced around it and instead to assert the centrality of teaching to our work as scholars and professionals.

"New Media Scholarship and Teaching: Challenging the Hierarchy of Signs" by Ellen Cushman. *Pedagogy* 11.1 (2011).

Ellen Cushman's essay describes the culture of some English departments and the value system often attached to various forms of media in them. Examples of new media scholarship are offered to demonstrate the plurality of scholarship and teaching practices possible with new media. New media compositions privilege all sign systems equally to the alphabet; thus new media composing is an activity that potentially can change the cultural practices of knowledge production and teaching as it has taken place in English studies. This essay represents our journal's mission by illustrating how movements in English studies can be put in conversation with each other. New media studies is an area of scholarship embraced by composition and rhetoric scholars, but Cushman's piece places it not only within English studies broadly, but also in relation to pedagogy. Thus, it fulfills two goals of the journal.

10 New Media Scholarship and Teaching: Challenging the Hierarchy of Signs

Ellen Cushman

Scenario 1: Department Meeting

A digital video production scholar was trying to understand what a creative nonfiction scholar was saying: "Can you make that more opaque?"

"You mean *transparent*?" she asked. "No, I mean *opaque*."

"No, you mean *transparent*; *opaque* means unclear, cloudy." "No, I mean *opaque*, as in visible."

Scenario 2: Department Meeting

Describing why film production, writing, and new media will never be taught in the English department, the chair said, "English will have nothing to do with the production of meaning."

You have to laugh. I knew where these speakers were coming from and have since realized that these statements reflect larger changes in intellectual work in English studies. I have been in and out of English departments most of my career. My PhD was granted from a language, literature, and communication department; I have taught in writing programs that ranged from specialized, intensive writing training for incoming, at-risk freshmen to classic vertical writing programs offering BAs up to PhDs in writing and rhetoric; I have taught in English departments as a rhetoric and composition scholar and an English education scholar; and I have taught a few classes in literacy and teacher education in schools of education. I research with and in communities (Cushman 1998, 1999a, 1999b; Cushman and Grabill 2009), my tribe (Cushman 2005, 2008), and nonprofit organizations (Cushman 2002, 2006) at the intersection of literacy, technology, culture, and praxis (Cushman 2006; Cushman and Green 2010).

For some time, I have been considering the role of the public intellectual in English studies and the ways in which English studies has promoted or discouraged these roles (Cushman 1999b, 2003a, 2003b). I have produced and taught new media and have had a long-standing interest in the struggle and the tools, the complexities of learning new sign systems, and discursive conventions used to negotiate asymmetrical power relations.

So when I hear my colleagues discuss the opacity and transparency of a statement, I know that one is referencing semantic clarity of speech, and the other, the visual density of dots in digital information. To make some- thing more opaque in visual information, one toggles the transparency of the dots, thus saturating the digital information with data that reflect the light: the more light reflected by the data, the more opaque it becomes, thus the more visible and apparent. In the first scenario, my colleagues worked from equally important, though completely different, epistemological perspectives on the technical nature of the sign technologies with which they were most comfortable. In writing, one rephrases text to make a convoluted, or opaque, statement clearer — more transparent and harmonious to the ear. In digital imaging, one increases opacity to make the image more visible. Enhanced perception is the goal of both processes, but the media and techniques used to achieve this differ. The good news is that my colleagues in this first scenario realized that they were seeking the same goal and eventually came to a shared understanding with mutual respect.

The second scenario ended not as well. When the chair of the English department said, "English will have nothing to do with the production of meaning," he meant that the English department should focus on literary critique, history, and theory. This emphasis privileges the disinterested critique of literature and history. However, the intellectual activities centered on a "production of meaning" might include film and digital video production *and* composition and rhetoric — any discipline of English studies that, in other words, explores and reveals how individuals use multiple media to teach and create meaning. As was the case in this particular English department, resources, incentives, and new initiatives would continue to emphasize scholarly activities related to disinterested critique rather than those that might have to do with the production of meaning. Two years after the sociolinguists left the English department, and one year after the department turned down a proposed PhD in rhetoric and writing, the English education scholars left the department for a newly created Department of Writing, Rhetoric, and American Cultures.

Regardless of their outcomes, though, both scenarios were rooted in a systemic problem of English studies. The discipline values the interpretation of text above the production of text, image, sound, and motion. Yet intellectual activities and media are intricately connected and mutually sustaining in what I call a hierarchy of signs. This hierarchy privileges the letter, text, and their consumption over image, film, public and student writing, and their production. Unfortunately, this hierarchy remains intact despite considerable challenges from both outside and inside the discipline, which have exposed and softened prejudices against media. English studies, on the whole, stays true to its hierarchy of signs, privileging text and its interpretation above all other forms of expression and their production. Change is slow in part because the intellectual activities surrounding text have not changed.

Making a case for English studies as having a rigid hierarchy of signs may seem like shooting fish in a barrel. Of course, English studies should be interested in the letter, the study of print, the book. But English studies has been influenced by cultural studies, opened to the study of multimodal artifacts (for example, film, art, photography, and material objects). If English studies has revised the artifacts it values for study, why have similar changes not taken place in the production of knowledge and methods of teaching English education?

Kathleen Welch offers a partial answer in her essay "Electrifying Classical Rhetoric: Ancient Media, Modern Technology, and Contemporary Composition" (1990: 25): "Many people now will routinely acknowledge the idea that film and video are 'artistic' media. However, their own responses to these media often indicate that these newer symbol systems are not in fact taken as seriously as symbol systems such as print or painting or music."

If newer symbol systems are not taken seriously, then how can multimodality possibly influence the scholarship produced and the teaching practices in English studies? This question is particularly important for English educators, the teachers of preservice 6 – 12 English teachers, who must require future teachers to achieve the professional standards to teach multimodality. Generations of students in high schools are learning to produce video, digital music, Web pages, slide shows, and a host of other media on their own time because English teachers typically are not equipped to teach them. If professors in English studies could produce multimodal scholarship and create more assignments that ask for multimodal products, then perhaps the hierarchy of signs could be leveled.

To explore and encourage such practices, I first describe the culture of English studies and the activities of making meaning that take place therein. I summarize the calls for change in these meaning-making practices and suggest why these calls have not yet affected the production of knowledge in English. I then illustrate possibilities inherent in new media compositions. New media compositions privilege all sign systems equally to the alphabet; thus, new media composition potentially can change the cultural practices of knowledge production and teaching in English studies.

To Be Lettered: Textuality in English Studies

To be literate in the institutional culture of English departments is to be lettered (for example, to write the essay well, to be highly specialized in a field of literary study, and to be well versed in an area of textuality such as a theory, genre, period, or author's work). Though not a surprise in a discipline that centers itself on the study of the written word, the intellectual pull of the written word has very real consequences for knowledge making and teaching practices. English departments maintain a hierarchy of sign technologies, with meaning making in letters and print afforded a good deal of instructional effort, accruing the highest status and receiving the most reward. Gunther Kress and Theo Van Leeuwen (2001: 1) might call this the "dominance of monomodality"; they might also note that the overreliance on monomodality "has begun to reverse" (1). Though many useful, enlightening, and engaging teaching practices and knowledge products have resulted from this dominance, the hierarchy of signs hinders knowledge making and teaching practices with multimodal discourses. Even though multimodal discourses and the sign technologies that allow their production are increasingly important to everyday acts of meaning making in schools, workplaces, and communities, the cultural practices of knowledge production in English still largely rely on the letter and print.

Here's Welch again on the ways in which this "class system in texts" manifests itself in curricular initiatives related to new media technologies:

> The most compelling evidence for this marginalization of newer discourse technologies lies in their nonintegration in general education requirements. They are regarded as peripheral concerns, unrelated to the study of print texts. When courses do appear in the electronic media, they tend to be segregated or marginalized.
>
> Their placement in the curriculum announces their secondary status. The written text of the canon reigns supreme; a remarkable sameness of response exists in the entrenched unawareness of the issues involved. (1990: 23)

To understand how new media might work as a challenge to the hierarchy of sign technologies, it is worth looking at scholarly and pedagogical activities that have taken textuality to task.

The daily life of the English scholar, resting as it does on print, reproduces and sustains itself as textuality, or practices of consumption indicated by critique, analysis, and interpretation of texts. In *The Rise and Fall of English*, Robert Scholes describes the four intellectual activities that take place in English studies: theorizing, historicizing, producing, and consuming texts:

> By theory I mean a canon of methods to be used in studying the other three aspects of textuality: how to situate a text (history), how to compose one (production), and how to read one (consumption). Theory, which has existed since ancient times, now consists of grammar, rhetoric, dialectic, poetics, hermeneutics, semiotics, grammatology, and other modes of understanding textuality. If English is to be a discipline, theory must be at the center of our teaching. (1998: 147)

While Scholes believes that these four activities should be balanced and practiced equally, such is rarely the case. English studies scholars who interpret and theorize are overrepresented at faculty meetings and find the idea of the production in whatever form (for example, film, creative writing, composing, speaking) abhorrent.

To be fair, this problem with textuality has been described from within and outside the discipline of English studies. Reseeing the page and book, Johanna Drucker (1995) directs the reader's eye to the letter and its products as images themselves through her analysis of artists' books. When print is divorced from the image it is, it becomes unseen as image and is viewed instead as transparently direct communication from one mind to another. To wed the letter to its material presence, as Drucker does, is to recognize it again, to chip away at its status by no longer ignoring it. W. J. T. Mitchell (1995) follows a similar path in his insistence on image/text as changing the ways textuality structures intellectual activities in English studies. Mitchell discusses the need to change the discipline but offers little in terms of possibility: "The pictorial turn is not just about the new significance of visual culture; it has implications for the acts of reading, literature, and literacy. This means that literary studies cannot simply 'add on' the study of film, television, and mass culture to its lists of courses without changing the whole map of the discipline" (418). Changing the discipline requires significant reflection on and modifications to the intellectual activities of English studies. Such a change, though, cannot take place if the discipline maintains a hierarchy of signs and its concomitant hierarchy of differentially valued activities: theory, history, consumption, and production.

Jay Bolter and Richard Grusin (2000: 30) find that Mitchell's "picture theory finally assimilates images to words more than the reverse." In short, knowledge production in print alone reinforces the supremacy of letters, the habits of mind cultivated with this tool (textuality), and the artifacts of knowledge produced and delivered with this tool (print). Even if the content of the message challenges the hierarchy of signs, as Mitchell's picture theory attempts, the challenge is delivered predominately in the media and form that it seeks to critique. Knowledge-making practices could be reformed so that critiques of cultural practices, such as Mitchell's, might find articulation and value in other sign technologies.

Scholars who have pointed out the dominance of the letter, writing, and the book are illustrative of a growing resistance to the hierarchy of signs. These studies also suggest that challenges to the hierarchy of signs made in print and with the letter may not be as potent a challenge as hoped, given the limitations of the media in which they are issued. Writing, print, and textuality are transparently ubiquitous in English studies, adding to their taken-for-granted nature. With new media scholarship and the teaching of new media, however, scholars are in a better position to level the hierarchy of signs used for knowledge making by valuing other sign technologies as equal to the letter and by changing knowledge-making practices to include multiple sign technologies.

Found in many fields, the resistance to print's prominence as premiere sign technology for meaning making lays the groundwork for new media composing as a scholarly and teaching endeavor. I will not argue for replacing print with other sign technologies, as some do (see Stephens 1990). I do think, however, that print must be seen and valued in equal relation with other media if scholars are to imagine and then enact the potential of knowledge making and teaching with new media.

New Media Scholarship: The Production of Meaning

Perhaps the greatest obstacle to leveling the hierarchy of signs rests in the reluctance of English scholars to engage in production as Scholes describes it, a reluctance so stated by the former chair of my former English department in scenario 2 that opened this article. Setting aside the implication that literary interpretation is meaningless, his statement reflects a belief that English scholars have long held, that textuality includes theory about and consumption of textual objects above historicizing and producing. Unfortunately, even when literary scholars, students, and a host of external audiences ask for a revaluation of the kinds of objects studied, produced, and taught within English studies, the production of meaning takes place primarily in and around print.

What might a multimodal digital essay look like, and how could it work to destabilize the hierarchy of signs in knowledge-making practices? In what ways might new media technologies untidy the neat lines of print? In what ways does knowledge production with new media make more complex, robust, and inclusive the ideas represented through a layering of semiotic systems? Scholars in English studies are beginning to understand visual rhetoric and its relation to design (Hocks 1999, 2003; Wysocki 2001, 2002, 2005), its relation to other sign technologies (Faigley 2003; Hocks and Kendrick 2003), and its relation to argument (George 2002).

Mary Hocks's "Understanding Visual Rhetoric in Digital Writing Environments" (2003) is particularly important for my purposes here, because in it she pays attention to knowledge-making practices made possible with new media. She examines two pieces of hypertextual scholarship,

Anne Frances Wysocki's 1998 *Kairos* essay "Monitoring Order" and Chris Boese's 1998 hypertextual dissertation from Rensselaer Polytechnic Institute, and finds that "both essays use the hypertextual form to underscore reflexively the arguments they make about conventions and about cultures" (643). Because the knowledge-making practices possible with new media technologies must necessarily differ from conventions available with print, authors work at a place in the semiotic process. That is, when image, video, sound, voice, and graphics are intertwined in new media compositions, the meanings that each sign technology indicates are intermingled and coexistent. If the medium is the message, as Marshall McLuhan claimed, then new media composing involves a sensitivity to the ways sign technologies index, interrelate, and create polysemic possibilities through their relations to each other in addition to their relations to the signified. Creating knowledge with new media, then, demands a reflexive underscoring of the ways that letter and print conventions work as signifiers, the ways that other media signify, and the ways that relations among media signify — no small feat. Along the way, the supremacy of the letter, textuality, and print is necessarily destabilized.

Two caveats: First, I am not calling for more scholarship about new media, though that would be useful. With Cheryl Ball (2004), I am calling for more new media scholarship. Composition and new media scholars write about how readers can make meaning from images, typefaces, videos, animations, and sounds . . . but most scholars don't compose with these media. It is evident from the scholarship available that

> compositionists are interested in new media. Yet, they do not seem to value creating new media texts for scholarly publications to explore the multimodal capabilities of new technologies. The linear tradition of composition scholars' publications about new media techniques causes me to suggest that this type of scholarship should not be called new media scholarship but should, more accurately, be labeled scholarship about new media. (407)

Ball rightly points out that the scholarship based on interpretation of new media as objects is not the same as production of new media scholarship. Composition scholars too fall into the textuality trap that stabilizes the hierarchy of signs by privileging interpretation above production. We do need to understand how signs work within new media composition, but that under- standing is too easily and frequently spoken of — in print rather than through production of new media scholarship. The production of new media scholar- ship stands a better chance of changing from inside the institution the ways in which knowledge products come to be valued, produced, and disseminated. Authors of new media scholarship may be hard pressed to produce this kind of scholarship when tenure committees do not necessarily value, or even under- stand, how complicated, time consuming, and difficult it is to produce new media. Because Ball describes this unforgiving cycle well, suffice it to say that tenured professors are better situated to produce new media scholarship.

Second caveat: New media scholarship is not the same cat as creating an avatar to inhabit a Second Life island, or posting a YouTube video of otters holding hands, or updating Facebook or MySpace pages, or posting a new album of photos to a Flickr site. The potential for new media scholar- ship in these Web 2.0 arenas remains, and Wikipedia is a fine example of this potential in the process of being realized. However, new media scholarship is richly layered and rhetorically dense in its convergences of media (see Jenkins

2001, 2006). New media scholarship rests on textuality, because it develops work with multiple sign technologies that reflects theorizing, historicizing, producing, and interpreting meaning. New media scholarship involves untold numbers of rhetorical decisions concerning the form and content of various sign technologies at every point of the creative process and makes knowledge that is subject to peer review. Two examples of new media scholarship will help illustrate.

In "Web 2.0 . . . The Machine is Us/ing Us," cultural anthropologist Michael Wesch (2007) uses screen captures, stills, and text to illustrate the ways in which the collaboratively authored Web 2.0 connects data by seamlessly, invisibly, tagging users' moves (see fig. 1). Internet code allows computers to follow our navigational paths and brings together the data we have accessed. In short, users unwittingly organize immense amounts of data through their daily explorations on the Internet; we create the machine, the collaboratively authored Web 2.0 that is using us to create it. Central to this process of building a Web 2.0, metadata tags of keywords or other media are meshed together by computer code that scans across thousands of separate pages to find recurring instances of data. In Wesch's example, metamediation happens when computer systems trace and tag users' paths. The machine that we are is very much uncritically, unconsciously, working to create links between shared pathways of exploration. More important, Wesch's work was subject to review, comment, and revision in a process of comment and response similar to that found under the history tabs of any Wikipedia page. He responds to the comments by showing his sources and explains the revisions he makes to the content accordingly. That versions of his particular piece, when taken together, have been viewed several million times to date suggests an interesting revision to the academic notion of peer review, but that's another article.

Figure 1. Screenshot of a draft of Michael Wesch's new media scholarship, "Web 2.0 . . . The Machine is Us/ing Us." Note that the number in the lower-right corner shows that this draft has been viewed more than 11 million times. The final draft has been viewed more than 1 million times since June 2010.

In another example of new media scholarship, "Technotreason" (Cushman 2004) destabilizes the hierarchy of signs by creating dissonant harmonies through a layering of media in ways that displace the supremacy of the letter. Layers of sign technologies (for example, music, voice, transition, images, and film effects) saturate meanings in order to illustrate the semiotic process of new media. In one section of "Technotreason," Magritte's *The Treason of Images* plays in tandem with They Might Be Giants' song "I Can Hear You." This song was recorded at the Thomas Edison National Historical Site in West Orange, New Jersey, using an early form of recording technology. The singers projected their music into elephant-ear-sized brass horns that recorded the vibrations of their voices onto wax cylinders without electric amplification ("Lost and Found Sounds" 1999). The song itself is a reflexive play on the development of communication technologies: We can just barely hear the lead singer because of the quality of Edison's early recording technology. The lyrics are all drawn from distant presences that have been possible with the development of subsequent sound technologies: "This is a warning. Step away from the car. This car is protected by Vipor," and later, "What's your order? I can supersize that. Please bring your car around." The band juxtaposes the recording technology at Edison's laboratory with subsequent digital and telecommunication devices used to record, produce, and transmit "speech." Thus, they set in dialectical tension the aural sign technologies and emphasize the social distances produced by these. The speaker not only is a distant presence from the words uttered but also is, in the car's case, not a speaker at all but a software program projected through the car, all of which we can barely hear thanks to Edison's wax-based encoding technology. The lyrics and the recording itself are playfully convergent and divergent from Réne Magritte's *The Treason of Images*.

In "Technotreason," text is never left to speak for itself in the transparent fashion so often seen in writing. Whenever text plays on the screen in Technotreason, lyric, music, rolling text, and moving lens flares (de)emphasize the letter's supremacy. For instance, in the segment of this new media composition that reads "in signification, technology makes all the différance," the lens flare enters the scene in the upper-left corner and slowly moves across and down the "page" that is a "movie screen" that is the "computer screen," destabilizing the left-to-right order presumed by textuality. The phrase "the différance" enters from the lower-right corner and moves from the right to the left, delaying the text's taken-for-granted immediate transmission of meaning.

The music's gritty sound quality demands that the audience listen hard in order to decode the lyrics playing during this frame sequence. In this segment, a person on an airplane calls a friend to say, "Guess where I am? I'm calling from the plane. I'll call you when I get there." The first two lines suggest that the person has called not to convey a message at all but to use the phone embedded in the seat. When placed in the context of the relatively poor quality of the lyrics themselves, the novelty of the airplane communication system again comments on the evolution of communication technologies. The decoding action needed to understand both the music and the text defer and call attention to the viewer's reliance on textuality and the technology of writing. Embedded throughout the piece is a digital recording of a voice repeating Magritte's insight: "This is not a pipe." This voiceover has a flange filter (a device that makes words sound as though they're echoing in a chamber), and its volume was controlled to be heard "behind" the music — another distant presence. Motion, voice, and sound play with text to decenter the supremacy of the letter as a privileged technology. In this new media piece, text is unfixed from its place by equally prominent sign technologies.

New media essays have the potential to treat all sign technologies equally. Wysocki's new media scholarship has described well the transparency of the letter, linking it to habits of mind that develop from the ordering of letters across a page (2002). Her new media scholarship and scholarship on new media (2005) work to destabilize the hierarchy of signs and produce meaning beyond that available in print alone, especially by focusing attention on the impossibly distinct, print-based, binaries of form and content that no longer obtain in new media scholarship. By situating images, video, film, music, and voiceover in moving dialectic, these signs converge with and diverge from each other and, as a result, saturate the signification process with interdirectionality. The dissonant harmony of "Technotreason" discombobulates, and it does so with the twofold purpose of (re)seeing sign technologies and disrupting the hierarchy of signs.

Teaching New Media and preservice Teacher Education

In addition to new media scholarship, English scholars might consider another way to engage the production of meaning: the teaching of future English teachers to produce, interpret, and historicize various media. (Elsewhere I have argued that activist research and service learning might be additional activities used to diversify the production work of English studies.) In this section, I explore how new media might be included in the cadre of teaching practices used to educate preservice teachers.

The production of new media scholarship could engage English scholars in all aspects of textuality, as Scholes discusses it, a process that could also inform the types and kinds of assignments and products preservice teachers are asked to create. Scholes offers one reason why the production of texts has not typically been a valued aspect of English studies: production relates to writing, a skill necessary in the creation of meaning. Skill — now there's a loathsome word to scholars of textuality because it is seen as separate and separable from knowledge, the real goal of learning. Scholes argues, though, that "the opposition between skill and knowledge is a red herring. . . . Knowledge that is not usable and regularly used is lost. The knowledge that we retain is the knowledge that we can and do employ" (1998: 148). Skills and knowledge are intricately connected and enable learning and retention: "What we take in through our eyes and ears must emerge from our hands and mouths if we are to hold on to it. It is a curious property of information that we keep it only if we give it away" (148). We keep what we learn only if we give it away, and that "giving away" is possible in composing and teaching, two forms of learning that relate to the production of texts. If English scholars are serious about leveling the hierarchy of signs, then the production of meaning through composing and teaching cannot be eschewed as trifling skills, as mere tertiary activities of English studies.

New media production can work at the nexus of the intellectual activities of textuality in ways that give future teachers insight into the meaning- making potentials of various media while serving to address these students' professional needs. At the undergraduate level, the preponderance of English majors hope to become teachers of English at the high school or elementary level, yet too few classes in the English curriculum address the teaching of English, let alone the teaching of new media textuality. Still, preservice teachers must perform to professional standards that demand fluency with various meaning-making technologies in order to be able to share and learn with their students. Two such policy guidelines for multimodality have been developed by national organizations. The National Council of Teachers of English suggests that twenty-first-century readers and writers need to

- Develop proficiency with the tools of technology
- Build relationships with others to pose and solve problems collaboratively and cross-culturally
- Design and share information for global communities to meet a variety of purposes
- Manage, analyze and synthesize multiple streams of simultaneous information
- Create, critique, analyze, and evaluate multi-media texts
- Attend to the ethical responsibilities required by these complex environments (NCTE Executive Committee 2008)

In addition, the National Board for Professional Teaching Standards (2003: 57) describes in Standard XI the ways that "accomplished Adolescence and Young Adulthood/English Language Arts teachers enable students to critically read, evaluate, and produce messages in a variety of media." They go on:

- Accomplished teachers help students understand the unique characteristics of a variety of media, as well as the commercial, social, and political messages embedded in these texts, and they prepare students to become more competent and sophisticated consumers and producers of communication in different media. (58)
- Accomplished teachers know that a vital component of any media literacy program is a production component. Teachers help students analyze the advantages and limitations of various media so students can purposefully select the medium — written, oral, visual, or some combination — that best suits the message to be communicated. (59)

These activities for critically informed production, critique, and interpretation of a variety of texts fall in line with the idea of English studies that Scholes provides. These national organizations are expecting that teachers graduating from English departments today have the kinds of fluency with new media interpretations, production, and consumption that will allow them to engage their students in these practices. Yet few English scholars at the university level are themselves prepared to teach their students, many of whom will go on to teach high school language arts, in the textuality of new media. Although it is possible to interpret new media works using a theoretical lens without actually producing new media scholarship, it is difficult to teach others to produce new media without actually knowing the basic ways that the software works or understanding what process of creation students might use with these technologies.

In general, new media are created when the computer (a medium and a tool for production) repurposes old media (image, sound, film, text, speech, and music) to form a compilation of sign technologies layered together. This kind of knowledge production challenges the hierarchy of signs using a process of "remediation" proposed by Bolter and Grusin (2000: 55–56):

1. Media are continually commenting on, reproducing, and replacing each other. . . .
2. All media remediate the real. Just as there is no getting rid of mediation, there is no getting rid of the real. . . .
3. The goal of remediation is to refashion or rehabilitate other media.
4. Furthermore, because all mediations are both real and mediations of the real, remediation can also be understood as a process of reforming reality as well.

Because new media reproduce, comment on, and replace each other, this process mitigates against the supremacy of print because it reforms the reality produced by the old media of letter and delivery vehicle of print. With new media, print no longer stands alone but is commented on as image, is juxtaposed to sound, is reshaped by intonation, is mitigated by video clip, and so on. New media compositions can include products such as Web pages, digital movies on CD or DVD, interactive software or interfaces, and digital art installations.

When we ask our students to produce and teach them how to produce these new media compositions, they begin to engage in precisely the kinds of intellectual activities that textuality demands. The guidelines for accomplished teachers offered by the National Board for Professional Teaching Standards argue that the very kinds of new media productions described above should be available in today's language arts classrooms: "Teachers might extend the reading of a novel by having students select a pivotal scene and create a storyboard, video, or multimedia presentation to represent their interpretation, or might have students select and sequence a series of photo- graphs to accompany a poem or short story selection, justifying their choices" (59). A digital video or Web page might prompt a student to provide an interpretation of a poem using a critical theory of technology to create a knowledge product similar to the very ones recommended by the National Board for Professional Teaching Standards. New media pieces lend themselves well to literary interpretation and a host of additional genres as they add to the forms of production, consumption, and analysis that have been part and parcel of textuality in those rare English departments that do value all four areas of English studies equally. Given the delivery vehicles found in Web 2.0, such as YouTube, blogs, and social networking sites, English scholars who com- pose new media scholarship and teach students to do the same can now reach audiences beyond the initiated few. It is interesting to consider what kinds of impact new media scholarship might have when it has the potential to be viewed millions of times.

IMPLICATIONS

The hierarchy of signs seems less tenable during this historical moment when new media technologies are better positioned (that is, more accessible and deliverable than they were a decade ago) to facilitate the knowledge production process for individual scholars and teachers. For this to happen, knowledge production and teaching with new media can be and need to be integrated into work in English studies. New media opens up possibilities for a plurality of representation and teaching practices, leveling the hierarchy of signs in English studies. The arguments made in the new media compositions discussed here could not have been made in print alone and required some familiarity with art, film production, music production, photography, and design.

This brings me to a second implication: new media might allow literary humanists another way to enter the Web 2.0 era, to make knowledge with and for publics using a plurality of media. Multimodal knowledge production could allow scholars to craft meaning more accessible to publics outside of academe because it uses the semiotic systems used regularly in homes, com- munities, and workplaces to shape meaning and representations. English scholars might position themselves better to acknowledge and appreciate multimodal communication strategies already taking place if they themselves were producing multimodal compositions and teaching others to do so in these ways.

As with the production of new media scholarship, the teaching of new media maps onto the activities already undertaken as routine practices of textuality: when producing multimedia projects, students can engage in historicizing the signs they are using in order to draw upon the historically rooted meanings and values attached to these signs; they could theorize the works they are interpreting and produce multiple ways of representing this interpretation. Taken together, then, producing meaning through composing and teaching with new media might help level the hierarchy of signs through both recognition of the problem and a concomitant change in intellectual activities that have sustained it.

WORKS CITED

Ball, Cheryl. 2004. "Show, Not Tell: The Value of New Media Scholarship." *Computers and Composition* 21: 403 – 25.

Boese, Chris. 1998. "The Ballad of the Internet Nutball: Chaining Rhetorical Visions from the Margins of the Margins to the Mainstream in the Xenaverse." PhD diss., Rensselaer Polytechnic Institute.
Bolter, J. David, and Richard Grusin. 2000. *Remediation: Understanding New Media*. Cambridge, MA: MIT Press.
Cushman, Ellen. 1998. *The Struggle and the Tools: Oral and Literate Strategies in an Inner City Community*. Albany: State University of New York Press.
—. 1999a. "Critical Literacy and Institutional Language." *Research in the Teaching of English* 33: 245 – 74.
—. 1999b. "The Public Intellectual, Activist Research, and Service-Learning." *College English* 61: 68 – 76.
—. 2002. "Sustainable Service Learning Programs." *College Composition and Communication* 64: 40 – 65.
—. 2003a. "Beyond Specialization: The Public Intellectual, Outreach, and Rhetoric Education." In *The Realms of Rhetoric: Inquiries into the Prospects for Rhetoric Education*, ed. Deepika Bahri and Joseph Petraglia, 171 – 89. Albany: State University of New York Press.
—. 2003b. "Vertical Writing Programs in Departments of Rhetoric and Writing." In *Composition Studies in the New Millennium*, ed. Lynn Z. Bloom, Donald A. Daiker, and Edward M. White, 121 – 29. Carbondale: Southern Illinois University Press.
—. 2004. "Technotreason." East Lansing, MI. www.msu.edu/~cushmane/newmedia/technotreason4.rm (accessed 2 October 2009).
—. 2005. "Face, Skins, and the Identity Politics of Rereading Race." *Rhetoric Review* 24: 378 – 82.
—. 2006. "Toward a Praxis of New Media: The Allotment Period in Cherokee History." *Reflections on Community-Based Writing Instruction* 4.3: 124-43.
—. 2008. "Toward a Rhetoric of Self-Representation: Identity Politics in Indian Country and Rhetoric and Composition." *College Composition and Communication* 60: 321 – 65.
Cushman, Ellen, and Jeffrey T. Grabill, eds. 2009. "Theories of Community Literacy." Special Issue of *Reflections* 7.4.
Cushman, Ellen, and Erik Green. 2010. "Knowledge Work with the Cherokee Nation: Engaging Publics in a Praxis of New Media." In *The Public Work of Rhetoric: Citizen- Scholars and Civic Engagement*, ed. John M. Ackerman and David J. Coogan. Columbia: University of South Carolina Press.
Drucker, Johanna. 1995. *The Century of Artist's Books*. New York: Granary Books.
Faigley, Lester. 2003. "The Challenge of the Multimedia Essay." In *Composition Studies in the New Millennium*, ed. Lynn Z. Bloom, Donald A. Daiker, and Edward M. White, 174 – 87. Carbondale: Southern Illinois University Press.

George, Diana. 2002. "From Analysis to Design: Visual Communication in the Teaching of Writing." *College Composition and Communication* 54: 11 – 39.

Hocks, Mary. 1999. "Toward a Visual Critical Electronic Literacy." *Works and Days* 17: 157 – 72.

—. 2003. "Understanding Visual Rhetoric in Digital Writing Environments." *College Composition and Communication* 54: 629 – 57.

Hocks, Mary, and Michelle Kendrick. 2003. "Introduction: Eloquent Images." In *Eloquent Images: Word and Image in the Age of New Media*, ed. Mary Hocks and Michelle Kendrick, 1 – 19. Cambridge, MA: MIT Press.

Jenkins, Henry. 2001. "Convergence? I Diverge." *Technology Review* 105.5: 93.

—. 2006. *Convergence Culture*. New York: New York University Press.

Kress, Gunther, and Theo Van Leeuwen. 2001. *Multimodal Discourse: The Modes and Media of Contemporary Communication*. London: Arnold.

"Lost and Found Sounds: Twenty-First Century Cylinders." 1999. Produced by David Nelson and Nikki Silva. National Public Radio.

Mitchell, W. J. T. 1995. *Picture Theory*. Chicago: University of Chicago Press.

National Board for Professional Teaching Standards. 2003. *Adolescence and Young Adulthood English Language Arts Standards*. 2nd ed. Washington, DC: National Board for Professional Teaching Standards.

NCTE Executive Committee. 2008. "The NCTE Definition of Twenty-First-Century Literacies." NCTE Position Statement. 15 February. www.ncte.org/positions/ statements/21stcentdefinition.

Scholes, Robert. 1998. *The Rise and Fall of English*. New Haven, CT: Yale University Press. Stephens, Mitchell. 1990. *The Rise of the Image: The Fall of the Word*. New York: Oxford University Press.

Welch, Kathleen. 1990. "Electrifying Classical Rhetoric: Ancient Media, Modern Technology, and Contemporary Composition." *Journal of Advanced Composition* 10: 22 – 38.

Wesch, Michael. 2007. "Web 2.0 ...The Machine is Us/ing Us." 31 January. www.youtube.com/watch?v=6gmP4nk0EOE&feature=channel (accessed 28 May 2008).

Wysocki, Anne Frances. 1998. "Monitoring Order: Visual Desire, the Organization of Web Pages, and Teaching the Rules of Design." *Kairos* 3.2. english.ttu.edu/Kairos/3.2.

—. 2001. "Impossibly Distinct: On Form/Content and Word/Image in Two Pieces of Computer-Based Interactive Multimedia." *Computers and Composition* 18: 137 – 62.

—. 2002. "A Bookling Monument." *Kairos* 7.3. english.ttu.edu/Kairos/7.3/binder2.html?coverweb/wysocki/index.html.

—. 2005. "awaywithwords: On the Possibilities in Unavailable Designs." *Computers and Composition* 22: 55 – 62.

REFLECTIONS

> *Reflections* | *A Journal of Public Rhetoric, Civic Writing, and Service* is on the Web at http://reflectionsjournal.net/

Reflections, a peer reviewed journal, provides a forum for scholarship on civic writing, service-learning and public rhetoric. Originally founded as a venue for teachers, researchers, students and community partners to share research and discuss the theoretical, political and ethical implications of community-based writing and writing instruction, *Reflections* publishes a lively collection of essays, empirical studies, community writing, student work, interviews and reviews in a format that brings together emerging scholars and leaders in the fields of community-based writing and civic engagement. We welcome materials that report on research; showcase community-based and student writing and/or artwork; investigate and represent literacy practices in diverse community settings; discuss theoretical, political and ethical implications of community-based writing; explore connections between service-learning, civic engagement, and current scholarship in composition studies and related fields

"Found" Literacy Partnerships: Service and Activism at Spelman College" by Zandra L. Jordan. *Reflections* 10.2 (Spring 2011)

Zandra L. Jordan's essay was chosen for two reasons. First, while service-learning scholarship often seems focused on historically white institutions, Jordan's essay reminds our field of the important work of historically Black colleges and universities, demonstrating a longer historical connection to such work than is typically recognized. This was the general focus of a two-part series by Reflections on the African-American contributions to service learning/community partnership work. Moreover, Jordan's work demonstrates how service-learning can lead to informed activism by students, providing them with a rich and informed understanding of such work as they leave school and become 'full time citizens."

11 "Found" Literacy Partnerships: Service and Activism at Spelman College

Zandra L. Jordan

Abstract

This article discusses found literacy partnerships—collaborations around literacy practices that emerge unexpectedly when Spelman College students enact the spirit of service and activism that has defined the historically black liberal arts college for women since its inception. Through an examination of institutional rhetoric, a required general education course and three student cases, the article considers the relationship between doing and becoming as students' literacies align with the interests of community agencies. Literacy partnerships are not always planned; they can emerge from a spirit of service and commitment to activism that encourages students not just to do service, but to become, through their doing, civic-minded women who use their literacies to promote positive social change.

Established in 1881, Atlanta Baptist Female Seminary, now Spelman College,* began in the basement of Friendship Baptist Church, then the largest black Baptist church in Atlanta, GA. The pastor, Reverend Frank Quarles, offered the basement to the school's founders, Sophia B. Packard and Harriet E. Giles, who started the school with just "eleven students—ten women, some former slaves, and one girl" (*History and Traditions* 5). Packard and Giles, both missionaries and teachers,

---

* In 1884, the name was changed to Spelman Seminary in honor of longtime antislavery activists Laura Spelman Rockefeller and her parents Harvey Buel and Lucy Henry Spelman. The name was changed again in 1924 to Spelman College.

were part of "the wave of Northern missionaries coming South to provide education and Christian training to more than one million freed people" (3). This historic church-school partnership is endemic of the kinds of literacy partnerships that are part of Spelman's continuing legacy. For more than a century, Spelman students, emboldened by the example of alumnae like Marion Wright Edleman, have partnered with local communities and agencies to support the literacy education of those living in nearby neighborhoods.

The 1971 Summerhill reading clinic is one example among many of Spelman's rich history of literacy partnerships. On Saturdays from 9 a.m. to 12 noon, approximately "80 Black tutors" from Spelman and other Atlanta University Center* institutions, as well as Emory University and Georgia State University, conducted a reading clinic at the Postal Street Academy on Capitol Avenue for children living in Summerhill, a predominantly Black, inner city neighborhood near downtown Atlanta. Coordinated by Spelman sophomore Virginia Davis, the tutors worked with approximately 85 children ranging in age from five to thirteen.

Although teaching reading skills was the primary purpose of the clinic, some of the larger structural issues impacting the achievement of Summerhill children, such as cultural dissonance between classroom teachers and students and limited access to educational and cultural experiences outside of Summerhill, were reflected in the clinic objectives: "to promote self-awareness, to create situations conducive to study, to improve scholastic performance, to bridge the gap between teacher and student, to encourage parental concern, and to expose the child to his environment" (Peters 33).

The former Virginia Davis, now Virginia Davis Floyd, developed the reading clinic objectives in collaboration with community activist and now Atlanta City Councilman C. T. Martin. The reading clinic was an offshoot of the Atlanta Postal Street Academies, which Martin initiated in 1970 to address the growing high school dropout rate among Black youth. Martin "worked for the Post Office," Floyd recalls, "and somehow convinced them to lend Post Office resources to identify high school dropouts and form the Postal Street Academy."

---

* Spelman College is part of the Atlanta University Center, a consortium of historically Black institutions that includes Clark Atlanta University, the Interdenominational Theological Seminary, Morehouse College and Morehouse School of Medicine.

Figure 1. Peoplestown and Summerhill children, early 1970s.*

---

* Courtesy of Emmaus House, an Episcopal community center situated in the Peoplestown and Summerhill neighborhoods, this photo depicts local children on the Emmaus House porch in the early 1970s. Herman Shackleford (center) and his sister (far left) grew up in the Peoplestown-

One of the original college tutors recruited by Martin, Floyd was an Academy tutor for a semester when she suggested that the program might be more successful if they started with younger children. Martin promptly put Floyd in charge of developing a reading clinic (Floyd, personal interview).

Under Floyd's leadership, each Saturday the Summerhill reading clinic tutors prepared breakfast and lunch for the children, mindful that "the growl of a stomach is much too distracting" for the children to ignore (Peters 33). They visited the children at home to assess their needs. Recognizing one child's delayed speech development, the tutors connected the child's family with "a speech and hearing specialist." To promote exercise, they brought the children to "Spelman's gymnasium for swimming, basketball, tumbling...and other activities." The tutors also organized a health clinic "with the assistance of Dr. Audrey Forbes Manley,* [Spelman alumna and] wife of the president of Spelman College, Dr. Albert E. Manley. Dr. Forbes [Manley], an outstanding pediatrician, Dr. Clinton Warner, Spelman College physician, and Dr. James Densler, an Atlanta surgeon" conducted health exams and provided services, including "dental work and eyeglasses" (33).

When Floyd received a Merrill Scholarship to study abroad, she entrusted the reading clinic to her Spelman classmate and best friend Darnell Ivory (personal interviews), who was "one of the original tutors of the program" ("Street Academy Clinic" 1). Under Ivory's direction, each session started and concluded "with a chant of blackness to instill in the children a sense of togetherness" (1). The clinic curriculum was "divided into four different 'classes' [on] black history, math, science and reading" (1). According to Ivory, the tutors also spent time in Summerhill playing softball with the children and visiting with their families (personal interview). "Twice a month," the tutors took the children on field trips to cultural events, baseball games, the Spelman College Biology Department and other campus facilities ("Street Academy Clinic" 1; Ivory, personal interview). They even held

---

Summerhill community. The identities of the other children pictured are unknown.

* In addition to many other professional accomplishments, Dr. Audrey Forbes Manley served as the President of Spelman College from 1997 until her retirement in 2002. She is the first alumna to hold the elected position ("History in Brief").

a Christmas celebration for the children in the Spelman College gymnasium that was catered by Spelman's dining service (Ivory, personal interview).

Neither Floyd nor Ivory know what became of the clinic after they graduated in 1973, but it made a lasting impression on them both (personal interviews). Reflecting upon her deep investment in the Summerhill reading clinic and the support that Spelman College provided, Floyd exclaimed, "I learned at Spelman that college is much more than grades. Spelman was a resource to the community in which it sits... Once you are touched like this, wherever you go you have to do this kind of work" (personal interview). The recipient of "numerous awards for her leadership in health policy, advocacy of the under-served, and as a medical educator" ("Biography"), Floyd has continued "to do this kind of work" by becoming a resource to communities in need at home and abroad. The Atlanta Postal Street Academies have also continued their work well into the 21st century. Now known as Communities in Schools, Inc., the Academies have garnered national distinction.*

Like Spelman alumnae Virginia Davis Floyd and Darnell Ivory, today's Spelman students "enter to learn and exit to serve."** They are encouraged by the College mission and related programs not only to volunteer, but also to see themselves as women who can promote social change through their life-long involvement with local and global communities. Spelman College's commitment to developing student leaders who engage in service to "change the world" presents an institutional context quite different from those described in some service-learning scholarship.

According to Bickford and Reynolds' survey of service-learning practitioners in "Activism and Service-Learning: Reframing Volunteerism As Acts of Dissent," students rarely connect their service with activism, that is, comprehend and "seek to change the social climate and structures that make volunteerism necessary" (238). They explain,

---

* The Atlanta Postal Street Academies became Exodus, Inc. in 1972, under the leadership of Neil Shorthouse, Bill Milliken and David Lewis. In 1977, Cities in Schools, Inc. "was created to manage [the academies'] national expansion." By 1989, "the program thrived nationally" and changed its name once more to Communities in Schools, Inc. In 2007, Cities in Schools of Atlanta formed a new partnership with Atlanta Public Schools ("History," *Communities in Schools of Atlanta*).

** "Enter to learn and exit to serve" is the Office of Community Service and Student Development slogan.

"few students understand their service as a contribution to structural social change" (238), because "the process of institutionalization obscures...the activist potential of service-learning." In other words, in their efforts to get students involved in community service, institutions often overemphasize "the volunteer ethos, a philanthropic or charitable viewpoint that ignores the structural reasons to help others" (230); thus, students learn to value service, but they may miss the possible connections between service and activism. Paula Mathieu and Bruce Herzberg make similar observations.

In *Tactics of Hope: The Public Turn in English Composition*, Paula Mathieu argues that some institutional approaches to sustaining service learning, like "repeat[ing] service projects" and using the academic calendar to determine a year in advance the type of service projects available to students (99), unwittingly fall short of the mark. While institutionalized service-learning has its benefits, such as "measurable success, broad institutional presence, and sustainability" (98), Mathieu argues that "today's colleges and universities" tend to prefer "long-term, top-down, institutionalized service-learning programs" (96) that, by virtue of institutional agendas and protocols, may exchange authentic opportunities "to respond to communities' needs and ideas" (98) for "benign," prescribed service "task[s]" (99).

Considering how students interpret their service, Bruce Herzberg, in "Community Service and Critical Teaching," questions what service-learning teaches students "about the nature of the problems that cause [community] organizations to come into existence" (138). Quoting Susan Stroud, he argues that community service projects, even in the context of a course, promote charity, not social change, if they are "'not structured to raise the issues that result in critical analysis'" of social problems (139). Indeed, if the goal of service-learning is to promote social change, then instructors and institutions must have structures in place that help students critique the specific social problems that create community needs. Peck et al. also suggest that students may need assistance understanding both their agentive potential and the process of social change.

In their description of the Pittsburgh Community Literacy Center*—"a community/university collaborative between the Community House and The National Center for the Study of Writing and Lit-

---

* For more on the Pittsburgh Community Literacy Center, see Flower's (2008) *Community Literacy and the Rhetoric of Public Engagement*.

eracy at Carnegie Mellon" (200), Peck et al. identify "social change" as one of the key aims of "community literacy" (205). Community literacy—"literate acts that could yoke community action with intercultural education, strategic thinking and problem solving, and with observation-based research and theory building" (200),—encourages students to use writing as a tool for producing social change with real "personal and public consequences" (208). However, Peck at al. caution against "assum[ing] that teenagers come prepared to enter such a discourse, to move from complaint or assertion to strategic, savvy action, to understand how the slow wheels of public persuasion work, to value persistence, or even to believe in the power of their own voice or see that writing can make a difference" (208). This caveat alludes to the need for pedagogical strategies that help students develop their rhetorical skills, their awareness of social change processes, and a vision of themselves as social change agents.

Whereas scholars report a disconnect between students' commitment (and/or that of colleges and universities) to volunteerism and their awareness of the larger structural issues underscoring the need for activism, Spelman's positioning of students as change agents works to align service with activism. This article discusses "found" literacy partnerships—collaborations around literacy practices that emerge unexpectedly when Spelman College students enact the spirit of service and activism that has defined this historically black liberal arts college for women since its beginning. Through these partnerships we see students in the process of becoming civic-minded women who use their literacies to promote "positive social change" (*History and Traditions* 1).

"A CHOICE TO CHANGE THE WORLD": INSTITUTIONAL IDENTITY AND COMMUNITY SERVICE

From its mission and grounds to its traditions and curriculum, Spelman College instills in its students the mantra of change. Students learn from the College mission statement that they will become leaders who make the choice to change the world.

> An outstanding historically Black college for women, Spelman promotes academic excellence in the liberal arts and develops the intellectual, ethical and leadership potential of its students. Spelman seeks to empower the total person, who

appreciates the many cultures of the world and commits to positive social change. (*History and Traditions* 1)

Students also see the message of change displayed prominently on the drive leading up to Spelman's front gates and on campus walkways. Banners juxtaposing the triumphant faces of Spelman students and faculty with the slogan "A Choice to Change the World" remind students that to attend Spelman is to make the choice to be an agent of change. Upon entering the gates, students see banners along walkways asserting "Change Means Action," "Change Means Strength," "Change Means Growth," "Change Means Success," and "Change Means Service."*

The Spelman College Glee Club often performs the song "A Choice to Change the World" during annual Founder's Day celebrations and Commencement exercises. Written by Sara Stephens, C' 2007 and arranged by both Dr. Kevin Johnson, Director of the Spelman College Glee Club, and Sara Stephens, the stirring song exhorts Spelman's daughters to choose activism:

---

* The banners are part of The Campaign for Spelman College. See http://www.changemeansaction.com/index.php

"A Choice to Change the World"*

Chorus	Verse Two
It's my choice	Within this institution
And I choose to change the world	We are women of change
It's my voice	The shoulders that we stand upon
And I'll speak with pride and courage	Never received applause or fame
I'll be the change I wanna see	But in their honor I will live
I'll scream out loud and say	Each day better than before
It's my choice	And show just how it takes a choice
And I choose to change the world	To change yourself and so much more
Verse One	**Bridge**
Why put off for tomorrow	The change begins today
What I can do today	With every choice that I make
Why wait for another	Spelman look around and see
When I can pave the way	Where the changes need to be
No matter how young or old	End poverty
I hold the power of change	Fighting overseas
Rather large or small, few or all	Another dies from a disease
My choice remains the same	End hypocrisy
	Starving on the streets
	And no one does a single thing

In its many iterations, the call for Spelman students to change the world speaks to systemic change that may begin with a single encounter, a community service experience, but ultimately aims to impact underlying structures. This kind of change is unlikely to occur within a semester or even a year. As the Summerhill tutors recognized, theirs would need to be an "on-going" program, "continu[ing]...as long as the need exists" (Peters 34). It is this awareness of social change as a process and a long-term commitment that I see in Spelman's rhetoric of change and its infusion in first-year student experiences. Chief among these is the First-Year Experience Seminar.

---

* The complete lyrics of "A Choice to Change the World" are available in "Spelman Blends Old and New Voices to Change the World." See Works Cited.

First-Year Experience Seminar (FYE) is a two-semester general education requirement that "exposes students to the tenets of academic excellence, leadership and service, which are the cornerstones of Spelman College." As the common course syllabus informs students, the 2009-2010 FYE Seminar took part of its title, "'When and Where I Enter': Becoming a Free Thinking Spelman Woman," and its inspiration from "Paula Giddings's (1984) seminal book on African American women's socio-political activism amidst severe racial and gender inequality." Seminar activities, which include Convocations/Assemblies, class discussions, reflection essays, community service, and the First-Year Writing Portfolio, "[encourage] students to think critically about 'when and where [they] enter' as ethical leaders and agents of social change" (syllabus 1).

One Seminar objective, "attain practical experience as change agents" (syllabus 3), is best reflected in the community service requirement and reflection essay. With the assistance of the Bonner Office of Community Service and Student Development, students "identify at least one local community service agency, program or activity that reflects her social change interests" (3). Minimally, first-year students make an eight-hour commitment to the selected agency and, upon completion of those hours, reflect upon their experience. A key part of the reflection process is composing the Community Service Reflection essay. Students receive the following instructions:

> As you know, your community service during the first year constitutes an important source of discovery and self-evaluation. Your interactions with the organization you chose constitute important moments for examining the values of the community and your own personal goals and values.
>
> Compose a reflective essay about your community service experience this year and the new understandings you have derived from it. Include an assessment of the mission of the agency where you volunteered, how your service helped to fulfill the agency's mission, what you hoped to learn from the experience (from your Community Learning Agreement), and the extent to which your learning goals were achieved. Also, describe your current understanding of how social change occurs, using your agency's work as an example, if you choose. Finally, if you were directing the agency, describe how

you might improve the way it functions. Examine the actions you would take as such a leader—and how those actions relate to your experience and observation.

You will be evaluated on your ability to analyze your experience and present specifics about your own goals and the potential achievements of the agency you worked for. At the same time, good critical thinking and writing depend upon a clear, direct, and concrete use of language.*

The community service requirement and reflection, which are repeated in the Sophomore Experience Seminar, illustrate the College's commitment to developing student leaders who serve as part of an activist agenda. Students choose a community agency that reflects their own social interests. They assess the agency's mission, thinking critically about how their contributions advanced that mission. They articulate the relationship between their personal goals and values and the agency's mission. Significantly, they reflect on the process of social change and what they might do if they were the agency director.

FYE Community Service reflections make visible students' thoughts on becoming change agents, their contemplations of shifting identity and expanding conceptions of service. As the three cases presented here illustrate, students are at different stages of understanding the relationship between activism and their "found" literacy partnerships—unexpected ways that the students used their literacies to support the mission of community agencies.

"Found" Literacy Partnerships: Making the Activist Connection

Erica and the Auburn Avenue Research Library

Erica's** reflection essay describes her service with the Auburn Avenue Research Library on African American Culture and History (AARL). The AARL is the first public library in the Southeast to provide specialized reference and research, archives and programs about African

---

* Obtained from the "FYE SpEl.Folio Assignments 2010-2011" webpage (see Works Cited), this FYE Community Service Reflection description is the same one used in the 2009-2010 FYE Seminar.
** All student names are pseudonyms. Portions of the students' 2009-2010 FYE Community Service Reflections are referenced with their permission.

American culture and history ("Auburn Avenue Research Library"). Previously unfamiliar with the AARL and its mission, Erica chose this site for its commitment to addressing social issues. She explains,

> The act of conducting community service is not just merely cleaning up the community, but one must assess the issues affecting their society. After reflecting on the issues affecting my society, I was in search of an opportunity that addressed the problems facing the community and also the problems facing the African American community as well.

Erica's reasons for choosing AARL suggest a greater motivation than just performing community service. Her willingness to serve is connected to her burgeoning awareness of her own activist potential. Rather than being disconnected from the "structural reasons to help others" (Bickford and Reynolds 230), Erica recognizes that service begins with identification of social problems in one's communities.

Erica worked with the AARL's 2010 Ashley Bryan Children's Literary Festival, an event co-sponsored by the National Black Arts Festival. She reports that "children, parents, caregivers, educators and others" participated in the three-day event, which "celebrat[ed] the sensitive and authentic representation of the African Diaspora in the genre of children's and young adult literature." According to Erica, organizers hoped the Festival would "promote literacy in the African American community by providing the children with characters in the literary works that they could relate to." Erica considered this goal laudable for several reasons. She observes, "These children were from all walks of life and vast socio-economic backgrounds. Many [people] may not know that racial and class disparities contribute to the success a child has with literacy." She also notes that "[she] was never awarded the opportunity to engage in literary works that focused on the African Diaspora until [she] came to Spelman College."

Erica's recognition that one's acquisition of literacy skills is influenced by socio-cultural and economic factors, like race and class, reflects her awareness of some of the social problems that give AARL purpose. As Erica noted, even though the "children [at the Festival] were from all walks of life" and some of them may "read under grade level," they shared in "common" a "passion for literacy and [their] race." What they seemed to lack, as she had at their age, is opportunities to engage literature and other works that celebrate African heritage.

Although Erica was told that she would be "registering participants, welcoming and greeting guests, handing out flyers, and directing guests to workshops," she was pleased to find occasions to "become more involved with the children." It was during these unexpected encounters that she used her academic literacies in support of the Festival's aims. She reflects,

> I met many young girls and I was able to discuss and analyze literary works with them that focused on African American women in society. One of the works we discussed was a documentary entitled, A Girl Like Me, by filmmaker Kiri Davis. This film explored the standards of beauty imposed on today's black girls and how these standards affect their self-image. I was able to explain to these young girls the [concept] of intersectionality and how it was a form of oppression that stemmed from slavery days and still has a negative effect on black women today. Although my duties were clearly set upon my arrival at the library, I met many young girls who I was able to mentor…

Erica credits her African Diaspora and the World* course for enabling her to speak knowledgeably about transatlantic slavery and its effects on black women and how such knowledge could empower the children to "make a positive contribution on the world and leave a legacy." Erica sees herself as accomplishing this same goal with the Festival participants. Reflecting upon the impact of her service, she writes,

> I was able to exercise my creativity to express to the young girls the importance of learning about black women in history and how they combated issues because these issues are ongoing. My demonstration to these young girls expressed my compassion for the problems facing the African American community such as literacy in our youth and the plight of black women. Giving back is a major part of community service and I was able to give encouragement to girls in my community to ensure that the[y] surpass the restrictions placed on them and reach their full potential.

---

* African Diaspora and the World is a two-semester general education requirement that engages students in reading and writing about the African Diaspora.

Erica identifies the girls as belonging to "[her] community," and therefore needing her to "give back" what she has received. Through "creativity" and "compassion," Erica encourages the girls to do what Spelman is equipping her to do—"surpass the restrictions placed on [her] and reach [her] full potential." The help that Erica provides are tools that the girls can use to resist institutional racism and sexism, societal forces that threaten to deny the girls agency. Having the tools to resist such forces positions the girls to take part in creating structural changes.

While Erica is still discovering her activist potential, her service experience with the AARL has done much to shape her emerging awareness of how social change occurs. Evaluating the AARL's effectiveness, she posits,

> Social change arises when an advocating individual realizes there is a problem affecting the community at an epidemic rate and takes the initiative to promote change. This event served as a catalyst to support literacy and growth of cultural competencies in the African American community. The work that this organization does truly denotes social change. Their objective is to make African American children aware at an early age [of] their historical background so they too can empower the world around them. Instilling these notions in children at a young age provide[s] them with a greater understanding of the social and cultural impact of people of color in today's literature and the world.

To Erica, social change is achievable when individuals recognize social problems and choose to act. An individual act or event, like the AARL's literary festival, can be just the "catalyst" needed to initiate a change process. Beyond helping the participants, the Festival, as Erica sees it, promotes knowledge of African American history and literature so that the children can one day "empower the world around them."

Sidney and the Atlanta University Center Neighborhood Association

Sidney's reflection essay describes her service with the Atlanta University Center Neighborhood Association (AUCNA). According to Sidney, the AUCNA focuses on community improvement by addressing a broad range of social issues. As an aspiring teacher and counselor, Sidney was drawn to the AUCNA's mentoring and tutoring program for middle school students. She reflects, "The mentoring motto of 'providing leadership in representing the interest of the Atlanta University Center Neighborhood Association to the City of Atlanta and the community at large' lured me unto this project, and I was motivated to go about leading and helping students reach their highest potential."

As a mentor, Sidney identified "patience, the ability to reason, humor and discipline" as essential for success. She credits these qualities for enabling her to be "very interactive" with her mentees and to "assist" them with completing homework. During one tutoring session, Sidney found that assistance could be reciprocal. Rather than positioning herself as the expert and therefore the only one capable of making a contribution, she was open to learning from her young mentee. She writes, "I helped my mentee with his Harlem Renaissance project. I also learned a lot from him in using computers. He taught me how to explore the internet in a more effective way, while I helped him with his writing and citing skills."

Sidney notes that the student's self-motivation and "ambition to get things right" grew after this encounter, remind[ing] [her] of how [she] used to be as a middle school student." "Enlighten[ed]" by this found literacy partnership, Sidney decided that "exact day" that she would "always come back to help." She explains, "I became attached in a sense, being that I didn't want to leave this student. His capabilities reminded me of how I use to be as a child and this experience left me with a feeling of happiness because I understood that I had something to offer."

Although Sidney initially seems to focus solely on volunteerism, her service experience and subsequent realization that she could make a meaningful contribution through service played an integral role in her coming to see herself as "an agent of social change." She reflects,

> Before starting at AUCNA, I understood social change to be a big movement, something that many people worked tirelessly to create to make lives better for many people. What I learned from working at AUCNA is that social change can be as small as picking up trash, taking an elderly neighbor's dog for a walk, or even working with local programs to tutor youth. My experience has changed my perception of social change as a big movement. Now, I understand it as many people doing

> what is possible in order to make their communities decent places to live and learn. I now see myself as an agent of social change as I have, as Spelman's logo attests, made "a Choice to Change the World."

Sidney's recognition that her service is a form of activism illustrates what Bickford and Reynolds wish more students understood. They contend,

> Many of our students appear to recognize activism only as participating in huge events planned by global or national organizations: marches, rallies and the like. They imagine activists as heroes, courageous and dedicated in ways that seem impossible to emulate. They do not recognize grassroots efforts as activism, and they do not see themselves as potential actors in either local or larger arenas. (238)

On the contrary, Sidney recognizes herself and her mentee as engaged in acts of social change in a local arena. Having made the connection between her service and activism, Sidney is more likely to continue seeing herself as someone who can make a difference because she does indeed "have something to offer."

Imagining the difference that she could make as the agency director, Sidney recommends greater disclosure of the agency's programs and greater visibility of the agency leader.

> After serving at the AUCNA, I can say that I have gained a greater understanding about what it means to be a mentor and how being one makes me an agent of progressive social change. I wish, however, that the agency would have provided us with more information about the other services that they provide for the community. If I were the leader of this agency, I would provide an introductory course for all volunteers so that they could see the functions of the facility and how all of the programs work together to help the community. I think that showing all volunteers the basic functions of all of the programs may boost participation because volunteers would be able to tell their friends about their volunteer experiences and other opportunities that the AUCNA offers. I wanted to meet the leader of the organization as well and to see him or her working in some capacity on the volunteer level. I know

that the leader has many administrative duties to attend to, but I think that when volunteers see a leader working amongst them, it raises the respect and shows that the work is important to the agency as well. I think that these two things, having a feel for other volunteer opportunities and actually seeing the leader, would have enhanced my volunteer experience and my observations as a whole.

When the focus is only on volunteering, perhaps it is enough to serve where one is assigned. However, as an activist in the making, Sidney is not satisfied with serving blindly. She wants to know all of her options and understand how the AUCNA's many community initiatives work together to meet community needs. Additionally, her interest in the leader's visibility suggests concern for volunteer morale, which influences the sustainability of programs. Sidney's call for understanding the role of all AUCNA programs and concern for volunteers is linked to the need for structural changes. Pushing the boundaries of a volunteer rhetoric, Sidney's observation suggests that students need to be made aware of the larger structural issues undergirding service efforts and how certain programs help to address those issues.

Mya and Friday Night Live

Mya's reflection essay describes her service with Friday Night Live (FNL)—a prevention program that aims to reduce the rate of teen driving deaths by discouraging drinking and smoking while driving. According to Mya, FNL began in 1984 as a pilot program. Proving successful, FNL gained its first statewide office in 1988. By 1990, "there were a lot of schools that held the program." FNL's motto is, "Remember there is no such thing as a small act of kindness. Every act creates a ripple with no logical end." Mya believes that this motto reflects "the good Friday Night Live does to help give students knowledge that will be useful to them in the future."

To promote FNL's mission, Mya and other volunteers created "Buckle Up." Mya explains, "Buckle Up was a project that we came up with to help educate children on why it is important to buckle up their seat belts." After interviewing children about their car safety habits, searching the Internet for resources, and adapting factual information so that "children [could] understand" it, Mya and other volunteers created posters and pamphlets that they later used in presentations to elementary and middle school students.

Prior to serving with FNL, Mya "did not know any facts about teenage driving." She was "inspired" by how much she learned, not only about teen driving, but also about collaborating with others. Mya reflects, "I also learned that it takes a lot of work to come up with ideas when being in a group with other students. I feel like I learned a lot about myself while doing this project. This project made me have a drive to do anything I put my mind to."

Mya's literacy partnership is what Thomas Deans calls "writing-*for*-the-community." In "English Studies and Public Service," an excerpt from his book *Writing Partnerships: Service-Learning in Composition*, Deans distinguishes three types of community writing performed in a range of service-learning programs and courses: "writing-*for*-the-community," "writing-*about*-the-community," and "writing-*with*-the-community" (108-110). When students write *for* the community, they work collaboratively with the community agency to produce documents that advance the community's mission. Often rooted in the nonprofit agency, these learning sites tend to privilege "academic and workplace literacies" (110). When writing *about* the community, students produce essays based upon their "lived experience" through "traditional community service" (108). Since the classroom is usually the primary learning site, "academic and critical literacies" are privileged (110). When students write *with* the community, they work "directly with community members (rather than through established nonprofit or governmental agencies) to research and address pressing local problems" (110). Typically anchored in community centers, these learning sites privilege "academic, community, and hybrid literacies" (110).

Mya sees her writing-for-the-community as performing a service, but, unlike Erica and Sidney, she does not explicitly connect her service with activism. Instead, she articulates values consistent with the agency's motto and a volunteer ethos.

> To me, community service means helping not only your community, but also your school, state, and country. It means to be kind and caring toward others, to help out those who are less fortunate. Community service is what drives a person to take time out of their day to better their community and ultimately themselves. It will also better people not only physically, but mentally while improving your surroundings.

Mya recognizes a connection between her local service and the welfare of her "school, state, and country," but she does not yet understand (or articulate) her service as connected to an activist agenda. At this stage of becoming, she acknowledges ethical reasons for serving—kindness and caring—as well as some personal benefits, such as how one can improve "physically" and "mentally" while working to "better their community." Mya later notes that "being involved and helping organizations fulfill their goals makes [her] feel good as a person."

Mya's one reference to social change comes when she considers what she might do as the agency leader. She writes, "Social change that I would take action on is having a mandatory class that is dedicated to learning about teen driving. I would have a video and talk to elementary and middle school students about safe teen driving so that they can be prepared for when it is [their] time to start driving." Even though she does not yet connect policy change with activism, Mya is recommending a change of policy that would require young students to learn about teen driving safety before they are of age to drive. Besides this brief mention, Mya focuses on service as an act of benevolence.

Literacy, Service, and Activism: What Taking Up the Rhetoric Means

Between participating in a literacy partnership and reflecting in writing on the experience, Erica, Sidney and Mya performed multiple literate acts. Erica participated in an African American literary festival and found that she could use her knowledge of literary analysis and the African Diaspora to promote literacy. Sidney mentored and tutored middle school children to improve academic achievement and found in the process that she gained computer literacy. Mya found herself working in a group to conceive, develop and present an original project that required the production of several literate texts. These performances are significant first steps in the process of becoming civic-minded women who use their literacies to promote social change. As we see in their written reflections, the students' emerging awareness of their activist potential is at different stages of development.

Erica's reflection indicates some awareness of the larger structural issues influencing the AUCNA's mission and the need for an African American literary children's festival. She is also able to articulate an understanding of how social change occurs, aligning herself with "advocating individuals" who recognize a need and act on it. Sidney's reflection does not acknowledge structural reasons that make her service necessary, but, like Erica, she has an epiphany about social change. No longer seeing it as a big movement, she recognizes that she can be one of many individuals who make a difference. Mya, on the other hand, represents a counter example. She neither mentions larger structural issues related to teen driving deaths, nor makes clear an understanding of social change processes. Whether Mya did not understand social change as well as the others or simply did not address the reflection prompt carefully is indeterminable from the reflection alone. Even so, these differences raise the question of what is gained when students take up the rhetoric of social change, when they begin to articulate an understanding of the connection between service and activism and even assert an activist identity?

Soviet psychologist Lev Vygotsky's learning theory is instructive in this regard. Vygotsky explains that children reach higher developmental levels by learning from more knowledgeable others. "The more skilled adult" gives the child activities "slightly" above her current level of development to help her mature. Adults help children bridge the gap between where they are and a higher level of development "by means of prompts, clues, modeling, explanation, leading questions, discussion, joint participation, encouragement…" (Miller 379-380). Vygotzky called this gap, or the "distance" between developmental levels, the zone of proximal development.

> The zone of proximal development defines those functions that have not yet matured but are in the process of maturation, functions that will mature tomorrow but are currently in an embryonic state. (380, Vygotsky qtd. in Miller)

The FYE community service requirement and reflection are activities that faculty use to bridge the gap between students' current understandings of service as simply the ethical or moral thing to do and service also as a tool for social change. By presenting students with the message of change and activism, Spelman College endeavors to help students develop activist sensibilities, including awareness of the structural reasons for volunteering and a sustained commitment to promoting social change.

Thus, while faculty should not assume that students become activists after one service experience, even if students mistakenly assume so, and faculty must acknowledge that students sometimes write what they think faculty want them to, taking up activist language is a significant performance in the process of becoming. As students have more service experiences and explore social problems, ideally in the context of service-learning courses, their understanding of the possible link between service and activism will continue to mature. Like Mya, it may take some students more time than others to articulate a connection between their service and activism; however, given multiple opportunities for engaging social problems and practicing activist discourses, students will have the tools needed to make the choice to change the world.

Works Cited

"Auburn Avenue Research Library on African American Culture and History." *The New Georgia Encyclopedia*. Georgia Humanities Council and the University of Georgia Press, 2010. Web. 1 Nov. 2010. <http://www.georgiaencyclopedia.org/nge/Article.jsp?id=h-3544>

Bickford, Donna M., and Nedra Reynolds. "Activism and Service-Learning: Reframing Volunteerism As Acts of Dissent." *Pedagogy: Critical Approaches to Teaching Literature, Language, Composition, and Culture* 2.2 (2002): 229-252. Web. 23 Oct. 2010

"Biography: Dr. Virginia Davis Floyd." *Changing the Face of Medicine: Celebrating America's Women Physicians*. National Library of Medicine. Web. 22 Dec. 2010. <http://www.nlm.nih.gov/changingthefaceofmedicine/physicians/biography_116.html>

"History." *Communities in Schools of Atlanta*. Web. 12 Dec. 2010. <http://www.cisatlanta.org/aboutUs/aboutUs_history.cfm>

Deans, Thomas. "English Studies and Public Service." Ed. Thomas Deans, Barbara Roswell, and Adrian J. Wurr. *Writing and Community Engagement: A Critical Sourcebook*. Boston: Bedford/St. Martins, 2010. 97-116. Print.

"FYE SpEl.Folio Assignments 2010-2011." *SpEl.Folio*. Spelman College. Web. 12 Nov. 2010. <http://www.spelman.edu/spelfolio/assignments.shtml>

Flower, Linda. *Community Literacy and the Rhetoric of Public Engagement*. Carbondale: Southern Illinois University Press, 2008. Print.

Floyd, Virginia Davis. *Personal Interview*. 20 Dec. 2010.

Herzberg, Bruce. "Community Service and Critical Teaching." Ed. Thomas Deans, Barbara Roswell, and Adrian J. Wurr. *Writing and Community Engagement: A Critical Sourcebook*. Boston: Bedford/St. Martins, 2010. 138-148. Print.

History and Traditions Reference Guide. The Spelman College Office of Alumnae Affairs. Web. 28 Oct. 2010. <http://www.spelman.edu/about_us/news/publications.shtml#historytraditions>

"History in Brief." *Facts.* Spelman College. Web. 1 Jan. 2011. <http://www.spelman.edu/about_us/facts/>

Ivory, Darnell. *Personal Interview.* 18 Dec. 2010.

Mathieu, Paula. *Tactics of Hope: The Public Turn in English Composition.* Portsmouth: Boynton/Cook Publishers, Inc., 2005. Print.

Miller, Patricia H. *Theories of Developmental Psychology.* 3rd ed. New York: W. H. Freeman and Company, 1993. Print.

Peck, Wayne Campbell, Linda Flower, and Lorraine Higgins. "Community Literacy." *College Composition and Communication* 46.2 (1995): 199-222. Web. 8 Dec. 2010

Peters, Katura. "Summerhill Project." *Spelman Messenger* 87.3 (1971): 33-34. Print.

"Spelman Blends Old and New Voices to Change the World." *Spelman Messenger* 119.2 (2008): 2-3. Web. 20 Dec. 2010 <http://www.spelman.edu/about_us/news/publications.shtml#messenger>

"Street Academy Clinic." *Spelman Spotlight* 40.2 (1973):1, 4. Print.

"Summerhill History." *The Organized Neighbors of Summerhill: Summerhill Neighborhood Association of Atlanta, GA,* n.p. n.d. Web. 1 Nov. 2010. <http://www.onsummerhill.org/summerhill-history/>

"When and Where I Enter: Becoming a Free Thinking Spelman Woman." *First-Year Experience Syllabus.* Spelman College, 2009-2010. 1-5. Print.

WRITING ON THE EDGE

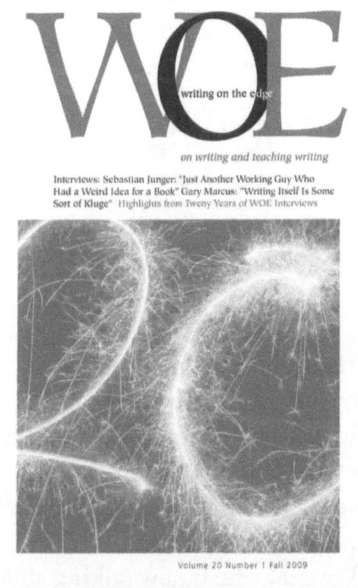

Writing on the Edge is on the Web at http://woe.ucdavis.edu/

Writing on the Edge, now in its 22nd year, is a University of California at Davis sponsored journal about writing and the teaching of writing. We publish articles, essays, creative nonfiction, cartoons, short stories, poems, collages, and whatever else. In each issue we also publish interviews with writers (e.g. Toni Morrison, Calvin Trillin, John McPhee) and writing teachers (e.g. Peter Elbow, Linda Flower, David Bartholomae). We think writing about composition does not have to be boring, that it can be interesting and lively. We are a journal to be read for pleasure rather than duty. We give annual $500 prizes for the best interview and the best anything else.

"In Our Names: Rewriting the U.S. Death Penalty" by Kimberly K. Gunter. *WOE* 21.2 (2011)

As our name implies, *Writing on the Edge* seeks to publish works that occupy the edges, within and between genres, styles, themes, etc. "In Our Names: Rewriting the U.S. Death Penalty," by Kimberly K. Gunter: It's rare that we run across a piece that fuses teaching craft with creative nonfiction with political persuasion to take an incisive look at the storytelling, teaching, and the death penalty. Through the raw power of her imagery, action, and insight, Gunter manages an organic union among disparate elements.

12 "In Our Names": Rewriting the U.S. Death Penalty

Kimberly K. Gunter

The stench of death is strong. Like the reek that hangs after a day of hog-killing, the dense, sickly sweet smell thickens the air. It's almost as if I could reach out and grab a handful of that odor and slide it into my pocket. Before either my students or I can ask, the prison guard cum tour guide, Lt. Bowden, offers, "We've tried to do something about the smell. We've cleaned. We've painted. But nothing works."

Jorge has slipped away from Lt. Bowden, who is now talking about last meals. He has instead ventured inside Cell C, the cell that houses North Carolina's condemned for the final 72 hours of their lives. Tattoos of skulls and flames running between his elbows and wrists, Jorge has outstretched his arms so that his fingertips touch the opposite walls of the tiny room. He's seen documentary footage of inmate Antonio James performing this same ritual in his own death row cell in Louisiana's Angola prison. Bowden catches up to us and, nodding at the flimsy, stained mattress upon which Jorge now sits, offers, "That's the bed where all of North Carolina's executed prisoners have slept. People like, say..." Bowden searches his memory and hits upon, "Velma Barfield." Samantha nods. All semester she has studied the dialectic created by gender and the U.S. death penalty, and she recognizes Barfield's name, the so-called "Death Row Granny" and the first woman executed after the United States' 1976 reinstatement of capital punishment.

My students are a curious bunch, and Bowden's having some trouble corralling them all. Erica has spun away and stands peering into another cell here in the death house. "You're using this one for storage?" she asks, incredulous. Staring at the brooms and mops and buckets and paint cans that tumble on top of one another in a second death house cell, Erica raises her eyebrows in cynical dismay. "That's one expensive janitor's closet," I whisper to her.

Bowden hastens us onward and into the death chamber itself. Until 1998, North Carolina still used lethal gas to kill its condemned inmates; however, any number of logistical concerns, not the least among them leakage of the cyanide gas from the chamber and into the lungs of the innocent observers, convinced the state to swap for lethal injection. The guards on the prison's execution team no longer, then, tousle the inmate's hair while he remains, dead, strapped into a chair below which minutes earlier dropped a pellet of cyanide into sulfuric acid; the purpose of what might have looked to onlookers like some gruesome fatherly gesture was in fact to dispel trapped cyanide gas. Instead, the old gas chamber has been reconfigured to serve as North Carolina's current death chamber. Ventilation ducts and gas barometers remain. Now, however, a hospital gurney dominates the former gas chamber, and my students and I can squeeze in, only three or four at a time. Jorge, starting at the gurney, whispers to me, "Dr. Gunter: touch it," as if it's some wild animal or ancient relic. "I don't wanna touch it," I hiss back. But I do run my fingers over the crisp hospital sheets. I stare at a patch of gauze taped to one of the gurney's steel rods. And I try to imagine how it must feel, to lie here, strapped down.

The death chamber itself is pierced by two Plexiglas windows set high into its cinderblock walls. The gurney is jacked up so that the inmate's prone body lies flush with the window sills. The larger of the two windows, maybe three feet high by four feet long, allows the inmate to glance to his right and into the witness room. Or, more precisely, the window allows the witnesses to stare in at the inmate. Up to sixteen people can pack into the witness' antechamber. Therein, the victim's family sit shoulder to shoulder with the inmate's family. Journalists, prison staff, prosecutors, defense attorneys, and "four respectable citizens...[who] serve as official witnesses" ("Selection of Execution Witnesses") fill the rest of the seats. Directly in front of the condemned hangs the death chamber 's second window. Much smaller than the other and intentionally angled so as to remain hidden from the witnesses, this window is a peephole into the next-door nook that houses the executioner. Two IV lines snake through a hole bored in a shared wall, lines through which flow the three-drug cocktail that will kill this woman or, more often, this man, now pronounced a monster.

Bowden teases Kimberly, probably because, cherubic, she looks the youngest of my students: "Jump up here and we'll show you what it feels like to be strapped in," he offers, laughing and patting the gurney's mattress. "Wouldn't that be special?" he asks, uttering a phrase that will pepper his talk all afternoon.

Our sojourn in Central Prison's, and North Carolina's only, death house and execution chamber comes early in our tour of this maximum security penitentiary. My composition students and I spend another three hours walking the prison grounds. We stand in the paved, razor wire-encrusted prison yard and peer skyward at the watchtowers. Inmates play basketball around us as Bowden points up to the guards and explains that they are trained to fire no warning shots. Filing through the gymnasium, on all sides the clanks of inmates lifting weights, I notice that lift records are carefully recorded on the walls in letters cut from construction paper. We slip into the auditorium to listen to a visiting Christian evangelist. The auditorium is full, the prisoners, racially segregated, listening to calls to Jesus, the preacher singing promises of a spiritual life that supersedes prison walls, backed by a tinny cassette of piped-in karaoke music. We walk through the non-air-conditioned infirmary, and I hear a nurse respond to one of my students, "There ain't nobody innocent here." We sit in the holding cells where groups of prisoners remain on first arrival at Central Prison. Bowden, chuckling, notes how uncomfortable it would be to linger in one of these crowded holding tanks for the five or six hours necessary, especially if one of the inmates defecated in the public toilet in the cell's corner. "Schew!" he exclaims, waving his hand underneath his nose. We meet the imposing prison guard who oversees the "prison within the prison" where the worst offenders end up, those who couldn't get along in general population or those who are on suicide watches. We stand not simply peering into cellblocks of death row inmates but walking within arms reach of them, no bars or steel doors between us. They are color-coded in their red jumpsuits, or in green shorts and t-shirts for those who are allowed outside to do landscaping, Ashley, my five foot dynamo of a student, whose e-mail handle is "callmetatertot," murmurs in my ear, "If these guys are the worst of the worst and so dangerous that we must execute them, then why are we allowed to stand right beside them with nothing between us for protection?" We walk through the no-contact visitation center and through the prison chapel. We learn that there are no on-site educational programs and that the prison employs only a Christian chaplain but no religious advisors of other faiths. We listen to the mental health unit supervisor explain that prison guards are empowered by physicians and the state to forcibly medicate inmates against their will, all the while a lone inmate moaning and screaming in the background. A line of slack-jawed and wall-eyed men slugs past us, and one of my students reports later that the mental health guards had mocked, "Time to feed the bugs."

Late in the day's tour, I fall back so that I can talk with Bailey, the guard who assists Bowden, bringing up the rear. A guard at Central Prison for only three months, it is a good job for Bailey, one with health care benefits and a state retirement plan, but she's come to the prison because she thinks she can do some good, too. "Any one of us could have ended up here," she says quietly.

Back on the bus, I'm counting heads, and the students are fired up. We pass Germ-X hand sanitizer back and forth, and exclamations about the day echo off the bus's riveted walls: "Dr. Gunter, did you hear it when the dispatcher came over the Lieutenant's radio and announced there'd been a stabbing?" Grey asks, wide-eyed. "I couldn't believe they didn't even make us walk through the metal detector," Samantha marvels. I respond that I don't think the metal detector has been installed yet, that the prison hadn't even had a metal detector on my first two tours. "Were your tours with other students the same as this one?" Tiffany asks. No. I tell them how tour guides make all the difference-how Bowden's authority to take us anywhere in the prison was diluted by what seemed to be a transparently standard PR script. "For instance, he out and out said that rape isn't much of a problem in that prison, but last year, another guard, a big barrel-chested sergeant who kept saying, 'I like to fight,' told me that, while guards ruled the prison during the day, the prisoners ruled the prison at night, and that prisoner rape was widespread and unchecked while the cell blocks were on nightly lockdown." "Well," Erica chimes up, aping Bowden, "isn't that special?" We laugh in what is as much nervous relief as anything else.

This field trip has come in April. These composition students entered this class in January, and most of them were adamantly in favor of the U.S. death penalty, too. Now, near the end of our fifteen-week study of America's system of capital punishment, fully 90% of these students oppose the practice. But how did we get here? To the prison?

Sure, on a 60-seat luxury bus normally used by the university's athletic teams. But how did we get to abolition?

First, via a course structure intent on empowering students to become rhetorical power-players. In American first-year composition programs, we largely teach a single genre: academic writing. Moreover, if academic writing is our destination, process pedagogies are often the vehicle forgetting there. Too often, though, "academic writing" remains arbitrary, oppressive, exclusionary, or, perhaps worse, undefined, and processes remain prescriptive. Bucking, for instance, a regulatory textbook industry and restrictive estimations of students, the best way to teach students to write as academics is to regard them as academics, all the while rending apart exactly what "academic writing" means. Single-themed composition courses, especially when they also employ writing groups, provide one viable means for doing so. Students write more complex, intricate essays and take up more complex, critically in formed arguments because they have had the time to conduct expanded research, to assimilate what they've l earned, to position themselves in the discourse, to hear dissensus in the classroom, to be challenged by knowledgeable readers during workshops, and to write multiple drafts and also various essays on the same subject matter.

Second, the notion of the student as author was fundamental to this course, and not simply as authors of essays but as (collaborative) authors of selves and of this class. If we remind ourselves that literacy isn't just a storehouse of knowledge but a kind of action and that discourse isn't printed text alone but also a way of being in the world, the ideological nature of all discourse is apparent; moreover, if we look at literacy (here, academic literacy specifically) as what we do, not only is literacy a social action, but it is a social call to action. Thus, discourse's creative power (that is, discourse as our means of being in the world, the enactment of the story we tell ourselves about ourselves), less it become hegemonic, must really be shared with students. Therefore, in this class, students compiled our course textbook by researching and selecting class readings. Students led all discussions and moderated all classroom debates. Student groups wrote their own essay assignments in group conferences with me. Students chose the subtopics on which they wrote all semester. Students co-wrote portions of the syllabus. This course demanded, then, not just a student-centered classroom but a student-propelled classroom. And if students' early choices (sometimes) emerged from a performative impulse (for example, if they designed essay assignments that seemed to represent the types of papers that students "ought" to write), they were at worst learning to use academic language, eventually learning to insert themselves into and change it, exploiting the language but not being subsumed by it.

Third, my students and I dismantled the walls of the insular classroom. We abandoned the insinuation of academia as an ivory tower, unsullied by material conditions. Instead, we took to the streets and invited the streets into our classroom, and doing so was vital to our scrutiny of America's death penalty. Yes, we left the campus to inspect North Carolina's Central Prison, but into our classroom came attorneys on both sides of the capital punishment debate: the words of Bruce Cunningham, an abolitionist attorney who cautioned my students, "If you're gonna kill somebody in this country, don't be poor," were contested by Assistant District Attorney Joe Osman who described for my students the atrocities committed by the men whose deaths he seeks as a routine part of his job. Asked to coordinate a lecture series,

I invited to campus and into our classroom Scott Langley, Amnesty International's Death Penalty Abolition Coordinator for the state of North Carolina and a photojournalist who has amassed an enormous collection of photographs documenting America's capital system. My students, in search of real-world sources for their essays and for the themed magazines they were producing, spread across the campus and into local communities. For instance, one group surveyed over 250 of their fellow college students in an opinion poll that sought to trace students' opinions on the death penalty and correlations between those opinions and students' race and religion. Students interviewed parole officers and prison psychologists, theology scholars and small-town preachers. They even began to correspond with death row inmates. In w hat was perhaps the course's pinnacle moment, after attending her lecture in Raleigh, students descended on Sister Helen Prejean with such animation and enthusiasm that it felt more like I was backstage at a Jay-Z show in Madison Square Garden instead of in the chapel of St. Francis of Assissi. This course became a borderland where sorority girls and honors students talked to convicted murderers and Catholic nuns- it was sometimes surreal but always exhilarating.

Finally, this class was shaped by a willing surrender, surrender of space, surrender of power, and, in some ways, surrender of course outcomes. The class was not unlike a giant trust fall, with m e falling backwards and into the arms of my students, hoping we wouldn't all end up on our asses. Sometimes frustratingly so, social justice cannot be decreed. It was my unabashed yet unspoken hope that encounters with the facts that surround and indict America's death penalty would convince students of its catastrophic legal, practical, diplomatic, and ethical failings. However, I didn't want to mimic a warden, with my students playing prisoners to my epistemology. Instead, I relinquished my s take in students' final positions on the death penalty. What's more,

I refused to posit myself, as the classroom 's font of knowledge. Only the students could truly say what it was they wanted to accomplish in a given piece of writing, so why not ask them to write their own assignments? Students really did know more about their semester-long topics that I did by semester 's end, and why shouldn't they? Instead, my students and I (to the extent possible in a culture where course grades are the currency and the GPA is the bottom line) operated as colleagues in a fifteen-week research project. This course embodied the unfolding of individual research agendas; writing to learn; and, ultimately, the composing of academic selves within a vigorous, critical community. Education came to mean, in the words of Victor Villanueva, "a way of attempting to make sense out of the senseless, to become more, rather than to become other" (53). By course's end, I'm not sure who had

l earned more-my students or me-but [can't help but wonder if the respect they were shown, irrespective of, for example, their stance on the death penalty or their institutional position as first -year students in a general education course, didn't foster the very compassion and thoughtfulness that most of these students would demonstrate toward the worst among us.

On the last day of c lass, Erica confided the difficulty that s he and her group- mates had had in naming their semester magazine. She told us, " I called my mom for suggestions. She's heard me talk about this class so much this semester, I thought she might have an idea. You know what she said?" Erica dismayed, continued: "She said, 'Call it Fry ' Em All.'" Through class laughter, Erica moaned and said, "I told her, 'Mom, we're against the death penalty.' So then she says, 'Okay. Then call it The Bleeding Heart.'" Half laughing, half jeering, my students and I were familiar with these ready caricatures of death penalty proponents and opponents and also with the easy answers to violent crime so often suggested by our fellow Americans. But these students, through fifteen weeks of research and composing, had learned the impossibility of easy answers. They knew too much for those now, too much about the racism, the classism, the sexism, the homophobia, the capriciousness, the corruption, the politics, the costs, the hyperbolic media coverage, too much about the mistakes. Moreover, they knew they themselves were culpable, that the state was committing executions, in Samantha's words, "in our names." My students, though, had recast the state's actions, had recast the terms of the entire debate, away from the punishment of monsters and-to the punishment of monstrous deeds, away from whether killers deserve to die to whether we deserve to kill them, and in so doing, they didn't just imitate them but instead they became academic writers.

Works Cited

"Selection of Execution Witnesses." Central Prison. North Carolina Department of Corrections, n.d. http: //www.doc.state.nc.us/DOP/ deathpenalty/witness.htm. 14 Apr. 2010.

Villanueva, Victor. Boots traps: From an American Academic of Color. Urbana, IL: NCTE, 1993.

About the Editors

Steve Parks is an Associate Professor of Writing and Rhetoric at Syracuse University. He is the author of *Class Politics: The Movement for a Students' Right To Their Own Language* and *Gravyland: Writing Beyond the Curriculum in the City of Brotherly Love*. With Paula Mathieu and Tiffany Rousculp, he co-edited *Circulating Communities: The Tactics and Strategies of Community Publishing*. Working with Samantha Blackmon and Cristina Kirklighter, he has co-edited *Listening to our Elders: Writing and Working for Change,* a research project supported by NCTE. He has also published in *College English, Journal of College Composition and Communication*, and *Community Literacy Journal*. Over the past ten years, he has directed New City Community Press (newcitypress.com).

Brenda Glascott is an Assistant Professor at California State University, San Bernarding specializing in Composition/Rhetoric. She is working on a book project about gender and nineteenth century evangelical literacy practices. She is publishing articles about nineteenth century evangelical constructions of literacy, about public writing and the public sphere, and about service learning. She is part of an editorial collective starting a new scholarly journal, *Literacy in Composition Studies*. Glascott was named a Finalist for the 2008 NCTE Promising Researcher Award for her historical research on nineteenth-century evangelical literacy narratives.

Brian Bailie is a PhD candidate in the Composition and Cultural Rhetoric program at Syracuse University. His work focuses on the intersections of protest and media, technology and transnationalism, identity and material rhetoric, and the ways activists exploit, expand, resist, and utilize these intersections to their advantage. Bailie has served as contributor, associate editor, and special issue editor for *Reflections: A Journal of Writing, Service-Learning, and Community*

Literacy. His most recent publications have appeared in the *KB Journal* nd *Composition Forum.*

Heather Christiansen is a PhD student in the Rhetoric, Communication and Information Design program at Clemson University. Her research interests include visual rhetoric, the rhetoric of branding, identity, user experience design, consumer behavior and social influence. She currently serves as the managing editor for *The WAC Journal.*

Stacey Waite is currently Assistant Professor of English in Rhetoric and Composition at the University of Nebraska—Lincoln. Waite's essays on the teaching of writing have appeared in *Writing on the Edge, Reader,* and *Feminist Teacher.* Waite has also published three collections of poems: *Choke* (winner of the 2004 Frank O'Hara Prize), *Love Poem to Androgyny* (Main Street Rag, 2006), and *the lake has no saint* (Tupelo Press, 2010). Other honors include an Andrew Mellon Dissertation Fellowship Award, the Elizabeth Baranger Excellence in Teaching Award, three Pushcart Prize nominations, and a National Society of Arts & Letters Poetry Prize. Waite has an interview online at *Pilot Light: A Journal of 21st Century Poetics and Criticism* and a forthcoming collection of poems, *Butch Geography,* from Tupelo Press in 2013.

www.ingramcontent.com/pod-product-compliance
Lightning Source LLC
Chambersburg PA
CBHW031704230426
43668CB00006B/100